CONTRACT FORMATION AND PARTIES

THE OXFORD-NORTON ROSE
LAW COLLOQUIUM

CONTRACT FORMATION
AND PARTIES

Edited by

ANDREW BURROWS

*Norton Rose Professor of Commercial Law in the University of Oxford;
Fellow of St Hugh's College, Oxford*

and

EDWIN PEEL

Fellow and Tutor in Law, Keble College, Oxford

OXFORD
UNIVERSITY PRESS

OXFORD

UNIVERSITY PRESS

Great Clarendon Street, Oxford OX2 6DP

Oxford University Press is a department of the University of Oxford. It
furthers the University's objective of excellence in research, scholarship, and
education by publishing worldwide in

Oxford New York

Auckland Cape Town Dar es Salaam Hong Kong Karachi
Kuala Lumpur Madrid Melbourne Mexico City Nairobi
New Delhi Shanghai Taipei Toronto

With offices in

Argentina Austria Brazil Chile Czech Republic France Greece
Guatemala Hungary Italy Japan Poland Portugal Singapore
South Korea Switzerland Thailand Turkey Ukraine Vietnam

Oxford is a registered trade mark of Oxford University Press
in the UK and in certain other countries

Published in the United States
by Oxford University Press Inc., New York

British Library Cataloguing in Publication Data

Data available

Library of Congress Cataloging in Publication Data

Data available

Typeset by Glyph International, Bangalore, India
Printed in Great Britain
on acid-free paper by
CPI Group (UK) Ltd, Croydon, CR0 4YY

ISBN 978–0–19–958370–6

3 5 7 9 10 8 6 4 2

Foreword

A law of contract is a necessity for the successful conduct of business. It is essential that any such law should be clear, easy to ascertain, and yet be sensitive to business expectations. This volume of essays addresses the law relating to the formation of legally binding contracts and relationships between contracting parties and third parties and is based on papers delivered at the eighth Oxford-Norton Rose Colloquium at St Hugh's College, Oxford in September 2009. Its immediate predecessor dealt with the problems of ascertaining and defining enforceable terms of a contract while the colloquium before that dealt with the consequences of breach. Important as those topics are, they must yield, at least, chronological precedence to the questions discussed in this admirable collection.

In *Associated Japanese Bank (International) Ltd v Credit du Nord SA* [1989] 1 WLR 255, Steyn J, as he then was, said that a primary function of the law of contract is to meet the reasonable expectations of honest businessmen. This axiom is easy to state but not always so easy to apply in practice. The Oxford-Norton Rose Colloquium brings together distinguished academic lawyers and legal practitioners (concepts which are often separate but can occasionally unite in a single personality) very largely to flush out the ramifications of Lord Steyn's dictum. The reader will find attention being given in these pages to subjects as diverse as letters of intent, agreements to negotiate in good faith, electronic offer and acceptance, promissory estoppel, liability (if any) for pre-contractual non-disclosure, unjust enrichment if a contract is expected but fails to materialise, assignment, agency, and third party rights.

But they are all attempts to apply Lord Steyn's guiding principle. The fact that they started out as papers read to those attending the colloquium means that they have all been refined by intellectual debate and even, on occasion, hearty disagreement from the participants. As someone privileged to be invited to chair one of the sessions, I can only say that I have been deeply impressed by the quality of the contributions, one more senior academic member being able to say, in the course of a spirited discussion of promissory estoppel, precisely what Lord Denning had told him he had and had not meant to say in a well-known case. Perhaps the real distinguishing feature of these colloquia is that they afford a forum for academics and practitioners to exchange views on matters of legal moment in commercial law and I know of no other forum in which this is done so congenially or so impressively.

The resulting essays should be read and digested by every contract lawyer and can hardly fail to continue to merit further important debate on the topics which they cover, up to and indeed beyond the date of the next colloquium. As Megarry J has reminded us, 'by good disputation shall the law be known'.

Lord Justice Longmore

Preface

The Eighth Oxford-Norton Rose Colloquium at which the papers in this book were presented was held at St. Hugh's College, Oxford on Friday and Saturday, 18-19 September 2009. As with the previous colloquia the participants consisted of a mix of academics and practitioners brought together to examine and discuss an area of commercial law.

As with the last colloquium (on contract terms) the focus of the papers was predominantly on the law of contract, or, more accurately, the law relating to the process of contract formation and the position of 'third parties'. The format remained the same. The papers prepared by academics were distributed in advance. Each author was given a short time to present his or her paper and, after one or two papers, the floor was open for extensive discussion, usually lasting between 45 minutes and an hour. The debate was never less than lively, interesting, informative, and practical and was conducted with no little good humour.

We would like to take this opportunity to thank all the participants and especially the chairmen (Lord Justice Longmore, Mr Justice Blair, and Mr Justice Hamblen) for their expert handling of the proceedings. We would also like to thank Lord Justice Longmore for being the guest speaker at the colloquium dinner and for writing the Foreword to this book. Thanks are also due to St. Hugh's College for its excellent hospitality throughout the colloquium; to Norton Rose for its funding and support of this event; to Laura Hodgson who produced a summary of the discussions for us; to Lyn Hambridge for her assistance in organizing the colloquium and compiling the lists of contributors and participants; and to Joanna Scott and Benjamin Roberts at OUP for seeing the papers through to publication.

Andrew Burrows
Edwin Peel
4 February 2010

Contents

List of Contributors   xi
List of Participants at the Colloquium   xii
Table of Cases   xv
Table of Legislation   xxvii

A. INTRODUCTION

1. Overview   3
   ANDREW BURROWS AND EDWIN PEEL

B. FORMATION

2. Letters of Intent   17
   MICHAEL FURMSTON

3. Agreements to Negotiate in Good Faith   37
   EDWIN PEEL

4. Offer and Acceptance in the Electronic Age   61
   DONAL NOLAN

5. A Bird in the Hand: Consideration and
   Contract Modifications   89
   MINDY CHEN-WISHART

6. Promissory Estoppel and Debts   115
   BEN MCFARLANE

7. Liability in Tort for Pre-Contractual Non-Disclosure   137
   JOHN CARTWRIGHT

8. Liability in Unjust Enrichment where a Contract
   Fails to Materialize   159
   JAMES EDELMAN

C. PARTIES

9. Problems in Assignment Law: Not Yet Out of the Wood?   183
   ANDREW TETTENBORN

10. Agency Law for Muggles: Why There is no Magic in Agency   205
    THOMAS KREBS

11. A Review of the Contracts (Rights of Third Parties) Act 1999   225
    HUGH BEALE

   Index   251

List of Contributors

HUGH BEALE is Professor of Law at the University of Warwick and Visiting Professor at the University of Oxford and the University of Amsterdam.

ANDREW BURROWS is Norton Rose Professor of Commercial Law in the University of Oxford and Fellow of St Hugh's College, Oxford.

JOHN CARTWRIGHT is Professor of the Law of Contract and Tutor in Law, Christ Church, Oxford; Professor of Anglo-American Private Law, University of Leiden.

JAMES EDELMAN is Professor of the Law of Obligations, and Fellow and Tutor in Law, Keble College, Oxford; Conjoint Professor, University of New South Wales.

MICHAEL FURMSTON is Professor of Law and Dean of the Law School at Singapore Management University.

THOMAS KREBS is Fellow and Tutor in Law, Brasenose College, Oxford.

BEN McFARLANE is Law Fellow and Tutor in Law, Trinity College, Oxford.

DONAL NOLAN is Fellow and Tutor in Law, Worcester College, Oxford.

EDWIN PEEL is Fellow and Tutor in Law, Keble College, Oxford.

PROFESSOR ANDREW TETTENBORN is the Bracton Professor of Law at the University of Exeter.

MINDY CHEN-WISHART is Fellow and Tutor in Law, Merton College, Oxford.

List of Participants at the Colloquium

Chairmen

Lord Justice Longmore
The Honourable Mr Justice Blair
The Honourable Mr Justice Hamblen

Speakers

Professor Hugh Beale	University of Warwick
Professor John Cartwright	University of Oxford
Professor James Edelman	University of Oxford
Professor Michael Furmston	Singapore Management University
Thomas Krebs	University of Oxford
Ben McFarlane	University of Oxford
Donal Nolan	University of Oxford
Edwin Peel	University of Oxford
Professor Andrew Tettenborn	University of Exeter
Mindy Chen-Wishart	University of Oxford

Oxford Law Faculty

Professor Susan Bright	University of Oxford
Professor Andrew Burrows	University of Oxford
Professor Timothy Endicott	University of Oxford
Tom Furlong	University of Oxford
Joshua Getzler	University of Oxford
Imogen Gould	University of Oxford
Louise Gullifer	University of Oxford
Henry Mares	University of Oxford
Julie Maxton	University of Oxford
Professor Ewan McKendrick	University of Oxford
Professor Charles Mitchell	University of Oxford
Jonathan Morgan	University of Oxford
Maureen O'Neill	University of Oxford
Professor Francis Reynolds	University of Oxford
Wolf-George Ringe	University of Oxford
Adam Rushworth	University of Oxford
Andrew Scott	University of Oxford

Norton Rose

Hamish Anderson
Chris Bates
Richard Calnan
Barthélemy Cousin
Sam Eastwood
Fiona Evans
James Foale
Laura Hodgson
Stephen Parish
John Shelton
Lorraine Watson
Carl Werner

Guests

The Honourable Mr Justice Beatson	
Georges Affaki	BNP Paribas
Neil Andrews	University of Cambridge
Professor Michael Bridge	London School of Economics
Sarah Cameron	Pinsent Masons
Jonathan Cotton	Slaughter and May
Wendy Critchlow	Slaughter and May
Professor Nelson Enonchong	University of Birmingham
Steven Elliott	One Essex Court Chambers
Richard Farnhill	Allen and Overy
Henry Forbes-Smith	One Essex Court Chambers
Anthony de Garr Robinson	One Essex Court Chambers
Professor Roger Halson	University of Leeds
Professor Richard Hooley	University of Cambridge
Sabastian Isaac	One Essex Court Chambers
Simon James	Clifford Chance
Kira King	Law Commission
Sam Krafft	Allen and Overy
James Lee	University of Birmingham
Bridget Lucas	Fountain Court Chambers
Professor Gerard McMeel	University of Bristol
Stephen Moriarty QC	Fountain Court Chambers
Kate Norgett	Clifford Chance
Professor Eoin O'Dell	Trinity College, Dublin
Tim Parkes	Herbert Smith LLP
Richard Pike	Baker & McKenzie

David Reed	Shearman and Sterling
Professor Francis Rose	University of Bristol
Michael Scargill	Shearman and Sterling
Joanna Scott	Oxford University Press
Akhil Shah	Fountain Court Chambers
Marcus Smith	Fountain Court Chambers
Professor Robert Stevens	University College London
Ben Strong	One Essex Court Chambers
Professor Graham Virgo	University of Cambridge
Stephen Watterson	London School of Economics

Table of Cases

24 Seven Utility Services Ltd v Rosekey Ltd [2003] EWHC 3415 (QB) 188, 193
453416 Ontario Inc v White (1984) 42 CPC 209 189
528650 Ontario Ltd v Hepburn (2003) 124 ACWS (3d) 16 189
A-G v McMillan v Lockwood Ltd [1991] 1 NZLR 53 238
AB Corp v CD Co (The Sine Nomine) [2002] 1 Lloyd's Rep 805. 94
Abrahams v Herbert Reiach Ltd [1922] 1 KB 477 57
Abu Dhabi National Tanker Co v Product Star Shipping Ltd (No 2)
    ('The Product Star') [1993] 1 Lloyd's Rep 397 . . . . 5, 51–2, 54
AC Controls v British Broadcasting Corp (2002) 89 Con LR 52 27–8
Adam Opel GmbH and Renault SA v Mitras Automotive (UK) Ltd [2008]
    EWHC 3205 91
Adler v Dickson [1955] 1 QB 158 230
Advanced Technology Structures Ltd v Cray Valley Products Ltd [1993]
    BCLC 723. . . . . 184, 189, 190
Al-Kandari v JR Brown & Co [1988] QB 665 (CA) 145
Alfred McAlpine Construction Ltd v Panatown Ltd [2001] 1 AC 518 246
Allied Maples v Simmons & Simmons [1995] 1 WLR 1602 . . . . 57, 102
Antons Trawling Co Ltd v Smith [2003] 2 NZLR 23 . . . . 92, 105–7, 112
Appleby v Myers (1867) LR 2 CP 651 163
Arctic Shipping v Mobilia [1990] 2 Lloyd's Rep 51 220
Arkwright v Newbold (1881) 17 Ch D 301 (CA) 141, 144, 147
Armitage v Nurse [1998] Ch 241 200
Associated British Ports v Ferryways NV [2009] EWCA Civ 189; [2009]
    1 Lloyds Rep 595 . . . . 5, 35
Athenaeum Life Ass'nce Co v Pooley (1853) 3 D & J 294. 199
Attorney-General for England and Wales v R [2002] 2 NZLR 91 106
Attorney-General of Hong Kong v Humphreys Estate (Queen's Gardens) Ltd
    [1987] AC 114 161
Attorney-General v Blake [2001] 1 AC 268. . . . . 93, 94
Attwood v Small (1838) 6 Cl & Fin 232; 7 ER 684 151
Australian Steel & Mining Corpn Pty Ltd v Corben [1974] 2 NSWLR 202 151

Baird Textiles Holdings Ltd v Marks & Spencer plc [2002] 1 All ER
    (Comm) 737; [2001] CLC 999 130
Baker v Baker [1993] 2 FLR 247 132
Banbury v Bank of Montreal [1918] AC 626 (HL) 140
Bank of Credit and Commerce International SA v Ali [1999] ICR 1068. 105
Bank of New Zealand v Ginivan [1991] 1 NZLR 178 35
Banque Brussels Lambert v Australian National Industries Ltd (1989)
    21 NSWLR 502 34
Banque Keyser Ullmann SA v Skandia (UK) Insurance Co Ltd [1990] 1 QB 665,
    CA; on appeal [1991] 2 AC 249 (HL) 9, 143, 144–5, 148, 150, 154
Barbados Trust Co v Bank of Zambia [2007] EWCA Civ 148; [2007]
    1 Lloyd's Rep 495 . . . . 11, 198–9, 200, 202, 203
Barclays Bank Ltd v W J Simms Son & Cooke (Southern) Ltd [1980] 1 QB 677 176
Barton v County NatWest Ltd [1999] Lloyd's Rep Bank 408 (CA) 151
Basham, Re [1986] 1 WLR 1498 130

Beatty v Brash's Pty Ltd [1998] 2 VR 201 . . . . 188, 193
Beckham v Drake (1849) 2 HLC 579 193
Bell v Lever Brothers Ltd [1932] AC 161 (HL) 146, 172
Bernuth Lines Ltd v High Seas Shipping Ltd (The Eastern Navigator) [2005]
    EWHC 3020 (Comm); [2006] 1 Lloyd's Rep 537 . . . . 72, 79
Biggerstaff v Rowatt's Wharf Ltd [1896] 2 Ch 93 196
Birmingham & District Land Co v London & NW Railway Co (1888)
    40 Ch D 268 . . . . 120, 123, 124, 125, 126
Blackburn, Low & Co v Vigors (1866) 17 QBD 553 145
Blakeley v Muller & Co [1903] 2 KB 760 163
Bluzwed Metals Ltd v Trans-World Metals Ltd [2006] EWHC 143 41
Boardman v Phipps [1967] 2 AC 46 206
Bolton Partners v Lambert (1889) LR 41 Ch D 295 . . . . 12, 214–15, 216–17, 220, 221
Boston Deep Sea Fishing and Ice Co v Ansell (1888) 39 Ch D 339 215
Bottiglieri di Navigazione SpA v Cosco Qingdao Ocean Shipping Co
    ('The Bunga Saga Lima') [2005] EWHC 244 (Comm); [2005] 2 Lloyds Rep 1 . . . 117
Bower v Bantam Investments Ltd [1972] 1 WLR 1120 41
BP Exploration Co (Libya) Ltd v Hunt (No 2) [1979]
    1 WLR 783 . . . . 116, 117, 121, 124, 129
Brace v Calder [1895] 2 QB 253 195
Bradford Third Equitable Building Society v Borders [1941]
    2 All ER 205 (HL) 141, 144
Bressan v Squires [1974] 2 NSWLR 460 (NSWSC) 65
Brewer Street Investments Ltd v Barclays Woollen Co Ltd [1954]
    1 QB 428 . . . . 160, 168–9, 170
Brice v Bannister (1878) 3 QBD 569 200
Bridgeman v Green (1757) Wilm 58; 97 ER 22 173
Brikom Investments Ltd v Carr [1979] QB 467 96
The Brimnes: Texas Steamship Co v The Brimnes (Owners) [1975]
    1 QB 929 (CA) 71, 73, 74
Brinkibon Ltd v Stahag Stahl mbH [1983] 2 AC 34 (HL) 64, 65, 66, 74, 77
British Eagle International Airlines Ltd v Compagnie Nationale Air
    France [1975] 1 WLR 758 . . . . 238, 239
British Russian Gazette and Trade Outlook Ltd v Associated
    Newspapers Ltd [1933] 2 KB 616 105
British Steel Corp v Cleveland & Bridge Engineering Co Ltd [1984]
    1 All ER 504 . . . . 4, 22–4, 33, 169
Brockbank, Re [1948] Ch 206 . . . . 200, 202
Brown v Gould [1972] Ch 53 43
Brownlie v Campbell (1880) 5 App Cas 925 . . . . 144, 147
Brownton Ltd v Edward Moore Inbucon Ltd [1985]
    3 All ER 499 . . . . 186, 189, 190, 193
The Bunga Saga Lima: Bottiglieri di Navigazione SpA v Cosco Qingdao
    Ocean Shipping Co [2005] EWHC 244 (Comm); [2005] 2 Lloyds Rep 1 117
Burgess v Rawnsley [1975] Ch 429 165
Byrne v Van Tienhoven (1880) 5 CPD 344 (CPD) 70

C & P Haulage v Middleton [1983] 1 WLR 1461 58
Camdex International Ltd v Bank of Zambia [1998] QB 22 188
Campbells Cash & Carry Pty Ltd v Fostif Pty Ltd (2006) 229 CLR 386 191
Canadian Pacific Railway Co v The King [1931] AC 414 127

Cantiare San Rocco SA v Clyde Shipbuilding and Engineering Co [1924]
AC 226 . . . . 163–4, 173
Cantor Fitzgerald International v Horkulak [2004] EWCA Civ 1287; [2005]
ICR 402. . . . . 52, 57
Caparo Industries plc v Dickman [1991] 2 AC 605 (HL) 141
Carlill v Carbolic Smoke Ball Co [1893] 1 QB 256 (CA) 81, 100
Carter v Boehm (1766) 3 Burr 1905; 97 ER 1162. . . . . 145, 155
CCC Films (London) Ltd v Impact Quadrant Films Ltd [1985] QB 16 58
Central London Property Trust Ltd v High Trees House Ltd
[1947] KB 130. . . . . 7–8, 102, 104, 118, 120, 121, 127, 134
Chandler v Webster [1904] 1 KB 493 163
Channel Home Centers v Grossman (1986) 795 F. 2d 291 . . . . 39, 40, 41, 54
Chapelton v Barry UDC [1940] 1 KB 532 (CA) 62
Chaplin v Hicks [1911] 2 KB 786 57
Chartbrook Ltd v Persimmon Homes Ltd [2009] UKHL 38; [2009]
3 WLR 267 . . . . 36, 173
Chemco Leasing SPA v Rediffusion [1987] 1 FTLR 201 34
Chillingworth v Esche [1924] 1 Ch 97. 170
Chwee Kin Keong v Digilandmall.com Pte Ltd [2004] SGHC 71; [2004] 2 SLR
594 (*affd*: [2005] SGCA 2; [2005] 1 SLR 502) 61, 62, 67, 69, 80, 81, 82, 83–4, 107
Circuit Systems Ltd v Zuken-Redac (UK) Ltd (1994) 11 Const LJ 201 189
City and Westminster Properties (1934) Ltd v Mudd [1959] Ch 129 96
Civil Service Co-operative Society v General Steam Navigation Co [1903]
2 KB 756. 163
Clark v BET [1997] IRLR 348 57
Cleveland Mfg Co Ltd v Muslim Commercial Bank Ltd [1981]
2 Lloyd's Rep 646. 220
Collier v P & MJ Wright (Holdings) Ltd [2007] EWCA Civ 1329; [2008]
1 WLR 643 . . . . 7, 8, 92, 102–5, 109, 112, 115, 120–1, 122, 128, 133, 134
Comfort v Betts [1891] 1 QB 737 187
Compton v Allward [1912] 1 WWR 452 193
Confetti Records v Warner Music UK Ltd [2003] EWHC 1274; [2003] EMLR 35 174
Conlon v Simms [2006] EWHC 401 (Ch); [2006] 2 All ER 1024; *on appeal*
[2006] EWCA Civ 1749; [2008] 1 WLR 484 . . . . 9, 137, 147–8
Coulls v Bagot's Executor and Trustee Co Ltd (1967) 119 CLR 460 229
Countrywide Communications Ltd v ICL Pathway Ltd [2000] CLC 324 162
Courtney & Fairbairn Ltd v Tolaini Bros (Hotels) Ltd [1975]
1 WLR 297 . . . . 37, 43, 44, 46, 47, 50, 56
Cowan v O'Conner (1888) 20 QBD 640 (QB) 65
Crabb v Arun District Council [1976] Ch 179 129–30
Cressman v Coys of Kensington (Sales) Ltd [2004] EWCA Civ 47; [2004]
1 WLR 2775 . . . . 159, 171
Culina v Giuliani [1972] SCR 343. 202
CW v Norton [2001] BCTC 478 194

D&C Builders v Rees [1966] 2 QB 617. . . . . 102, 104, 105
Daley, Re, *ex p* National Australia Bank Ltd (1992) 37 FCR 390 . . . . 188, 189
Damon Cia SA v Hapag-Lloyd International SA, The Blankernstien [1985]
1 All ER 475. 26–7
Darlington BC v Wiltshier Northern Ltd [1995] 1 WLR 68 246
Daulia Ltd v Four Millbank Nominees Ltd [1978] Ch 231. 99

David Securities Pty Ltd v Commonwealth Bank of Australia (1992)
    175 CLR 353 176
Davison v Vickery's Motors Ltd (1926) 37 CLR 1 . . . . 215–16, 217
De Pothonier v De Mattos (1858) E B & E 461 202
Debtors, Re (Nos 4449 and 4450 of 1998) [1999] 1 All ER (Comm) 149 42
Defries v Milne [1913] 1 Ch 98 188
Deglman v Guaranty Trust Co of Canada and Constantineau [1954] SCR 725 179
Deloitte Touche Tohmatsu v Cridlands Pty Ltd (2003) 204 ALR 281 192
Derry v Peek (1889) 14 App Cas 337 (HL) 140
Deutsche Morgan Grenfell Group plc v Inland Revenue Commissioners
    [2006] UKHL 49; [2007] 1 AC 558 . . . . 163, 176, 177
Devefi v Mateffy Pearl Nagy (1993) 113 ALR 225 195
Dextra Bank & Trust Company Limited v Bank of Jamaica [2002]
    1 All ER (Comm) 193 177–8
Diamond Build Ltd v Clapham Park Homes Ltd [2008] EWHC 143 (TCC);
    (2008) 119 Con LR 32 26
Dibbins v Dibbins [1896] 2 Ch 348 . . . . 216, 217
Didymi Corporation v Atlantic Lines and Navigation Co Inc. [1988]
    2 Lloyd's Rep 108 47–8
Dillwyn v Llewellyn (1862) 4 De GF & J 517 133
Dimond v Lovell [2002] 1 AC 384 179
Director General of Fair Trading v First National Bank Plc [2001] UKHL 52;
    [2002] 1 AC 481 51
Dodsworth v Dodsworth (1973) 228 EG 1115 132
Doherty v Murphy [1996] 2 VR 553 201
Don King Productions Ltd v Warren [2000] Ch 291 . . . . 197–9, 200, 202, 203
Donwin Productions Ltd v EMI Films Ltd *The Times*, 9 March 1984 43–4
Doyle v Olby (Ironmongers) Ltd [1969] 2 QB 158 (CA) 140
Dunlop Pneumatic Tyre Co v Selfridge [1915] AC 847 208
Durham Fancy Goods Ltd v Michael Jackson (Fancy Goods) Ltd and
    another [1968] 2 QB 839 124

Eaglehill Ltd v J Needham Builders Ltd [1973] AC 992 (HL) 74
Easat Antennas Limited v Racal Defence Electronics Limited (Unreported
    Hart J, Chancery, 28 March 2000) 160, 169
East v Maurer [1991] 1 WLR 461 58
The Eastern Navigator: Bernuth Lines Ltd v High Seas Shipping Ltd [2005]
    EWHC 3020 (Comm); [2006] 1 Lloyd's Rep 537 . . . . 72, 79
Edgington v Fitzmaurice (1885) 29 Ch D 459 38
Edmonton (City) v Lovat Tunnel Equipment Inc (2000) 260 AR 140 188
Ellis v Torrington [1920] 1 KB 399 189
Emcor Drake & Scull v Sir Robert McAlpine [2004] EWCA Civ 1733;
    (2004) 98 Con LR 1 33
Empress Engineering Co, Re (1880) 16 Ch D. 125 202
English & Scottish Mercantile Investment Co Ltd v Brunton [1892]
    2 QB 700 204
Entores v Miles Far East Corp [1955] 2 QB 327 (CA) 64, 65–6, 67, 74, 76
Errington v Errington [1952] 1 KB 290 . . . . 99, 100
Essery v Cowlard (1884) 26 Ch D 191 165
Esso Petroleum Co Ltd v Mardon [1976] QB 801 (CA) 141, 142
Esso Petroleum Co Ltd v Niad Ltd [2001] EWHC 458 (Ch) 94

The Eurymedon: New Zealand Shipping Co Ltd v AM Satterthwaite &
 Co Ltd [1975] AC 154. 230
Experience Hendrix LLC v PPX Enterprises [2003] EWCA Civ 323;
 (2003) EMLR 25. 94

Fibrosa Spolka Akcyjna v Fairbairn Lawson Combe Barbour Ltd
 [1943] AC 32 164
Fiona Trust & Holding Corporation v Privalov [2007] Bus LR 1719 222–4
First Energy (UK) Ltd v Hungarian International Bank Ltd [1993]
 2 Lloyd's Rep 194. 39
Fisher v Bell [1961] 1 QB 394 (QB). 81
Fitzpatrick Contractors Ltd v Tyco Fire and Integrated Solutions (UK) Ltd [2008]
 EWHC 274 (TCC); (2008) 119 Con LR 155 26
Fitzroy v Cave [1905] 2 KB 364. 187
528650 Ontario Ltd v Hepburn (2003) 124 ACWS (3d) 16 189
Fleming v Bank of New Zealand [1900] AC 577 217
Foakes v Beer (1884) LR 9
 App Cas 605 . . . . 9, 92, 93, 102, 103, 104, 105, 118, 119, 120, 122,
 128, 132, 134, 135
Foamcrete (UK) Ltd v Thrust Engineering Ltd [2002] BCC 221 . . . . . 11, 195–6, 197, 203
Fostif Pty Ltd v Campbells Cash & Carry Pty Ltd (2005) 218 ALR 166;
 63 NSWLR 203 . . . . 166, 187
Fredrickson v Ins Corp of BC (1988) 28 DLR (4th) 414. 189
The Front Comor [2005] 1 CLC 347; [2005] EWHC (Comm) 454 200
Fulham v M'Carthy (1848) 1 HLC 703 185

Gan Insurance Co Ltd v Tai Ping Insurance Co Ltd (No.2) [2001] EWCA Civ 1047;
 [2001] 2 All ER (Comm) 299 52
Garnac Grain Co Inc v HMF Faure and Fairclough Ltd [1968] AC 1130 205–6
Gay Choon Ing v Loh Sze Ti Terence Peter [2009] SGCA 31 107
Gibson v Winter (1833) 5 B & Ad 96 202
Gilbert & Partners v Knight [1968] 2 All ER 248 166
The Gladys [1994] 2 Lloyd's Rep 402 43
Glegg v Bromley [1912] 3 KB 474. . . . . 185, 193, 203
Gloucester CC v Richardson [1969] 1 AC 480 239
Gore v Van der Lann [1967] 2 QB 31 230
Graham v Johnson (1869) LR 8 Eq 36 199
Grant v Bragg [2009] EWHC 74 (Ch) (*decision reversed on other grounds*: [2009]
 EWCA Civ 1228; [2009] 1 All ER (Comm) 674) 25–6
Great Peace Shipping Ltd v Tsavliris Salvage (International) Ltd
 (The 'Great Peace') [2002] EWCA Civ 1407; [2003] QB 679 . . . . 138, 173
Griffith v Tower Publishing Co Ltd [1897] 1 Ch 21. 195
Guinness Mahon v Kensington and Chelsea RLBC [1999] QB 215 . . . . 167, 176
Guy v Churchill (1889) 40 Ch D 481 192

Ha v New South Wales [1997] HCA 34; (1997) 189 CLR 465 167
Hagedorn v Oliverson (1814) 2 M & S 485. 215
Hamilton v Allied Domecq plc [2007] UKHL 33; 2007 SC (HL) 142. 146
Harling v Eddy [1951] 2 KB 739. 96
The Harriette N: Statoil ASA v Louis Dreyfus Energy Services LP [2008]
 EWHC 2257 (Comm); [2008] 2 Lloyd's Rep 685 138

Hedley Byrne & Co Ltd v Heller & Partners Ltd [1964]
    AC 465 (HL) 140, 141, 142, 145
Helstan Securities Ltd v Hertfordshire County Council [1978]
    3 All ER 262. 194
Henderson v Merrett Syndicates Ltd [1995] 2 AC 145 (HL) 142
Henthorn v Fraser [1892] 2 Ch 27 (CA). 64, 70
Hickman v Haynes (1875) LR 10 CP 598 125
High Trees case: Central London Property Trust Ltd v High Trees
    House Ltd [1947] KB 130. . . . . 7–8, 102, 104, 118, 120, 121, 127, 134
HIH Casualty and General Insurance Ltd v Chase Manhattan Bank [2001]
    EWCA Civ 1250; [2001] 2 Lloyd's Rep 483; *on appeal* [2003] UKHL 6; [2003]
    2 Lloyd's Rep 61 . . . . 9, 145, 147, 152
Hillas & Co Ltd v Arcos Ltd (1932) 147 LT 503; 43 Lloyd's Rep 359. . . . . 43, 46, 58
Hoenig v Isaacs [1952] 2 All ER 176. 101
Holwell Securities Ltd v Hughes [1974] 1 WLR 155 (CA) 65
The Household Fire and Carriage Accident Insurance Co v Grant (1879)
    4 Ex D 216 (CA) 64
Howard Marine & Dredging Co Ltd v A Ogden & Sons (Excavations) Ltd [1978]
    QB 574 (CA) 142
Hughes v Metropolitan Railway Co (1877)
    2 App Cas 439 . . . . 8, 102, 117, 120, 123, 124, 125, 126, 127, 128, 135

IBM United Kingdom Ltd v Rockware Glass Ltd [1980] FSR 335 41
Imperial Land Co of Marseilles, Re (Townsend's case) (1871) LR 13 Eq 148 77
Investors' Compensation Scheme Ltd v West Bromwich Building Society [1998]
    1 WLR 896 . . . . 199, 222
Inwards v Baker [1965] 2 QB 29. 133
The Ion: Nippon Yusen Kaisha v Pacifica Navegacion SA [1980]
    2 Lloyds Rep 245 131–2
Ireland v Livingston (1871–72) LR 5 HL 395 222
Itek Corp v Chicago Aerial Industries 248 A 2d 625 (Del. 1968). 39

The Jay Bola [1997] CLC 993. 200
JD Wetherspoon plc v Van de Berg & Co Ltd [2007] EWHC 1044 (Ch);
    [2007] PNLR 28. 148
Jeffs v Day (1866) LR 1 QB 372. 185
Jennings and Chapman Ltd v Woodman, Matthews & Co [1952]
    2 TLR 409. . . . . 160, 170
Jennings v Rice [2002] EWCA Civ 159; [2003] 1 P & CR 100 131
John Taylors (A Firm) v Masons (A Firm) [2001] EWCA Civ 2106 198
Jorden v Money (1854) 5 HL Cas 185 128
JSC Zestafoni v Ronly Holdings Ltd [2004] EWHC 245 (Comm);
    [2004] Lloyd's Rep 335 (QB) 68
Junior Books Ltd v Veitchi Co Ltd [1983] 1 AC 520. 239

The Kanchenjunga: Motor Oil Hellas (Corinth) Refineries SA v Shipping
    Corporation of India [1990] 1 Lloyds Rep 391. 136
Al-Kandari v JR Brown & Co [1988] QB 665 (CA) 145
Keech v Sandford (1726) Sel Cas T King 61 198
Kenneth Wright Distributors Pty Ltd (in liq), Re 185, 189
Kitchen v Royal Air Force Association [1958] 1 WLR 563 57

Kleinwort Benson Ltd v Lincoln County Council [1999] 2 AC 349 176–7
Kleinwort Benson Ltd v Malaysia Mining Corp Bhd [1988] 1 All ER 714;
    [1989] 1 WLR 379 . . . . 4–5, 34

Laemthong International Lines Company Ltd v Artis (The Laemthong Glory)
    (No 2) [2005] EWCA Civ 519; [2005] 1 Lloyd's Rep 688 . . . . 227, 235
Lalani v Crump [2007] EWHC (Ch) 47; (2007) EG 136 133
Lampet's case (1613) 10 Co Rep 46b, 48a 185
Lane v O'Brien Homes Ltd [2004] EWHC 303. 94
Laurent v Sale & Co [1963] 1 WLR 829 187
Lefkowitz v Great Minneapolis Surplus Stores 86 NW 2d 689 (Minn 1957). 82
Les Affréteurs Réunis SA v Leopold Walford Ltd [1919] AC 801 198
Levey & Co v Goldberg [1922] 1 KB 688. 125
Linden Gardens Trust Ltd v Lenesta Sludge Disposals Ltd [1994]
    1 AC 85. . . . . 194–5, 196, 203, 204, 239, 242
Little v Courage (1995) 70 P & CR 469 . . . . 41, 42
LJ Korbetis v Transgrain Shipping BV [2005] EWHC 1345 (QB). 77
London & Regional Investments Ltd v TBI plc Belfast International
    Airport Ltd [2002] EWCA Civ 355. . . . . 41, 161
Luo v Hui Shui See [2008] HKEC 996 (Court of Final Appeal of Hong Kong,
    June 2008): noted Lee & Ho (2009) 125 LQR 25 131
Luxor (Eastborne) Ltd v Cooper [1941] AC 108 99–100
Lymington Marina Ltd v Macnamara [2007] EWCA Civ 151 52

McCormick v Grogan (1869) LR 4 HL 82 122
McEvoy v Belfast Banking Co Ltd [1935] AC 24 229
McRae v Commonwealth Disposals Commission (1951) 84 CLR 377 59
Maharaj v Chand [1986] AC 898 131
Mallozzi v Carapelli SpA [1976] 1 Lloyd's Rep 407 . . . . 46–7, 54, 55
Mamidoil-Jetoil Greek Petroleum SA v Okta Crude Oil Refining AD [2001]
    EWCA Civ 406; [2001] Lloyd's Rep 76 37
Maple Leaf Macro Volatility Master Fund v Rouvroy [2009] EWHC 257 (Comm);
    [2009] I Lloyds Rep 475 26
Margart Pty Ltd, Re [1985] BCLC 314 196
Margetts v Timmer Estate (1999) 178 DLR (4th) 577. . . . . 189, 193–4
Maskell v Horner [1915] 3 KB 106 174
Massai Aviation Services v Attorney General of the Bahamas [2007]
    UKPC 12; [2007] 5 LRC 179. . . . . 187, 189, 190, 191
Master v Miller (1791) 4 TR 320 . . . . 184, 185
May & Butcher v R [1934] 2 KB 17n 45
Mendelssohn v Normand Ltd [1970] 1 QB 177 96
Miles v Wakefield Metropolitan District Council [1987] AC 539 174
Minister of Health v Bellotti [1944] 1 KB 298. 125
Mobil Oil Australia Ltd v Wellcome International Pty Ltd and Others (1998)
    153 ALR 196 . . . . 100, 101, 102
Monk Construction v Norwich Union Life Insurance Society (1992)
    62 BLR 107. 34
Monk v Australia & New Zealand Banking Group Ltd (1994) 34 NSWLR 148 191
Morrison Shipping Co v The Crown (1924) 20 Ll L Rep 283 . . . . 100, 102
Motor Oil Hellas (Corinth) Refineries SA v Shipping Corporation of India
    (The Kanchenjunga) [1990] 1 Lloyds Rep 391 136

MSM Consulting Limited v United Republic of Tanzania [2009]
    EWHC 121 (QB) 160, 170–1
Mulchrone v Swiss Life (UK) Plc [2005] EWHC 1808 (Comm). 236
Multiplex Constructions UK Ltd v Cleveland Bridge UK Ltd [2006]
    EWHC 1341 (TCC); 107 Con LR 1 41–2
Mulvenna v Royal Bank of Scotland [2003] EWCA Civ 1112 57
Murphy v Zamonex Pty Ltd (1993) 31 NSWLR 439 201
Murray v ABT Associates 18 F. 3d 1376 (1994) 28

Napier and Ettrick (Lord) v Hunter [1993] AC 713. 172
National Mutual Association of Australasia Ltd v Walsh (1987) 8 NSWLR 586. 176
The New York Star: Port Jackson Stevedoring Pty Ltd v Salmond &
    Spraggon Pty (Australia) Ltd [1981] 1 WLR 138 231
New Zealand Shipping Co Ltd v AM Satterthwaite & Co Ltd
    (The Eurymedon) [1975] AC 154 230
Newfoundland Government v Newfoundland Railway Co (1888)
    LR 13 App Cas 199 199
Newman Tours Ltd v Ranier Investment Ltd [1992] 2 NZLR 68 96
Nile Co for the Export of Agricultural Crops v H & J M Bennett
    (Commodities) Ltd [1986] 1 Lloyd's Rep 555. 37
Nippon Yusen Kaisha v Pacifica Navegacion SA [1980] 2 Lloyds Rep 245 131–2
Nisshin Shipping Co Ltd v Cleaves & Company Ltd [2003] EWHC 2602;
    [2004] 1 Lloyd's Rep 38 . . . . 227, 228
Nissho Iwai Petroleum Co Inc v Cargill International SA [1993]
    1 Lloyd's Rep 80 42
Nokes v Doncaster Amalgamated Collieries Ltd [1940] AC 1014. 195
Norglen Ltd (In Liquidation) v Reeds Rains Prudential Ltd [1999] 2 AC 1 189
Norglen Ltd v Reeds Rains Prudential Ltd, 3 February 1994 (unreported) 189
Norwich Union Fire Insurance Society Ltd v WH Price Ltd [1934] AC 455 175
NV Stoomv Maats 'De Maas' v Nippon Yusen Kaisha (The Pendrecht) [1980]
    2 Lloyd's Rep 56 (QB) 71, 72

453416 Ontario Inc v White (1984) 42 CPC 209 189
528650 Ontario Ltd v Hepburn (2003) 124 ACWS (3d) 16 189
Ord v Upton [2000] Ch 352. 193
Overseas Tankship (UK) Ltd v Morts Dock & Engineering Co
    (The 'Wagon Mound') [1961] AC 388 (PC). 140, 142

The Pamela: Schelde Delta Shipping BV v Astarte Shipping Ltd [1995]
    2 Lloyds Rep 249 (QB). 71, 74
Pan Atlantic Insurance Co Ltd v Pine Top Insurance Co Ltd [1995]
    1 AC 501 (HL). 139
Panchaud Freres SA v Etablissements General Grain Co [1970]
    1 Lloyds Rep 53 117
Pao On v Lau Yiu Long [1980] AC 614 97–8
Paragon Finance plc v Nash [2001] EWCA Civ 1466; [2002] 1 WLR 685 52
Parker v Parker [2003] EWHC (Ch) 846 131
Partridge v Crittenden [1968] 1 WLR 1204 (QB) 81
Paula Lee Ltd v Robert Zehil Ltd [1983] 2 All ER 390 57
Pavey & Matthews Pty Ltd v Paul (1987) 162 CLR 221 179
Peek v Gurney (1873) LR 6 HL 337 . . . . 141, 144, 147

The Pendrecht: NV Stoomv Maats 'De Maas' v Nippon Yusen Kaisha [1980]
2 Lloyd's Rep 56 (QB) 71, 72
Penwith District Council v V P Developments Ltd [2005] 2 BCLC 607 201
Performing Right Society Ltd v London Theatre of Varieties Ltd [1924] AC 1 198
Petromec Inc v Petroleo Brasileiro SA Petrobas [2005] EWCA Civ 891; [2006]
1 Lloyd's Rep 121 . . . . 6, 39, 44–6, 48, 50, 57, 60, 139
Pharmaceutical Society of Great Britain v Boots Cash Chemists (Southern) [1953]
1 QB 401 (CA) 80–1
Phillips Petroleum Co UK Ltd v Enron Europe Ltd (1997) CLC 329 . . . . 48–50, 53
Photo Production Ltd v Securicor Transport Ltd [1980] AC 827 230
Pinnel's Case (1602) 5 Co Rep 117a 90, 92, 97, 119
The Pioneer Container [1994] 2 AC 324 233
Pitt v PHH Asset Management Ltd [1993] 1 WLR 327 37
Plevins v Downing (1876) 1 CP 220 116
Port Jackson Stevedoring Pty Ltd v Salmond & Spraggon Pty (Australia) Ltd
(The New York Star) [1981] 1 WLR 138 231
Poulton v Commonwealth (1953) 89 CLR 540 188
Pridean v Forest Taverns (1996) 75 P&CR 447 161
The Product Star (No 2): Abu Dhabi National Tanker Co v Product
Star Shipping Ltd (No 2) [1993] 1 Lloyd's Rep 397 . . . . 5, 51–2, 54
Prudential Assurance Co Ltd v Ayres [2007] EWHC 775 (Ch); [2007] L & TR 35;
reversed [2008] EWCA Civ 52; [2008] L & TR 30 225
PSC Industrial Services Canada Inc v The Queen in right of Ontario (2005)
258 DLR (4th) 320 . . . . 188, 193

Queensland Electricity Generating Board v New Hope Collieries Pty Ltd [1989]
1 Lloyd's Rep 205 . . . . 40, 43

Rae Lambert v HTV Cymru (Wales) Ltd [1998] FSR 87 41
Rama Corpn v Proved Tin and General Investments Ltd [1952] 2 QB 147 220
Raymond Burke Motors Ltd v Mersey Docks and Harbour Board Co [1986]
1 Lloyd's Rep 155 231
Redgrave v Hurd (1881) 20 Ch D 1 (CA) 138
Regalian Properties v London Docklands Development Corp [1995]
1 WLR 212 . . . . 10, 160–1, 170
Rennick v O.P.T.I.O.N. Care Inc (1996) 77F 3d 309 19
Reynell v Lewis (1846) 15 M & W 517 219–20
Rickard Constructions Pty Ltd v Rickard Hails Moretti Pty Ltd (2004)
188 FLR 278 190
The Rijn [1981] 2 Lloyd's Rep 267 57
Rizzo & Rizzo Shoes Ltd, Re (1998) 38 OR (3d) 280 190
Rose v Buckett [1901] 2 KB 449 193
Roxborough v Rothmans of Pall Mall Ltd (2001) 208 CLR 516 . . . . 164, 167, 173
Royal Bank of Scotland plc v Etridge (No 2) [2001] UKHL 44; [2002]
2 AC 773 152
Royscot Trust Ltd v Rogerson [1991] 2 QB 297 (CA) 142
RTS Flexible Systems Ltd v Molkerei Alois Muller GMBH & Co KG [2009]
EWCA Civ 26, (2009) 123 Con LR 130; [2009] 2 All ER (Comm) 542 . . . . 4, 24–5

Sabemo Pty Ltd v North Sydney Municipal Council [1977] 2 NSWLR 880 . . . . 161, 168
Scaptrade, The [1981] 2 Lloyd's Rep 425 37

Schelde Delta Shipping BV v Astarte Shipping Ltd (The Pamela) [1995]
    2 Lloyds Rep 249 (QB) 71, 74
Schweppe v Harper [2008] EWCA Civ 442 102
Scruttons v Midland Silicones Ltd [1962] AC 446 208
Sears Tooth (A Firm) v Payne Hicks Beach (A Firm) [1997] 2 FLR 116 188
Seear v Lawson (1880) 15 Ch D 426. 192
Selectmove, Re [1995] 1 WLR 474 . . . . 103, 105, 118
Sempra Metals Ltd v Inland Revenue Commissioners [2007] UKHL 34;
    [2008] 1 AC 561 166
Sheffield District Railway Co v Great Central Railway Co (1911) 27 TLR 471 41
Shogun Finance v Hudson [2004] 1 AC 919. 217
Sigma Finance Corporation, Re [2009] UKSC 2. 36
Smith New Court Securities Ltd v Citibank [1997] AC 254 (HL) 140, 142
Smith v Chadwick (1884) 9 App Cas 187 141
Smith v Hughes (1871) LR 6 QB 597 . . . . 138, 146, 151, 152–3
Socimer International Bank Ltd v Standard Bank London Ltd [2008]
    EWCA Civ 116; [2008] 1 Lloyd's Rep 558 . . . . 52, 53, 59
Soulsbury v Soulsbury [2007] EWCA Civ 969; [2008] 2 WLR 834 . . . . 99, 101
Southern Water Authority v Carey [1985] 2 All ER 1077 . . . . 230, 231
Stack v Dowden [2007] UKHL 17; [2007] 2 AC 432. 165
Standard Chartered Bank v Pakistan Shipping Co (Nos 2 and 4) [2002]
    UKHL 43; [2003] 1 AC 959 151
Statoil ASA v Louis Dreyfus Energy Services LP (The 'Harriette N') [2008]
    EWHC 2257 (Comm); [2008] 2 Lloyd's Rep 685 138
Stilk v Myrick (1809) 2 Campbell 317 . . . . 90, 91, 92–3, 104
Stocznia Gdanska SA v Latvian Shipping Co Ltd [1998] 1 WLR 574 169
Strover v Strover [2005] EWHC 860; [2005] NPC 64 130
Stubbs v The Holywell Railway Company (1867) LR 2 Exch 311 163
Swift v Dairywise Farms Ltd [2000] 1 WLR 1177 198

Talbot v Von Boris [1911] KB 854 173
Tate v Williamson (1866) LR 2 Ch App 55 138
Texaco Inc v Pennzoil Co 729 S.W. 2d 768 (1987) 4, 28–32
Texas Steamship Co v The Brimnes (Owners) (The Brimnes) [1975]
    1 QB 929 (CA). 71, 73, 74
Thompson v Liquichimica of America Inc 481 F. Supp. 365 (EDNY 1979) 40
Thorner v Majors [2009] UKHL 18; [2009] 1 WLR 776 . . . . 130, 136
Thornton v Shoe Lane Parking [1971] 2 QB 163 (CA). 63, 79, 210–11
Timothy's Pty Ltd, Re [1981] 2 NSWLR 706. 188
Tool Metal Manufacturing Co Ltd v Tungsten Electric Co Ltd [1955]
    1 WLR 761 . . . . 126, 127
Total Liban SA v Vitol SA [1999] 2 Lloyd's Rep 700 188
Trendtex Trading Corp v Crédit Suisse [1982]
    AC 679 . . . . 184, 186–7, 188, 189, 190, 191, 193
24 Seven Utility Services Ltd v Rosekey Ltd [2003] EWHC 3415 (QB) 188, 193
Tye v House [1997] 2 EGLR 171 37

Ulrich v Ulrich and Felton [1968] 1 WLR 180 165
UNISON v Allen [2007] IRLR 975 195
Universe Tankships Inc of Monrovia v International Transport Workers
    Federation (The Universe Sentinel) [1983] 1 AC 366 111

Upton-on- Severn Rural District Council v Powell [1942] 1 All ER 220. . . . . 165, 166

Vandepitte v Preferred Accident Insurance Corporation of New York [1933]
   AC 70 . . . . 198, 200
Vedatech Corporation v Crystal Decisions (UK) Ltd [2002] EWHC 818 169

W & J Alan & Co v el Nasr Export [1972] 2 QB 189 120
Wagon Mound case: Overseas Tankship (UK) Ltd v Morts Dock &
   Engineering Co [1961] AC 388 (PC). 140, 142
Walford v Miles [1992]
   2 AC 128 (HL) 5, 37–9, 40, 42, 44, 46, 47, 50–1, 52, 53–4, 55–6, 58, 60, 139
Waltons Stores (Interstates) Ltd v Maher (1988) 164 CLR 387. 130
Warmington v Miller [1973] QB 877 204
Waste Not Wanted Inc v The Queen in right of Canada [1988] 1 FC 239. 191
Watford Electronics Ltd v Sanderson Ltd [2001] EWCA Civ 317; [2001]
   1 All ER (Comm) 696 41
Watson v Mid-Wales Ry Co (1867) LR 2 CP 593 199
Way v Latilla [1937] 3 All ER 759 . . . . 168, 170, 179
West of England Fire Insurance Co v Isaacs [1897] 1 QB 226 202
White & Carter Ltd v McGregor [1962] AC 413. 102
White v Jones [1995] 2 AC 207 89
Whittle Movers Ltd v Hollywood Express Ltd [2009] EWCA Civ 1189 4
William Lacey (Hounslow) Ltd v Davis [1957] 1 WLR 932 . . . . 166, 169
Williams v Roffey Brothers Ltd [1991]
   1 QB 1. . . . . .7, 91, 92, 95, 96, 98–9, 104, 105, 106, 111, 112, 113
Willis Management (Isle of Man) Ltd v Cable & Wireless Plc [2005] EWCA Civ 806;
   [2005] 2 Lloyd's Rep 597 45
Wiluszynski v Tower Hamlets LBC [1989] ICR 493 175
Withers v General Theatre Corp [1933] 2 KB 536 57
WJ Vine Pty Ltd v Paul [1973] VR 161. . . . . 185, 189
Woodhouse AC Israel Cocoa Ltd SA v Nigerian Produce Marketing Co [1972]
   AC 741 . . . . 115, 119
Woolwich Equitable Building Society v Inland Revenue Commissioners
   [1993] AC 70 174
Wrotham Park v Parkside Homes [1974] 1 WLR 798 94
WWF World Wide Fund for Nature v World Wrestling Federation
   Entertainment Inc [2007] EWCA Civ 286; [2008] 1 WLR 445. 94

Yeoman's Row Management Ltd v Cobbe [2008] UKHL 55; [2008]
   1 WLR 1752 . . . . 10, 130, 161–2, 170

Zuniga v Groce, Locke & Hebdon 878 SW2d 313 189

Table of Legislation

Arbitration Act 1950
  s 27 132
Arbitration Act 1996
  s 7 . . . . 222, 223
Carriage of Goods by Road
  Act 1965 244
  s 14(2) 245
Carriage of Goods by Sea
  Act 1992 . . . . 232, 245
Companies Act 1948
  s 108 124
Consumer Protection (Distance Selling)
  Regulations 2000 83
Contracts (Rights of Third Parties)
  Act 1999 . . . . . . 3, 12, 13, 89, 225, 250
  s 1 . . . . 232, 234
  s 1(1)(a) 227
  s 1(1)(b) 225, 241, 248
  s 1(2) 226, 227, 248
  s 1(3) 228
  s 1(4) 229
  s 1(5) 13, 229
  s 1(6) 232
  s 2 13
  s 6(5) 232
  s 6(5)(b) 244
  s 8 233–4
  s 8(1) 233
  s 8(2) 233
Criminal Law Act 1967
  s 14(2) 184
Electronic Commerce (EC Directive)
  Regulations 2002
  reg 9(1)(a) 85
  reg 9(4) 85
  reg 11 83
  reg 11(2) 84
  reg 11(2)(a) 72, 84
Electronic Communications Act 2007
  ss 7–8 62
Fire Prevention (Metropolis) Act 1774
  s 83 235
Insolvency Act 1986
  s 127 196
  Sch 4, Pt III, para 6 192
  Sch 5, Pt II, para 9 192
Judicature Acts 197

Law of Property (Miscellaneous
  Provisions) Act 1989
  s 2(1) 161
Limitation Act 1980
  s 32(1)(c) 176
Marine Insurance Act 1906
  s 18 139
Married Women's Property Act 1882
  s 11 235
Misrepresentation Act 1967 . . . . 144, 157
  s 2(1) . . 9, 140, 142, 143–4, 149, 155, 156
  s 2(2) 140
Road Traffic Act 1948
  s 148(7) 235
Sale of Goods Act 1979 45
  s 8(2) 45, 179
  s 14 152
Statute of Frauds 1677 116
Third Parties (Rights Against Insurers)
  Act 1930 . . . . 235, 238–9
Third Parties (Rights Against Insurers)
  Act 2010 235
Unfair Terms in Consumer Contracts
  Regulations 1999 56
  reg 5(1) 51, 86

OTHER COUNTRIES

AUSTRALIA

Electronic Transactions Act 1999
  s 14(3) 72

FRANCE

French Civil Code 209
  Art 953 110
  Art 955 110
  Art 1102 110

GERMANY

German Civil Code
  **167–68 209
  **320–26 110
  *120 209
  *519 110
  *530(1) 110

GREECE

Greek Civil Code
*211 209

ITALY

Italian Civil Code
Art 1387 209

JAPAN

Japanese Civil Code
*99 209

SWITZERLAND

Swiss OR
Art 32 209

UNITED STATES

Restatement of Agency (Third)
*4-05(1) 217
Restatement (Second) of Contracts (1981)
*64 64
*66 76
*68 71–2
*90 130
Uniform Commercial Code
*1-201(26) 72
Uniform Computer Information
    Transactions Act
s 102(a)(52)(B)(II) 72
s 203(4) 69
s 206 63

EUROPEAN UNION

Directive 2004/39/EC (Markets in
    Financial Information) 245

CONVENTIONS

Brussels Convention
Art 17 233
Hague-Visby Rules
Art IV *bis* 232
UN Convention on Contracts for the
    International Sale of Goods
Art 14(2) 81
Art 18(2) 71
Art 20(1) 76
Art 24 71
UN Convention on the Use of Electronic
    Communications in International
    Contracts
Art 10(2) 72, 73, 75, 79
Art 11 81
Art 12 63
UN Model Law on Electronic
    Commerce
Art 2(f) 72
Art 15(2) 72
Unidroit Principles of International
    Commercial Contracts
Art 1.7 39
Art 1.9(3) 71
Art 2.1.15 19

PART A

Introduction

1
Overview

ANDREW BURROWS AND EDWIN PEEL

PART A. INTRODUCTION

This book is concerned with the formation of contracts and their relationship with, or effect upon, certain 'third parties'. While Part B deals
with 'formation', much of the focus is not on formation itself, but
rather the consequences of a failure to reach a binding contract. In that
sense it is concerned with the 'formation process': limits on the parties' freedom to negotiate, or not to negotiate as they see fit; whether,
and what, obligations they owe to each other at the pre-contract stage;
whether, and what, forms of binding obligation they can create short
of the full contract towards which they are negotiating. So far as formation itself is concerned, two chapters look closely at the 'modification' of an existing contract, in particular in the context of the payment
of debts, whether via contractual or non-contractual means, and a
last is concerned with the application of the well established, if not
always entirely certain, rules of offer and acceptance to the formation
of contract through the media of new technology. Part C deals with
third parties and three types of tri-partite arrangements in particular:
contracts conferring benefits on non-party beneficiaries; assignment;
and contracts made through an agent. Although there are just three
chapters in Part C, they range across a broad spectrum of issues: the
effectiveness and use being made of the Contracts (Rights of Third
Parties) Act 1999; equitable assignment and trusts; construction; and
the rules of offer and acceptance (it is perhaps fittingly ironic that one
of the chapters in 'Parties' is more concerned with 'formation' in the
strict sense than some of the chapters in 'Formation').

In this introductory chapter we aim to provide an overview of the
various papers and to indicate the main issues that were aired in the
discussions that followed.

PART B. FORMATION

The proceedings began with Chapter 2 by Michael Furmston in which
he seeks to analyse the legal effect of the many kinds of preliminary
documents which may be loosely labelled as 'Letters of Intent'. As he

points out, parties may use the language of 'letter of intent', or similar terms such as 'Heads of Agreement', 'Memorandum of Understanding', or 'Agreement in Principle', but not necessarily always understand them to have the same meaning from one transaction to the next. He concludes that the only general rule is that there is no general rule. Everything must depend on an objective analysis of what the parties have said and done. If one also allows, as he says, for a distinction in attitude to contracts between businessmen and lawyers, it is not surprising to find that the employment of letters of intent can produce a variety of results: that there is no contract, though acts of performance may lead to restitutionary effects ('the most common case', eg *British Steel Corp. v Cleveland Bridge Engineering Co*[1]); that the letter of intent, though in a sense preliminary, nevertheless leads to a complete contract (eg perhaps most famously, or controversially, *Texaco Inc v Pennzoil Co*[2]); or that the document falls short of the full contract, but nevertheless has some contractual effects (eg a simple contract for a price, or agreements as to the course of negotiations).

Much of the discussion focused on two well known cases. The first was the *Cleveland Bridge* case. Michael Furmston suggested that the case would not necessarily be decided the same way today, but recent cases have tended to emphasize the availability of restitutionary relief and stressed that judges should not feel constrained to find a contract where evidence of the parties' intention falls short of that.[3] It will be interesting to see if this 'trend' is continued by the Supreme Court in its forthcoming decision in *RTS Flexible Systems Ltd v Molkerei Alois Muller.*[4]

The second case was *Kleinwort Benson Ltd v Malaysia Mining Corp Bhd*[5] in which the Court of Appeal decided that the 'letter of comfort' provided by the parent company did not amount to a guarantee of the subsidiary's obligation. Much like the courts in the case itself,[6] there was a quite stark difference of opinion about the correctness of the decision among participants. A reference to the binding nature of letters of comfort in French law led to the observation from Georges Affaki that this has been the source of some uncertainty, particularly in

[1] [1984] 1 All ER 504.

[2] 729 S W 2d 768 (1987).

[3] See, eg *Whittle Movers Ltd v Hollywood Express Ltd* [2009] EWCA Civ 1189.

[4] Appeal heard by the Supreme Court on 2 December 2009. For the earlier proceedings, see: [2009] EWCA Civ 26, [2009] 2 All ER (Comm) 542.

[5] [1989] 1 WLR 379.

[6] Hirst J, at first instance ([1988] 1 All ER 714) had found that the letter of comfort was enforceable.

banking, and he expressed the hope that England would not go down this route. One unresolved question was as to the precise nature of a 'binding' letter of comfort, if it is not simply a guarantee.[7]

Michael Furmston's reference to agreements as to the course of negotiations leads naturally into Edwin Peel's chapter on the status of agreements to negotiate in good faith. In the first part, he seeks to show that the current position is that, strictly speaking, there is no enforceable agreement to negotiate in good faith, notwithstanding attempts to limit the decision of the House of Lords in *Walford v Miles*[8] to so-called 'bare' agreements to negotiate. The willingness to seek out such limitations is itself an indication of a certain judicial disquiet as to the correctness of the decision in *Walford*, and in the second part of Chapter 3 Edwin Peel suggests a possible standard of good faith by which even agreements to negotiate may have some legal content. He does so by drawing an analogy with the limit imposed by the courts on the exercise of 'contractual discretion', namely that such discretion must not be exercised arbitrarily, capriciously, unreasonably, or for an improper purpose.[9] This is a fairly minimal standard which may give legal content to agreements to negotiate so that they are at least enforceable, but will not often result in a finding of breach given that it is a standard which allows parties to take account of their own commercial interest. He concludes by considering the possible remedies in the event of breach and suggests that this may be an area where an award of damages on the basis of the 'reliance' measure may be more commonplace.

Although there was some difference of opinion, a majority of those who spoke shared the sense of disquiet that English law should seem to know nothing, or very little in the way, of an enforceable agreement to negotiate. This led to discussion of whether the standard proposed by Edwin Peel's chapter should be viewed as *the* standard or whether it was better viewed as a minimum standard from which the parties could depart if it were clear that their intention was to impose more onerous obligations. In this regard, reference was made to a paper by Alan Berg and the proposition therein that it is precisely by agreeing to negotiate in good faith that the parties have undertaken not to, or at least to limit, the pursuit of their own commercial self-interest.[10]

---

[7] See, in this respect, the very recent decision of the CA in *Associated British Ports v Ferryways NV* [2009] EWCA Civ 189, [2009] 1 Lloyds Rep 595.

[8] [1992] 2 AC 128.

[9] Based on decisions such as that in *Abu Dhabi National Tanker Co v Product Star Shipping Ltd (No 2) ('The Product Star')* [1993] 1 Lloyd's Rep 397.

[10] A Berg, 'Promises to Negotiate in Good Faith' (2003) 119 *LQR* 357.

On this there was a greater difference of opinion and, as if to reinforce that the problem is one of the uncertainty of having the courts impose the appropriate standards, it was the difference of opinion between two participants from the bench which is perhaps most noteworthy.[11]

In Chapter 4 Donal Nolan assesses how a contract is formed when made through the medium of email, or a website. As he points out the overarching question may be *how*, and more particularly how to apply the rules of offer and acceptance, but it is asked so as to determine the questions which matter in practice, which are *whether, when*, and *where* such contracts are made. Guided by what he regards as the three principal considerations—the need for certainty, the protection of autonomy, in particular the preservation of freedom of manoeuvre during contract negotiations, and the protection of the reasonable expectations of those involved—he concludes that the 'default' rule for acceptance by email should be when the email arrives on the server which manages the offeror's email; not when the email is read by the offeror, or when the email ought reasonably to have come to the offeror's attention.

So far as websites are concerned and, in particular, the more difficult scenario where performance does not immediately follow the placing of the customer's order,[12] he does not advocate a general rule as such. He notes that the normal understanding, as with goods advertised in a shop, must be that it is the customer who makes the offer in response to an invitation to treat posted on the website. As for any acceptance, the answer is 'less obvious' and he emphasizes how this is an area where on-line retailers can do much to pre-determine the precise moment of acceptance with an appropriately drafted clause.

Donal Nolan stresses that what he proposes for acceptance by email is a 'default' rule and, as a default rule, the moment the email arrives on the server which manages the offeror's email should be preferred primarily on the grounds of certainty, at least when compared to any alternative. But, as a default rule, he also acknowledges that it may be necessary to depart from it when, as he says, 'things go wrong'. It was the scope, or force, of the default rule and the possible exceptions to it

---

[11] This did not include Longmore LJ who chaired a later session, but in a sense it was his view that such agreements should be regarded as enforceable (in *Petromec Inc v Petroleo Brasileiro SA Petrobas* [2005] EWCA Civ 891; [2006] 1 Lloyd's Rep 161, at [121], discussed in Ch 3) which was the subject of debate.

[12] He contrasts this with the more 'straightforward' scenario which involves digital products, such as software, music, or videos, where a consumer goes onto the retailer's website and downloads the product in return for payment. Once the buyer's order has been placed, performance of the contract by the retailer is likely to begin immediately, as the product is downloaded onto the buyer's computer, so that the buyer will have little or no opportunity to alter or cancel the transaction.

which was the principal topic of discussion, particularly if one also had to allow for the subtle technological differences in email systems (some of which, one suspects, were lost on some participants (including both of the editors)). To the extent that the proposed solutions for when things go wrong turned primarily on the relative fault of offeror and offeree some questioned whether, in fact, the rule really being advocated was one of whether the email ought reasonably to have come to the offeror's attention. While acknowledging that it may just be a question of degree, Donal Nolan emphasized the desirability of a simple, clear rule to begin with.

Given a degree of overlap in the chapters by Mindy Chen-Wishart and Ben McFarlane, a summary of both chapters may be helpful before noting the key points of the discussion which considered the arguments they had raised. The principal focus of Chapter 5 by Mindy Chen-Wishart is the problem of 'one-sided contract modifications'; one-sided in the sense that one party promises to give more for the same reciprocal obligation (an 'adding modification', as exemplified by *Williams v Roffey Brothers Ltd*[13]), or to accept a reduced reciprocal obligation (a 'subtracting modification', as exemplified by *Collier v P & MJ Wright (Holdings) Ltd*[14]) from the other party. How can the decisions in both cases be reconciled with the doctrine of consideration? Mindy Chen-Wishart's solution is not to dilute the need for consideration in a bilateral contract via the introduction of a test of 'practical benefit' (*Roffey*),[15] nor to distort the true role of promissory estoppel (*Collier*), but to recognize that in each case the courts were simply giving effect to a unilateral contract, ie one made only on *actual* performance: *if* you complete the flats I will pay you a sum which represents an additional £575 on the original price (*Roffey*); *if* you pay your share of the partnership's debt, I will release you from the balance of the debt (*Collier*).

In Chapter 6, Ben McFarlane takes the decision of the Court of Appeal in *Collier v Wright* as his starting point and also considers whether it is a decision which can best be explained as an application of promissory estoppel. He decries the idea of a unitary doctrine, or general principle, of promissory estoppel. Instead, he identifies at work in the cases at least three distinct principles: (i) acceptance by A of a substitute performance by B—a form of waiver which rests on the need for finality and which he considers best explains Denning J's obiter view in *Central London Property Trust Ltd v High Trees House Ltd*[16] that,

---

[13] [1991] 1 QB 1.
[14] [2007] EWCA Civ 1329, [2008] 1 WLR 643.
[15] Particularly, if that includes the mere *promise* to perform a pre-existing duty.
[16] [1947] KB 130.

had the landlord claimed arrears for 1940 to 1944 (the period in which the tenant had offered, and the landlord had accepted, a reduced rent) such a claim would have failed; (ii) limits on A's acquisition, or enforcement, of a right as a result of B's action or inaction, in circumstances where B's conduct was influenced by a promise by A that, if B acted or failed to act in that way, A would *not* acquire, or would not enforce, the right in question—exemplified by *Hughes v Metropolitan Railway Co*[17] (indeed, he refers to this as the *Hughes* principle); (iii) the prospect of B's suffering a detriment as a result of B's reasonable reliance on A's promise—a principle which is close to promissory estoppel save in its potential to create a new duty for A, which outcome is usually confined to proprietary estoppel.

This categorization of the cases and the principles for which he contends they stand leads Ben McFarlane to a specific conclusion that, while the *Hughes* principle cannot apply to a promise to accept a lesser sum in satisfaction of a debt, the other two may and it is the first of them which best explains the decision of the Court of Appeal in *Collier v Wright*. It also leads him to the general conclusion that the law will continue in a confused state if these quite different principles continue to be applied as if they were part of a unitary doctrine of promissory estoppel.

Given the prominence of *Collier v Wright* in both chapters, it is not surprising that it was the subject of some of the discussion which followed; all the more so as this session was chaired by Lord Justice Longmore.[18] Both chapters see the *actual payment* of the lesser sum as crucial: Mindy Chen-Wishart in support of a consideration-based analysis, which sees the arrangement between the parties as resting on a unilateral contract; Ben McFarlane in support of a principle akin to waiver (though he maintains that his first principle is not waiver itself[19]). The sense that something would be wrong if[20] the creditor had clearly represented that he would not seek the balance of the debt if the debtor paid his share, but would be free to do so even when he had been paid that share was widely accepted,[21] but there was far less agreement as to the most appropriate basis for prevention. Some preferred the apparent simplicity of effectively abolishing the need for

---

[17] (1877) 2 App Cas 439.

[18] Who heard the appeal with Mummery LJ and Arden LJ.

[19] This begs the obvious question about what one means by the elastic concept of waiver, but that is a debate for another day.

[20] And as Longmore LJ pointed out in *Collier*, this not only may, but should, be a big 'if': [2007] EWCA Civ 1329, [2008] 1 WLR 643, at [48].

[21] But not universally so.

consideration for the modification of an existing contract, but that of course would require the setting aside of the decision of the House of Lords in *Foakes v Beer*.[22] The unilateral contract analysis was well received, but some felt that it may lead to difficult questions about if, or when, the unilateral offer could be revoked once the offeree had commenced, but not yet completed performance.[23] A noticeable feature of the discussion of Ben McFarlane's chapter was the sense from the practitioners in the audience that to strive for a unitary doctrine of promissory estoppel was no bad thing; a tendency to focus on particular cases is what had made this such an uncertain area.

In Chapter 7 John Cartwright engages with the traditional view that there can be no liability in the tort of deceit for non-disclosure. He notes that very little prominence has been given to the decision of Lawrence Collins J in *Conlon v Simms*,[24] holding for the first time by way of ratio,[25] that damages are available in the tort of deceit for fraudulent breach of a duty of disclosure. He argues that such a proposition finds very little support in the earlier authorities,[26] and goes on to consider the full implications of the underlying reasoning, namely that the duty of disclosure is assimilated to misrepresentation: a failure to fulfil the duty to disclose 'is tantamount to an implied representation that there is nothing relevant to disclose'. His conclusion is that the decision in *Conlon* is 'right, but not for the right reasons'; there should be liability in the case of a deliberate (fraudulent) breach of a duty of disclosure. Whether liability should extend to a negligent breach of a duty of disclosure he regards as a further issue which needs to be addressed separately, and any prospect of applying the underlying reasoning to s 2(1) of the Misrepresentation Act 1967 would seem to require an amendment of the wording since it currently requires a 'misrepresentation' to have been 'made' by the other party to the contract.[27]

In the discussion which followed there was widespread agreement with the proposition that where a defendant breaches a recognized duty of disclosure and does so with the level of culpability required of fraud, or indeed other torts, damages should be available as a remedy. There was, inevitably, far less agreement on what John Cartwright had

---

[22] (1884) LR 9 App Cas 605.

[23] See Ch 5, part 2(d) where Mindy Chen-Wishart argues that this simply raises an issue of construction, to be decided on a case by case basis.

[24] [2006] EWHC 401 (Ch), [2006] 2 All ER 1024.

[25] He also notes support for the idea from Lord Bingham in *HIH Casualty and General Insurance Ltd v Chase Manhattan Bank* [2003] UKHL 6, [2003] 2 Lloyd's Rep 61, at [21].

[26] Most notably, *Banque Keyser Ullmann SA v Skandia (UK) Insurance Co Ltd* [1990] 1 QB 665, CA.

[27] A point emphasized by the Court of Appeal: *ibid*, at 790.

identified as the larger (and quite different) question of whether the scope of the existing duties of disclosure should be broadened—both for the remedy of rescission and for the claim for damages in tort. The different positions adopted on this question matched in many ways those adopted when debating the scope of any obligation to negotiate in good faith. This is not surprising given that they both go to the fundamental question about the extent of 'freedom of negotiation'.

In Chapter 8 James Edelman assesses when it is that one party should be entitled to a claim in restitution in circumstances when the parties have been negotiating towards a contract which fails to materialize. On the assumption that the defendant has been enriched,[28] he criticizes what he calls the conventional 'risk analysis', ie an approach under which the court asks: did the claimant take the risk that if no contract was reached he would not be paid? The question he prefers to ask is: did the claimant perform on the objective basis that such performance would be remunerated? This, he argues, is a question which will better determine *why* it is that the finding should be that the claimant did or did not take the risk of payment. It is a question which places the relevant cases[29] into the category of 'failure of consideration' for the purpose of determining why it is that the enrichment of the defendant is unjust.

As James Edelman explains, his analysis makes explicit the exercise which courts are implicitly undertaking when asking which party 'bore the risk' of unremunerated work. It was this contention that was the principal subject of the discussion which followed. Some questioned whether the 'objective' basis approach was any less 'conclusory' than the conventional risk analysis since both require the courts to take into account 'all the circumstances' and determine whether the claimant was or was not entitled to remuneration. Some wondered whether the entirely objective approach to failure of basis failed to take account of the fact that, at its starting point, the question of risk was a subjective one and some pondered the difference, if any, between an 'objective basis' and a contract. Perhaps inevitably, no firm conclusions were reached but the very lively debate was an appropriate way to bring to an end the first day's deliberations.

---

[28] He deals with this question elsewhere: J Edelman, 'The Meaning of Loss and Enrichment' in R Chambers, C Mitchell, and J Penner (eds), *Philosophical Foundations of Unjust Enrichment* (Oxford: OUP, 2008) ch 8.

[29] Cases such as *Yeoman's Row Management Ltd v Cobbe* [2008] UKHL 55; [2008] 1 WLR 1752 and *Regalian Properties v London Docklands Development Corp* [1995] 1 WLR 212.

PART C. PARTIES

In Chapter 9, Andrew Tettenborn addresses the question of what rights are assignable and when. He argues that the present rules preventing or limiting assignment do not make much sense and are, in some respects, unclear. He favours removing many of the restrictions on assignability while allowing the parties to make contract rights unassignable through anti-assignment clauses. Those clauses should, in his view, be upheld; and he suggests ways in which those drafting such clauses might make them fully effective so as to outflank the controversial reasoning in cases such as *Foamcrete (UK) Ltd v Thrust Engineering Ltd*[30] and *Barbados Trust Co v Bank of Zambia*.[31]

In the discussion there was disagreement between participants as to whether in this context there is a valid distinction to be drawn between an assignment and a declaration of trust. It was pointed out that, whether there is a conceptual distinction or not (and some argued that there is), the courts have been applying different approaches (for example, as to who can enforce the right) so that in practice the two are being treated as if different.

In respect of anti-assignment clauses and Andrew Tettenborn's support for these being upheld, there was an impassioned plea to the contrary by Georges Affaki on the ground that, as a practical matter, such clauses are extremely disruptive in relation to the factoring of large amounts of receivables.[32] It is arguable, however, that one could deal with that by creating a policy-based exception in relation to factoring without altering the basic principle that a no assignment clause should be valid.

In Chapter 10 Thomas Krebs argues that agency is not an independent source of rights and obligations. The contractual liability of a principal to a third party (and vice versa) can be explained by using a simple offer and acceptance model. It also follows in his view that agency pure and simple is not an exception to privity. He argues that a realization of this makes it much easier to understand much of agency law. There is only one doctrine, commonly characterized as part of the law of agency, which cannot be explained without recourse to 'magic': the undisclosed principal doctrine. He argues that this should not obscure the nature of the whole law of agency and goes on

---

[30] [2002] BCC 221.
[31] [2007] EWCA Civ 148, [2007] 1 Lloyd's Rep 495.
[32] For this sort of argument, see Goode, 'Contractual prohibitions against assignment' [2009] *LMCLQ* 300.

to consider three additional problem areas, asking whether the offer and acceptance model can usefully be applied: ratification, apparent authority, and the construction of actual authority.

During the discussion, the question was raised whether the approach advocated by Thomas Krebs and relying on offer and acceptance might, perversely, make it harder to explain actual authority than apparent authority because there is no outward appearance in relation to actual authority. It was also pointed out that, as his paper stressed, the impact of the analysis is to wipe away retrospective ratification because there was no offer and acceptance at the time the contract was entered into. The response to this was that that is indeed the law in some other countries and the English law on ratification would do well to follow suit by departing from *Bolton v Lambert*.[33]

Another line of questioning pondered how far the offer and acceptance analysis was intended to go. In particular, it was argued that one would surely still need special agency rules in the context of companies where one has to think in terms of fictions because the company is not a legal person. Thomas Krebs agreed that his analysis was not intended to displace the need for special rules dealing with the internal structure of a company. He also clarified that one plainly cannot explain the doctrine of the undisclosed principal except by 'magic'. But the purpose of his approach was to see how far so-called agency rules in contract are explicable by normal rules before one has to resort to the more problematic realm of special (magic) rules.

Ten years on from the coming into force of the Contracts (Rights of Third Parties) Acts 1999, Professor Hugh Beale in the final chapter examines the use being made of the Act, as well as some difficulties with it. From enquiries made of practitioners, he presents a novel picture of where the Act is being used. He also draws on that usage to refute some objections of principle put against the reform. His overall conclusion is that the Act is useful but remains underused.

One question of minor detail posed by his chapter is one that one of us can answer. Hugh Beale asks where the inspiration came from to move the focus from enforcement of the contract to enforcement of a term of the contract. The answer is that this emerged during a conversation between Phillip Capper (formally Law Fellow at Keble College, Oxford and now a partner specializing in Construction Law at White & Case) and Andrew Burrows, who was the Law Commissioner in charge of the Privity project. The former put forward the idea as one

---

[33] (1889) LR 41Ch D 295.

that could be used to allay the fears of some of those in the construction industry who were opposing the Bill.

In discussion Robert Stevens, a well-known critic of the 1999 Act, raised a fundamental question of principle about the remedies available to the third party (C) in an example where A and B contract to build a house worth £1 million on C's land and C is given the right to enforce the contract. If A commits a repudiatory breach and B accepts the repudiation so that A is unpaid, what remedy is C entitled to under the 1999 Act? It was suggested that the answer to this is that, just as if B had been suing, the contract price that A would have been paid must be deducted from the expectation damages that C would be entitled to. Although some doubted how that sensible answer could be reached under the 1999 Act, it would seem that there are straightforward ways of arriving at that desired solution. So, for example, s 1(5) states that C will have 'any remedy that would have been available to him … if he had been a party to the contract'. This would allow the courts, by analogy to what the position would have been had B been suing A for B's loss, to take into account, in assessing C's damages in C's action against A, that the contract price has not been paid to A.

Another question raised was whether the provisions in s 2 of the Act on variation are satisfactory for those drafting contracts. But as those provisions allow the parties expressly to apply whatever regime for variation they wish (including making the contract irrevocable as regards third party rights) it is hard to see that this should pose any problem in practice.

PART B

Formation

2

Letters of Intent

MICHAEL FURMSTON*

1. INTRODUCTION

This paper seeks to analyse the legal effect of the many kinds of preliminary documents which may be loosely labelled as 'Letters of Intent'.[1]

Many contracts arise without any negotiation between the parties. The supermarket shopper arrives at the checkout with her trolley and empties the goods onto the space in front of the cashier. The cashier enters them into the till and states the price. Little if anything will be said. Whether we characterize the arrival at the till as the offer or an acceptance, it is clear that the transaction has moved very quickly from no contract to contract.

In most countries it would be a surprise if the shopper arrived at the checkout and said to the cashier 'I will give you $100 for these'. But this is a matter of culture and not of law. Even in England we would not be surprised if a potential buyer of a second-hand car offered the dealer less than the marked price. In England if one was in a shoe shop looking at shoes one would be unlikely to ask the assistant for a discount; in Singapore in a physically very similar shop with identical shoes one would not be at all surprised if the assistant offered 10 per cent off if one looked likely to leave the shop without making a purchase.[2]

In some of these cases there will be no negotiation at all. In others there will be brief negotiations about the price but the parties will still move quickly from no contract to contract. This is largely the situation which classical contract law deals with, but it is by no means the whole range of transaction for which contract law has to provide rules.

* Professor of Law and Dean of the Law School at Singapore Management University. This chapter is based on a chapter in M Furmston and G Tolhurst, *Contract Formation* to be published by OUP in March 2010. It tries to take some account of discussion at the conference and of some recent cases.

[1] R Lake and U Draetta, *Letters of intent and other pre-contractual documents* (2nd edn, London: Butterworths, 1995) (hereafter 'Lake and Draetta'); A Farnsworth, 'Precontractual Liability and Preliminary Agreements: Fair Dealing and Failed Negotiations' (1987) 87 *Columbia L Rev* 217; S Ball, 'Work carried out in pursuance of letters of intent—contract or restitution' (1983) 99 *LQR* 572.

[2] I once asked a Singapore shopkeeper why he marked the price of goods if he offered me a discount as I entered the store and he replied 'those prices are for Japanese'.

Many contracts are the product of months or years of negotiations, often involving consideration of many side issues and involving teams of experts and advisors. Such situations give rise to a whole set of extra problems.

One relatively simple possibility is that the parties will make a deal but postpone its coming into legal effect until some further event. A well known example is the standard method of English house purchase. Here the most common scenario is that the parties negotiate about the price, often with the assistance of estate agents but usually without that of lawyers. Once the price is agreed there is said to be an agreement 'subject to contract' and things are handed over to the parties' lawyers, who do the things that lawyers normally do in this situation, including the preparation of the contract. It is accepted that neither side is bound until copies of the contract are prepared, signed, and exchanged.

It is important to understand that this practice is in most circumstances for the benefit of the buyer. The buyer usually needs to borrow money to complete the purchase and binding offers cannot usually be obtained from lenders until a specific property and an agreed price can be proposed. Further the buyer's lawyer needs to make sure that the seller actually owns the property and that there is not a plan to build a motorway through the back garden. Nevertheless neither party is legally bound and from time to time on rising markets, sellers decide at the last minute to refuse to sign the contract unless the price is increased. This practice, known as 'gazumping', not surprisingly causes fury among buyers but the English Law Commission advised that the problem was not sufficiently serious to be attacked by legislation.[3] In falling markets the reverse practice by which buyers refuse at the last minute to sign unless the price is reduced is not unknown but does not seem to have attracted so much publicity or a perjorative name (perhaps gazundering).

In many cases the parties make written statements of provisional agreement during the negotiation. The names given to such provisional statements are many and various: 'Letters of Intent'; 'Heads of Agreement'; 'Memorandum of Understanding'; 'Agreement in Principle'; and so on. I will for convenience usually call them 'letters of intent'.

The problem appears to occur across all legal systems but the results are not necessarily exactly the same. An invaluable survey was carried

---

[3] See Law Com 65 (1975).

out by a group led by Professor Marcel Fontaine.[4] Their report was for many years available only in French but since 2006 it is also available in English.[5] A major factor is whether the governing law is one which imposes a duty to negotiate in good faith or which permits the parties to make a binding agreement to negotiate in good faith. Many civilian systems require the parties to negotiate in good faith and such a requirement is now often found in Statements of Contract Law intended for international use.[6] It is typically contrary to good faith to enter into or continue negotiations with no real intention of reaching an agreement with the other party.[7] Such notions have found significant degrees of acceptance in the United States version of the common law. English law appears not even to allow the parties to agree to negotiate in good faith but it is far from certain that this rule will survive.[8]

Perhaps the only general rule is that there is no general rule, that is that one cannot say in advance that a letter of intent has or has not legal effect and, if it does, what the effect would be. Everything must depend on an objective analysis of what the parties have said and done.[9]

In their consideration, the working group on International Contracts looked at 26 examples. These examples fall, however, into a rather smaller number of groups. We may consider first cases where the letter of intent does not give rise to a contract; then those where on the contrary it gives rise to a full contract, and then consider situations which fall in between. As we shall see this third group falls into a number of sub groups.

Before we come on to this analysis it is worth saying a little about the practical problems which give rise to the difficulties. One is that in many business situations there are many parties and contracts involved. So if a hotel chain wishes to build a new hotel it will typically enter into a contract with someone who is usually called a main contractor but the hotel will not be built by the main contractor or its employees.

---

[4] The working group on international contracts.

[5] M Fontaine and F De Ly, *Drafting International Contracts* (Transnational Publishers Inc, 2006) (hereafter 'Fontaine and De Ly').

[6] Unidroit Principles for International Commercial Contracts Art 2.1.15; Draft Common Frame of Reference (DCFR) 3.301 (2).

[7] Unidroit Principles 2.1.15 (3); DCFR 3:301 (3).

[8] See M Furmston and G Tolhurst, *Contract Formation* (Oxford: OUP, 2010), ch 12 and the discussion by Edwin Peel in Ch 3 of this book.

[9] The United States Court of Appeals for the ninth circuit come quite close in *Rennick v O.P.T.I.O.N. Care Inc* (1996) 77F 3d 309 to saying that there is a presumption that a letter of intent is not legally binding but reading the opinion as a whole supports rather the proposition in the text.

Nearly all the work, the building of the foundations; the erection of the framework of the building, the windows, the roof, the electrical appliances, the plumbing, the lifts, and so on will be done by specialists. Most of these will be sub-contractors to the main contractor or sub-sub-contractors to the sub-contractors. It is inconceivable that all the contracts could come into existence at the same time. Typically the main contractor will quote a price to the customer (usually called the employer) based on quotations obtained from sub-contractors but he will certainly not want to bind himself to the sub-contractors until he has a binding contract with the employer. In practice there is often pressure to start work before the contracts are all in place. As we shall see many problems arise from this pressure.

In other cases the contract will depend on some governmental permission or on obtaining finance and it is not possible to obtain such finance or permission without having carried the contract-making process forward.

Even where the contract is being negotiated simply between the parties, the negotiation may be long and complex running over weeks or months. In such cases it is common to divide the negotiation up into stages. In such cases what has been agreed at each stage may well be treated as binding but there may be serious practical problems in giving effect to such an assumption.

It is also important to bear in mind that the underlying assumptions of lawyers and businessman in these circumstances are by no means the same.[10]

For lawyers a contract is a mixture of rights, obligations, and remedies for breach. For businessmen, however, it is 'primarily a facilitative device within an economic cycle which turns on such processes as the acquisition of materials, the production of finished goods, marketing and sales, finance and payment'.[11] Thus, businessmen believe that they need not insist on the rights associated with the contractual relationship if some other device or method can achieve their goals.

Therefore, we might conclude that businessmen insist on receiving letters of intent which deny any legally binding effect because they expect that, regardless of legal force, such a document obliges the other party to abide by what he has promised.

Letters of intent can be binding ethically, if not legally. Indeed, it seems that businessmen frequently do not take the legal effect of a

---

[10] S Macaulay, 'Non-contractual Relations in Business: A Preliminary Study' (1963) 28 *Am Soc Rev* 55, at 61. H Beale and A Dugdale, 'Contracts between Businessmen: Planning and the Use of Contractual Remedies' (1975) 2 *British Jl of L and Society* 45.

[11] J Tillotson, *Contract Law in Perspective* (4th edn, London: Cavendish, 2004) 3.

document into consideration and are rarely conscious of the legal position when they insert provisions which deny legal effect. This explains why such documents are often so vague and ambiguous in terms of their legal effect.

This vagueness in expressing the legal effect of a document can also be attributed to the fact that a letter of intent may be an 'un-gentlemen's agreement' which is intended to bind one party while giving the other a free hand. In many instances businessmen wish to obtain the other party's acceptance before binding themselves to conclude the contract. They seek to achieve this by inserting a clause such as, 'This offer is subject to formal approval by our Board of Directors' into the offer. Letters of intent can therefore seek to bind one party whilst leaving the other free. For example, some drafters of letters of intent do not allow the other party a right to negotiate in parallel with a third party, but expressly reserve their own right to do so. As an example, main contractors often try to bind sub-contractors but remain uncommitted themselves. Main contractors calculate their figures based upon particular sub-contractors' estimates and expect the sub-contractor to abide by his assurance that he will not withdraw that estimate. However, since the award of the main contract is not guaranteed, the main contractor does not wish to give any assurance that a contract will be concluded with the sub-contractor. Therefore in letters of intent any commitment on the part of the main contractor is skillfully avoided, yet a promise not to withdraw the estimate is demanded from the sub-contractor.

2. CASES WHERE THE LETTER OF INTENT DOES NOT CREATE A CONTRACT

This must in practice be the most common case. Many letters of intent are no more than measures of goodwill and encouragement. To a lawyer this might not seem worth much but this is too simple a view. If a contractor or sub-contractor who is competing for a job receives a letter of intent, he knows (unless the sender is a complete crook) that he is now the only person being effectively considered. His chances of getting the job have gone up from say 20 per cent to 80 per cent. If he has a boss, he can send it to his boss and hope to be popular for a day or two.

Examples 14 to 19 of the Fontaine working group appear to be of this kind. Example 14 assesses the use of the phrase 'subject to contract' which in English law has the effect of denying a legally binding agreement[12] and example 15 includes an express statement that the document is not to be contractual. This also appears to be clear from the remaining content of the letter in example 15, which indicates that this is early in the negotiation process with many uncertainties still to be resolved:

> We shall of course need to discuss the details of all these documents ...; but if our proposal seems to you to be a starting point for negotiations, we should be glad if you would return to us the enclosed copy of this letter with your signature, which should be preceded by the remark, 'valid as a letter of intent only, without being contractual'.

The commentary assesses this as thoughtful drafting and compares it to example 8 ('We hereby inform you of our intention to award you in due course the order...').

Examples 16 and 17 illustrate further methods of achieving a denial of legal effect. Example 16 indicates that there is not agreement on terms but in any event includes the following: 'In case no agreement is reached on all terms and no contract is signed before ... we reserve the right to cancel this award, without any right for indemnification from your part.'

Example 17 denies any obligation and for good measure excludes any liability (other than for fraudulent conduct) in the event that the matter does not proceed: 'It is clearly understood that so far as concerns our company, no decision has been taken about this acquisition, any such decision being subject to various considerations about the prospects.... It is further understood that in the event that we should not proceed with these proposals ... we would be free of any obligation to you ...'.

Finally, an individual negotiator may indicate that he does not have authority to bind his organization by including a form of wording such as 'subject to the approval of the Board of Directors of Company A'.[13]

An important English case illustrating this is *British Steel Corp v Cleveland Bridge Engineering Co.*[14] In this case Cleveland Bridge and Engineering Co. Ltd (CBE) entered into negotiations with British Steel Corp. (BSC) for the manufacture of a variety of cast-steel nodes for a project in Saudi Arabia. BSC prepared an estimated price and telexed production and delivery information to CBE. After further discussions

---

[12] Fontaine and De Ly, above, n 5, 20.
[13] *Ibid*, 24.
[14] [1984] 1 All ER 504.

on technical aspects and specifications, CBE sent the following letter
of intent to BSC:

> We are pleased to advise you it is the intention of Cleveland Bridge Engi-
> neering Co. Ltd to enter into a Sub-contract with your company, for the
> supply and delivery of the steel castings which form the roof nodes on
> this project. The price will be as quoted in your telex dated 9th February
> '79 . . . The form of Sub-contract to be entered into will be our standard
> form of sub-contract for use in conjunction with the ICE General Condi-
> tions of contract, a copy of which is enclosed for your consideration. . . .
> We understand that you are already in possession of a complete set of our
> node detail drawings and we request that you proceed immediately with
> the works pending the preparation and issuing to you of the official form
> of sub-contract.

[The ICE Conditions provided for unlimited liability for consequential loss due to late delivery by BSC.]

BSC would not have agreed to unlimited liability for late delivery
and intended to submit a formal quotation for individual prices once it
had the full set of drawings from which it could make calculations.

Anticipating that a formal order would follow shortly, BSC went
ahead with the request to commence manufacture.

CBE then indicated for the first time that it required the nodes to
be delivered in a particular sequence. There were further discussions
and negotiations between the parties over the specifications but no
final agreement was reached. BSC sent CBE a formal quotation on its
standard form, quoting an increased price and stating that delivery
dates were to be agreed. CBE rejected this. Meanwhile BSC went ahead
with the casting and delivery of nodes in stages in an effort to comply
with requirements for delivery.

Although agreement was eventually reached on price, there was no
agreement on liability for consequential loss or on progress payments.
By 28 December 1979 BSC had delivered all but one of the nodes, the
last node being held back by BSC to ensure that payment would be
made by CBE. Owing to a steelworker's strike, the last node was not
delivered to CBE until April 1980. CBE claimed damages from BSC
for late delivery and refused to make any payment for the nodes. BSC
claimed the value of the nodes on a *quantum meruit* basis, contending
that no binding contract had been entered into. CBE claimed that a
binding contract could be found in the various documents including
the letter of intent, and by conduct in proceeding with the manufacture of the nodes.

On the general effect of a letter of intent Robert Goff J stated that
'There can be no hard and fast answer to the question whether a letter

of intent will give rise to a binding agreement: everything must depend on the circumstances of the particular case'. He continued by analysing the particular letter of intent: 'In that letter, the request to BSC to proceed immediately with the work was stated to be "pending the preparation and issuing to you of the official form of sub-contract", being a sub-contract which was plainly in a state of negotiation, not least on the issues of price, delivery dates, and the applicable terms and it was impossible to say with any degree of certainty what the material terms of [the formal] contract would be'. Accordingly he rejected the submission that BSC, by starting work, was contractually bound.

This case is commonly treated as one of the leading English cases on letters of intent. In the light of the distinction of Robert Goff this is not surprising and the statement that there is no general rule and that everything turns on an objective analysis of the words used in their actual context is surely correct. Further the actual decision that BSC was not liable for being late because they had never agreed to a timetable for delivery seems right. There are, however, difficulties with the view that there was no contract at all. Let us change the facts a little. Suppose that after the nodes had been delivered and incorporated in the building, one of them proved defective and the building collapsed. The owner of the building would certainly have had a claim against the builder, who would have had a claim against Cleveland Bridge. It is very hard to believe that on such facts Cleveland Bridge would not have an action against British Steel. There is a conceivable action in tort but this would require proof of negligence. The essence of any claim is that the nodes were not as they had been agreed to be. This is in its nature a contract claim.

It is clearly easier to hold that there is no contract where there has been no performance than where the contract, if there were one, had been largely performed, but the problem is a recurring one as is shown by *RTS Flexible Systems Ltd v Mockerei Alois Muller GMBH & Co KG*.[15] In this case the defendant was a leading dairy product supplier. The claimant specialized in the supply of automated machines for packaging and product handling. There were lengthy and elaborate negotiations for the design, installation, and commission of lines for the packaging of multi-packs of yoghurt. A fixed price of £1,682,000 was agreed and it was intended to have a written contract based on the form MF/1 but with substantial modifications and many schedules. The conclusion of negotiation proved elusive and it was agreed to start work in February 2005 on the basis of a letter of intent, originally to

---

[15] [2009] EWCA Civ 26; (2009) 123 Con LR 130.

last for 4 weeks but later extended several times. The parties eventually fell out by which time the letter of intent had run out and some 70 per cent of the purchase price had been paid. No written contract had ever been concluded. A preliminary issue was ordered as to the contractual position.[16]

At first instance the parties argued for alternative views of what the contract was but on appeal RTS was allowed to argue and did argue that there was no contract.

The Court of Appeal accepted this argument. For the court the decisive consideration was that the parties had been negotiating around the MF/1 conditions and that clause 48 provided:

> This contract may be executed in any number of counterparts provided that it shall not become effective until each party has executed a counterpart and exchanged it with the other.

The Supreme Court allowed Muller's appeal. They thought that on an objective analysis of the parties' behaviour it was clear that they intended to be contractually bound.

It is clear that the parties can, and often do, agree that there is no contract until something has been signed. But it is equally clear that they can, and often do change their minds. Christopher Clarke J thought that this was exactly what the parties had done. He thought that the fact that the parties had carried on performing but had not signed anything showed that they had abandoned the idea of contracting on MF/1.[17] The Supreme Court agreed with the trial judge that there was a contract but disagreed as to its content. They thought it did include most of the MF/1 conditions but not clause 48—basically all the terms which had been agreed up to 5 July and a subsequent variation agreed on 25 August.

A recent case in which the parties did change their minds is *Grant v Bragg*.[18] In this case the parties each owned 50 per cent of the shares in a company which was a quasi-partnership. There was a shareholders' agreement which gave one party a right to buy out the shares of the other if that other was the victim of long-term sickness. The precise scope of these provisions was far from clear but the judge thought that illness did not cause an automatic transfer. The claimant was seriously ill and in due course the defendant sought to exercise his right to buy the claimant's shares. There were some difficult negotiations

---

[16]   The substantive issue between the parties is not clear from the report.

[17]   Paras [73]-[76] of his judgment quoted at (2009) 123 Con LR 147.

[18]   [2009] EWHC 74 (Ch) (decision reversed on other grounds: [2009] EWCA Civ 1228; [2009] 1 All ER (Comm) 674).

and it is clear that at one stage the parties envisaged a signed contract. However, what in fact happened was an exchange of emails which was treated by the judge as completing a contract.

The judge said:[19]

> where parties are proceeding in anticipation of execution of a formal document then the normal inference will be that the parties will not be bound unless and until both of them sign the document. However, that inference will change if the facts change so that it can be objectively ascertained, on a balance of probabilities, that the continuing intention of the parties is, now, to be contractually bound immediately and not following formal execution of the document.

3. CASES WHERE THE LETTER OF INTENT DOES CREATE A CONTRACT

The English case of *Damon Cia SA v Hapag-Lloyd International SA, The Blankernstien*[20] is a good example of a situation where, despite the reference to a formal contract, it was evident that agreement had already been reached between the parties.

Negotiations had taken place between the sellers and the Raftopoulos brothers for the sale of three ships to a prospective purchaser whose identity was not disclosed. The principal terms of the sale had been agreed with the exception of the name of the purchasing company. The purchase price was to be US $2,364,000 with a 10 per cent deposit. The sellers sent a memorandum of agreement incorporating the agreed terms and stating that the 10 per cent deposit was payable on signing the contract. A Panamanian company was then nominated as the purchaser and the sellers were requested to prepare a new memorandum of agreement on that basis which they sent to the buyer's broker. Telexes were sent to the sellers indicating the company's intention to go ahead with the purchase but the memorandum was not executed.

A few days later the sellers gave the buyers notice to sign the agreement and pay the deposit and stated that, if this were not done, the contract would be rescinded. The buyers did not respond and the sellers claimed to be entitled to the deposit on the grounds that the buyers had rescinded.

---

[19]   See also *Maple Leaf Macro Volatility Master Fund v Rouvroy* [2009] EWHC 257 (Comm); [2009] I Lloyds Rep 475; *Diamond Build Ltd v Clapham Park Homes Ltd* [2008] EWHC 143 (TCC); (2008) 119 Con LR 32, *Fitzpatrick Contractors Ltd v Tyco Fire and Integrated Solutions (UK) Ltd* [2008] EWHC 274 (TCC); (2008) 119 Con LR 155.

[20]   [1985] 1 All ER 475.

The question for the court to determine was whether there was any concluded contract between the parties. The purchaser company claimed that there was no contract because they had not signed the memorandum or paid the deposit and since clause 2 of the memorandum only required the deposit to be paid 'on signing' the contract, the sellers could not recover the deposit amount.

However, the Court of Appeal held that all the terms of the sale had been agreed before the memorandum was sent and there was no indication that this agreement was to be subject to the execution of a memorandum. As a result, the fact that the memorandum was not signed did not prevent a binding contract existing. The deposit requirement was a term of the agreement itself so that it could not be argued that it was a condition precedent to the existence of the contract. There was also evidence that the shipping market would regard such an agreement as a binding contract without the necessity for a signed memorandum.

Fox LJ explained the position of the memorandum as follows:[21]

> That they contemplated and indeed agreed on the execution of a written memorandum I accept. But that, of itself, is not conclusive. It is open to parties to agree to execute to a formal document incorporating terms which they have previously agreed. That is a binding contract. In the present case, on 8 July all the terms of the sale were agreed. And it seems to me that all the indications are that they were not intended to be subject to the execution of the memorandum.

Significantly, therefore, the Court of Appeal denied that the agreement between the parties was in any way conditional.

In *AC Controls v British Broadcasting Corp*[22] the BBC wished to install a centrally controlled software access system to 57 of its properties. ACC submitted a tender for £3,118,074.14. Under BBC internal controls it was not permissible to incur an obligation to make payments until a contract had been entered into. No formal contract was ever entered into though the BBC indicated its preferred form of contract.

On 4 June 1999 authorized representatives of both parties signed what was referred to (though not in the document itself) as a letter of intent. By this time some £400,000 of work had been done. The BBC did not want to enter into a formal contract until the programme of work had been devised. This could not be done without significant survey work which ACC would not do without either payment or binding assurances of payment. Matters were made more difficult because the BBC wished to adhere to a strict and ambitious timetable. There was

---

[21]   [1985] 1 All ER 475, at 481.
[22]   (2002) 89 Con LR 52.

provision for payments against certifications by an independent consultant.

On 7 July 1999 a second letter was sent authorizing further works up to an additional value of £500,000. His Honour Judge Anthony Thornton QC held that there was a contract for ACC to do the work subject to the BBC's right to stop work once the existing cap had been exceeded. The provision for payment based on the independent consultant's assessment must involve an obligation to pay a reasonable sum for work done.

A famous American case is *Texaco Inc v Pennzoil*.[23] Negotiations had taken place between Pennzoil, a company which had sought to acquire the stock of Getty Oil, and the two main shareholders of Getty Oil, Gordon Getty and the Getty Museum. The purpose was to persuade Pennzoil to withdraw its bid for Getty Oil. Following negotiations a document, referred to as a 'Memorandum of Agreement', was signed on 2 January, the outcome of which was that there would be only two shareholders of Getty Oil, namely Pennzoil and Gordon Getty. The 'Memorandum', which I shall now set out, detailed various steps and commitments with the object of achieving joint restructuring of the company.

> The following plan (the 'Plan') has been developed and approved by (i) Gordon P. Getty, as Trustee (the 'Trustee') of the Sarah C. Getty Trust dated December 31, 1934 (the 'Trust'), which Trustee owns 31,805,800 shares (40.2% of the total out standing shares) of Common Stock, without par value, of Getty Oil Company (the 'Company'), which shares as well as all other out standing shares of such Common Stock are hereinafter referred to as the 'Shares', (ii) The J. Paul Getty Museum (the 'Museum'), *which Museum owns 9,320,340 Shares (11.8% of the total out standing Shares) and (iii) Pennzoil Company ('Pennzoil'), which owns 593,900 Shares through a subsidiary,* Holdings Incorporated, a Delaware corporation (the 'Purchaser'). The Plan is intended to assure that the public shareholders of the Company and the Museum will receive $110 per Share for all their Shares, a price which is approximately 40% above the price at which the Company's Shares were trading before Pennzoil's subsidiary announced its Offer (hereinafter described) and 10% more than the price which Pennzoil's subsidiary offered in its Offer for 20% of the Shares. The Trustee recommends that the Board of Directors of the Company approve the Plan. The Museum desires that the Plan be considered by the Board of Directors and has executed the Plan for that purpose.

---

[23] 729 S.W. 2d 768 (1987) cf *Murray v ABT Associates* 18 F. 3d 1376 (1994), a decision of 7th Circuit Court of Appeals (Posner CJ, Easterbrook J, and Ripple J).

(i) Pennzoil agreement. Subject to the approval of the Plan by the Board of Directors of the Company as provided in paragraph 6 hereof, Pennzoil agrees to cause the Purchaser promptly to amend its Offer to Purchase dated December 28, 1983 (the 'Offer') for up to 16,000,000 Shares so as:

(a) to increase the Offer price to $110 per Share, net to the Seller in cash and

(b) to increase the number of Shares subject to the Offer to 23,406,100 (being 24,000,000 Shares less 593,900 Shares now owned by the Purchaser).

(ii) Company agreement. Subject to approval of the Plan by the Board of Directors of the Company as provided in paragraph 6 hereof, the Company agrees:

(a) to purchase forthwith all 9,320,340 Shares owned by the Museum at a purchase price of $110 per Share (subject to adjustment before or after closing in the event of any increase in the Offer price or in the event any higher price is paid by any person other than the Company who hereafter acquires 10 percent or more of the outstanding Shares) payable either (at the election of the Company) in cash or by means of a promissory note of the Company, dated as of the closing date, payable to the order of the Museum, due on or before thirty days from the date of issuance, bearing interest at a rate equivalent to the prime rate as in effect at Citibank, N.A. (the 'Company Note' and backed by an irrevocable letter of credit (the 'Company Note').

(b) to proceed promptly upon completion of the Offer by the Purchaser with a cash merger transaction whereby all remaining holders of Shares (other than the Trustee and Pennzoil and its subsidiaries) will receive $110 per Share in cash, and

(c) in consideration of Pennzoil's agreement provided for in paragraph 1 hereof and in order to provide additional assurance that the Plan will be consummated in accordance with its terms, to grant to Pennzoil hereby the option, exercisable at Pennzoil's election at any time on or before the later of consummation of the Offer referred to in paragraph 1 and the purchase referred to in (a) of this paragraph 2, to purchase from the Company up to 8,000,000 Shares of Common Stock of the Company held in the treasury of the Company at a purchase price of $110 per share in cash.

(iii) Museum agreement. Subject to the approval of the Plan by the Board of Directors of the Company as provided in paragraph 6 hereof, the Museum agrees to sell to the Company forthwith all 9,320,340 Shares owned by the Museum at a purchase price of $110 per Share (subject to adjustment before or after closing in the event of any increase in the Offer price) as provided in paragraph 2(a)) payable either (at the election of the Company) in cash or by means of the Company Note referred to in paragraph 2(c).

(iv) Trustee and Pennzoil agreement. The Trustee and Pennzoil hereby agree with each other as follows:

(a) <u>Ratio of Ownership of Shares</u>. The Trustee may increase its holdings to up to 32,000,000 Shares and Pennzoil may increase its holdings to up to 24,000,000 Shares of the approximately 79,132,000 outstanding Shares. Neither the Trustee nor Pennzoil will acquire in excess of such respective amounts without the prior written agreement of the other, it being the agreement between the Trustee and Pennzoil to maintain a relative Share ratio of 4 (for the Trustee) to 3 (for Pennzoil). In connection with the Offer in the event that more than 23,406,100 Shares are duly tendered to the Purchaser, the Purchaser may (if it chooses) purchase any excess over 23406,000; *provided, however,* (i) the Purchases agrees to sell any such excess Shares to the Company (and the Company shall agree to purchase) forthwith at $110 per Share and (ii) pending consummation of such sale to the Company the Purchaser shall grant to the Trustee t he irrevocable proxy to vote such excess Shares.

(b) <u>Restructuring plan</u>. Upon completion of the transactions provided for in paragraphs 1, 2 and 3 hereof, the Trustee and Pennzoil shall endeavor in good faith to agree upon a plan for the restructuring of the Company. In the event that for any reason the Trustee and Pennzoil are unable to agree upon a mutually acceptable plan on or before December 31, 1984, then the Trustee and Pennzoil hereby agree to cause the Company to adopt a plan of complete liquidation of the Company pursuant to which (i) any assets which are mutually agreed to be sold shall be sold and the net proceeds there from shall be used to reduce liabilities of the company and (ii) individual interests in all remaining assets and liabilities shall be distributed to the shareholders pro rata in accordance with their actual ownership interest in the Company. In connection with the plan of distribution, Pennzoil agrees (if requested by the Trustee) that it will enter into customary joint operating agreements to operate any properties so distributed and otherwise to agree to provide operating management for any business and operations requested by the Trustee on customary terms and conditions.

(c) <u>Board of Directors and Management</u>. Upon completion of the transactions provided for in paragraphs 1, 2 and 3 hereof, the Trustee and Pennzoil agree that the Board of Directors of the Company shall be mutually agreeable to the Trustee and Pennzoil (which Directors may include certain present Directors) and who shall be nominated by the Trustee and Pennzoil, respectively, in the ratio of 4 to 3. The Trustee and Pennzoil agree that the senior management of the Company shall include Gordon P. Getty as Chairman of the Board, J. Hugh Liedtke as President and Chief Executive Officer and Baine P. Kerr as Chairman of the Executive Committee.

(d) <u>Access to information.</u> Pennzoil, the Trustee and their representatives will have access to all information concerning the Company necessary or pertinent to accomplish the transactions contemplated by the Plan.

(e) <u>Press releases.</u> The Trustee and Pennzoil (and the Company upon approval of the Plan) will coordinate any press releases or public announcements concerning the Plan and any transactions contemplated hereby.

(v) Compliance with regulatory requirements. The Plan shall be implemented in compliance with applicable regulatory requirements.

(vi). Approval by the Board of Directors. This Plan is subject to approval by the Board of Directors of the Company at the meeting of the Board being held on January 2, 1984 and will expire if not approved by the Board. Upon such approval, the Company shall execute three or more counterparts of the 'Joinder by the Company' attached to the Plan and deliver one such counterpart to each of the Trustee, the Museum and Pennzoil.

Note that, by clause 6, the plan was subject to the approval of the Plan by the Board of Directors of the Company (Getty Oil). This approval was secured on 3 January. On 4 January a press release was issued.

On 5 January secret negotiations were commenced by the two shareholders with Texaco and on 6 January it was announced that Texaco had signed an agreement to take over the company. Texaco were offering $125 a share. Pennzoil brought an action against Texaco alleging that Texaco had intentionally interfered with its existing contract and had induced the breach of contract. It was therefore necessary for Pennzoil to establish that there was a valid contract contained in the 'Memorandum of Agreement'.

The jury found that 'from a preponderance of the evidence' there was an intention to be bound by an agreement containing the terms of this 'Memorandum'. Pennzoil was awarded the considerable figure of $7.53 billion in damages, plus punitive damages of $3 billion. On appeal the Texas Court of Appeal upheld the $7.53 billion actual damages award but reduced the punitive damages to $1 billion. It held that the jury had been correctly instructed and that the verdict was open to the jury on the evidence.

Whether there was an intention to be bound was a question of fact to be determined by the jury in the light of all the circumstances of the case. The court concluded that 'the release as a whole is worded in indicative terms, not in subjective or hypothetical ones'. In particular, the court found that the words 'after the execution and delivery of this Agreement' was simply a phrase used before a statement of each party's obligations to indicate the timing of acts that were to occur and 'did not impose any express precondition to the formation of a contract'.

The division of function between judge and jury which no longer exists in other common law systems is clearly of great significance in this case. Since there are plausible arguments either way as to the correct result it is hard to see that either side was entitled to a directed verdict. Pennzoil was not suing the Getty interests for breach of contract but Texaco for inducing breach but clearly the existence of a binding contract was an essential part of its case. There was a possible second line of defence for Texaco that it did not know there was a contract. Texaco led evidence that it had been told that there was no contract but clearly this evidence was not accepted. Indeed the size of the punitive damage award shows that the jury formed a very hostile view of the behaviour of Texaco.

Texaco argued that the addition of the words 'in principle' after the word 'Agreement' meant that the transaction was not intended to be legally binding and led evidence that on Wall Street everybody knew that 'agreement in principle' meant not binding but it seems dangerously simplistic to rely on such a formula in such a case. As can be seen the Memorandum of Agreement was very detailed and expressly provided that it was subject to the approval of the Board. Once the Board approved it is perhaps not surprising that the jury thought that it had become binding.

It is not surprising that about a case involving such vast sums there has been much discussion[24] including it is said, at least three books, one by one of the jurors. It is perhaps unlikely that the case will inspire any common law jurisdiction to restore jury trials in such matters[25] but the factual situation could occur in any jurisdiction. It would be bold to assert that in a case tried by a judge alone, the result would be certain. The most striking feature of the facts is that in the key meeting between Pennzoil and the representatives of the various Getty interests, which went on for many hours and was deeply populated by lawyers, no-one took adequate steps to make the legal status of the agreement clear.

---

[24]   See Lake and Draetta, above, n 1, 130-44; Ansaldi, 27 *Houston LR* 733; R Weintraub, 9 *Review of Litigation* 371; M Gergen, 9 *Review of Litigation* 441.

[25]   It is hard to believe that an English judge would have taken such a wide view of the jury's function at any time in history. For this purpose the legal effect of the Memorandum of Agreement would surely have been treated as a question of law.

4. CASES WHERE THE LETTER OF INTENT HAS SOME LEGAL EFFECT

(a) Letter of intent followed by performance

As explained above, there will be many cases where there are commercial pressures to start performance before negotiations are complete. If performance confers benefits on the other party there will usually be at least a restitution remedy as in *British Steel v Cleveland Bridge* but quite often instructions to proceed will be treated as promises to pay for the work done. In *Emcor Drake & Scull v Sir Robert McAlpine*[26] the claimant was the M&E sub-contractor on a major hospital contract on which the defendant was the main contractor. The defendant indicated from an early stage that the claimant was its preferred sub-contractor and a price of £34.25 million was soon agreed but there were long and complex negotiations over the terms. The parties never signed a formal contract. The defendants sent a number of letters which the claimant was invited to sign but it did not sign any of them. The defendant issued a letter instructing the claimant to start work and promising to pay up to £1 million. There was no dispute about the scope of work. The claimant started work and there were successive letters raising the authorized payments up to £14 million before the parties fell out. The Court of Appeal held that no contract for the whole work had ever been concluded. There was a string of contracts under which the claimant was entitled to a reasonable sum for work of a good and workmanlike quality up to a maximum. This is a classic example. There was never a final contract but there was a series of interim contracts in which there was identifiable work to be done and an agreed price for the work.

Where there is an instruction to start work and the work is of a kind for which, objectively speaking, payment is reasonably expected there will be a contract of this kind. If a price is not stated it will still usually be possible to hold that there is a promise to pay a reasonable price.

(b) Letters of comfort

Suppose an English company is dealing in England with the English subsidiary of a large American company. Discreet searches reveal that the English subsidiary does not itself have much money. Caution

---

[26] [2004] EWCA Civ 1733; (2004) 98 Con LR 1.

suggests that it would be wise to check whether the American company will stand behind its English subsidiary. The foolproof way to do this is to request a parent company guarantee but there may be resistance to doing this and instead the American company may offer a letter of comfort. What is the effect of such a letter?

The orthodox answer must be that it all depends on an objective construction of what the letter says but something may turn on the approach. The leading English case is *Kleinwort Benson Ltd v Malaysia Mining Corp Bhd*[27] where the defendant parent company had issued a 'Letter of Comfort' which stated 'it is our policy to ensure that the business of [the subsidiary company] is at all times in a position to meet its liabilities to you [under the loan agreement]'. When the subsidiary became insolvent the plaintiff bank claimed that the defendant should cover the subsidiary's indebtedness to them in accordance with the comfort letter.

Hirst J, at first instance,[28] treated the question of the enforceability of the comfort letter as resting on whether there was any intention to create legal relations. This was a commercial agreement where it was difficult to rebut the presumption of an intention to create legal relations and Hirst J held that the presumption had not been rebutted. However, the Court of Appeal considered this approach to be incorrect and preferred a test involving an examination of the words used in the comfort letter to determine if a promise was being made. The Court of Appeal held the words in question to be only a statement of current policy and intention and that the words used did not amount to a promise to abide by this statement of policy. In its view the presumption of an intention to create legal relations in commercial agreements could only arise if the words used were clearly promissory.

In the decision of the Commercial Division of the Supreme Court of New South Wales in Australia in *Banque Brussels Lambert v Australian National Industries Ltd*[29] this approach was forcefully criticized by Rogers CJ as leading to uncertainty in commercial contracts and as placing the enforceability of bargained for comfort letters in the realms of clauses binding in honour only without there being any express statement to this effect.

---

[27] [1989] 1 WLR 379. See also: *Chemco Leasing SPA v Rediffusion* [1987] 1 FTLR 201; *Monk Construction v Norwich Union Life Insurance Society* (1992) 62 BLR 107; F Reynolds, 104 *LQR* 353; B Davenport, [1988] *LMC LQ* 290; D Prentice, 105 *LQR* 346; Ayres and Moore, [1989] *LMCLQ* 281; Tyrre, 2 *JCL* 279; Brown, [1990] *JBL* 281.

[28] [1988] 1 All ER 714.

[29] (1989) 21 NSWLR 502.

In *Bank of New Zealand v Ginivan*[30] the New Zealand Court of Appeal considered the *Kleinwort Benson* decision but rejected an argument to apply it to the mixed wording of the comfort letter in that case. The comfort letter stated that 'Our policy is that this company will conduct its affairs in a responsible manner, maintain a sound financial condition and meet its obligations promptly and will use our "best endeavours" to see that the company continues to do so'. The New Zealand Court of Appeal appeared to suggest that despite the reference to the future in the last sentence, ie 'will use', the existence of a best endeavours clause indicated a legally binding obligation.

The distinction between guarantees and letters of comfort occurs equally in French practice.[31] The President of the Association of Banks (in France) issued an opinion stating that a letter of comfort should be 'considered as providing in practical terms security comparable to a guarantee'.

It is worth stopping to consider the commercial realities here. There are undoubtedly many situations in which someone invited to give a guarantee might sensibly hesitate to do so. I was once asked by a bank manager to guarantee my eldest daughter's overdraft. When I asked why this would be good for me or indeed my daughter, to whom he had already lent more than was sensible, he could make no coherent response and I politely declined.[32] But the position in the parent company guarantee/letter of comfort situation is not of this kind. If Malaysia mining company had said explicitly that they never stood behind their subsidiaries Kleinwort Benson would probably have behaved differently.

In its recent decision in *Associated British Ports v Ferryways NV*[33] the Court of Appeal held that the words 'letter of comfort' normally connoted a non-binding assurance. This ruling was clearly obiter since the document in question had not been labelled a 'letter of comfort' and the primary question was whether it was a guarantee or an indemnity.

There is a puzzle here, however. We are dealing in this area with commercially astute people with access to good legal advice. It is not clear why any such person should be comforted by a letter of comfort which has no effect. Of course a holding company can put statements in red on its notepaper 'We never stand behind our subsidiaries' but can it achieve the same purpose by weasel words? There are sensible

---

[30] [1991] 1 NZLR 178.
[31] Fontaine and De Ly, above, n 5, 6-8.
[32] And my daughter went to another bank.
[33] [2009] EWCA Civ 189; [2009] 1 Lloyds Rep 595.

arguments for saying that if one wants to make meaningless assurances one should do so clearly.

In two recent cases, the House of Lords has overturned the Court of Appeal and held that clear words must yield to commercially sensible results.[34] It is a question whether this reasoning may reach this area. In principle if clear words should yield unclear words should do so more quickly.

(c) Agreements imposing obligations as to the course of the negotiations

In long and complex negotiations the parties may very well make binding agreements which are separate from the main negotiations.[35] So they may agree that the details of the negotiation are to be confidential. There are good reasons why such an agreement should be binding at once. Similarly they might enter into binding obligations not during the negotiation to enter into negotiations about the same subject matter with anyone else.

The process of negotiation is often itself expensive. The general rule is no doubt that usually each party bears its own costs but there is no reason why in exceptional circumstances the parties cannot make another agreement. So a letter of intent may produce this effect. Similarly it may impose on one party specific duties, such as obtaining the consent of third parties.

5. CONCLUSION

There are at least three possible effects which may arise from a letter of intent.

(1) There is no contract (though acts of performance may lead to restitutionary effects).
(2) The letter of intent, though in a sense preliminary, nevertheless leads to a complete contract.
(3) The document falls short of the full contract but nevertheless has some contractual effects.

---

[34] *Chartbrook Ltd v Persimmon Homes Ltd* [2009] UKHL 38; *Re Sigma Finance Corporation* [2009] UKSC 2.
[35] Fontaine and De Ly, above, n 5, examples 20-5.

3

Agreements to Negotiate in Good Faith

EDWIN PEEL*

1. INTRODUCTION

Any assessment of the status of agreements to negotiate in good faith must start with the decision of the House of Lords in *Walford v Miles*.[1] The defendants agreed that, while negotiating with the claimants for the sale of their business and property, they would not enter into negotiations with any third party; sometimes referred to as a 'lock out' agreement. The finding of the trial judge was that the defendants had, in fact, continued negotiations with a third party with whom they then entered into an agreement to sell, after having informed the claimants that they were breaking off negotiations with them. The claimants sued and put their claim on two grounds: breach of the lock out agreement and misrepresentation.

The House of Lords accepted that a lock out agreement can be enforced in circumstances where it is supported by consideration and limited to a specified time.[2] The difficulty for the claimants in *Walford v Miles* was that no time limit had been specified and the most that could be said was that the lock out would last for as long as the defendants and claimants were negotiating in good faith. This required it to contain an element of locking in (agreement *to* negotiate with the claimants), as well as an element of locking out (agreement *not* to negotiate with third parties). The House of Lords followed a number of earlier cases in holding that an agreement to negotiate, like an agreement to agree, is unenforceable because it lacks certainty.[3] In a lengthy, but important, passage Lord Ackner, with whom the other Lords agreed, said:

> The reason why an agreement to negotiate, like an agreement to agree, is unenforceable is simply because it lacks the necessary certainty. The same

---

* Fellow & Tutor in Law, Keble College, Oxford; Consultant, Clifford Chance LLP.

[1] [1992] 2 AC 128.

[2] As was subsequently the case in *Pitt v PHH Asset Management Ltd* [1993] 1 WLR 327; cf *Tye v House* [1997] 2 EGLR 171.

[3] *Courtney & Fairbairn Ltd v Tolaini Bros (Hotels) Ltd* [1975] 1 WLR 297, at 301; *The Scaptrade* [1981] 2 Lloyd's Rep 425, at 432; *Nile Co for the Export of Agricultural Crops v H & J M Bennett (Commodities) Ltd* [1986] 1 Lloyd's Rep 555, at 587; and see subsequently, *Mamidoil-Jetoil Greek Petroleum SA v Okta Crude Oil Refining AD* [2001] EWCA Civ 406; [2001] Lloyd's Rep 76, at [53], [59].

does not apply to an agreement to use best endeavours. This uncertainty is demonstrated in the instant case by the provision which it is said has to be implied in the agreement for the determination of the negotiations. How can a court be expected to decide whether, subjectively, a proper reason existed for the termination of negotiations? The answer suggested depends upon whether the negotiations have been determined 'in good faith'. However, the concept of a duty to carry on negotiations in good faith is inherently repugnant to the adversarial position of the parties when involved in negotiations. Each party to the negotiations is entitled to pursue his (or her) own interest, so long as he avoids making misrepresentations. To advance that interest he must be entitled, if he thinks it appropriate, to threaten to withdraw from further negotiations or to withdraw in fact in the hope that the opposite party may seek to reopen the negotiations by offering him improved terms. Mr Naughton of course, accepts that the agreement upon which he relies does not contain a duty to complete the negotiations. But that still leaves the vital question: how is a vendor ever to know that he is entitled to withdraw from further negotiations? How is the court to police such an 'agreement'? A duty to negotiate in good faith is as unworkable in practice as it is inherently inconsistent with the position of a negotiating party. It is here that the uncertainty lies. In my judgment, while negotiations are in existence either party is entitled to withdraw from these negotiations, at any time and for any reason. There can be thus no obligation to continue to negotiate until there is a 'proper reason' to withdraw. Accordingly, a bare agreement to negotiate has no legal content.[4]

The claim for breach of the lock out agreement therefore failed.

The claimants did, however, recover damages in their claim for misrepresentation. It is noted in the Court of Appeal that it was dealt with rather summarily by the trial judge and is rejected by Bingham LJ,[5] as well as being doubted by Stocker LJ in the majority.[6] It depended on a finding that when the defendants entered into the lock out agreement, they did not, even at that time, have any intention of not negotiating with any third party,[7] ie the misrepresentation of fact was the false statement as to their own state of mind.[8] Since this

---

[4] At 138.

[5] (1991) 62 P & CR 410, at 423.

[6] *Ibid*, at 427.

[7] Dillon LJ held that the judge had not made all of the findings necessary in this regard, but that since he had expressed no reservations about the evidence of the defendant, the Court of Appeal was in as good a position as the judge to make those findings.

[8] *Edgington v Fitzmaurice* (1885) 29 Ch D 459: 'There must be a mis-statement of an existing fact; but the state of a man's mind is as much a fact as the state of his digestion. . . . A misrepresentation as to the state of a man's mind is, therefore, a mis-statement of fact', Bowen LJ, at 482.

almost certainly also amounts to a finding of deceit,[9] on the basis that the defendant must know that his statement is false, it is not lightly to be reached[10] and one suspects that, in most cases, a court will not feel able to make such a finding.

Notwithstanding the established line of authority upon which it was based, the decision in *Walford v Miles* has come in for adverse comment from other members of the judiciary. Writing extra-judicially, Lord Steyn has cited the decision as one which is 'surprising' and against the 'thread' which 'runs through our contract law that effect must be given to the reasonable expectations of honest men'.[11] This is a view recently echoed in the obiter dictum of Longmore LJ in the *Petromec* case who observed that: 'it would be a strong thing to declare unenforceable a clause into which the parties have deliberately and expressly entered.'[12]

It is a decision which is said to leave English law out of line with other common law jurisdictions,[13] and with other European legal systems.[14] Article 1.106(1) of the *Principles of European Contract Law* states that 'in exercising his rights and performing his duties each party must act in accordance with good faith and fair dealing'.[15] More specifically, in the *Draft Common Frame of Reference*, Article II—3:301 states: 'A person who is engaged in negotiations has a duty to negotiate in accordance with good faith and fair dealing and not to break off negotiations contrary to good faith and fair dealing. This duty may not be excluded or limited by contract.'

This paper has two principal aims. First, to determine the scope of the decision of the House of Lords in *Walford v Miles* and whether it amounts to the principle of 'blanket unenforceability', as it is sometimes described.[16] Second, whether any change to the law may be appropriate. In this regard, consideration is given to what might be

---

[9] Though, curiously, Dillon LJ refers to it as a claim founded on 'negligent misrepresentation': (1991) 62 P & CR 410, at 432.

[10] Or pleaded.

[11] 113 *LQR* 433. This is a theme about which his Lordship has also written judicially: *First Energy (UK) Ltd v Hungarian International Bank Ltd* [1993] 2 Lloyd's Rep 194, at 196.

[12] *Petromec Inc v Petroleo Brasileiro SA Petrobas* [2005] EWCA Civ 891; [2006] 1 Lloyd's Rep 161, at [121]. *cf Butters v BBC Worldwide Ltd* [2009] EWHC 1954 (Ch), at [144]-[154].

[13] Such as the US: *Channel Home Centers v Grossman* (1986) 795 F. 2d 291; *Itek Corp v Chicago Aerial Industries* 248 A 2d 625 (Del. 1968). See, further: Kessler and Fine, 77 *Harv L Rev* 401 (1964).

[14] For a helpful survey, see R Zimmermann and S Whittaker, *Good Faith in European Contract Law* (CUP, 2000), Case 3.

[15] *cf UNIDROIT Principles for International Commercial Contracts*, Art 1.7.

[16] *Petromec Inc v Petroleo Brasileiro SA Petrobas* [2005] EWCA Civ 891; [2006] 1 Lloyd's Rep 161, at [119], *per* Longmore LJ.

meant by 'good faith' in the context of an agreement to negotiate, if, contrary to the view of Lord Ackner, it is an agreement with some legal content.

2. SCOPE

Lord Ackner appears to suggest two limits to the scope of his decision. First, he distinguishes an 'agreement to use best endeavours' and, second, by way of conclusion, he states only that a *bare* agreement to negotiate has no legal content. The first proves to be no limit at all and the second not much more.

(a) The 'best endeavours' fallacy

It is not entirely clear what Lord Ackner meant by his reference to an agreement to use best endeavours. It is preceded by his discussion of the decision of the United States' Court of Appeal, Third Circuit, in *Channel Home Centers v Grossman*,[17] about which he says: 'the Court of Appeal appears to have proceeded on the basis that an agreement to negotiate in good faith is synonymous with an agreement to use best endeavours and as the latter is enforceable, so is the former.'[18] He describes that as an 'unsustainable proposition' because, as he goes on to state at the start of the passage cited above, whereas an agreement to negotiate lacks certainty, an agreement to use best endeavours does not. If by this, he meant to distinguish between an agreement to negotiate and an agreement to use best endeavours to agree, or negotiate, it is this distinction which cannot be sustained. Patrick Neill argued as such, writing shortly after the decision in *Walford v Miles*.[19] He did so to conclude that both types of agreement should be regarded as *enforceable*. The courts have subsequently held that there is no distinction between the two so that they must both be regarded as *unenforceable*.

---

[17] (1986) 795 F. 2d 291.

[18] [1992] 2 AC 128, at 138. One assumes that Lord Ackner must have reached this conclusion about the reasoning employed by the Court of Appeal on the basis of its citation of the following passage from *Thompson v Liquichimica of America Inc* 481 F. Supp. 365 (EDNY 1979), at 366: 'Unlike an agreement to agree, which does not constitute a closed proposition, an agreement to use best efforts [or to negotiate in good faith] is a closed proposition, discrete and actionable.' There is no other reference to an agreement to use best endeavours.

[19] 108 *LQR* 405, based in part on the decision of the Privy Council in *Queensland Electricity Generating Board v New Hope Collieries Pty Ltd* [1989] 1 Lloyd's Rep 205.

The subsequent approach of the courts takes Lord Ackner to have been referring, by way of distinction, only to an agreement to use best endeavours in the *performance* of a contract,[20] eg where an admitted contract between A and B requires A to use his best endeavours to make a computer software system supplied by A work, or to procure C to enter into a contract with B,[21] rather than in seeking the *formation* of a contract.[22] There is no doubt that terms such as the former can impose a legal obligation on A.[23] But where the question is whether any contract has come into existence, a number of decisions now support the view that an agreement to use best or reasonable endeavours to agree on the terms of a contract is no more than an agreement to negotiate, and therefore lacks contractual force.[24] The distinction is best summed up by Millett LJ in *Little v Courage*:

> An undertaking to use one's best endeavours to obtain planning permission or an export licence is sufficiently certain and is capable of being enforced: an undertaking to use one's best endeavours to agree, however, is no different from an undertaking to agree, to try to agree, or to negotiate with a view to reaching agreement; all are equally uncertain and incapable of giving rise to an enforceable obligation.[25]

It has recently been applied by Jackson J in the Wembley Stadium litigation[26] to find unenforceable a provision in an interim settlement agreement in which it was said:

> the parties shall use reasonable endeavours to agree to re-programme the completion of the subcontract works and to agree a fixed lump sum

---

[20] There is room for this in that Lord Ackner refers only to 'an agreement to use best endeavours' without more, but the context and, in particular, his earlier discussion of the decision in the *Channel Home Centers* case do seem to imply that he had in mind an agreement to use best endeavours *to agree.*

[21] cf *Rae Lambert v HTV Cymru (Wales) Ltd* [1998] FSR 87; *Bluzwed Metals Ltd v Trans-World Metals Ltd* [2006] EWHC 143.

[22] *Little v Courage* (1995) 70 P & CR 469, at 475 (based on earlier dicta of Goff LJ in *IBM United Kingdom Ltd v Rockware Glass Ltd* [1980] FSR 335, at 348, and *Bower v Bantam Investments Ltd* [1972] 1 WLR 1120).

[23] See *Watford Electronics Ltd v Sanderson Ltd* [2001] EWCA Civ 317; [2001] 1 All ER (Comm) 696, at [45]. For the meaning of 'best endeavours', see: *Sheffield District Railway Co v Great Central Railway Co* (1911) 27 TLR 471; *IBM United Kingdom Ltd v Rockware Glass Ltd*, above, n 22, at 339, 343.

[24] See *Little v Courage* (1995) 70 P & CR 469; *London & Regional Investments Ltd v TBI plc Belfast International Airport Ltd* [2002] EWCA Civ 355, at [39]; *Multiplex Constructions UK Ltd v Cleveland Bridge UK Ltd* [2006] EWHC 1341 (TCC); 107 Con LR 1.

[25] *Ibid*, at 475.

[26] *Multiplex Constructions UK Ltd v Cleveland Bridge UK Ltd* [2006] EWHC 1341 (TCC); 107 Con LR 1.

and/or reimbursable subcontract sum for the completion of subcontract works…

It has been suggested[27] that an agreement to use best endeavours could be interpreted as referring to the *machinery* of negotiation, whereas one to negotiate in good faith is more plausibly interpreted as referring to its *substance*. On this basis, a promise to use best endeavours might, for example, oblige a party to make himself available for negotiations, or at least not deliberately prevent the other from communicating with him, eg by not picking up the telephone.[28] This distinction might have been employed in the Wembley Stadium case where the evidence suggests that, far from not making reasonable endeavours to agree, the main contractors made no endeavours at all. However, on the basis of the authorities referred to above,[29] Jackson J found that the relevant clause created no enforceable obligation at all.[30]

(b) Bare agreements to negotiate

The implied agreement to negotiate in *Walford v Miles* was a 'bare' agreement in two ways. First, in the absence of any binding contract in the form of an agreement to negotiate, there was no contract at all between the parties, either because the agreement for the sale of the business was incomplete, or, in any event, it was 'subject to contract'. The position may be different where the parties have entered into a contract which is otherwise enforceable and the agreement to negotiate relates to some inessential or subsidiary matter. Secondly, the only limit on the parties' negotiations was that they should be conducted 'in good faith', and, as Lord Ackner explained, such a limit is too uncertain. Here, the position may be different where the parties have, in addition, imposed some objective criteria, or machinery, by reference to which any disagreement should be resolved. In a number of cases, it has been said that the decision in *Walford v Miles* or the earlier authorities upon which it is based can be distinguished on one, or other, or both, of these grounds.

---

[27] Treitel, *The Law of Contract* (12th edn, London: Sweet & Maxwell, 2007) para 2-107. The suggestion was first made by Professor Treitel in the ninth edition.

[28] Example based on *Nissho Iwai Petroleum Co Inc v Cargill International SA* [1993] 1 Lloyd's Rep 80, where such conduct was held to amount to a breach of a party's duty to cooperate in the *performance* (not in the *formation*) of a contract. cf *Re Debtors (Nos 4449 and 4450 of 1998)* [1999] 1 All ER (Comm) 149, at 158 (implied obligation to use 'best endeavours' to conclude an agreement required the party 'not unreasonably to frustrate' its conclusion).

[29] ie *Walford v Miles* and *Little v Courage*.

[30] [2006] EWHC 1341 (TCC), 107 Con LR 1, at [623].

(i) Where an agreement to negotiate is not 'bare' because there is, otherwise, an enforceable contract between the parties

An agreement is not incomplete and, therefore, unenforceable merely because it calls for some further agreement between the parties. The agreement already reached by the parties will be binding if it may stand without more, ie the outstanding matters are regarded as subsidiary, or non-essential,[31] or if such outstanding matters can be resolved without the agreement of the parties, ie by reference to some objective criteria,[32] or machinery.[33] In such cases, it would be very surprising if an incomplete agreement which would otherwise be binding is rendered unenforceable because the parties had agreed to negotiate the outstanding terms. It is, however, important to stress the limited nature of this proposition: it is the agreement otherwise reached by the parties which is, and remains, enforceable; not the agreement to negotiate. A number of cases may be considered by way of illustration.

In *Donwin Productions Ltd v EMI Films Ltd*[34] the parties negotiated for the defendant to distribute a film produced by the claimant. Although the parties contemplated that they would enter into a formal distribution agreement, Pain J found that this was a case where, prior to any formal contract, the parties had already concluded a bargain by which they intended to be bound. He described it thus:

> It is true that it would be a rather rough and ready contract, which would require to be filled out by a written agreement in due course ... I think it would by necessary implication be a term of such a contract that the parties would negotiate in good faith about the further terms to be inserted in the written agreement ... I am not overlooking the decision in *Courtney Ltd v Tolaini Bros*,[35] that the law does not recognise a contract to negotiate. But I do not think that decision prevents the implication of such a term as I have suggested once a firm agreement has been made and a further fuller agreement is in contemplation.

---

[31] Since, however, it remains a question of the intention of the parties, they may make it clear that they do not intend to be bound until agreement on any outstanding matters has been reached: *The Gladys* [1994] 2 Lloyd's Rep 402.

[32] Such criteria may be specified in the agreement (see *Hillas & Co Ltd v Arcos Ltd* (1932) 147 LT 503; *Brown v Gould* [1972] Ch 53), or by statute (see, eg, the power of the courts to determine a 'reasonable price' in a contract for the sale of goods: Sale of Goods Act 1979, s 8(2)).

[33] For example, by reference to a third party such as a valuer, or an arbitrator: *Queensland Electricity Generating Board v New Hope Collieries Pty Ltd* [1989] 1 Lloyd's Rep 205.

[34] *The Times*, 9 March 1984.

[35] [1975] 1 WLR 297, ie the forerunner of *Walford v Miles*.

The point to be stressed about the *Donwin* case is that Pain J was only required to determine the question of liability and, more specifically, liability under a contract *without* the further terms about which he said the parties would have to negotiate. What would be the position if the parties failed to reach agreement on the further terms? Would it be possible for either of them to claim that the other was in breach of the implied agreement to negotiate in good faith? It is submitted that, for the reasons given later by Lord Ackner in *Walford v Miles* and at the time of the *Donwin* decision by Lord Denning MR in *Courtney v Tolaini*, they would not. In fact, the most that can be said in a case where the parties have reached an incomplete, but nonetheless binding, contract is that they might be *expected* to resolve any outstanding details; an implied *term* is really unnecessary because they can be under no enforceable *obligation* to do so.

Nor, it is submitted, should the position be any different if the parties have included an express term to negotiate any outstanding matters. In the *Petromec* case,[36] under clause 12 of a Supervision Agreement, the parties had agreed that work would be done to upgrade an oil production platform and that the respondent would pay 'the reasonable costs'. The agreement then went on to state, under clause 12.4, that the respondent 'agrees to negotiate in good faith with (the appellant) the extra costs referred to'. Longmore LJ found that any negotiations that the parties had conducted fell outside the scope of clause 12 so that no issue arose as to its enforceability.[37] Nonetheless, he went on to consider this question and it is in that context that he distinguished *Walford v Miles* as a case involving a 'bare' agreement to negotiate.

Clause 12.4 was not a bare agreement in the sense contemplated in this part, ie it formed part of an agreement that was otherwise enforceable, but the Supervision Agreement of which it formed part was only itself an enforceable agreement because clause 12.4 was not a bare agreement in the other sense explained above, ie in the absence of any agreement it provided an objective criterion in the form of 'reasonable costs'. As Longmore LJ explained:[38]

> The first objection, that the obligation is an agreement to agree, carries little weight in the present case. It is contained in the Supervision Agreement

---

[36] Above, n 12.

[37] He suggested that such a clause should, perhaps, be interpreted *contra proferentem*: 'It is, moreover, fair to say that since the traditional view is that any obligation to negotiate is, to say the least, problematic in its enforceability, it is inevitable that if any such obligation could be held to exist, it will be restrictively construed in accordance with its exact wording' (at [114]).

[38] At [117].

which is itself legally enforceable. (No one suggested that, if the obligation to negotiate the cost of the upgrade is unenforceable, that affects the rest of the agreement.) The obligation only relates to the cost to Petromec of the Roncador upgrade over and above the South Marlim upgrade and the cost of any variation orders. The 'cost to Petromec' is comparatively easy to ascertain (especially if no element for profit is to be included). If agreement is not reached, the court will itself have to ascertain what the reasonable cost of such upgrade should be.

There is an element of construction required to reach this conclusion. It requires a finding that the 'price' to be paid for the upgrade is 'cost', but that the parties will also attempt in the first instance to agree what that figure should be. That is rather different from a finding that the price is 'cost *as agreed*' by the parties. On that basis, there would be no more than an agreement to negotiate since 'cost' cannot be divorced from what is meant by the parties and assessed objectively.[39] But if the former is the correct construction of the parties' agreement, it results in the very limited proposition advanced above, ie it is the agreement otherwise reached by the parties which is, and remains, enforceable; not the agreement to negotiate. In the context of *Petromec*, the parties had agreed to the upgrade of the platform at 'cost'; it would indeed be very surprising if that became an unenforceable contract because they also agreed that they would first attempt to negotiate what that figure should be (and, as Longmore LJ noted, it was not even suggested). What this does not amount to is a finding that the agreement to negotiate is itself enforceable.

In the *Petromec* case, however, Longmore LJ seemed to go further and suggest that the agreement to negotiate may itself have been enforceable when he considered that cost might be found to include some element of 'uplift' by way of profit. That too could be determined by the courts alone (see, eg the power to determine a reasonable price under s 8(2) of the Sale of Goods Act 1979), but Longmore LJ refers to it in the *Petromec* case as the figure which the parties would have reached if they had fulfilled the obligation to negotiate in good faith. At this

---

[39] cf *May & Butcher v R* [1934] 2 KB 17n., where the House of Lords found unenforceable an agreement for the sale of tentage which provided that the price, dates of payment and manner of delivery should be agreed from time to time: 'Had the agreement simply been silent on these points, they could perhaps have been settled in accordance with the provisions of the Sale of Goods Act 1979; or by the standard of reasonableness; but the parties showed that this was not their intention by providing that such points were to be settled by further agreement between them', *Treitel*, above, n 27, para 2-098. Similarly, in *Willis Management (Isle of Man) Ltd v Cable & Wireless Plc* [2005] EWCA Civ 806; [2005] 2 Lloyd's Rep 597 the parties agreed that one would take a 'fair' share of losses incurred by the other, but the evidence indicated that parties meant fair share *to be agreed*.

point, one has not just a basis for distinguishing *Walford v Miles* but a direct challenge to its authority and this must call into doubt Long-more LJ's view that, notwithstanding *Walford v Miles*, clause 12.4 itself was enforceable, or at least not 'completely without legal substance'.[40] It is, perhaps, mindful of this that Longmore LJ also referred, seemingly with approval, to Lord Steyn's suggestion that *Walford v Miles* should be reconsidered.[41]

That an agreement to negotiate outstanding terms in a contract which is otherwise enforceable is not itself enforceable is confirmed by the only case in which, it seems, an attempt has been made at enforcement. In *Mallozzi v Carapelli SpA*[42] the parties entered into contracts for the sale of oats and maize cif free out one safe port west coast Italy excluding Genoa which further provided, as to the discharging port: 'First or second port to be agreed between sellers and buyers on the ship passing the Straits of Gibraltar.' The buyers nominated Naples as the port of discharge, but the sellers also wished to call in to Genoa to deliver parcels which were the subject of other sale contracts with different buyers. Because of congestion at both ports and the attendant risk of demurrage,[43] it suited the buyer for Naples to be the second port; conversely, it suited the seller that Genoa should be the second port. There were no negotiations as such and the seller simply adhered to the decision which suited them. The ship therefore first called into Naples.

The Court of Appeal found that there was no breach of contract by the sellers because there was no legally binding obligation upon them to negotiate. At first instance[44] Kerr J had found otherwise,[45] but his decision was handed down before the decision of the Court of Appeal in *Courtney & Fairbairn Ltd v Tolaini Bros (Hotels) Ltd*.[46] For the purposes of the present discussion, Roskill LJ noted that in *Courtney's* case the court was concerned with whether the parties were *ad idem* and had reached an enforceable binding contract (ie it involved a 'bare' agreement to negotiate), whereas in *Mallozzi v Carapelli* there was 'no doubt at all that the parties had reached an enforceable binding contract and ... the provision ... with which we are concerned appears in

---

[40] At [121].

[41] *Ibid.*

[42] [1976] 1 Lloyd's Rep 407.

[43] Though none was found to be owed for other reasons.

[44] [1975] 1 Lloyd's Rep 229.

[45] Based on the dictum of Lord Wright in *Hillas v Arcos* (1932) 43 Lloyd's Rep 359, which is considered below: text to n 80.

[46] [1975] 1 WLR 297.

a contract otherwise binding'.[47] Nonetheless, he held that that did not make any difference in principle.[48] Similarly, Goff LJ, having cited the well known passage from Lord Denning in *Courtney's* case stated:[49]

> It is clear that the words 'First or second port to be agreed' ... cannot do more than import an agreement to negotiate with a view to agreeing that particular point. That is exactly covered, in my judgment, by the words which I have just cited; and none the less so because the words are a term in a particular, existing contract. It follows, in my judgment, that there cannot be any *separate head of liability for breach of that term*. That, of course, is wholly independent of other questions which arise in this case whether the sellers may not be liable for breach of other express or implied terms in the contract; but ... those words cannot give rise to any enforceable liability for breach of contract to negotiate.

This, it is submitted, is the limit of the proposition that the principle in *Walford v Miles* (and *Courtney's* case before it) is confined to bare agreements to negotiate, ie those cases where an agreement to negotiate represents the only agreement between the parties. Since it is not enforceable, there is no contract at all. Where there is, otherwise, a binding and enforceable contract, that will not be affected by any further agreement to negotiate, but the agreement to negotiate itself remains unenforceable.

(ii) Where an agreement to negotiate is not 'bare' because the parties have agreed to a further objective restriction on their right to negotiate

The implied agreement to negotiate in *Walford v Miles* was also 'bare' in the sense that the only restriction on the parties' right to negotiate was 'good faith'. It is sometimes said that their agreement is enforceable when, in addition, it imposes some objective criteria, or machinery, by reference to which they should seek to reach agreement. A simple illustration is provided by *The Didymi*.[50]

The owner's vessel was chartered for five years at a daily hire of US $5,800 during the first year, rising to US $7,000 during the last period of the charter. The charter also provided, under clause 30, that if the speed and fuel consumption of the vessel fell below the figures stated in the charter, the 'hire shall be equitably decreased by an amount to be mutually agreed'; conversely, if the vessel performed better than the stated figures, the owners were to be 'indemnified by way of increase

---

[47] At 414.
[48] *Ibid.*
[49] [1976] 1 Lloyd's Rep 407, at 415 (emphasis added).
[50] *Didymi Corporation v Atlantic Lines and Navigation Co Inc.* [1988] 2 Lloyd's Rep 108.

of hire, such increase to be calculated in the same way as the reduction provided in the preceding sentence' (ie 'equitably... to be mutually agreed'). The owners maintained that the performance of the vessel exceeded the figures given in the charter and claimed for additional hire under clause 30. The Court of Appeal rejected the charterers' submission that clause 30 was unenforceable as an agreement to negotiate. It did not represent a 'bare' agreement to negotiate in the sense considered above, in that it formed a 'relatively minor aspect' of the parties' 'close and continuing contractual relationship for five years'.[51] More relevant to the present discussion, and the reason why clause 30 might itself have been regarded as enforceable, is that it was not a bare agreement in the sense that the negotiations on additional hire were left only to the good faith of the parties. As Hobhouse J put it at first instance:[52]

> The words of this paragraph (clause 30) do not disclose an intention merely to require an agreement. The words 'to be mutually agreed' are directory or mechanical and do not represent the substance of the provision. The substance of the provision is that there shall be an equitable decrease in hire.

Just as the parties in the *Petromec* case had agreed to an upgrade at 'reasonable cost' which they would first attempt to agree, the parties in *The Didymi* had agreed to additional hire at an 'equitable' (ie fair and reasonable[53]) rate which they would first attempt to agree. Furthermore, if they did not, the matter could be referred to arbitration so that this was also a case where there was 'no mere agreement to agree without machinery to resolve any failure to agree'.[54] But this too is a limited proposition. It is not so much that the parties' agreement to negotiate is enforceable, but that, in the absence of any agreement, there is an objective basis upon which the courts can reach agreement for them.

As noted above when discussing *Petromec*, whether the parties have reached no more than an agreement to negotiate subject only to 'good faith', or whether they have agreed to some objective standard will be a matter of construction. *The Didymi* was regarded by the Court of Appeal as a case where the construction was straightforward. A more difficult case, at least in the sense that it divided the judges, is presented by *Phillips Petroleum Co UK Ltd v Enron Europe Ltd*.[55]

---

[51] At 112, col 2, *per* Bingham LJ.
[52] [1987] 2 Lloyd's Rep 166, at 169.
[53] [1988] 2 Lloyd's Rep 108, at 119 col 1, *per* Dillon LJ.
[54] *Ibid*, col 2.
[55] (1997) CLC 329.

The parties entered into a gas sales agreement, under which commencement of supply depended on the seller and buyer each completing the facilities necessary to allow for the supply and receipt of the gas. The date on which supply would commence was agreed by the parties, under clause 2.2, as follows:

> The Buyer and the Seller shall use reasonable endeavours to agree, as much in advance as possible but in any case not less than thirty (30) days in advance, the date on which the Seller (and the other Sellers) will commence deliveries of Natural Gas to the Buyer (herein referred to as the 'Commissioning Date') … If the Seller and the Buyer are unable to agree, prior to 25 August 1996, as to the Commissioning Date … then the Commissioning Date shall be 25 September 1996...

The agreement as a whole was clearly enforceable because, failing any agreement of the parties, the supply of gas would commence on 25 September 1996 (the 'fall-back' provision). By the beginning of 1996 the necessary facilities had been completed so that supply could have commenced at an earlier date if the parties reached agreement. The seller proposed an earlier date which the buyer rejected on the basis of the very substantial loss it would suffer due to a severe fall in the short term market resale price of gas. The seller sought, and obtained from Colman J at first instance,[56] a declaration that it was a breach of clause 2 for the buyer to fail to agree to an earlier Commissioning Date on the basis of its own 'financial interest', or for any reason other than one based entirely upon the technical or operational practicality of the proposed date. On appeal, Sir John Balcombe agreed with Colman J, but the majority found for the buyer. Lord Justice Kennedy noted that the buyer did not have to go so far as to establish an unfettered entitlement to refuse to agree; only that the relevant wording in clause 2 did not require it to disregard its own financial position when endeavouring to agree a Commissioning Date. Neither he nor Potter LJ could find anything in the contractual setting which would support the implication of such a restriction. The present case was very different to *The Didymi*, as Potter LJ explained:[57]

> The standard of fairness and reasonableness is an objective criterion to which the Court is frequently willing to resort when determining a price or other sum not specifically agreed but readily assessable by reference to market rates and prices in the relevant sphere. No such straightforward or well-established exercise arises in a 'one-off' case of this kind, in which no criteria have been specified and there are a variety of considerations which

[56] 8 May, 1996 (unreported).
[57] At p 10, transcript.

may legitimately operate in the minds of the parties in relation to their ability or willingness to agree upon a specific date.

Some of the further observations of the majority on agreements to negotiate will need to be considered below.

3. ANALYSIS

To recap on the current status of agreements to negotiate: an agreement to negotiate in good faith is unenforceable and is no more enforceable when it is couched in terms of an agreement to use best or reasonable endeavours to agree. When the parties have entered into an agreement which is otherwise enforceable, it will not become unenforceable simply because the parties have agreed to negotiate any outstanding terms, but the agreement to negotiate is not itself enforceable. Such an agreement may be 'enforceable' when the parties have set out objective criteria, or machinery for resolving any disagreement, but the reality is that the agreement to negotiate is then irrelevant and the court simply completes the agreement by reference to such objective criteria or the machinery stipulated. In sum, for all the emphasis in some cases that *Walford v Miles* and *Courtney v Tolaini* only involved a 'bare' agreement to negotiate, the fact remains that no agreement to negotiate in good faith is enforceable as a matter of English law. This part attempts to analyse why this is so and whether there is any room for change, as advocated by Lord Steyn and Longmore LJ.

It is Longmore LJ who helpfully summarizes the reasons which may be given for the current state of the law:[58]

> The traditional objections to enforcing an obligation to negotiate in good faith are (1) that the obligation is an agreement to agree and thus too uncertain to enforce, (2) that it is difficult, if not impossible, to say whether, if negotiations are brought to an end, the termination is brought about in good or in bad faith, and (3) that, since it can never be known whether good faith negotiations would have produced an agreement at all or what the terms of any agreement would have been if it would have been reached, it is impossible to assess any loss caused by breach of the obligation.

The first of these may be regarded as the 'obligation analysis', the second the 'breach analysis', and the third the 'remedy analysis'. The first two overlap to a very great extent. There can be no breach if there is no obligation in the first place and the main reason given by Lord Ackner why there is no obligation created by an agreement to negotiate

---

[58] *Petromec*, above, n 12, at [116].

is the unwillingness of the courts to determine whether the conduct of the defendant departed from a standard of good faith, ie whether there was any breach. They will therefore be considered together as part of the obligation analysis.[59] This will be followed by the remedy analysis.

(a) Obligation

The key passage in Lord Ackner's dictum cited in full above is his observation that: 'while negotiations are in existence either party is entitled to withdraw from those negotiations, at any time and *for any reason.*' As Patrick Neill points out, the words 'while negotiations are in existence' must in context mean 'while good faith negotiations are in existence'. This results in a 'zero content' to the duty of good faith.[60] There seems little doubt that Lord Ackner would accept this; his reasoning is meant to be that stark. The parties' negotiations are subject to restrictions imposed by law, eg not to make misrepresentations, or not to fail to disclose in the exceptional circumstances where there is a duty of disclosure, but no more. The parties' self-imposed standard of good faith is 'inherently repugnant to the adversarial position of the parties when involved in negotiations' and is impossible for the courts to police. If there is little doubt that this is exactly what Lord Ackner meant, there is also little doubt that it is open to challenge, not least because it is inconsistent with other areas of the law of contract where the courts have accepted the need to police for good faith.

The most telling comparison is to be made between the approach of the courts to agreements to negotiate and their approach to the exercise of a discretion conferred on one of the parties to a valid and enforceable contract, since both tend to arise largely in the context of commercial contracts.[61] The latter approach is summed up by Leggatt LJ in *The Product Star*[62] as follows:

> Where A and B contract with each other to confer a discretion on A, that does not render B subject to A's uninhibited whim. In my judgment, the

[59] Though, as will be seen, on at least one occasion a judge has preferred to adopt the breach analysis to illuminating effect: text to n 68.

[60] 108 *LQR* 405, at 411.

[61] It is for this reason that no consideration will be given in this paper to the standard of good faith imposed by the Unfair Terms in Consumer Contracts Regulations 1999, reg 5(1). On which, see: *Director General of Fair Trading v First National Bank Plc* [2001] UKHL 52; [2002] 1 AC 481.

[62] *Abu Dhabi National Tanker Co v Product Star Shipping Ltd (No 2)* [1993] 1 Lloyd's Rep 397.

authorities show that not only must the discretion be exercised honestly and in good faith, but, having regard to the provisions of the contract by which it is conferred, it must not be exercised arbitrarily, capriciously or unreasonably.

This is now a well established approach, to which has been added the requirement that the discretion should not be exercised for an 'improper purpose'.[63] Although 'good faith' appears in this list as a separate requirement, in practice it is itself likely to be defined by reference to the others, ie it is consistent with good faith for a contractual discretion to be exercised honestly and not arbitrarily, capriciously, or unreasonably. In this context, 'reasonably' does not mean with reasonable care, but is akin to *Wednesbury* unreasonableness, ie not so unreasonable that no reasonable party would have exercised discretion in that way.[64]

If this were to be imported as the meaning of 'good faith' in the context of agreements to negotiate, it raises two questions: first, would it make a great deal of difference in practice; second, would it go far enough and would English law have been brought in line with other legal systems with which it is often compared in this regard?

As to the first, it would, at one level, make a great deal of difference to English law if the courts were to recognize that there is *a* standard of good faith which can be applied to agreements to negotiate. Such agreements would then have *some* legal content and the courts would at least have to entertain the prospect of a claim for breach. It is at this level though, ie whether there has been any breach, that there may not be a great deal of difference in terms of outcome. There are two principal reasons for this.

First, it is clear that part of the suggested test of 'good faith', ie that the parties must negotiate honestly, is already required. As Lord Ackner acknowledged the parties must not make misrepresentations and, as *Walford v Miles* itself illustrates, this can include misrepresentation as to their intention to negotiate.

Second, the parties may prefer their own commercial self-interest and still comply with the suggested standard of good faith.

---

[63] See, inter alia: *Gan Insurance Co Ltd v Tai Ping Insurance Co Ltd (No.2)* [2001] EWCA Civ 1047; [2001] 2 All ER (Comm) 299; *Paragon Finance plc v Nash* [2001] EWCA Civ 1466, [2002] 1 WLR 685; *Cantor Fitzgerald International v Horkulak* [2004] EWCA Civ 1287; [2005] ICR 402; *Lymington Marina Ltd v Macnamara* [2007] EWCA Civ 151; *Socimer International Bank Ltd v Standard Bank London Ltd* [2008] EWCA Civ 116; [2008] 1 Lloyd's Rep 558.

[64] And, as a consequence, it probably adds nothing since such an exercise of discretion would be either dishonest, arbitrary, capricious, or for an improper purpose: *Paragon Finance*, above, at [41], *per* Dyson LJ.

For example, in the *Socimer* case,[65] the buyer defaulted under a forward sale leaving the seller with a portfolio of securities in emerging
markets. The buyer was entitled to a credit for those securities against
any unpaid amounts due to the seller, but the valuation of those securities was left to the discretion of the seller. The Court of Appeal held
that, in reaching its valuation, the seller was 'entitled primarily to
consult its own interests'.[66] There is a comparison here with certain
dicta of Potter LJ in *Phillips v Enron*.[67] He expressed his conclusion
in that case on the orthodox basis that the agreement to use reasonable endeavours to agree the commissioning date was unenforceable in principle, ie it created no obligation at all. But he expressed
himself rather differently at the start of his judgment, by contemplat-
ing, in effect, whether the buyer was guilty of breach if there was an
obligation to negotiate:[68]

> The GSA was an agreement drawn up between international energy com-
> panies intended to regulate their trading and financial relationship over a
> period of at least 15 years and involving hundreds of millions of pounds
> worth of business. They were plainly the product of much arm's length
> negotiation and careful legal drafting, which appears to have been calcu-
> lated to provide sequentially for every contractual eventuality which might
> occur at the various stages of the development and operation of the supply
> contract. That being so, I see no reason to suppose that it was the expecta-
> tion, let alone the obligation, of the parties that, in any area of activity in
> which room was left for manoeuvre or further negotiation, they were not
> at liberty to take into account their own financial position and act in the
> manner most beneficial to them, short of bad faith or breach of an express
> term of the contract.

If it is consistent with the requirement of good faith for a party to break
off negotiations when it suits its own commercial interests, this may
be acceptable to Lord Ackner since it meets his concern that '(e)ach
party ... is entitled to pursue his (or her) own interest'. It may also be
'acceptable', of course, because it results in an 'obligation' which can
never be breached and, hence, no obligation at all. For example, in
Walford v Miles, one of the reasons given by the defendants for breaking off negotiations with the claimant was that they were concerned

---

[65] *Socimer International Bank Ltd v Standard Bank London Ltd* [2008] EWCA Civ 116; [2008] 1
Lloyd's Rep 558.

[66] *Ibid*, at [112], *per* Rix LJ.

[67] Above, n 55.

[68] *Ibid*, at 335. It was also noted, above (text following n 56), that Kennedy LJ proceeded in
some sense on the basis that clause 2 did create an obligation, but the question was whether
the buyer was in breach by preferring its own financial interest.

whether they and their staff would get on with the claimants; if they failed to do so, they might lose staff and then fail to produce the £300,000 profit which was the subject of a warranty. This may have been a mis-judgment on their part, but it is surely not enough to make their decision arbitrary, capricious, or improper.

It is clear that the suggested standard of good faith can be breached in the context in which it is currently applied, ie in the exercise of contractual discretion. In *The Product Star (No 2)* the Court of Appeal was concerned with a provision in a charter under which the own-ers were given discretion to determine whether a loading or discharg-ing port was dangerous or impossible to reach. They were found to have exercised their discretion capriciously or arbitrarily in refus-ing to proceed to a port nominated by the charterers, with the result that they had repudiated the charter.[69] Among the factors taken into account by the court were: the owners made no attempt to consult the master of the vessel; the refusal was made at short notice; the charter allowed for trading in a known war risk zone and there was no evidence that the nominated port was any more at risk than any other port in that zone; and there was no explanation offered why the owners had traded another vessel in the same zone during the time in question. However, a feature of the discretion conferred on the own-ers is that it was only directed to an assessment of dangerousness; that, of itself, ruled out any prospect of the owners being allowed to refuse to proceed to a port simply on the grounds of commercial self-interest. This may be contrasted with *Mallozzi* where, even if the agree-ment to agree on the order of the ports had been enforceable, there would have been no breach on the basis of the suggested standard of good faith because the owners nominated Genoa as the second port on the grounds of commercial self-interest (ie a possible liability for demurrage).

It remains the case therefore that any breach of an agreement to negotiate in good faith, where good faith has the same meaning as given to it in the context of contractual discretion, is likely to be very rare. Patrick Neill has referred to the 'arbitrary' decision of the defen-dant to break off negotiations in the *Channel Home Centers* case, but even in that case it seems clear that the decision was based on the offer of a higher rent from elsewhere.[70]

It is not in every case that it would be necessary to assess whether negotiations breached the standard of good faith suggested. In some,

[69] Though the charterers succeeded on liability, they failed to prove any loss.
[70] 795 F. 2d. 291, at 296, fn 3.

the defendant may fail to negotiate at all, though even then it may be argued that any such failure is no breach if it was based on commercial self-interest and was not arbitrary, capricious, or for an improper purpose (as seems to have been the case in *Mallozzi*). In others, it is not the agreement *to* negotiate which will be in issue. For example, there would have been an actionable breach in *Walford v Miles*. It will be recalled that the claimants sued for breach of a lock out agreement and the judge found that the defendants had continued to negotiate with the third party to whom they ultimately sold the business. The recognition of *a* standard of good faith for negotiations would be sufficient to remove the uncertainty about the duration of the lock out and the claim would be for breach of the lock out element, not the lock in. This would then, of course, lead to the further question of what remedy might be appropriate, which is considered below.

If the test of good faith suggested for agreements to negotiate is unlikely to make a lot of difference in terms of outcome, it rather begs the second of the questions raised above: does it go far enough and would it bring English law in line with other legal systems? If one starts with the second part of this question, the answer depends on exactly what it is that one is comparing. For example, the one concrete example given in the Draft Common Frame of Reference is that it is contrary to good faith and fair dealing for a person to enter into or continue negotiations with no real intention of reaching an agreement with the other party.[71] That may already be covered in English law by misrepresentation, as demonstrated by *Walford v Miles*. But in its general definition of 'good faith and fair dealing' the DCFR goes further:[72]

> The expression 'good faith and fair dealing' refers to a standard of conduct characterised by honesty, openness and consideration for the interests of the other party to the transaction or relationship in question.

Here there is obvious room for divergence. It can perhaps be put in the form of a concrete example provided by Professor Sir Guenter Treitel, based on *Walford v Miles*. He noted that the claimants sought damages of £1 million on the basis that having agreed, subject to contract, to buy the business and property for £2 million, it was in fact worth £3 million (by reason of facts known to them but not the defendants). He went on to state:[73]

---

[71] Para II-3:301(4).

[72] Para I-1:103(1).

[73] In earlier editions of *Treitel*, but this is the form in which it appears in the twelfth edition, at para 2-106.

If a duty to negotiate in good faith exists, it must be equally incumbent on both parties, so that it can hardly require a vendor to agree to sell a valuable property for only two-thirds of its true value when the facts affecting that value are known to the purchaser and not disclosed (as good faith would seem to require) to the vendor. The actual result in *Walford v Miles* (in which the purchasers recovered the sum of £700 in respect of their wasted expenses as damages for misrepresentation, but not the £1 million which they claimed as damages for breach of contract) seems with respect, to be entirely appropriate on the facts…

It is submitted that when parties to negotiations agree to negotiate in good faith, they are very unlikely to have intended the sort of 'openness', or 'consideration for the interests of the other party' which would require the disclosure to which Professor Treitel alludes in this passage.[74] The most they intend, in the absence of anything more express, is that they will adhere to a standard of good faith *consistent with the negotiating process*, in which it may be said they have discretion over the *formation* of the contract. That, it is submitted, should be seen as the same standard as the courts have imposed on parties who have discretion in the *performance* of a contract. This may be less than what is meant by good faith in other areas,[75] or in other legal systems.

(b) Remedy

The difficulty of formulating an appropriate remedy for breach of an agreement to negotiate in good faith has featured prominently in the reasoning of some judges. As Lord Denning stated in *Courtney v Tolaini*:

…if the law does not recognize a contract to enter into a contract … it seems to me that it cannot recognize a contract to negotiate. The reason is because it is too uncertain to have any binding force. No court could estimate the damages because no one can tell whether the negotiations would be successful or would fall through; or, if successful, what the result would be. It seems to me that a contract to negotiate … is not a contract known to the law…

---

[74] cf A Berg, 'Promises to Negotiate in Good Faith' (2003) 119 *LQR* 357 who argues that this may depend on the precise factual setting. See also: E McKendrick, 'The Meaning of Good Faith' in M Andenas *et al* (eds), *Liber Amicorum Guido Alpa: Private Law Beyond the National Systems* (London: BIICL, 2007).

[75] Eg under the 1999 Regulations, above, n 61. A feature of the discretion test is that it is context-specific ('having regard to the provisions of the contract by which it is conferred' (see dictum of Leggatt LJ, above (at n 62)), so that, if applied to agreements to negotiate, it could allow for the fact that one of the parties negotiates as a consumer.

With respect to the distinguished judge, this approach starts at the end and not the beginning. If an agreement to negotiate is too uncertain to be unenforceable, the uncertainty must lie, as Lord Ackner argues, with the obligation. If, *ex hypothesi*, there is an obligation to negotiate, damages may be difficult to assess but they cannot be so uncertain as to negate the existence of any obligation in the first place.

It is nonetheless unarguable that damages would be difficult to assess. Based on the reform suggested above, a defendant would have to have conducted negotiations in a way which was arbitrary and capricious, or for an improper purpose. The defendant could then argue that, even if it had negotiated in good faith, particularly bearing in mind its entitlement to consult its own financial interest, the parties would not have entered into the contract which was the subject of negotiation. As Longmore LJ noted in the *Petromec* case there are echoes here of a claim for loss of chance and that is something which it is not 'uncommon' for the courts to have to assess.[76] The analogy is not complete since such claims turn on an assessment of the way a third party would have behaved,[77] whereas in a claim for breach of an agreement to negotiate it turns on an assessment of the way the defendant would have behaved. Here it is necessary to take account of a further principle that where a contract entitles the party in breach to perform in alternative ways, damages are, as a general rule, assessed on the assumption that he would have performed in the way that is least burdensome to himself and least beneficial to the other party.[78] However, the alternative relied upon by the defendant to diminish or extinguish any damages must constitute a valid performance and will be limited to a mode of performance which could in all the circumstances be regarded as reasonable.[79] In the present context, the defendant would not be allowed simply to say that he would not have concluded the contract under negotiation; he would have to establish that he would not have concluded it on grounds that were not arbitrary or capricious. It seems to have been this sort of consideration which led Bingham LJ

---

[76] At [118].

[77] Eg the decision of the courts if the defendant had conducted the claimant's case properly (*Kitchen v Royal Air Force Association* [1958] 1 WLR 563); or of the other party to a deal if the defendant had advised the claimant properly (*Allied Maples v Simmons & Simmons* [1995] 1 WLR 1602); or even the decision of a judge in a talent contest if the defendant had not prevented the claimant from taking part (*Chaplin v Hicks* [1911] 2 KB 786).

[78] *Abrahams v Herbert Reiach Ltd* [1922] 1 KB 477; *Withers v General Theatre Corp* [1933] 2 KB 536; *The Rijn* [1981] 2 Lloyd's Rep 267.

[79] *Paula Lee Ltd v Robert Zehil Ltd* [1983] 2 All ER 390; *Mulvenna v Royal Bank of Scotland* [2003] EWCA Civ 1112; *Clark v BET* [1997] IRLR 348; *Cantor Fitzgerald International v Horkulak* [2004] EWCA Civ 1287; [2005] ICR 402.

to assess the likely damages as follows in his dissenting judgment in the Court of Appeal in *Walford v Miles*:

> The plaintiffs are entitled to be placed in the same position as if the defendants had performed their obligation, *albeit in the manner most favourable to themselves*. Depending on the facts as found by the court, the proper inference might be that the parties would probably not have come to terms even if the defendants had complied with their obligation or that the defendants would have decided not to sell; in that event the plaintiffs' damages would be nominal. But the proper inference might be that if the defendants had complied with their obligation the parties would probably have come to terms because all potential points of difference would have been compromised or conceded.[80] If that were the correct factual inference, the plaintiffs' damages could, I think, be more than nominal.[81]

This difficulty in assessing damages is, of course, confined to the 'expectation' or 'performance' interest, ie an award of damages to put the claimant in the same position as if the defendant had negotiated in good faith. It would not be encountered if damages were confined to the 'reliance' interest, ie the expenditure wasted by the claimant in conducting negotiations with the defendant.[82] A claimant has this option,[83] but if he exercises it he will not recover any expenditure which the defendant can prove he would not have recouped even if the contract had been performed.[84] In this context that means he will not recover if the defendant can prove that, even if he had negotiated in good faith, the parties would *not* have entered into the contract under negotiation. The difference is, of course, that the burden will be on the defendant and, given the inherent uncertainty referred to above, this will not be an easy burden to discharge. Even if the claimant does not exercise his option to claim reliance damages and seeks expectation damages instead, the court may at its option confine him to

---

[80] In a case like *Walford v Miles* where the terms for sale appear largely to have been agreed, it would have been more a case of assessing whether the parties would have moved beyond the stage of 'subject to contract'.

[81] (1991) 62 P & CR 410, at 423. cf the earlier well known dictum of Lord Wright in *Hillas and Co v Arcos Ltd* (1932) 147 LT 503, at 515: '... in the event of repudiation by one party the damages may be nominal, unless a jury think that the opportunity to negotiate was of some appreciable value to the injured party.'

[82] A claimant may of course wish to include in his reliance loss the loss of the opportunity to negotiate with *another party* and argue that that opportunity had a value which should be recognized as part of his reliance loss. This rather speculative claim is largely confined to claims for fraudulent misrepresentation: see, eg *East v Maurer* [1991] 1 WLR 461.

[83] *CCC Films (London) Ltd v Impact Quadrant Films Ltd* [1985] QB 16.

[84] See *C & P Haulage v Middleton* [1983] 1 WLR 1461. One way of ensuring recovery without restriction may be to provide expressly for a 'break off' fee, by way of an indemnity.

reliance and will do so where expectation damages are too speculative,[85] which may be thought, by definition, to be the case with breach of an agreement to negotiate. It may therefore be assumed that a claimant who has been able to establish breach of an agreement to negotiate in good faith would almost always recover his wasted expenditure, either at his option or that of the court. In *Walford v Miles* of course the claimants recovered their wasted expenditure by way of an action for misrepresentation, but as explained above this was the subject of some doubt in the Court of Appeal and it is not an action which would always be available. By contrast, an award of reliance damages for breach of an agreement to negotiate would, it is submitted, be available as a matter of routine; what would not be routine is establishing that the defendant was in breach in the first place.

4. CONCLUSION

This paper has first sought to assess the current status of agreements to negotiate in good faith and has done so largely by considering the so-called limits to the decision of the House of Lords in *Walford v Miles*. In fact, there are no real limits and agreements to negotiate are not themselves enforceable in any of the guises they may take. It has then considered whether any change to the law might be appropriate and has done so largely by asking a question which is surprisingly conspicuous in its absence: what might be meant by 'good faith' in the context of an agreement to negotiate? It is submitted that, given the nature of the negotiating process, particularly in the context of the commercial dealings where such agreements tend to be employed, 'good faith' can only be given the same limited meaning as it has in cases where a contract confers discretion on one of the parties.[86] This would be enough to acknowledge that agreements to negotiate are enforceable, but a breach would be a relatively rare occurrence and the claimant is likely to be confined to the recovery of his wasted expenditure.

---

[85] *McRae v Commonwealth Disposals Commission* (1951) 84 CLR 377.

[86] In due course, and in line with the analogy drawn herein with 'contractual discretion', the standard proposed may be recognized as a minimum which can be added to depending on the circumstances of the case, cf A Berg, 'Promises to Negotiate in Good Faith' (2003) 119 *LQR* 357 who argues for a more extensive meaning of 'good faith'. In *Socimer International Bank Ltd v Standard Bank London Ltd* [2008] EWCA Civ 116; [2008] 1 Lloyd's Rep 558 (see discussion in text following n 65) an argument that the minimum standard of good faith should be supplemented by an implied term that the portfolio of securities be valued with reasonable care was unsuccessful.

This would represent a limited reform, but what this paper has thus far studiously avoided is any indication of whether even this limited reform should be implemented. That is because this is the hardest question to answer. One can agree with Longmore LJ's assessment that a finding of fraudulent misrepresentation of the type found to have been made in *Walford v Miles* would make good faith fall away as a separate obligation and that, in its absence, it is 'perhaps less likely that there will have been bad faith in terminating negotiations'.[87] It is less easy to agree with his assessment that 'it will not be particularly difficult to tell whether there was or not'.[88] On this issue, the assessment of Lord Ackner is to be preferred. But parties do not normally enter into agreements on the basis that they are entirely unenforceable[89] and for this rather unconvincing reason, if no other,[90] the limited reform suggested herein is put forward for consideration.

---

[87] *Petromec*, above, n 12, at [119].

[88] *Ibid*.

[89] There is, of course, a sense of self-fulfilling prophecy about the decision in *Walford v Miles*. The longer it remains unchallenged the easier it will become to conclude that the parties must have entered into an agreement to negotiate on the basis it provides no more than comfort, rather than anything legally enforceable.

[90] Save perhaps the aim of promoting a consistent approach within English law, if not between English law and other legal systems.

4

Offer and Acceptance in the Electronic Age

1. INTRODUCTION

The fact that the essentially nineteenth century construct which we refer to as the requirement of 'offer and acceptance' in contract formation has survived into the twenty-first century is a testament to the flexibility of a model of agreement which has proven relatively straightforward in its application to new modes of communication. In the twentieth century, these new modes included the telex and the fax, technologies now largely superseded by the development of email and the internet. There is no reason to suppose that the application of the offer and acceptance rules to these more recent electronic technologies will give rise to any particular difficulty, and we can confidently expect that the model will continue to operate effectively in the future. There are nevertheless a number of unanswered questions about the application of the offer and acceptance rules to these new means of communication, and in this paper I set out what I think these questions are, and try to find answers to them.

Before I begin looking at these questions, however, there are some preliminary issues which should be dealt with. One is the practical significance of the offer and acceptance rules. There are a number of reasons why the questions under consideration may be important in practice. First and foremost, of course, the offer and acceptance rules tell us not only whether a contract was formed at all, but they also tell us when a contract was formed and where that took place. Whether there was a contract at all may be significant for a whole host of reasons, such as whether an online retailer is bound by an apparent agreement to sell goods at a significant undervalue arising out of a pricing error on its website.[1] The precise time at which a contract was made

* Fellow and Tutor in Law, Worcester College, Oxford. I am grateful to the participants in the Oxford-Norton Rose Colloquium for their comments on an earlier draft of this paper. Particular thanks are due to Sir William Blair, Sam Krafft, and Eoin O'Dell for their valuable assistance. The usual caveat applies.

[1] A number of such incidents have been reported in the press, and the subject of legal commentary. For discussion of two well known English examples, involving Argos and Kodak, see Kevin Rogers, 'Snap! Internet "Offers" Under Scrutiny' (2002) 23 *Bus L Rev* 70. See also *Chwee Kin Keong v Digilandmall.com Pte Ltd* [2004] SGHC 71, [2004] 2 SLR 594 (affd: [2005]

may determine issues such as whether or not a party's standard terms have been validly incorporated by notice,[2] and whether a term requiring completion of work within a particular interval from the moment of contract formation has been satisfied.[3] Finally, the place where a contract was formed may still be of importance for the purposes of jurisdiction in a limited category of cases.[4] More generally, online retailers keen to maintain control over with whom they contract—preferring to deal only with consumers in the same jurisdiction, for example—will have an interest in delaying the moment of contract formation in order to preserve their freedom of manoeuvre in this respect.

Another preliminary issue is the scope of the paper, which is limited in two ways. The first is that I consider only transactional activity effected through communication between computers. The focus is therefore on contract formation by email and through websites. Contracts formed via electronic data interchange and instant messaging do not appear to raise any distinct issues with regard to offer and acceptance, and so I have not given these forms of communication separate consideration, although some of the material relating to emails and websites will apply to them by analogy. The second limit on the scope of the paper is that it deals only with the offer and acceptance requirement, and does not extend to other issues relating to contract formation and computer technology, such as the validity of electronic signatures and the satisfaction of requirements of form.[5]

A third preliminary question is the significance of so-called automated message systems. There are at least two contexts in which these may be relevant to the issue under consideration. The first is in internet trading, where typically the customer interacts with an automated system on the retailer's website and a confirmation email is sent out automatically, so that there is no human intervention on the retailer's side during the process of contract formation. The second is electronic data interchange (EDI), where the parties have established an interactive transacting system whereby contracts are made by automated systems (or 'electronic agents') on both sides. Needless to say, the latter are used only where there is an existing trading relationship between

---

SGCA 2, [2005] 1 SLR 502), discussed below, where a laser printer worth nearly Sing $4,000 had been offered for sale for just Sing $66.

[2] See, eg *Chapelton v Barry UDC* [1940] 1 KB 532 (CA).

[3] Similarly, the precise moment at which an offer is held to have been communicated will determine when the period within which the offer must be accepted begins.

[4] See Jonathan Hill, *Cross-Border Consumer Contracts* (Oxford: OUP, 2008) para 1.56.

[5] See further, Law Commission, *Electronic Commerce: Formal Requirements in Commercial Transactions* (2001); and the Electronic Communications Act 2007, ss 7–8.

the parties—for example, between a retailer and a supplier—and the terms of the contracts made have been agreed in advance. Although it is sometimes suggested that the use of automated systems for contract formation gives rise to doctrinal difficulties,[6] it is hard to see why this should be thought to be the case. Programmed action by a computer objectively signifies the consent of the person on whose behalf the computer was programmed to entry into the relevant contract,[7] and discussion of the 'intention' of the computer or its status as an agent is entirely superfluous.[8] In this respect, an automated computer system is no different from a vending machine, or the ticket machine at the entrance to the car park in *Thornton v Shoe Lane Parking*.[9] The only real difficulty which systems of this kind pose for contract law is the extent to which a contracting party is bound by the unintended actions of such a system under its control, but even here one would expect the normal rules to apply, so that the party in question would be bound by the objective manifestation of its consent as expressed by the system unless the situation fell within an established exception, such as the 'snapping up' of an offer known not to have been intended.

Finally, a note on methodology. The absence of direct authority on the questions under discussion means that it is necessary to reason from first principles and by analogy. In doing so, the three principal considerations which will be borne in mind are the need for certainty; the protection of autonomy, in particular the preservation of freedom of manoeuvre during contract negotiations; and the protection of the reasonable expectations of those involved. The analysis is structured around the technologies under scrutiny, and the paper is therefore divided into two main parts, the first dealing with contracts formed by email exchanges, and the second with contracts formed through websites.

---

[6] See, eg Amelia Boss and Wolfgang Kilian, *The United Nations Convention on the Use of Electronic Communications in International Contracts: An In-Depth Guide and Sourcebook* (Austin, Texas: Wolters Kluwer, 2008) 349.

[7] In *Chwee Kin Keong*, above, n 1, Rajah JC said (at [134]) that 'It is not really in issue ... that programmed computers sending out automated responses can bind the sender'. Article 12 of the UN Convention on the Use of Electronic Communications in International Contracts stipulates that contracts may be formed as a result of actions by automated message systems, even if no natural person reviewed or intervened in each of the individual actions carried out by the systems or the resulting contract, but it is questionable whether this provision was necessary. See similarly the US Uniform Computer Information Transactions Act, s 206.

[8] See Steve Hedley, *The Law of Electronic Commerce and the Internet in the UK and Ireland* (London: Cavendish Publishing, 2006) 245.

[9] [1971] 2 QB 163 (CA).

2. CONTRACTING BY EMAIL

Because the basic structure of email communication is similar to that of older methods of communication—such as the post—the extension of the offer and acceptance model to email should not pose too many difficulties.[10] The principal issues such an extension seems to raise are as follows: (1) whether the postal rule applies to email; (2) if not, when exactly an email acceptance takes effect; and (3) what the position should be when things go wrong. When looking at these questions, we should bear in mind that any rules that emerge will represent only the default position, and that an offeror generally has the power to control the effectiveness of any communication of acceptance.

(a) Does the postal rule apply to email?

Although the general rule is that an acceptance must be communicated to the offeror,[11] there is a well established exception for posted acceptances, which (at least for some purposes)[12] take effect on posting.[13] Since, superficially, there are similarities between electronic mail and mail delivered by post, it has been argued that this 'postal rule' should be extended to email, with the result that an email acceptance would be effective when sent, and the contract formed then and there.[14]

---

[10] See Jonathan Hill, above, n 4, para 1.53: 'A contract concluded by an exchange of emails is not substantially different from a contract concluded by an exchange of letters; the fact that the parties communicate via computer technology rather than by another method of communication changes neither the fundamentals of the legal relationship nor the legal issues to which it gives rise.'

[11] *Entores v Miles Far East Corp* [1955] 2 QB 327 (CA), at 335 (Birkett LJ); *Brinkibon Ltd v Stahag Stahl mbH* [1983] 2 AC 34 (HL), at 41 (Lord Wilberforce), at 48 (Lord Brandon).

[12] See Treitel, *The Law of Contract* (12th edn, London: Sweet & Maxwell, 2007) para 2-033, where it is said that 'there is no single or universal rule which determines the effect of a posted acceptance', and that the effect of such an acceptance has to be considered as against various competing factors, such as withdrawal of the offer and loss or delay of the acceptance.

[13] *The Household Fire and Carriage Accident Insurance Co v Grant* (1879) 4 Ex D 216 (CA); *Henthorn v Fraser* [1892] 2 Ch 27 (CA).

[14] See eg Paul Fasciano, 'Internet Electronic Mail: a Last Bastion for the Mailbox Rule' (1997) 25 *Hofstra L Rev* 971; and Valerie Watnick, 'The Electronic Formation of Contracts and the Common Law "Mailbox Rule"' (2004) 56 *Baylor L Rev* 175. Paul Fasciano in particular puts forward very considered arguments for the application of the postal rule to email, but the significance of his analysis for the present discussion is limited by the outdated assumption he makes (at 1001) about the speed of email transmission ('it will typically take minutes, hours, or in some cases, days') and by the fact that the US Restatement, Second, Contracts (1981) § 64 limits the application of the alternative 'receipt rule' to instances of 'substantially instantaneous two-way communication', which he interprets as requiring that there must be

However, such an extension of the postal rule appears highly unlikely, and the arguments against it overwhelming.[15]

It is noteworthy that since the introduction of the postal rule in the nineteenth century, it has been extended to only one other form of communication, the telegraph.[16] Far from extending the rule, the courts have tended to limit its scope, both by developing exceptions to the operation of the rule in the postal context,[17] and by refusing to apply it to faster modes of communication, such as telex.[18] Furthermore, the leading English cases on the application of the rule to other technologies, *Entores v Miles Far East Corp*[19] and *Brinkibon v Stahag Stahl mbH*,[20] provide little support for the extension of the rule to email.

In *Entores*, the plaintiffs had sent an offer to buy copper cathodes by telex to the Dutch agents of the defendants, and the offer had been accepted by a telex received by the plaintiffs in London. The Court of Appeal had to decide for jurisdiction purposes whether the contract had been made in the Netherlands, where the acceptance had been sent, or in England, where the acceptance had been received. It was held that the postal rule did not apply, and so the contract had been made in England. At the beginning of his judgment, Denning LJ distinguished contracts made by telephone and telex from contracts made by post on the grounds that the former were 'virtually instantaneous and stand on a different footing'.[21] He posited the example of two people making a contract in each other's presence, where the acceptance was drowned out, saying that in such a case no contract would be made. The same would be true where the parties were speaking on the telephone and the line went dead before the offeror heard the words of acceptance. In the case of a telex, he continued, if the line went dead or the ink at the receiving end failed, this would generally be apparent to the offeree, in which case there would be no contract

the possibility of interaction between the two parties, allowing each to ensure that there has been understanding by the other. As we shall see, this is not a condition of the application of the 'receipt rule' in English law.

[15] See Simone Hill, 'Flogging a Dead Horse—The Postal Acceptance Rule and Email' (2001) 17 *Jl of Contract L* 151.

[16] See *Cowan v O'Conner* (1888) 20 QBD 640 (QB).

[17] See, eg *Holwell Securities Ltd v Hughes* [1974] 1 WLR 155 (CA) 161 (Lawton LJ) (the rule probably does not operate if its application would produce 'manifest inconvenience and absurdity').

[18] 'It is true, I think, that courts in more recent times and in the light of modern means of communication have no disposition to extend the [postal rule] exception': *Bressan v Squires* [1974] 2 NSWLR 460 (NSWSC) 462 (Bowen CJ).

[19] [1955] 2 QB 327 (CA).

[20] [1983] 2 AC 34 (HL).

[21] [1955] 2 QB 327 (CA), at 332.

until the acceptance was repeated and received. In general, therefore, the rule for instantaneous communications was that the contract
was only complete 'when the acceptance is received by the offeror'.[22]
Birkett LJ agreed with Denning LJ, adding that the ordinary rule of
law, 'to which the special considerations governing contracts by post'[23]
were exceptions, was that the acceptance of an offer must be communicated to the offeror. Finally, Parker LJ said that there was no need
for the postal rule where the parties were in each other's presence or
where, though separated in space, communication between them was,
'in effect, instantaneous' and that although the dispatch and receipt
of a message by telex was 'not completely instantaneous', the parties
were 'to all intents and purposes in each other's presence' and there
was no reason to depart from the general rule.[24]

The decision in *Entores* not to apply the postal rule to telex communications was upheld by the House of Lords in the *Brinkibon* case. The
House again emphasized that the general rule required that the acceptance be communicated,[25] with Lord Wilberforce describing the postal
rule as 'an exception applying to non-instantaneous communication
at a distance'.[26] And although Lord Wilberforce emphasized that the
involvement of agents or other intermediaries and error or default at
the recipient's end might complicate matters, in 'the simple case of
instantaneous communication between principals',[27] the general rule
applied. According to Lord Brandon, the postal rule was based on considerations of commercial expediency which applied where there was
'bound to be a substantial interval between the time when the acceptance is sent and the time when it is received', but not where the means
of communication was instantaneous in nature.[28] And while Lord
Fraser pointed out that because typically the operator of a telex would
be a clerk with no authority to conclude contracts, the transmission of
the message between the principals would not in fact be instantaneous, he nevertheless agreed that the postal rule should not be applied.
It was not unreasonable to treat receipt of the telex on the offeror's
machine as effective delivery, since it was the principal's responsibility to arrange for prompt handling of messages within his own office.
Furthermore, the offeree could generally tell whether his message had

---

[22] *Ibid*, at 334.
[23] *Ibid*, at 335.
[24] *Ibid*, at 337.
[25] [1983] 2 AC 34 (HL), at 41 (Lord Wilberforce), at 48 (Lord Brandon).
[26] *Ibid*, at 41-2.
[27] *Ibid*, at 42.
[28] *Ibid*, at 48.

been received, whereas the offeror would not know that an unsuccessful attempt had been made to send an acceptance to him.

For the purposes of the present discussion, three points are worthy of note about these two decisions. The first is that the general rule requiring communication of acceptance is emphasized, and the postal rule presented as a special exception, justified by particular considerations of commercial convenience. The second is that the postal rule is held not to apply where the means of communication is 'instantaneous', with this concept being interpreted broadly, to include a mode of communication which was described as 'virtually' and 'not completely' instantaneous. Particularly noteworthy in this respect is Lord Brandon's description of the postal rule as based on considerations applicable where there is bound to be a substantial delay between the sending and the receipt of the acceptance. And the third is that some emphasis is attached to the fact that in the case of a telex, it is more likely that the offeree will be able to tell that his attempt to communicate has failed than that the offeror will be able to tell that there has been an unsuccessful attempt to communicate with him.

The implications for email seem clear. Since email is also 'virtually instantaneous'—in the words of one commentator, 'any delay in the electronic relaying of an email message is now infinitesimal'[29]—the general rule requiring communication of the acceptance should apply. Furthermore, the sender of an email is more likely than the recipient to be aware that it has not arrived, since in most cases he will receive a message telling him that there is a problem.[30] He is therefore in a

---

[29] Simone Hill, above, n 15, 159. See also Jonathan Hill, above, n 4, para 1.62 (long delays in the arrival of an email 'are rare'). A series of emails sent from an Italian email address to an English email address, and then accessed from Italy, took between two and three seconds to go from one computer's outbox to the other computer's inbox. It is sometimes argued that emails are not instantaneous because they usually pass through various servers, routers and internet service providers before reaching their destination (see eg the New Zealand Law Commission, *Electronic Commerce Part One: A Guide for the Legal and Business Community* (1998) para 71; *Chwee Kin Keong*, above, n 1, at [97] (Rajah JC), but telephone calls and faxes may also pass through a number of different exchanges, and it is not clear why the complexity of the transmission process should be thought to determine whether or not the transmission is 'instantaneous'. Similarly, although it is sometimes argued that email is not instantaneous because email messages sent over the internet are broken into smaller 'packets' of information which are sent along different routes to their destination (see eg Watnick, above, n 14, 200-1), it is not clear why this is thought to be relevant to whether or not they are 'instantaneous'.

[30] Commentators sometimes argue that the postal rule should apply to email because the sender of an email *may not* know whether or not the email has been received, but the same is true of the sender of a telex message, and in the *Entores* case, above, n 11, Denning LJ expressed the opinion (at 333) that where the offeror through no fault of his own did not

very different position from the sender of a letter, who will rarely have any indication that it has gone astray.[31] Finally, Lord Fraser's concern about delays in the passing of a telex message from a clerk to a principal has limited relevance to email (where the message will typically be sent directly to the principal's email account), and in the event that emails are handled by an intermediary, it would—as with telex messages—be the principal's responsibility to ensure that they are dealt with efficiently. These considerations are reinforced by the subsequent classification of fax transmissions as an instantaneous form of communication not subject to the postal rule,[32] despite the fact that they are subject to short delays similar to those involved in the sending of emails. All in all, it seems clear that emails resemble more the class of communications to which the postal rule does not apply than the class to which it does.[33]

A further argument against the extension of the postal rule to email is the fact that the rule itself is unpopular, and the justification for it obscure. In a report published in 1993, the Scottish Law Commission said that the postal rule 'gives rise to well-recognised difficulties', and that the law would be much more coherent if there were only one rule for all means of communication.[34] All the consultees who had expressed an opinion on the matter favoured the abolition of the postal rule, which the Commission recommended be replaced by a rule requiring that the acceptance reach the offeror. Academics have found it difficult to identify a justification for the rule,[35] and the most

receive a telexed acceptance, and yet the offeree reasonably believed that it had got through, there would be no contract.

[31] See Saul Squires, 'Some Contract Issues Arising from Online Business-Consumer Agreements' (2000) 5 *Deakin L Rev* 109, 109 ('a sender's knowledge of the transmission status of an email acceptance exceeds that of a postal acceptance'). Furthermore, as Deveral Capps has pointed out, it would be strange if the application of the postal rule to emails meant that a contract was held to have been concluded even though the offeree knew (through receipt of a non-delivery message) that his acceptance had not reached the offeror: 'Electronic Mail and the Postal Rule' (2004) 15 *Int'l Company and Commercial L Rev* 207, 209.

[32] *JSC Zestafoni v Ronly Holdings Ltd* [2004] EWHC 245 (Comm), [2004] Lloyd's Rep 335 (QB).

[33] John Dickie, 'When and Where are Electronic Contracts Concluded?' (1998) 49 *NILQ* 332, 332. See also Jonathan Hill, above, n 4, para 1.61 ('[A] contract concluded by e-mail has much more in common with a contract concluded by telephone than with a contract concluded by post').

[34] *Report on the Formation of Contract: Scottish Law and the United Nations Convention on Contracts for the International Sale of Goods* (Scot Law Com No 144, 1993) para 4.4.

[35] See, eg David Marshall Evans, 'The Anglo-American Mailing Rule: Some Problems of Offer and Acceptance in Contracts by Correspondence' (1966) 15 *ICLQ* 553, 561 (of the many justifications put forward for the rule, only one or two are of any merit); Michael

positive thing that is said about it in a leading text is that 'the rule is in truth an arbitrary one, little better or worse than its competitors.'[36] It follows that even if the analogy between the post and email communication were thought to be close, there would be little justification for extending the rule to the new method of communication.

In the light of these considerations, it is not surprising that the majority of commentators have come down against the application of the postal rule to email,[37] and it seems sensible to conclude that to be effective an emailed acceptance must be received by the offeror.[38] The first English case touching directly on the matter is consistent with this view. In *Greenergy SA v Memphis Biofuels*,[39] one of the issues was whether there was a good arguable case that contracts concluded by email were made within the jurisdiction of the English courts. Counsel for the two parties agreed that the contracts were made in the place where the offeror received the emailed acceptance, and in the light of this Blair J held that there was a good arguable case that the course

---

Furmston, Takao Norisada, and Jill Poole, *Contract Formation and Letters of Intent: a Comparative Assessment* (Chichester: John Wiley, 1997) 59 ('Various attempts have been made to justify this rule but none are convincing').

[36] Treitel, above, n 12, para 2-029.

[37] See eg Dickie, above, n 33, 332; Simone Hill, above, n 15; Jeff Dodd and James Hernandez, 'Contracting in Cyberspace' [1998] *Computer L Rev and Technology J* 1, 12; Squires, above, n 31, 110; Roger Halson, *Contract Law* (Harlow: Pearson Education, 2001) 151; Sharon Christensen, 'Formation of Contracts by Email—Is it Just the Same as the Post?' (2001) 1 *Queensland U of Technology L and Justice J* 22, 38; Capps, above, n 31, 212; E Allan Farnsworth, *Farnsworth on Contract* (3rd edn, New York: Aspen, 2004), vol I, para 3.22; Diane Rowland and Elizabeth Macdonald, *Information Technology Law* (London: Cavendish Publishing, 3rd edn, 2005) 281; Lawrence Collins (ed), *Dicey, Morris and Collins on The Conflict of Laws* (14th edn, London: Sweet & Maxwell, 2006) para 11-186; Faye Fangfei Wang, 'E-confidence: Offer and Acceptance in Online Contracting' (2008) 22 *Int'l Rev of L, Computers and Technology* 271, 277; David Bainbridge, *Introduction to Computer Law* (6th edn, Harlow: Pearson Education, 2008) 363; Jonathan Hill, above, n 4, paras 1.61-2; Christina Riefa and Julia Hörnle, 'The Changing Face of Electronic Consumer Contracts' in Lilian Edwards and Charlotte Waelde (eds), *Law and the Internet* (3rd edn, Oxford: Hart Publishing, 2009) 105. See also the US Uniform Computer Information Transactions Act, s 203(4) ('If an offer in an electronic message evokes an electronic message accepting the offer, a contract is formed (A) when an electronic acceptance is received …'); and HMRC, *Non-Residents Trading in the UK: Trading in the UK* <http://www.hmrc.gov.uk/manuals/intmanual/INTM263000.htm> (accessed 29 September 2009) ('it would seem that an e-mail acceptance should also be regarded as an instantaneous communication'). Cf Fasciano, above, n 14; Watnick, above, n 14; Paul Todd, *E-Commerce Law* (London: Cavendish Publishing, 2005) 180; and Jill Poole, *Textbook on Contract Law* (9th edn, Oxford: OUP, 2008) 75.

[38] The issue was left open by Rajah JC in *Chwee Kin Keong*, above, n 1. The learned judge said (at [98]) that while it could be argued cogently that the postal rule should apply to email acceptances, there were also 'sound reasons to argue in favour of … the recipient rule', noting that 'unlike a posting, e-mail communication takes place in a relatively short time frame'.

[39] 2 September 2008 (Com Ct).

of the negotiations had been such that the acceptances had taken effect in London, so that the contracts were made within the jurisdiction. It seems simply to have been assumed that the postal rule did not apply.

(b) When exactly is an email acceptance received by the offeror?

It might be thought that once it is clear that the postal rule does not apply to email acceptances, there is little more to say: the acceptance must be received by the offeror, and that is that. Unfortunately, the position is not so simple, as there are a number of different times at which it could be said that the offeror has 'received' an email. The three possibilities I will consider are the following:[40] (1) when the email is read by the offeror; (2) when the email arrives on the server which manages the offeror's email; and (3) when the email ought reasonably to have come to the offeror's attention.

Option one (when the email is read by the offeror) is extremely unlikely to be favoured by the English courts, for obvious reasons. Such a rule would give rise to evidentiary problems, since unless an acknowledgment is sent it is difficult to prove when a particular email was read—this information not generally being recorded by email software—and it would be unfair on the offeree, since it would seem to give the offeror the power to nullify the acceptance by deciding not to read it, or to delay its taking effect by putting off reading it. An 'information' rule of this kind can occasionally be found in other jurisdictions, but seems to be based on notions of subjective consent far removed from the objective principles underlying the English rules of offer and acceptance.[41] And although the courts have held that the revocation of an offer must reach the mind of the offeree before taking effect,[42] the considerations there are very different, and in any case it seems unlikely that the courts would apply this test literally; in practice, an approach closer to option three seems to be adopted.[43] Finally, option one would also be at odds with the more objective approach which the courts have taken in other contexts, such as the moment

---

[40] Another possibility would be when the acceptance email is downloaded onto the offeror's computer, but this can be ruled out on the grounds that it will not work where the offeror uses a web-based email system, and where, therefore, the email will usually not be downloaded at all.

[41] See PH Winfield, 'Some Aspects of Offer and Acceptance' (1939) 55 *LQR* 499, 506.

[42] *Byrne v Van Tienhoven* (1880) 5 CPD 344 (CPD). See also *Henthorn v Fraser*, above, n 13, 31-2 (Lord Herschell).

[43] See Treitel, above, n 12, para 2-060.

of 'receipt' by charterers of a telexed notice of withdrawal of a ship,[44] and the moment at which a telex notice is 'served' for limitation purposes.[45]

Option two (when the email arrives on the offeror's email server) is much more attractive. The moment at which the email arrives on the offeror's email server is recorded in the email itself, so this option provides the greatest clarity and raises few evidential difficulties. Although it will mean that the offeror may be bound before he realizes—or should have realized—that he is, the postal rule shows that in itself that is not a fatal objection as far as English law is concerned, and since (all being well) he will not be bound until he has at least had an opportunity to read the email, any injustice to him is likely to be minimal. Besides, it is open to the offeror to stipulate that an acceptance is not effective until it is read or acknowledged by him if he so wishes. This option also has the advantage of being consistent with a number of established rules relating to the 'receipt' of contractual communications in circumstances where the postal rule does not apply. An example is Article 24 of the UN Convention on Contracts for the International Sale of Goods, which states that an offer or acceptance 'reaches' the addressee when 'it is made orally to him or delivered by any other means to him personally, to his place of business or mailing address',[46] and which has been interpreted as meaning that an electronic communication 'reaches' the addressee when it has entered his server, provided the addressee has expressly or impliedly consented to receiving electronic communications of that type, in that format, and to that address.[47] Similarly, the second US Restatement of Contracts states that:

> A written revocation, rejection, or acceptance is received when the writing comes into the possession of the person addressed, or of some person authorized by him to receive it for him, or when it is deposited in some

---

[44] *Texas Steamship Co v The Brimnes (Owners) (The Brimnes)* [1975] 1 QB 929 (CA); *Schelde Delta Shipping BV v Astarte Shipping Ltd (The Pamela)* [1995] 2 Lloyds Rep 249 (QB).

[45] *NV Stoomv Maats 'De Maas' v Nippon Yusen Kaisha (The Pendrecht)* [1980] 2 Lloyd's Rep 56 (QB).

[46] See also the UNIDROIT Principles of International Commercial Contracts, art 1.9(3); and the Commission for European Contract Law's Principles of European Contract Law, art 1.303(3).

[47] CISG Advisory Council Opinion no 1, *Electronic Communications under CISG* (15 August 2003), Opinion on art 24. See also the Advisory Council's Opinion on art 18(2) ('An acceptance becomes effective when an electronic indication of assent has entered the offeror's server ....').

place which he has authorized as the place for this or similar communications to be deposited for him.[48]

And although (as we shall see) English law has in other contexts tended to prefer tests for 'receipt' of a communication closer to option three, it should be noted that it was held in *The Pendrecht*[49] that a telex notice was 'served' for limitation purposes when it was received at the registered office of the other party, whether or not this was during normal business hours. Finally, there is support for option two in some of the model legislation relating to electronic commerce—such as the UN Model Law on Electronic Commerce[50] and the US Uniform Computer Information Transactions Act[51]—and it would also be consistent with the Law Commission's 'initial view' that emails should be deemed to be received when the message reaches the recipient's internet service provider.[52]

A variation of option two would be to say that an email acceptance takes effect when the addressee is able to access it. This would have the advantage of being consistent with Article 10(2) of the UN Convention on the Use of Electronic Communications in International Contracts, which states that the time of receipt of an electronic communication is the time when it becomes capable of being retrieved by the addressee at an electronic address he has designated—this being presumed to happen when it reaches that address—and with the Electronic Commerce (EC Directive) Regulations 2002, under which acknowledgments of receipt of orders sent by web-based service providers are deemed to be received when the persons to whom they are sent are able to access them.[53] However, it is submitted that this variation ought not to be

---

[48] Restatement, Second, Contracts (1981) §68. See also the Uniform Commercial Code, §1-201(26) ('A person "receives" a notice ... when (a) it comes to his attention; or (b) it is duly delivered at the place of business through which the contract was made or at any other place held out by him as the place for receipt of such communications'); and Fasciano, above, n 14, 997 ('receipt may be proper where a letter ... is placed in the addressee's mailbox').

[49] Above, n 45. See also *Bernuth Lines Ltd v High Seas Shipping Ltd (The Eastern Navigator)* [2005] EWHC 3020 (Comm), [2006] 1 Lloyd's Rep 537, at [31] (Christopher Clarke J).

[50] See art 15(2), which lays down a default rule that where the addressee has designated an information system for the purpose of receiving data messages, receipt occurs at the time when the data message enters the designated information system (an 'information system' being defined in art 2(f) as 'a system for generating, sending, receiving, storing or otherwise processing data messages'). This provision was transposed into Australian law by s 14 of the Electronic Transactions Act 1999 (Cth), s 14(3).

[51] See s 102(a)(52)(B)(II), which defines 'receipt', in the case of an electronic notice, as 'coming into existence in an information processing system or at an address in that system in a form capable of being processed by or perceived from a system of that type by a recipient'.

[52] Above, n 5, para 3.56.

[53] (SI 2002/2013) reg 11(2)(a).

adopted, for two reasons. The first is that it would introduce a degree of uncertainty into option two, since there is scope for disagreement as to what it means to say that someone is 'able to access' an email.[54] And the second reason is that the only situations where this variation might make a difference would seem to be those where the email has arrived on the offeree's email server, but he is unable to access it because of a problem with his computer, the server, or the connection between the two; and that, in such cases, it seems fair that the offeree should none the less be bound, since the email is within what we might term his 'sphere of control'.[55]

Option three (when the email ought reasonably to have come to the offeror's attention) is also a plausible solution to the 'receipt' issue, but is not free from difficulty. Some support for this option is provided by two cases concerning the moment at which a telexed notice of withdrawal of a ship by the owners is deemed to have been received by the charterers. In *The Brimnes*,[56] the notice of withdrawal had arrived in the charterers' office before 6pm on a weekday, and even though it had gone unnoticed until the next morning, the Court of Appeal held that the notice had taken effect on arrival, since the charterers had advanced no reason why a message arriving at that time should not have been noted before the end of the working day. According to Megaw LJ, the relevant principle was as follows:[57]

> [I]f a notice arrives at the address of the person to be notified, at such a time and by such a means of communication that it would in the normal course of business come to the attention of that person on its arrival, that person cannot rely on some failure of himself or his servants to act in a normal businesslike manner in respect of taking cognisance of the communication so as to postpone the effective time of the notice until some later time when it in fact came to his attention.

---

[54] See the *Explanatory Note* written by the UNCITRAL Secretariat on the UN Convention on the Use of Electronic Communications in International Contracts, where the discussion of the art 10(2) 'capable of being retrieved' test in paras 180-4 is difficult to follow.

[55] See CISG Advisory Council Opinion no 1, above, n 47, para 15.3, where (in a discussion of the time at which an electronic communication of an *offer* takes effect) it is said that 'it is not appropriate to put the risk on the offeror for the offeree's technical problems'.

[56] Above, n 44.

[57] *Ibid*, 966-7. The reasoning of Cairns LJ was similar, although he expressly took as his starting point a general rule that the notice of withdrawal must reach the mind of the charterer, and then carved out some exceptions, for example, if the charterer deliberately refrained from opening a letter with a view to avoiding the receipt of the notice or if the notice were delivered by post on an ordinary working day and the office were closed all day. On the facts, he concluded, the charterers were not entitled to take advantage of their own failure to attend to the telex to say that they did not receive the notice when it arrived.

It seems reasonable to extrapolate from this negative proposition a positive rule to the effect that such a notice is deemed to be received when in the ordinary course of business it ought reasonably to have come to the attention of the charterer. This rule is also consistent with the reasoning in the second case, *The Pamela*,[58] where the telex arrived outside business hours, at shortly before midnight on a Friday evening. According to Gatehouse J, if the telex had been sent in ordinary business hours it would have taken effect on arrival, but the arbitrators in the case had been entitled to find that on the facts the notice of withdrawal had not been received until it was to be expected that it would be read at the start of business on the following Monday (the next working day).

However, although these decisions appear to be consistent with option three, it is submitted that they are of limited significance when it comes to choosing between options two and three in the contractual acceptance context. One reason is that in the leading decision, *The Brimnes*, the court was responding to the charterers' argument that the notice was only effective when it came to their attention, and so was not being asked to choose between the notice taking effect when it arrived on the telex machine and when the charterers ought to have read it. It follows that while the decision might be thought to be inconsistent with option one, it is not a strong authority for preferring option three over option two. More importantly, it does not follow that the principle adopted in the context of a notice of withdrawal in a charterparty should also apply to a contractual acceptance, since it might be argued that in the former case the receipt rule should be more heavily skewed in favour of the recipient.[59] It is significant in this respect that in *The Pamela*, Gatehouse J described the notice with which he was concerned as 'of a quite different type' from the telexed notices of acceptance at issue in the *Entores* and *Brinkibon* cases,[60] and rejected the charterers' contention that a universal rule should be adopted for telex communications, preferring to resolve the issue by reference to the particular circumstances.

---

[58] Above, n 44.

[59] Similarly, while it is noteworthy that in *Eaglehill Ltd v J Needham Builders Ltd* [1973] AC 992 (HL), the House of Lords held that a notice of dishonour of a bill of exchange was received by the drawers of the bill when it was opened in the ordinary course of business, or would have been so opened had the ordinary course of business been followed, this holding is arguably of limited significance in the offer and acceptance context. Cf *Chitty on Contracts* (30th edn, London: Sweet & Maxwell, 2008) para 2-047, where it is suggested that a similar rule to that adopted in *The Brimnes* and *The Pamela* would probably apply to determine the effectiveness of an emailed acceptance.

[60] Above, n 44, 252.

   The disadvantage of making the effectiveness of an emailed acceptance depend on the time when it ought reasonably to have come to
the offeror's attention is that it creates uncertainty.[61] The concept of
'ordinary business hours' is of limited utility in this regard.[62] Ordinary business hours may vary across different types of business, and
between businesses operating in the same field, and if the business
hours of the offeror differ from those of the offeree, for example, the
offeree may think that his acceptance has been communicated to the
offeror before it in fact has. Furthermore, it is questionable how much
significance should be attached to ordinary business hours in business
contexts where it is now common for those working in the field to
check their email in the evenings and at weekends, and the concept
will be of little use in non-business contexts, where many contracts
are of course concluded.[63] One particular issue that would have to
be resolved if option three were to be adopted would be the perspective from which the question of when the acceptance ought reasonably have come to the offeror's attention is to be judged. Suppose, for
example, that the offeror's business hours differed from the norm. In
this case, it would seem to make sense to say that if the offeree knew
or ought reasonably to have known this, an emailed acceptance would
take effect only within the offeror's actual business hours, but that
otherwise the 'ordinary business hours' principle would apply. That
would suggest that the appropriate perspective is that of the reasonable person in the offeree's position, with the result that if option
three were to be adopted the acceptance would take effect when the
offeree would reasonably expect it to have come to the attention of the
offeror.[64] Finally, since it is possible that an email acceptance could

---

   [61] See the UNCITRAL *Explanatory Note*, above, n 54, para 181 (the provision in the UN
Convention on the Use of Electronic Communications in International Contracts defining
the time of receipt of an electronic communication 'is not concerned with national public
holidays and customary working hours, elements that would have led to problems and to
legal uncertainty in an instrument that applied to international transactions').
   [62] See Furmston *et al*, above, n 35, 55.
   [63] According to Gerald Spindler and Fritjof Börner (eds), *E-Commerce Law in Europe and
the USA* (Berlin: Springer-Verlag, 2002) 164, German law adopts a version of option three to
determine the timing of receipt of a declaration of intent such as a contractual acceptance, the
test being whether 'it is within the recipient's sphere of dominion such that one can expect
that the recipient would become aware of it'. However, the authors point out that while
the recipient of an email relating to a commercial transaction is expected to be aware of the
declaration of intent on arrival of the email during normal business hours, in the case of a
private transaction, this will depend on the particular circumstances.
   [64] This would mean, for example, that if the offeror is away on holiday, the time that
the acceptance would take effect would depend on whether or not the offeree received an
automatically generated 'vacation reply' to this effect—if so, the acceptance would take

actually come to the attention of the offeror before the offeree might
reasonably expect it to, strictly speaking the test under option three
should be that the email acceptance takes effect either when it comes
to the attention of the offeror, or when the offeree would reasonably
expect it to have come to his attention, whichever is the earlier.

In the light of the additional uncertainty generated by option three,
the most sensible answer to the second question seems to be that an
email acceptance should in general be held to have been received
by the offeror when it arrives on the server that manages his email.
Furthermore, it is submitted that in circumstances where it is necessary
to identify the precise moment at which an *offer* sent by email takes
effect—as where the offeror lays down a time period within which his
offer must be accepted—the default rule should be the same, so that
the offer should generally take effect when it arrives on the offeree's
email server.[65]

(c) What if things go wrong?

No means of communication is foolproof, and email is no exception.
Some emails never arrive, or arrive in a garbled form, and others are
automatically deleted as 'junk mail'. While a default rule for the taking
effect of an emailed acceptance of the kind discussed in the previous
section is essential, it is also important to identify the principles which
apply when things go wrong, and an attempt at email communication
fails. It is submitted that three general principles should govern such
cases, the first two of which are adapted from Denning LJ's discussion
of failed attempts to communicate acceptance in the *Entores* case.

The first principle is that if the offeree knows or should know
that the email has not been received, he must send it again (and if
he does not, there is no contract). The second principle is that, if the
first principle does not apply—because the offeree has neither actual
or constructive knowledge of the failure of communication—then the
offeror is bound if it is his fault that he does not receive the email, but
if it is not his fault there is no contract.[66] And the third principle is that

effect on the offeror's return; if not, it would take effect immediately (if sent within business
hours).

[65] See CISG Advisory Council Opinion no 1, above, n 47, Opinion on art 20(1) ('A period of
time for acceptance fixed by the offeror in electronic real time communication begins to run
from the moment the offer enters the offeree's server').

[66] See *Entores*, above, n 11, 333. See also Simone Hill, above, n 15, 158 ('Actual communication is still the legal requirement, but communication might be deemed in the event that it is
the fault of the receiver that actual communication is thwarted'). This is also consistent with

a contract is also concluded if, although the offeror is not at fault, the problem lies within his 'sphere of control', as where the responsibility for what has happened lies with one of his employees or independent contractors.[67] On the assumption that the general test favoured here for 'receipt' of an email is adopted—namely that the email has arrived on the offeror's email server—what would be the outcome if these principles were applied to some of the things that can go wrong with email communication?

(i) The email does not arrive because the email address is incorrect

Here, it is likely that it is the offeree, rather than the offeror, who is at fault, either because he has mistyped the address, or because he has received an error message telling him that the email has not arrived, and then failed to resend the message after checking the address. In these circumstances, there would be no contract.[68] However, if it is the offeror who is at fault—because, for example, he gave the offeree the wrong address[69]—and the offeree is not (no error message having been generated), then it is submitted that a contract would be formed at the time when the email would have arrived on the offeror's server, but for the offeror's fault.

(ii) The email arrives on the offeror's email server, but cannot be accessed because it is blocked by the offeror's firewall or automatically deleted as 'junk-mail'

In this case the general test for 'receipt' is satisfied, and since the problem lies within the offeror's 'sphere of control', there is no reason why an exception should be made. There is therefore a contract.

---

the assumed position under the postal rule, where the default rule that the contract is formed on the posting of the letter is probably displaced where the offeree is at fault, for example because he has put the wrong address on the envelope: see the US Restatement, Second, Contracts (1981) §66; and *Chitty*, above, n 59, para 2-058.

[67] This seems consistent with Lord Fraser's observation in the *Brinkibon* case, above, n 11, 43, that once a telex message has been received on the offeror's machine, it is reasonable to treat it as delivered to the offeror, since it is his responsibility to arrange for the prompt handling of messages within his own office.

[68] See *LJ Korbetis v Transgrain Shipping BV* [2005] EWHC 1345 (QB), where it was held that a fax which never arrived because the appropriate international dialling code had not been entered was ineffective to conclude an agreement to nominate an arbitrator.

[69] As in an old case involving the post, where the offeror provided an incomplete address: *Re Imperial Land Co of Marseilles (Townsend's* case) (1871) LR 13 Eq 148 (V-C Malins).

*(iii) The email is rejected by the offeror's email server because the offeror's
email 'inbox' is full or because of a problem with the server*

In both these cases, although the test of arrival on the offeror's email
server is not satisfied, the problem lies within the offeror's 'sphere
of control', and so the acceptance should be deemed to have arrived
unless the offeree has been alerted to the problem.

*(iv) The email is rejected by the offeror's email server because it contains
a virus*

Since this could be said to be the responsibility of the offeree, the
default rule should be applied, and so no contract would come into
existence.

*(v) The email arrives but the contents are garbled, with the result that the
acceptance of the offer is not communicated*

In this circumstance, if the offeree knows or should know of the failure
of communication, then there is no contract. However, this is unlikely
to be the case, and where the offeree is oblivious to the problem, it is
clearly incumbent on the offeror to alert him to what has happened.
If the offeror fails to do so, there is therefore a contract. In this latter
scenario, an exception might perhaps be made where it is the offeree's
fault that the message has been corrupted, but on balance even here it
seems more reasonable to require the offeror to act.

*(vi) The email arrives on the offeror's email server, but the offeror does not
see the email because he was not expecting it to be sent to the email address
in question*

Where the offeror has multiple email addresses, it is submitted that an
emailed acceptance should take effect only when it reaches an email
address to which it was reasonable for the offeree to send the acceptance.[70] Where the offer was also made by email, it will usually only be
reasonable to reply to the email address from which the offer was sent;
where the offer was communicated by another means, it will usually
be reasonable to send the acceptance to any email address which the

---

[70] According to the UNCITRAL *Explanatory Note*, above, n 54, 'parties should be expected
not to address electronic communications containing information of a particular business
nature … to an electronic address they know or ought to know would not be used to process
communications of such a nature' (para 188).

offeror has held out as suitable for a communication of this kind.[71] If this reasonableness test is not satisfied, then it is submitted that the acceptance should take effect only when the offeror becomes aware that it has been sent to the email address in question.[72]

3. CONTRACTING THROUGH WEBSITES

The proliferation of internet trading over the last decade means that a substantial proportion of all transactional activity now takes place over the web. However, the formation of contracts online is in some respects quite different from earlier modes of contract formation, and the application of the offer and acceptance model to contracts made in this way raises a number of issues. It will be helpful to begin by describing the two principal ways in which such a contract can be made. In the first case, the offer and acceptance analysis is straightforward; in the second, it is more complex.

The first scenario involves digital products, such as software, music, or videos, where a consumer goes onto the retailer's website and downloads the product in return for payment. In this case, the website is essentially a 'digital vending machine', which responds to the user's actions in a predetermined manner.[73] Once the buyer's order has been placed, performance of the contract by the retailer is likely to begin immediately, as the product is downloaded onto the buyer's computer, so that the buyer will have little or no opportunity to alter or cancel the transaction. In such cases, the offer and acceptance analysis seems obvious: as with a real vending machine, the presence of the website is a standing offer, which the customer accepts by making the relevant payment.[74] The only difference is likely to be that whereas with a vending machine the terms of the offer are likely to be found in a

---

[71] See *The Eastern Navigator*, above, n 49, where it was held that an emailed notice of arbitration was effective notwithstanding the fact that it had never reached the relevant managerial or legal staff of the addressee company because it had been sent to an email address that the company had held out to the world as its email address, and that it was not necessary for service of the notice to be effective that the email address in question had been notified to the serving party as an address to be used in the context of the relevant dispute.

[72] See the UN Convention on the Use of Electronic Communications in International Contracts, art 10(2).

[73] See Boss and Killian, above, n 6, 429.

[74] See *Thornton v Shoe Lane Parking*, above, n 9, at 169 (Lord Denning MR): 'It can be translated into offer and acceptance in this way: the offer is made when the proprietor of the machine holds it out as being ready to receive the money. The acceptance takes place when the customer puts his money into the slot.'

notice placed on or near the machine, with a website the customer will usually be required to click a button expressing his agreement with the retailer's standard terms, so that the acceptance is strictly speaking expressing agreement with the standard terms and then making the appropriate payment.[75]

The second scenario is where the retailer's performance does not immediately follow the placing of the customer's order, but comes at a later time, as in the online sale of a book or an airline ticket. A description of such a transaction can be found in a Singaporean case concerning the purchase of laser printers from an online retailer, *Chwee Kin Keong v Digilandmall.com*:[76]

> To effect the purchase transactions on the respective websites, the plain-tiffs had to navigate through several web pages. In terms of chronologi-cal sequence, the initial page accessed was the shopping cart, followed by checkout-order particulars, checkout-order confirmation, check-out payment details and payment ... In the final stage of the process, after the payment mode was indicated, each of the plaintiffs was notified 'success-ful transaction ... your order and payment transaction has been processed'. Upon completing this sequence, each of the orders placed by the plain-tiffs was confirmed by automated responses from the respective websites stating 'Successful Purchase Confirmation from HP online'.

Although this form of transaction is set up to look like a self-service shop, the analogy is not an exact one, for two reasons; first, because here the delivery of the goods does not take place when the customer goes to the online 'checkout', but at a later time, typically at the cus-tomer's address; and, second, because self-service shops do not send out confirmation emails. In considering the appropriate offer and acceptance analysis in this scenario, it will be helpful to begin by trying to identify the offer.

(a) What is the offer in an online transaction?

At this stage the analogy of a shop is helpful. In *Pharmaceutical Society of Great Britain v Boots Cash Chemists (Southern)*,[77] the Court of Appeal

---

[75] One other possible difference between such a website and a vending machine is that websites of this kind may be programmed to reject orders from customers in certain juris-dictions. However, provided this limitation is made clear in the standard terms, this would be unlikely to affect the offer and acceptance analysis, as the website would still seem to amount to a standing offer, albeit one made only to potential customers in particular jurisdictions.

[76] Above, n 1, at [72] (Rajah JC).

[77] [1953] 1 QB 401 (CA).

held that the display of goods on the shelves of a self-service shop was an invitation to treat, rather than an offer, and in *Fisher v Bell*[78] it was held that the same was true of an item in a shop window accompanied by a ticket bearing a description and a price. According to Lord Parker CJ in the latter case, such a display was 'in no sense an offer for sale the acceptance of which constitutes a contract.'[79] The same is generally true of advertisements, catalogues, and the like.[80] As numerous commentators have pointed out, this principle would also seem to apply to the display of goods or services on a website, with the result that the offer is not made by the retailer, but by the customer when he places his order.[81] This conclusion is also consistent with Article 11 of the UN Convention on the Use of Electronic Communications in International Contracts, which states that a proposal to conclude a contract made electronically which is not addressed to one or more specific parties, but is generally accessible, is to be considered as an invitation to make offers, unless it clearly indicates an intention to be bound.[82] Furthermore, the operators of websites will frequently make

---

[78] [1961] 1 QB 394 (QB). For a different view, see Ellison Kahn, 'Some Mysteries of Offer and Acceptance' (1955) 72 *South African L J* 246, 250–3.

[79] *Ibid*, 399.

[80] See, eg *Partridge v Crittenden* [1968] 1 WLR 1204 (QB) (newspaper advertisement). An advertisement may, however, be construed as an offer of a unilateral contract, as in *Carlill v Carbolic Smoke Ball Co* [1893] 1 QB 256 (CA).

[81] See *Chitty*, above, n 59, para 2-014; and Simon P Haigh, *Contract Law in an E-Commerce Age* (Dublin: Round Hall, 2000) 13. Cf Christensen, above, n 37, 28 (likely that interactive websites will be interpreted as offers and not invitations to treat); and Riefa and Hörnle, above, n 37, 107 (arguing that the confirmation summary provided by an online retailer before the customer submits her payment may well amount to an offer because of the degree of specificity of the summary, and the fact that the retailer has had time to 'check their stock levels and that the price is the correct one'). In *Chwee Kin Keong*, above, n 1, Rajah JC compared a website advertisement to 'a billboard outside a shop or an advertisement in a newspaper or periodical', while also making the point that the internet 'conveniently integrates into a single screen traditional advertising, catalogues, shop displays/windows and physical shopping' (at [93]).

[82] This provision is based on art 14(2) of the UN Convention on Contracts for the International Sale of Goods, which provides that a proposal not addressed to one or more specific persons is to be considered merely as an invitation to make offers, unless the contrary is clearly indicated by the person making the proposal. There is a helpful discussion of the issues raised by the transposition of this principle to website trading in the UNCITRAL *Explanatory Note*, above, n 54, paras 200-4. According to the *Explanatory Note*, while UNCITRAL noted the argument that parties dealing with websites offering goods or services through interactive applications enabling immediate conclusion of a contract might reasonably assume that by placing an order they were concluding a binding contract, it considered that in the light of the 'potentially unlimited reach of the Internet' and the widespread practice of online traders indicating on their websites that they are not bound by these offers, the general principle should be applied.

it clear that the presentation of goods and services on their site is not intended to be binding. Of course, as with shop displays and advertisements, there may be exceptional cases where an online display of goods or services is construed as a binding offer, for example where the retailer states unequivocally that an item will be sold to the first ten customers whose orders are processed.[83] In these circumstances, the placing of the order by such a customer will constitute acceptance of the offer, and the contract will be formed at that time. However, in general a website provider will not be bound to deal with every customer who seeks to place an order, but may, for example, choose to decline an order if his supply of stock is limited, or if the customer is in a jurisdiction where it is illegal to sell the goods in question.

(b) What is the acceptance in an online transaction?

The precise moment at which the online retailer *does* become bound is less obvious. Since in general it will be the customer who makes the offer, the acceptance must in general come from the online merchant. Beyond this, however, the position becomes less clear-cut. One possibility is that by taking the customer's payment, the retailer will be held to have accepted the customer's offer by conduct.[84] Indeed, it might be thought to be unfair for the customer to have to pay for the goods before a contract has been formed.[85] (Conversely, where the retailer holds off on taking payment until the goods are delivered, that might be taken as an indication that the acceptance came only at that time.) Alternatively, the retailer's acknowledgment of the receipt of the order may constitute the acceptance,[86] although there will often be more than one of these, in which case a choice will have to be made between them. As in the transaction described above, it is usual for the website to display a message after payment has been accepted which says that

---

[83] *Chitty*, above, n 59, para 2-015. See eg *Lefkowitz v Great Minneapolis Surplus Stores* 86 NW 2d 689 (Minn 1957). See also *Chwee Kin Keong*, above, n 1, [94] (Rajah JC); and the UNCITRAL *Explanatory Note*, above, n 54, para 206. Although it has been suggested (Ewan McKendrick, *Contract Law: Text, Cases and Materials* (3rd edn, Oxford: OUP, 2008) 71-7) that the range and variety of sales that can take place over the internet may mean that less weight will be placed on the default rule 'and more on the words used in the particular advertisement', the wording of the advertisement is always determinative, and it is doubtful whether advertisements on the web are more likely to be interpreted as offers than those found elsewhere.

[84] On acceptance by conduct, see *Chitty*, above, n 59, para 2-030.

[85] At the very least, one would expect a retailer which took payment without intending to be bound to tell its customers that this was the case and that it would reimburse them if a contract did not materialize.

[86] See eg Jonathan Hill, above, n 4, para 1.58.

the customer's order has been processed, and for this to be followed by an automated email confirming that the order has been received. Indeed, the sending of such an email is a legal requirement in a wide range of internet transactions, by virtue of the Electronic Commerce (EC Directive) Regulations 2002.[87] Which, if either, of these acknowledgments will amount to a contractual acceptance must in the end be determined by their wording, the test being whether, judged objectively, they amount to 'a final and unqualified expression of assent to the terms' of the offer.[88] A mere acknowledgment that an offer has been received will not satisfy this test—*a fortiori* if the sending of the acknowledgment was a legal requirement—but an email confirming that the order has been successfully processed may well be interpreted as a clear expression of agreement, subject of course to the precise contents of the message. Where more than one acknowledgment sent by the retailer passes this test, the acceptance will be the one the customer receives first. If there is no acknowledgment that amounts to an acceptance, then the online trader will be at liberty to resile from the transaction until acceptance does take place later on, which will usually be when the goods are actually delivered, or when a message is sent confirming their dispatch.

The *Chwee Kin Keong* decision is a good illustration of the mechanics of contract formation online. The retailer argued that no contracts had been formed for the sale of the printers (which had been mistakenly offered at a very substantial undervalue) because the email confirmations had carried the notation 'call to enquire' under the heading 'Availability'. However, the judge at first instance, Rajah JC, said that the emails 'had all the characteristics of an unequivocal acceptance'. The caption in the emails saying 'Successful Purchase Confirmation from HP online' said it all, and this was reinforced by the text of the messages. It was clear from the circumstances that the words 'call to enquire' related to the timing of the delivery, and were not intended

---

[87] (SI 2002/2013) reg 11. Since the purpose of this requirement is presumably to safeguard consumers against errors they may have made when ordering goods or services online, it might be thought that it would be counter-productive to interpret such an email as a contractual acceptance, since this would mean that by the time the consumer had been alerted to a mistake, he or she would already be bound. However, this consideration is unlikely to have any bearing on the correct interpretation of the offeror's intention in sending the message, not least because, even if a contract has been formed, the consumer will almost certainly have the right to cancel it under the Consumer Protection (Distance Selling) Regulations 2000 (SI 2000/2334).

[88] *Chitty*, above, n 59, para 2-027 (definition of an acceptance).

to prevent the retailer coming under an obligation until it had had the chance to check whether suitable stock was available.[89]

Finally, there is no scope for the operation of the postal rule in online transactions. The communications between the customer and the website are usually instantaneous, the sender gets immediate feedback, and any problems should be readily apparent.[90] If, for example, the customer's web browser were to shut down after he clicked 'confirm', so that he did not know whether or not his order had been received, it would then be incumbent on him to make contact with the retailer, just as it would be if the line went dead immediately after he made an offer over the phone. And where an email acceptance is sent by an online retailer to a customer following an online transaction, the default rule should be the same as it is when a contract is formed through an exchange of emails, namely (as argued above) that the acceptance takes effect when the message arrives on the customer's email server.[91]

(c) To what extent can an online retailer control the contract formation process?

The final issue which we need to consider is the extent to which an online retailer can control the process of contract formation. There are a number of steps that a retailer can take in this respect. The first is to

---

[89] On appeal to the Singapore Court of Appeal, it was not disputed that prima facie a contract was concluded each time the placing of an order was followed by the recording of the transaction as a 'successful transaction': [2005] SGCA 2, [2005] 1 SLR 502 [29] (Chao Hick Tin JA).

[90] See *Chwee Kin Keong*, above, n 1, [101] (Rajah JC) ('Transactions over websites are almost invariably instantaneous and/or interactive. The sender will usually receive a prompt response. The recipient rule appears to be the logical default rule'); and Haigh, above, n 81, 30-1 ('The receipt rule would ... seem most suited to Internet/website contracting'). See further, Clive Gringras, *The Laws of the Internet* (2nd edn, London: LexisNexis Butterworths, 2003) 36-7.

[91] This test has the advantage of being broadly consistent with reg 11(2)(a) of the Electronic Commerce (EC Directive) Regulations 2002 (SI 2002/2013), which states that for the purposes of the obligation of a service provider to acknowledge receipt of an order laid down in that regulation, 'the order and the acknowledgement of receipt will be deemed to be received when the parties to whom they are addressed are able to access them'. Note that since this formulation is expressly limited to the purposes in question, it does not itself determine when a contractual acceptance takes effect (still less what amounts to a contractual acceptance in the first place). For a contrary view, see Robert Wegenek *et al* (eds), *E-Commerce: A Guide to the Law of Electronic Business* (London: Butterworths LexisNexis, 2002) 21-2 (arguing that if the retailer's acknowledgement does amount to a contractual acceptance, the time of contract formation will be as specified in reg 11(2)).

make it clear to viewers of its website that the presentation of goods and services on the website is an invitation to treat as opposed to an offer. And the second is to make clear the status of any email it sends to customers after receipt of an order. In some cases, the retailer will wish to defer the moment of contract formation, in order to retain the option of later refusing to fulfil the order. There are a number of reasons why a retailer might wish to do this, including its not having the goods ordered in stock, a problem with the customer's payment, a pricing error on its website, or the customer being in a different jurisdiction. In such cases, the retailer can make it clear that the email it sends out is merely an acknowledgment of receipt of the order, and that the contractual acceptance will follow later on. For example, the email which the online retailer Amazon.co.uk sends out includes the following statement:

> Please note that for items ordered from Amazon.co.uk this e-mail is only an acknowledgment of receipt of your order and your contract to purchase these items is not complete until we send you an e-mail notifying you that the items have been dispatched to you.[92]

On the other hand, other online retailers, such as airlines and hotels, may wish their customers to be bound immediately, so that they can be certain that a seat or room which has been booked has been taken, and plan accordingly. Such a retailer may therefore wish to make it clear that the email it sends out *is* intended as a contractual acceptance, so that the contract will be concluded upon its receipt.[93]

Finally, it is now commonplace for retailers to try to control the timing of the offer and acceptance by inserting a clause in their terms and conditions that purports to lay down how a contract made through their website is formed. Indeed, in some circumstances, the retailer is required to do this under the Electronic Commerce (EC Directive) Regulations 2002, which stipulate that where a contract is to be concluded by electronic means, a provider of an 'information society service' must (unless parties who are not consumers have agreed otherwise), before an order is placed by the recipient of the service, provide to that recipient information including 'the different technical steps to follow to conclude the contract'.[94] An example of a clause of this kind

---

[92] Email correspondence to author (16 December 2008).

[93] It is noteworthy that the confirmation email sent out by British Airways (ba.com) is described as an 'e-ticket receipt', and contains no caveats of the kind found in the email from Amazon.co.uk: email correspondence to author (9 August 2009).

[94] (SI 2002/2013) reg 9(1)(a). This requirement does not apply to 'contracts concluded exclusively by exchange of electronic mail' (reg 9(4)).

is provided by clause 14 of the terms and conditions of Amazon.co.uk, which says:

> When you place an order to purchase a product from Amazon.co.uk, we will send you an e-mail confirming receipt of your order and containing the details of your order. Your order represents an offer to us to purchase a product which is accepted by us when we send e-mail confirmation to you that we've dispatched that product to you (the 'Dispatch Confirmation E-mail'). That acceptance will be complete at the time we send the Dispatch Confirmation E-mail to you.[95]

Assuming that a clause along these lines is properly incorporated into the contract, it seems that it would be effective to determine the process of contract formation, since the customer's acceptance of the terms and conditions as part of the ordering process would turn this clause into a term of the offer made by the customer to the retailer, in which case only the 'acceptance' described in the clause would amount to a valid acceptance of the offer. If this is correct, then the widespread use of such clauses should mean that in many online transactions the offer and acceptance analysis will be relatively straightforward.[96]

4. CONCLUSION

As Jonathan Hill points out, there may be rather less to the legal issues surrounding electronic commerce than has sometimes been suggested. 'It is easy to be blinded by the technological wizardry which lies behind the Internet', he warns, 'and to reach the conclusion that the uniqueness of cyberspace gives rise to a range of complex and unique problems'.[97] I hope to have demonstrated in this paper that, while the proliferation of electronic commerce raises some interesting questions about the precise mechanics of contract formation by email and through websites, the offer and acceptance model is likely to prove

[95] Amazon.co.uk, 'Conditions of Use and Sale' <http://www.amazon.co.uk> (accessed 15 September 2009).

[96] Although it might be thought that a clause of this kind could potentially fall foul of the Unfair Terms in Consumer Contracts Regulations 1999 (SI 1999/2083) (for example, where the retailer has taken payment from the consumer but is keeping its own options open), it is doubtful whether a term that determines how the contract is made could be said to cause 'a significant imbalance in the parties' rights and obligations *arising under the contract*', as required by reg 5(1).

[97] Jonathan Hill, above, n 4, para 1.24. See also at para 1.53 ('it is important that the potential problems generated by the borderless and global nature of the Internet are kept in proportion').

sufficiently flexible to accommodate these new forms of communication without great difficulty. By reasoning from first principles, and by analogy with the rules governing older means of communication, the courts should prove well able to deal with the issues posed by offer and acceptance in the Electronic Age.

5

A Bird in the Hand: Consideration and Contract Modifications

MINDY CHEN-WISHART*

1. INTRODUCTION

English contract law has accepted for centuries that a sufficient reason for enforcing a promise is that it is part of a freely agreed exchange between two parties. It explains why a *promisee* is entitled to enforce the promise and why her remedy should be based on her expectation (the distinctively contractual measure of enforcement); namely, because she has paid for it. Formalities and reliance provide exceptional reasons for the (sometimes only partial) enforcement of promises, but bargain is overwhelmingly the usual one. Yet the literature on the consideration doctrine is conspicuous in the intensity and depth of the hostility it has inspired. It is described as an 'enormous and shapeless grab bag'; uncertain in scope, and in places overly technical, artificial, internally incoherent, and inconsistent with the parties' intentions.[1] It is commonly explained as a historical accident; the result of the tyranny exercised in English law by the mediaeval forms of action. Lord Goff observed in *White v Jones*[2] that: 'our law of contract is widely seen as deficient in the sense that it is perceived to be hampered by the presence of an unnecessary doctrine of consideration'.

Abolition has been urged.[3] The 1937 Law Revision Committee in its Sixth Interim Report[4] proposed extending the enforceability of promises in a wide range of circumstances. The Law Commission's report (implemented by the Contracts (Rights of Third Parties) Act 1999)

* Reader in Contract Law, University of Oxford, and Tutor in Law, Merton College, Oxford.

[1] See, eg P Atiyah, 'Consideration: A Restatement' in (ed) *Essays on Contract* (Oxford: Clarendon Press, 1986) 181; EW Paterson, 'An Apology for Consideration' (1958) 58 *Columbia L Rev* 929.

[2] [1995] 2 AC 207, at 262–3.

[3] L Wright, 'Should the Doctrine of Consideration Be Abolished?' (1936) 49 *Harv L Rev* 1225.

[4] Statute of Fraud and the Doctrine of Consideration (1937), Cmnd 5449, paras 26-40, 50. See similarly the Ontario Law Reform Commission *Report on Amendment of the Law of Contract* (Report No 85, 1987), ch 2.

commented that 'the doctrine of consideration may be a suitable topic for a future separate review'.[5] Professor Burrows concludes that:[6]

> The law would be rendered more intelligible and clear if the need for consideration were abolished and gratuitous promises which have been accepted or relied on were held to be binding (subject to the operation of normal contractual rules relating to, for example, the intention to create legal relations, duress, and illegality).

Nevertheless, the wholesale extermination of the consideration doctrine is unlikely any time soon. One reason is, paradoxically, the very reason for dissatisfaction with the consideration doctrine in the first place, namely, its uncertainty (or, which amounts to the same thing, its flexibility). The result is that, in practice, the consideration requirement causes little injustice or difficulty. My argument here is that, whatever we might ultimately conclude about the desirability of the consideration doctrine, we can resolve the most glaring target of criticism *within* the doctrine itself, without artificiality or deviation from the core idea of contract as exchange.

This is the problem traditionally posed by the requirement of consideration for the enforcement of one-sided contract modifications; one-sided in the sense that one party promises to give more for the same reciprocal obligation (an adding modification), or to accept a reduced reciprocal obligation (a subtracting modification) from, the other party. *Stilk v Myrick*[7] and *Foakes v Beer*[8] stand for the orthodox answer that such modifications are never enforceable because the promisee gives nothing in exchange for the modifying promise; she merely undertakes to perform (or partly perform) what she was already obliged to do. This apparently logical position has been described as 'the most harmful distortion' that has 'distracted attention from its central idea—bargain as a ground for enforcing promises.'[9] While the concern to protect the sanctity of contract and to prevent opportunistic exploitation point against enforcement, the stark reality is that change of circumstances (external or internal to the promisee) may make her

---

[5] Law Commission 'Privity of Contract: Contracts for the Benefit of Third Parties' (Law Com No 242 Cmnd 3329, 1996) para 6.17.

[6] 'Improving Contract and Tort: the View from the Law Commission' in A Burrows, *Understanding the Law of Obligations* (Oxford: Hart Publishing, 1998) 197, citing H McGregor, *Contract Code Drawn up on Behalf of the English Law Commission*, and the *Unidroit Statement of Principles for International Commercial Contracts*, art 3.1.

[7] *Stilk v Myrick* (1809) 2 Campbell 317.

[8] Traceable to *Pinnel's Case* (1602) 5 Co Rep 117a.

[9] J Dawson, *Gifts and Promises: Continental and American Law Compared* (Yale: Yale University Press, 1980) 4.

contractual performance practically impossible without some adjustment by the promisor. No less than Professors Treitel and Reynolds have observed that 'these cases are of great difficulty. The task of weighing these conflicting factors is a delicate one'.[10]

The enforceability of an agreement is subject to a two-stage test.[11] Stage one deals with formation and broadly requires the parties' intention to be bound and an exchange signified by the consideration requirement. Only after an agreement satisfies stage one does the question of vitiation arise at stage two; namely, whether a prima facie valid contract should nevertheless be set aside in the particular circumstances. It is here that the concern to prevent opportunistic exploitation by the promisee properly belongs, to be resolved under the rubric of duress. My concern is how we get past stage one. The modern case law has thrown up three main solutions which mirror the major reasons for some enforcement of promises; namely, bargain consideration, reliance, and serious intention.

2. CONSIDERATION

While *Williams v Roffey Brothers*[12] affirms the *Stilk v Myrick* requirement of fresh consideration for adding promises, it crucially overrules the decision by recognizing fresh consideration in the promisee's mere *promise* to perform his pre-existing contractual obligations where 'the promisor obtains in practice a benefit, or obviates a disbenefit'.[13] The risk of opportunistic exploitation was held to be adequately dealt with by reference to the doctrine of economic duress. I previously criticized the decision in *Williams v Roffey*.[14] While I stand by these criticisms, I now see them as resolvable by a refinement of the practical benefit approach; an approach which is preferable to the alternatives being mooted.

[10] F Reynolds and G Treitel, 'Consideration for the Modification of Contracts' (1965) 7 *Malaya L Rev* 1, 22.

[11] HLA Hart, 'The Ascription of Responsibility and Rights' in *Proceedings of the Aristotelian Society* (1948) 49; also in A Flew (ed), *Logic and Language—First Series* (Basil Blackwell, 1952) 145, 173.

[12] [1991] 1 QB 1.

[13] *Ibid*, 15-16; followed in *Adam Opel GmbH and Renault SA v Mitras Automotive (UK) Ltd* [2008] *EWHC* 3205.

[14] 'Consideration, Practical Benefit and the Emperor's New Clothes' in Beatson and Friedmann (eds), *Good Faith and Fault in Contract Law* (Oxford: Oxford University Press, 1995) 123–50.

(a) A bird in the hand

My main criticism was of *Roffey*'s acceptance that the mere promise to perform a pre-existing duty can confer practical benefit and so be good consideration for the reciprocal promise to pay more. A *re-promise* to do something already owed to the promisee really gives her nothing more than she had before. The crux of the widespread discontent with the traditional bar against one-sided modifications is our belief that: 'A bird *in the hand* is worth two in the bush';[15] the practice of selling debts at a discount on their face value tells us so. Logically, then, a bird in the hand must be worth more than *one* in the bush. This is recognized in *Williams v Roffey*,[16] and by those who deny that one-sided modifications are gratuitous.[17] This suggests that adding and subtracting promises should be enforceable *so long as the promisor receives the stipulated bird in the hand*. But precisely in what sense does this give the promisor 'more' than she had before?

To answer this question we need to fix the baseline against which to measure whether 'more' consideration has been given. Two are possible. First, the baseline can be fixed by reference to the 'eye of the law'. *Stilk v*

---

[15] *Foakes v Beer* 9 App Cas 607 at 622 (emphasis added): Lord Blackburn noted his 'conviction that all men of business, whether merchants or tradesmen, do every day recognise and act on the ground that prompt payment of a part of their demand may be more beneficial to them than it would be to insist on their rights and enforce payment of the whole. Even where the debtor is perfectly solvent, and sure to pay at last, this is often so. Where the credit of the debtor is doubtful it must be more so.' And see *Collier v Wright* [2007] EWCA Civ 1329, [2008] 1 WLR 643 at [3] where Arden LJ notes that *Pinnel's Case* frustrates the parties' expectations and makes it difficult to make modifications when this may 'be commercially beneficial for both parties to do'.

[16] *Ibid*, at 20-1, Purchas LJ notes that 'there were clearly incentives... to relieve [Williams] of his financial difficulties and also to ensure that he was in a position, or alternatively was willing, to continue with the sub contract works to a reasonable and timely completion.... Businessmen know their own business best even when they appear to grant an indulgence'. See also Russell LJ at 19.

[17] B Coote, 'Consideration and Benefit in Fact and in Law' (1990) 2 *Jl of Contract L* 23; FMB Reynolds and G Treitel, 'Consideration for the Modification of Contract' (1965) 7 *Malaya L Rev* 1; J Beatson, *Anson's Law of Contract* (28th edn, Oxford: Oxford University Press, 2002), 125-6; H Kotz and A Flessner, *European Contract Law*, vol 1 (Oxford: Oxford University Press, 1977), 68-71. In *Antons Trawling Co Ltd v Smith* [2003] 2 NZLR 23, at [92]: 'insofar as consideration serves to exclude gratuitous promise, it is of little assistance in the context of on-going, arms-length, commercial transactions where it is utterly fictional to describe what has been conceded as a gift, and in which there ought to be a strong presumption that good commercial "considerations" underlie any seemingly detrimental modification.' See also B Reiter, 'Courts, Consideration and Common Sense' (1977) 27 *U of Toronto L J* 439, 507; and MA Eisenberg, 'The Principles of Consideration' (1982) 67 *Cornell L Rev* 640, at 644: 'The proposition that bargains involving the performance of a pre-existing contractual duty are often gratuitous is empirically far-fetched.'

Myrick and *Foakes v Beer* take this approach. The 'eye of the law' sees a 'contract right' as the 'right to contractual performance' and this, in turn, is equated with the '*receipt* of performance'. On this view, the promisor gets nothing more when she gets her hands on the stipulated bird than she originally had (the right to the bird in the bush). The problem is that if you start with a legal fiction, you are bound to end up with some odd results. Here, you prevent the promisor from bargaining for actual performance or part performance because the promisee knows that the law will not enforce it.

We should be wary of tracking logical deductions beyond common sense. An analogy can be drawn with the perverse outcomes that would follow from rigid adherence to the 'postal acceptance rule'. An offeree who posts her acceptance, then immediately changes her mind and tells the offeror that she rejects the offer before her letter arrives would nevertheless be bound if the offeror insists (although the offeror is not prejudiced and the parties were never in agreement). If the offeror had relied on the offeree's apparent rejection and sells to another, he may be in breach if the offeree insists on her postal acceptance. It is unsurprising that 'few, if any, judges or writers have been prepared to follow all these deductions to their logical conclusion'.[18] Equating a *right to* performance with the *receipt of* performance creates a baseline against which the value of actual performance over the right to performance simply disappears. As Dawson observes, 'within the limits of the obligation their agreement had created, the parties had destroyed their own power to contract.'[19] We need an alternative baseline which is intellectually coherent, yet sufficiently open to account for human and legal realities.

The second, and preferable, baseline is fixed by reference to the 'eyes of the parties'. We bargain for performance, but what we get is a more fragile right in remedial terms. The unpalatable truth is that there is no straightforward equivalence between the two. In recognizing the possibility of gain-based damages for breach of contract in *Attorney-General v Blake*, Lord Nicholls[20] noted Lionel Smith's argument[21] that contract rights should be protected as strongly from expropriation by the defendant's breach as property rights (which traditionally yield

---

[18] *Treitel: The Law of Contract* (12th edn, London: Thomson Sweet & Maxwell, 2007) para 2-033.

[19] J Dawson, *Gifts and Promises: Continental and American Law Compared* (Yale: Yale University Press, 1980) 210.

[20] [2001] 1 AC 268, at 283.

[21] L Smith, 'Disgorgement of Profits of Contract: Property, Contract and "Efficient Breach"' (1995) 24 *Canadian Business L J* 121.

gains-based remedies). However, it is trite law that many features of contract law are inconsistent with the protection of an innocent party's performance interest.[22] Unless contractual performance comprises the payment of money, an innocent party's right to performance will not normally translate into actual performance or its moneys-worth in remedial terms. Against *this* baseline, the receipt of actual performance or part performance may well give the promisor *more* than she had before. Likewise, it may be a detriment for the promisee to perform a pre-existing duty. This is clear where a promisee would otherwise risk bankruptcy. But even when solvent, the promisee's performance might be more advantageously applied elsewhere and her liability for breach will generally bear no relationship to the extent of this advantage.[23] The potential availability of gain-based damages[24] does not substantially undermine this argument given its very exceptional nature, and the uncertainties surrounding its basis,[25] availability,[26] and measure.[27]

Professor Coote objects to this line of reasoning because it would necessitate 'some break in the link between a contract and its performance which is inherent in the concept of an enforceable legal obligation'.[28] It appears to contradict the idea of contract as creating binding obligations and to support the Holmesian heresy that the contractual obligation is only to perform or pay damages

---

[22] For example, the rarity of gain-based damages itself; the limited availability of specific performance; agreed damages clauses are unenforceable if they amount to penalties or indirect specific performance; agreed specific performance will generally be unenforceable; rules such as remoteness and mitigation cut back the expectation damages to leave the claimant's pecuniary losses inadequately compensated, meanwhile her non-pecuniary losses from the breach (anxiety, annoyance, and so on) and from seeking legal redress (typically delay, hassle, time, and effort) are not normally compensable at all; punitive damages are generally rejected; and the innocent party may even be prevented from affirming and performing the contract on the other's breach if it would be wholly unreasonable to do so.

[23] P Atiyah, *Essays on Contract* (Oxford: Clarendon Press, 1986) 190 quoting *Corbin on Contracts* (rev edn, 1963) vol 1, para 172.

[24] *Attorney-General v Blake* [2001] 1 AC 268.

[25] *Ibid*, at 920. The remedy is available when (i) contract remedies would be inadequate; (ii) the claimant has a 'legitimate interest' in preventing the defendant from making or retaining his profits, and (iii) 'all the circumstances of the case'.

[26] Contrast *Esso Petroleum Co Ltd v Niad Ltd* [2001] EWHC 458 (Ch) with *AB Corp v CD Co (The Sine Nomine)* [2002] 1 Lloyd's Rep 805.

[27] For example, 5% was awarded in *Wrotham Park v Parkside Homes* [1974] 1 WLR 798, 100% in *Attorney-General v Blake*; 30-50% in *Lane v O'Brien Homes Ltd* [2004] EWHC 303; the case was sent back for quantification of the reasonable user in *Experience Hendrix LLC v PPX Enterprises* [2003] EWCA Civ 323, (2003) EMLR 25 and for damage to the innocent party's reputation in *WWF World Wide Fund for Nature v World Wrestling Federation Entertainment Inc* [2007] EWCA Civ 286, [2008] 1 WLR 445.

[28] B Coote, 'Consideration and Benefit in Fact and in Law' (1990) 2 *J of Contract L* 23, at 28.

for non-performance.[29] Purchas LJ recognized in *Williams v Roffey* that it was 'open to the plaintiff to be in deliberate breach of the contract in order to "cut his losses" commercially'.[30] His Lordship conceded that 'the suggestion that a contracting party can rely on his own breach to establish consideration is distinctly unattractive'[31] and it is certainly arguable that exploitation of the inadequacies of contract remedies should not be recognized as valid consideration to support one-sided modifications.[32]

However, recognition that the contractual right will not always be vindicated by an order for specific performance or the cost of cure need not contradict the idea that contract law recognizes a duty to perform or mean that the remedy determines the right.[33] It is simply that the law on contractual remedies is not solely concerned with vindicating performance. The latter must be weighed against contract law's *other* concerns, for example, to avoid waste and unnecessary harshness to the contract-breaker; to encourage mitigation; to promote finality in dispute resolution, and to terminate hostile relationships. If we accept these concerns as important and legitimate, then 'inadequacy of remedies', on account of them, is inevitable. We can agree with Professor Friedmann that 'the essence of contract is performance. Contracts are made in order to be performed.'[34] But, this just fixes the starting point from which deviation is not only possible, but likely, in recognition of the other interests in play. Those who support the primacy of the performance interest nevertheless recognize the need to qualify its protection in many circumstances. No value is absolute; the fact that multiple policies are at work in our contract law means that trade-offs will be required. Thus, it is widely accepted that where harm can be remedied in different ways, the law should opt for that which is least restrictive of the defendant's liberty.[35]

---

[29] OW Holmes, *The Common Law* (1881) 298. See P Atiyah, 'Holmes and the Theory of Contract' in (ed) *Essays on Contract* (Oxford: Clarendon Press, 1986), 59ff.

[30] [1991] 1 QB 1, at 23.

[31] *Ibid*.

[32] S Williston, 'Successive Promises of the Same Performance' (1894-95) 8 *Harvard L Rev* 27, 30–1.

[33] As suggested by Holmes and Atiyah, above, n 29.

[34] D Friedmann, 'The Performance Interest in Contract Damages' (1995) 111 *LQR* 628, at 629; C Webb, 'Performance and Compensation: An Analysis of Contract Damages and Contractual Obligation' (2006) 26 *Oxford J of Legal Studies* 41.

[35] D Kimel, 'Remedial Rights and Substantive Rights in Contract Law' (2002) 8 *Legal Theory* 313. Compelling specific behaviour is more oppressive than requiring the payment of damages, particularly where the former is backed by a finding of contempt of court, potentially punishable by imprisonment. If a money award of a fine were the penalty, courts may be more prepared to order specific performance as in France or Germany. See H Beale,

To press the point, unless contract law is prepared to make specific performance the primary remedy, backed up by the cost of cure or account of profits from breach, then, ironically, in order to protect the promisor's performance interest, contract law should concede that obtaining actual performance will often be more valuable than simply having the right to sue for non-performance. The 'eye of the law' should defer to the 'eyes of the parties' so long as contract law does not fully protect the performance interest, particularly when the concern to prevent opportunistic exploitation can be controlled directly at stage two by the doctrine of economic duress.[36]

(b) The unilateral contract device

A bird in the hand is better than one in the bush. On this view, the promisor of additional payment is not intending to buy the same *right* twice. She is now bargaining for *actual performance*.[37] This describes a unilateral contract: the promisor's offer to pay more (or accept less) is only accepted if and when the promisee actually completes the stipulated part of the promisee's pre-existing contractual duty. The bilateral contract analysis in *Williams v Roffey* will not do the job. The Court of Appeal's acceptance of the promisee's mere *repromise* to perform her pre-existing contractual duty provoked Professor Coote's comment that consideration in a bilateral contract 'is required for the formation of a contract. Performance, *ex hypothesi*, comes too late to qualify'.[38]

However, a complete answer is provided by supplementing the original bilateral contract with a collateral unilateral contract to pay more (or accept less) *if* actual performance is rendered. This unilateral contract can prevail over an inconsistent term in the main written contract.[39] But if the unilateral contract does not eventuate, because the promisee fails to render the stipulated performance, then the original contract retains full force. This approach is also preferable because it avoids the absurd and unjust results of a bilateral contract analysis

---

A Hartkamp, H Kotz, and D Talon, *Ius Commune Casebook for the Common Law of Europe: Contract Law* (Oxford: Hart Publishing, 2002) 68081.

[36] TE Robison, 'Enforcing Extorted Contract Modifications' (1983) *Iowa L Rev* 699, 751.

[37] In *Newman Tours Ltd v Ranier Investment Ltd* [1992] 2 NZLR 68, at 80, Fisher J applied *Williams v Roffey Bros*, saying: 'the agreement to perform [its] existing contractual obligations, followed by actual performance in reliance upon that subsequent agreement, can constitute fresh consideration.'

[38] 'Consideration and Benefit in Fact and in Law' (1990–91) 3 *J of Contract L* 23, at 26.

[39] See *City and Westminster Properties (1934) Ltd v Mudd* [1959] Ch 129; *Brikom Investments Ltd v Carr* [1979] QB 467; *Harling v Eddy* [1951] 2 KB 739; *Mendelssohn v Normand Ltd* [1970] 1 QB 177.

which would leave a promisor of additional payment worse off than before because her damages would be reduced by the original *and additional* sums she undertook to, but now need not, pay.[40] A bilateral contract analysis of *relieving* promises yields the same perverse outcome. If the promisee fails to render the lesser performance, the promisor's claim would be confined to that lesser performance.[41]

Consistently, the Ontario Law Reform Commission states that where the promisee of additional payment fails to perform, the appropriate deduction is the *original sum* promised, and not the greater modified sum; 'it would be an implicit understanding between the parties that failure to comply with the terms of the new agreement would revive the old one.'[42] Likewise, subtracting promises are binding 'subject to actual performance' by the promisee.[43] The promisor 'has agreed to accept less on the ground that "a bird in the hand is worth two in the bush". It would be unfair, in such a case, to limit the rights absolutely to the single bird of the subsequent agreement'. The same reasoning underlies the 1937 Law Revision Committee's recommendation on reversing the effect of *Pinnel's Case*.[44] It would be more straightforward to say that, with both adding and relieving promises, the promisor's liability on the additional promise only crystallizes *on the promisee's performance* on a unilateral contract analysis.

A unilateral contract analysis avoids another potentially anomalous result, instanced by *Pao On v Lau Yiu Long*.[45] The parties exchanged shares in their companies. P also agreed to delay selling 60 per cent of the shares received for at least a year to avoid triggering a fall in their value; L agreed to *buy back* those shares at a fixed price at or before the end of the year. When P realized that he would be disadvantaged if the shares rose above the fixed price, he refused to proceed unless L agreed to a *guarantee by way of indemnity* (if the shares should fall below

---

[40] For example, X promises to pay Y £5,000 for a job; later X promises another £3,000 (total £8,000), but Y still does not perform and it would cost X £10,000 for substitute performance. The expectation damages under the original contract is £10,000–£5,000, while under the modified contract it would be £10,000–£8,000.

[41] X promises to accept £70 in discharge of Y's debt of £100 in the hope of actually getting £70, but, if Y disappoints, X's claim is confined to £70.

[42] Ontario Law Reform Commission 'Report on the Amendment of the Law of Contract' (No 82, 1987) 12–13, discussing the promise to accept part performance.

[43] *Ibid*, 10, 12–13.

[44] *Sixth Interim Report on the Statute of Frauds and the Doctrine of Consideration*, Cmd 5449, paras 33-5: 'It would be possible to enact only that actual payment of the lesser sum should discharge the obligation to pay the greater, but we consider that it is more logical and more convenient to recommend that the greater obligation can be discharged either by a promise to pay a lesser sum or by actual payment of it, but that if the new agreement is not performed then the original obligation shall revive.'

[45] [1980] AC 614.

the fixed price). L agreed in order to avoid the delay and loss of public confidence that a legal action against P would attract at a critical time in their company's restructuring. Moreover, L believed that the risk entailed in the modification was 'more apparent than real'. When the share price plummeted, L would neither buy back the shares under the original contract (alleging this arrangement was ended by the modification) nor indemnify P under the modified bilateral contract (alleging that it was voidable for duress). The modification was upheld. However, the Privy Council opined that, even if duress had been found, it would not have countenanced the 'stark injustice' of denying P 'the safeguard which all were at all times agreed [P] should have—the safeguard against fall in value of the shares'.[46] A unilateral collateral contract analysis of the modification would restrict the vitiating effect of any duress, leaving the original contract in place.

(c) The award in *Williams v Roffey*

A unilateral contract analysis of the promise to pay more comes closest to explaining the damages actually awarded in *Williams v Roffey*. Williams had already received more than 80 per cent (£16,200) of the £20,000 originally agreed for the work on the 27 flats when Roffey Brothers promised an extra £575 *if, as and when* he finishes *each* of the 18 remaining flats on time. Williams claimed his expectation of £10,847, which is slightly more than the additional sums for the remaining flats (18 x £575 = £10,300). This should have followed logically from the Court of Appeal's bilateral contract analysis (even with an 'entire obligations' overlay)[47] since it was Roffey Brothers' breach (by paying only £1,500 more although Williams had completed eight further flats) that entitled Williams to terminate.

However, the trial judge, with whom the Court of Appeal agreed, only awarded £3,500. Glidewell LJ explains the calculation:[48] the judge started with £4,600 (being 8 x £575) 'less some small deduction for defective and incomplete items'. Additionally, Williams was entitled to a reasonable proportion of the sum outstanding from the original price.[49] This entitled Williams to £5,000. From this is deducted

---

[46] *Ibid*, at 635.
[47] *Williams v Roffey Bros* [1991] 1 QB 1 at 8-10, 16-17; and 23.
[48] *Ibid*, at 6.
[49] This should be £3,800 although the trial judge said £2200 and Glidewell LJ said £2,300. The error probably occurred because Roffey Brothers made an additional payment of £1500 (£3,800–£1500 = £2,300). However, this was credited twice by being deducted again from Williams' original entitlement of £5,000.

the £1,500 already paid, leaving the final figure of £3,500. Since Roffey Brothers' offer is to pay a specific sum on completion of specified work, this can be interpreted as 18 separate unilateral offers. One interpretation is that Williams only accepted eight of these by substantial performance; by ceasing work, it accepted no more.

(d) Revocation of the unilateral offer

An alternative interpretation is that Roffey's breach (in not paying) amounts to an implied revocation of its unilateral offers in respect of the *incomplete* flats. There is no suggestion that Williams had commenced work on *these* flats nor that Roffey had prevented Williams from further performance, so there is nothing to stop Roffey from revoking its offer on the incomplete flats. A third interpretation is that Roffey's unilateral offer is for completion of all 18 flats. On this view, we would run into the supposed rule that a unilateral offer can be accepted 'as soon as the offeree has unequivocally begun performance of the stipulated act or abstention…, so that the offer can no longer be withdrawn'.[50] But, is there a universal rule to this effect?

On the 'yes' side is the judgment of Denning J in *Errington v Errington*.[51] A father promised his son and daughter-in-law that if they paid off the mortgage, amounting to two-thirds of the value of the house they were all living in, it would be theirs. When the father died nine years later and a substantial part of the mortgage had been paid, the Court of Appeal prevented his representatives from revoking the arrangement because the couple had commenced payment, provided that the couple's performance was not left 'incomplete and unperformed'.[52] Aside from this family case, there is only Court of Appeal dicta in *Daulia Ltd v Four Millbank Nominees Ltd*[53] (involving an unenforceable oral agreement for property) and *Soulsbury v Soulsbury*[54] (where no question of revocation arose because the stipulated performance of a family arrangement was completed). On the other side is *Luxor (Eastborne) Ltd v Cooper*.[55] The House of Lords denied a real estate agent's claim for a £10,000 commission payable on completion of a sale when the agent found buyers but the owners refused to complete. The commission was the equivalent of a Lord Chancellor's annual pay

---

[50] *Chitty on Contracts*, (30th edn, London: Sweet & Maxwell, 2008) para 2-079.
[51] [1952] 1 KB 290.
[52] *Ibid*, at 295.
[53] [1978] Ch 231, especially at 239.
[54] [2007] EWCA Civ 969, [2008] 2 WLR 834, at [50].
[55] [1941] AC 108.

for work done within eight or nine days. The court held that the common understanding was that estate agents take 'the risk in the hope of a substantial remuneration for comparatively small exertion'.[56]

It is tempting to opt for a clear rule prohibiting or permitting revocation of the modifying offer once performance has commenced. However, the answers 'never' or 'always' will sometimes yield unintended and unjust results. In *Morrison Shipping Co v The Crown*[57] the Lord Chancellor doubted: 'whether a conditional offer in general terms, whether made to the public (as in the *Carbolic Smoke Ball* case) or to a class of persons, is converted into a contract so soon as one of the persons to whom the offer is made takes some step towards performing the condition.' The Federal Court of Australia in *Mobil Oil Australia Ltd v Wellcome International Pty Ltd and Others*[58] declined to recognize a 'universal proposition that an offeror is not at liberty to revoke the offer once the offeree "commences" or "embarks upon" performance of the sought act of acceptance'. The issue is one of construction, but also of protecting a performing offeree from exploitation by the offeror.[59] These features will vary greatly from case to case. Relevant factors would include:

(i) *Construction*—The parties' intention or the prevailing convention (eg estate agents' contracts) as to whether the offeror should be able to withdraw at any time (ie a *locus poenitentiae*) which may be inferable from other relevant factors.

(ii) *The length of time* over which the offeror would have to keep the offer open without knowing whether the offeree will complete the act. *Errington v Errington*[60] involved a lengthy period but was a family property case where 'the parties were not considering future possibilities at arms length'.[61]

(iii) *Whether the stipulated performance requires the offeror's cooperation*—if so, it is less likely that the parties intended to bar revocation (eg real estate agents' contract and by analogy to the test of whether affirmation is available).

(iv) *The extent of performance*—The demands of justice will vary between an offeree who has completed 1 per cent of the stipulated performance and one who has completed 99 per cent.

---

[56] *Ibid*, at 126.

[57] (1924) 20 Ll L Rep 283, at 287.

[58] (1998) 153 ALR 196, at 228.

[59] This mirrors the concern to protect the promisor from the promisee's exploitation via duress.

[60] [1952] 1 KB 290.

[61] *Ibid*, at 293.

Revocation should be barred if the offeree has incurred significant reliance or change of position (eg by not declaring bankruptcy) or has substantially completed the stipulated performance (by analogy to the entire obligations rule).[62]

(v) *The extent of benefit conferred on the offeror* by the offeree's part performance.

(vi) *Acquiescence*—Whether the offeror knows of the offeree's commencement of performance. In *Soulsbury v Soulsbury*[63] Waller LJ thought it inconceivable that the offeror 'should be free to watch [the offeree] work once the offer had been made, take advantage of the work done' and then revoke the offer.

(vii) *Subsequent change of circumstances*—Revocation should be permitted if the modifying offer was made on a common assumption which is untrue or does not eventuate (eg you offer to pay more or accept less because of dramatic price increases which then fall back quickly to their original level) or the promisor has reason to lose confidence in the promisee's ability to perform and can salvage the situation with a substitute.

In *Mobil Oil Australia Ltd*,[64] franchisees of Mobil alleged that Mobil could not revoke its 'nine-for-six' offer (to give nine additional years of franchise free if the franchisee obtained at least 90 per cent in the annual 'Circle of Excellence' judging for six years). The court found no implied offer not to revoke because the act of acceptance was ill-defined and the franchisees were already obliged to achieve high standards in order to run an efficient business. The court questioned the suggestion 'that the attainment of 90 per cent in the first year or even perfect operation of the service station for a day, a week or a month, albeit by reference to the offer, represents a commencement of attainment of 90 per cent in all six years so it is immediately to bind Mobil not to revoke?'[65]

Even if an offeror has impliedly promised not to revoke on commencement of the stipulated performance, it does not follow that a purported revocation would be ineffective. In the absence of specific relief in respect of that implied promise, the offeror will simply be liable to damages; but on what measure? The most obvious is loss of expectation measured by the chance that the performance would have been

---

[62] *Hoenig v Isaacs* [1952] 2 All ER 176.
[63] [2007] EWCA Civ 969, [2008] 2 WLR 834, at [44].
[64] (1998) 153 ALR 196, at 228.
[65] *Ibid*, at 224.

completed[66] less the expenses saved or, where completion depends on the hypothetical acts of third parties, by reference to the offeree's loss of a chance.[67] *Chitty* puts forward 'an intermediate possibility'[68] by analogy to *White & Carter Ltd v McGregor*.[69] Namely, that the offeree should cease performance and recover damages amounting to his expenses unless she has a 'substantial legitimate interest' in completing performance. A third possibility is put forward by the Lord Chancellor in *Morrison Shipping Co v The Crown*:[70] 'It may be that, when work is done and expense incurred on the faith of a conditional promise, the promisor comes under an implied obligation not to revoke his promise, and if he does so may be sued for damages or on a *quantum meruit*.'

3. PROMISSORY ESTOPPEL IN *COLLIER V WRIGHT*

Lord Denning opened the way to using the promissory estoppel doctrine in *Hughes v Metropolitan Railway Co*[71] to enforce relieving promises in *Central London Property Trust v High Trees House Ltd*.[72] His Lordship staked further ground for the equitable doctrine in dicta in *D&C Builders v Rees*.[73] Namely, that it is in principle, although not on the facts, applicable to part payment of a debt agreed by the parties to discharge the whole debt. In *Collier v Wright*[74] the Court of Appeal applied the dicta in *Rees* to override the House of Lords decision in *Foakes v Beer*.[75] Collier and his two former business partners were jointly indebted to Wright for £46,800, each servicing his share. When Collier's former partners ceased paying, Collier alleged that Wright told him to continue his payments and Wright would chase the other debtors. Over four years later, when Collier had repaid his third of the debt, Wright demanded the other two-thirds from Collier.

---

[66] *Mobil Oil Australia Ltd v Wellcome International Pty Ltd and Others* (1998) 153 ALR 196, at 225.
[67] *Allied Maples v Simmons & Simmons* [1989] 1 WLR 1602; and see *Schweppe v Harper* [2008] EWCA Civ 442, at [53].
[68] *Chitty on Contracts* (30th edn, London: Sweet & Maxwell, 2008) para 2-086.
[69] [1962] AC 413; and see P Atiyah, 'Consideration: Restatement' in (ed) *Essays on Contract* (Oxford: Clarendon Press, 1988) 204.
[70] *Morrison Shipping Co v The Crown* (1924) 20 Ll L Rep 283, at 287.
[71] (1876-77) LR 2 App Cas 439.
[72] [1947] KB 130.
[73] [1966] 2 QB 617.
[74] [2007] EWCA Civ 1329; [2008] 1 WLR 643.
[75] (1883-84) LR 9 App Cas 605.

In a preliminary hearing, the Court of Appeal found that although Collier gave no consideration on the authority of *Foakes v Beer* and *Re Selectmove*,[76] he had established a 'genuine triable issue' on promissory estoppel. If Wright had given the alleged undertaking, which was unclear, Collier's subsequent part payment would, without more, bar Wright from suing for the balance. Arden LJ reformulated the promissory estoppel doctrine:[77]

> [I]f (1) a debtor offers to pay part only of the amount he owes; (2) the creditor voluntarily accepts that offer, and (3) in reliance on the creditor's acceptance the debtor pays that part of the amount he owes in full, the creditor will, by virtue of the doctrine of promissory estoppel, be bound to accept that sum in full and final satisfaction of the whole debt. For him to resile will of itself be inequitable. In addition, in these circumstances, the promissory estoppel has the effect of extinguishing the creditor's right to the balance of the debt.... To a significant degree it achieves in practical terms the recommendation of the Law Revision Committee chaired by Lord Wright MR in 1937.

Collier v Wright[78] is a clear break with precedent. In place of promissory estoppel's flexible weighing of the parties' conduct and potential losses, Arden LJ substitutes an absolute rule. Her Ladyship's approach substantially alters our understanding of the reliance requirement for the purposes of promissory estoppel. The trial judge found no relevant reliance by Collier.[79] Collier's claim, that absent Wright's assurance, he would have pursued the other debtors prior to their bankruptcy, struck the trial judge (and Longmore LJ)[80] as 'wild speculation' given Wright's 'inability to recover a single penny from them, despite being in possession of a judgment debt'.[81] Indeed, Arden LJ agreed that:[82]

> there is no evidence that Mr Collier's position now is in any material respect different from that immediately before the agreement was made. For instance, there is no evidence that he entered into any business venture or made any substantial investment on the strength of the agreement. Nor is there any evidence that he could not raise the money now to meet Wright's claim.

---

[76] [1995] 1 WLR 474.

[77] [2007] EWCA Civ 1329, [2008] 1 WLR 643, at [42].

[78] A Trukhtanov, '*Foakes v Beer*: Reform of Common Law at the Expense of Equity' (2008) 124 *LQR* 364.

[79] [2007] EWCA Civ 1329, [2008] 1 WLR 643, at [19].

[80] *Ibid*, at [46].

[81] *Ibid*, at [28].

[82] *Ibid*, at [36].

Neither did the trial judge think that Collier's *part payment* amounted
to relevant reliance. This is unsurprising since part payment has
never previously, *in itself*, been sufficient to raise promissory estoppel.
Otherwise, one would wonder what all the fuss surrounding *Foakes
v Beer*. Nevertheless, Arden LJ held that part performance *per se*, *does*
amount to the relevant reliance, *and* that this, *without more*, makes it
inequitable for the creditor to resile from the agreement, *and* completely
extinguishes the creditor's right to the balance of the original debt.
This makes the requirement of promisor unconscionability in resiling redundant and departs from the reliance basis of the doctrine. It
cuts the doctrine adrift from its justification. The analogy with
'pratical benefit' is inescapable; *Collier v Wright* undermines *Foakesv
Beer* in the same way that *Williams v Roffey Brothers* undermined
Stilk v Myrick.

Longmore LJ conceded that Lord Denning's dicta in *Rees* 'seems' to
have the effect attributed by Arden LJ,[83] but he was distinctly unen-
thusiastic about it. He doubted that Wright had *permanently* foregone
its original right or that Collier had 'relied … in any meaningful way'.
His Lordship recognized that it was arguably inequitable for Wright
to resile, but thought there was 'much to be said on the other side',
concluding that:[84]

> If, as Arden LJ puts it, the 'brilliant obiter dictum' of Denning J in the *High
> Trees* case [1947] KB 130 did indeed substantially achieve in practical terms
> the recommendation of the Law Revision Committee chaired by Lord
> Wright MR in 1937, it is perhaps all the more important that agreements
> which are said to forgo a creditor's rights on a permanent basis should not
> be too benevolently construed.

Lord Denning's dicta in *D & C Builders Ltd v Rees*[85] is weak precedent
for *Collier's* version of promissory estoppel. Lord Denning found his
own formulation inapplicable because Rees' bad faith meant that it was
not inequitable for the builders to resile. Thus, Rees' part payment did
not, *per se*, make the builders' resiling inequitable, contrary to Arden
LJ's formulation.[86] The greater part of Lord Denning's judgment simply applied *Foakes v Beer*. Danckwerts LJ's judgment spent just 14 lines
rejecting promissory estoppel (because there was no true accord and *no
detrimental change of position*).[87] Winn LJ, giving the longest judgment,

---

[83] *Ibid*, at [45]–[47].

[84] *Ibid*, at [48].

[85] [1966] 2 QB 617.

[86] Arden LJ could explain the outcome of *Rees* by saying that the builders made no promise to start with.

[87] *D & C Builders Ltd v Rees* [1966] 2 QB 617, at 627.

made no mention of promissory estoppel at all. It is, therefore, paradoxical that a case which applies *Foakes v Beer* should be interpreted in direct contradiction of it. All three judges agreed that the modification was unenforceable because there was no accord and satisfaction where: 'The accord is the agreement by which the obligation is discharged. The satisfaction is the consideration which makes the agreement operative.'[88] In contrast, Arden LJ[89] relies on Lord Denning's different use of the terminology of 'accord and satisfaction'[90] to mean 'agreement and part-payment'.[91]

Adopting the unilateral contract analysis in relation to both adding and subtracting would not only avoid the difficulties raised by *Collier v Wright*, it would also counter the glaring inconsistency between *Williams v Roffey*[92] and *Re Selectmove*[93] which *Collier v Wright* perpetuates. There is no functional difference between an adding and subtracting promise; in both cases the promisor is getting *proportionately* 'less' than his original entitlement and the promisee is getting 'more'. Moreover, the unilateral contract analysis is entirely consistent with outcome in *Collier v Wright* and Arden LJ's requirement of actual performance.

4. ABOLISHING CONSIDERATION IN ADDING MODIFICATIONS

Another way around the traditional obstacle to the enforcement of adding promises posed by the consideration requirement is to abolish the requirement. This is the approach advocated by the New Zealand Court of Appeal in *Antons Trawling v Smith*.[94] Smith was employed by Antons to fish for orange roughy. The standard agreement provided for payment as a percentage of the net value of the fish caught.

---

[88] *Chitty on Contracts*, (30th edn, London: Sweet & Maxwell, 2009) para 22-012. *British Russian Gazette and Trade Outlook Ltd v Associated Newspapers Ltd* [1933] 2 KB 616, at 643; *Bank of Credit and Commerce International SA v Ali* [1999] ICR 1068, at 1078.

[89] *Collier v* Wright [2007] EWCA Civ 1329, [2008] 1 WLR 643, at [33], [39], and [42].

[90] In *D&C Builders Ltd v Rees* [1966] 2 QB 617, at 625, Lord Denning MR held: 'Where there has been a true accord, under which the creditor voluntarily agrees to accept a lesser sum in satisfaction, and the debtor acts upon that accord by paying the lesser sum and the creditor accepts it, then it is inequitable for the creditor afterwards to insist on the balance.'

[91] [2007] EWCA Civ 1329, [2008] 1 WLR 643, at 644. According to the Weekly Law Reports, *Collier v Wright* held, inter alia, that Collier had raised a triable issue 'that there had been an accord and satisfaction in that he had paid his share of the debt and the company had voluntarily agreed to accept the payments on that basis'.

[92] [1991] 1 QB 1.

[93] [1995] 1 WLR 474.

[94] [2003] 2 NZLR 23, citing Chen-Wishart, 'The Enforceability of Additional Contractual Promises: A Question of Consideration' (1991) 14 *New Zealand U L Rev* 270 at [92].

When Smith realized the risk that this arrangement entailed when performing exploratory fishing, he requested a daily rate as he was entitled to do under the agreement. Antons declined but agreed to give Smith a 10 per cent share of any additional fishing quota allocated by the government to Antons as a result of Smith proving the existence of a commercial fishery. Antons argued that it was not bound by this additional promise because Smith was already paid to fish and so gave no consideration. The court endorsed the 'practical benefit' approach[95] of *Williams v Roffey*. However, acknowledging the trenchant criticisms of the decision, the court held, in the alternative, that consideration is unnecessary for the variation of a contract. Baragwanath J said:[96]

> [Denying enforcement] would be inconsistent with the essential principle underlying the law of contract, that the law will seek to give effect to freely accepted *reciprocal* undertakings.... Where the parties who have already made such intention clear by entering legal relations have *acted upon* an agreement to a variation, *in the absence of policy reasons to the contrary* they should be bound by their agreement.

Although the court did not choose between recognizing 'practical benefit' and dispensing with consideration, the two approaches are conceptually incompatible; one liberalizes consideration, the other abolishes it, albeit only in the context of adding modifications. The latter approach is objectionable on a number of fronts. First, Baragwanath J's view that '[t]he importance of consideration is as a valuable signal that the parties intend to be bound by their agreement, rather than an end in itself'[97] will be contested below.[98] Second, if 'the essential principle underlying the law of contract' is the parties' intention to be bound, then its logic should extend to both adding and relieving promises,[99] and even to contract formation. The fact that his Honour confines his abolition to adding promises where there is already 'freely accepted *reciprocal* undertakings'[100] shows that reciprocity is not dispensable to contractual enforcement. Third, the intention to be bound approach cannot explain why the enforceability of the promise should be conditional on the promisee *actually* performing her pre-existing obligations.

---

[95] Reference was made at [91] to a previous Court of Appeal's endorsement in *Attorney-General for England and Wales v R* [2002] 2 NZLR 91, at 109, which praised the approach as appropriately paying attention to the practical realities of the parties' circumstances rather than to 'legal niceties'.

[96] [2003] 2 NZLR 23, at [93] (emphasis added).

[97] *Ibid.*

[98] See text accompanying n 110–111.

[99] There is no suggestion that the court intended to abrogate the rule in *Foakes v Beer*.

[100] [2003] 2 NZLR 23, at [93] (emphasis added).

On the other hand, this condition is entirely consistent with the uni-lateral contract approach premised on consideration proposed in this essay. Indeed, Baragwanath J specifically held that 'the agreement about the issue of quota was a unilateral contract. Mr Smith did not assume the obligation of achieving the goals so as to expose oneself to liability if he failed'.[101] Lastly, there is no guidance as to the content of the additional qualification that enforcement of adding promises is subject to the 'absence of policy reasons to the contrary'.

5. ABOLISHING CONSIDERATION OUTRIGHT

An even more radical departure is signalled by the dicta of Andrew Phang Boon Leong JA of the Singapore Court of Appeal in *Gay Choon Ing v Loh Sze Ti Terence Peter*.[102] The case was decided on the basis that the parties had reached a valid compromise on the ordinary principles of contract law, there being 'no fundamental difficulties with respect to the doctrine of consideration'.[103] Nevertheless, his Honour went on to give an 11-page critique of the doctrine in anticipation of the day that 'the issue of reform does squarely arise before this court in the future'.[104] He explains that 'the doctrine might now be outmoded or even redundant, and that its functions may well be met by more effec-tive alternatives'.[105] In particular, 'the doctrines of economic duress, undue influence, and unconscionability appear to be more clearly suited not only to modern commercial circumstances but also (more importantly) to situations where there has been possible "extortion"'.[106] While recognizing the impossibility of enforcing all promises, his Honour's only stated restriction is that any agreement should be *seriously intended*[107] because '[t]he marrow of contractual relation-ships should be the parties' intention to create a legal relationship'.[108]

---

[101] *Ibid*, at [59]. This unilateral contract contains additional *legal* benefit for Antons; namely, the prospect of satisfying the Ministry of Agriculture and Fisheries of the existence of a com-mercial fishery in the area. The 10% deal was offered to encourage Smith to redouble his efforts and to agree to the extensive research programme and record keeping which the Ministry would require before issuing further quota, at [31]–[41].

[102] [2009] SGCA 31.

[103] *Ibid*, at [92].

[104] *Ibid*, at [94].

[105] *Ibid*, at [92].

[106] *Ibid*, at [113]. Another possible 'alternative doctrine' is promissory estoppel; see [111].

[107] *Ibid*, at [113].

[108] *Ibid*, at [86], citing VK Rajah JC in *Chwee Kin Keong v Digilandmall.com Pte Ltd* [2004] 2 SLR 594, at [139].

Consideration is dispensable because 'consideration is merely evidence of serious intention to contract'.[109]

The idea that consideration merely performs the functions of formalities has been standard fare since Fuller's famous article in 1941.[110] The idea is that consideration is a reasonably efficient indicator that a promise has actually been made (evidentiary), the promisor understood the consequences of making it (channelling), and took care in making it (cautionary). Now, it is true that, exceptionally, nominal consideration may *only* evince a serious intention to be bound, but it is a mistake to confine the role of consideration in this way. Even *with* consideration an oral promise may be very difficult to prove, given impulsively or without thought of the legal consequences. Conversely, the *absence* of consideration does not necessarily, or even normally, point towards a promise being perjured, careless, or unintended.[111] There can be no doubt about my seriousness in solemnly promising you £5,000 in front of witnesses, or even in writing. Yet, you cannot enforce my promise. In contract law, a promisor can change her mind *unless* the promisee has given or promised to give a reciprocal inducement for the promise.

The idea that an undertaking seriously made is sufficient to justify its enforcement is simply wrong as a description of contract law. If it were true, contract law would have little content. All contractual questions (When is there a contract? What are its contents? Is a contract vitiated? What are the remedies for breach?) would be answered by sole reference to the parties' serious intentions. The only issue becomes one of fact finding. We would wonder why contract books need to run to many hundreds, even thousands of pages. No legal system does or can enforce all promises and the idea of respect for seriously intended promises is not determinative of the promises which should be enforced.

Nor is the idea of enforcing every seriously intended promise normatively attractive. First, if we value freedom of choice then we should value equally highly an individual's subsequent abandonment of her initial choice. Why should we prioritize a past choice over a present one when both are equally valid expressions of her will?[112] Second, it would be a very different world from the one we know if we were 'bound by every promise, no matter how foolish, without any chance of letting increased wisdom undo past foolishness.

---

[109] *Ibid*, at [113].
[110] 'Consideration and Form' (1941) 41 *Columbia L Rev* 799.
[111] A Kull, 'Reconsidering Gratuitous Promises' (1992) 21 *J of Legal Studies* 39, 55.
[112] A Brudner, 'Reconstructing Contracts' (1993) 43 *U Toronto LJ* 1, 21.

Certainly, some freedom to change one's mind is necessary for free intercourse between those who lack omniscience'.[113] An integral part of any valuable autonomous life is the ability to learn, change, mature and recreate oneself. This may entail the rejection or alteration of previous beliefs or goals. Even when account is taken of the value of learning from one's mistakes, coerced performance of one's regretted promises may unduly compromise one's integrity and self-respect[114] (hence damages is the primary remedy for breach, rather than specific performance), or may jeopardize one's future autonomy (hence the invalidity of slavery contracts and unreasonable restraints of trade, and the facility of bankruptcy which allows a fresh start).

Even if we believe that the promisor should do as she promises (for example, as a matter of self-consistency), this does not explain why contract law should weigh in on behalf of the *promisee* as a matter of justice. For this, we need the doctrine of consideration.[115] Contract law will not generally assist a promisee *unless* she has given or promised to give the reciprocal inducement for the promise.

It is doubtful that a substantive requirement of intention to create legal relations 'will in the long run work any better than the rules of consideration'.[116] There is the risk of confusion with the misnamed doctrine of 'intention to create legal relations', which is more concerned to map the boundaries of appropriate legal involvement in private affairs[117] than to interrogate the parties' intentions. Moreover, to say that the question is the parties' 'intention to be bound' simply begs the question: bound to *what*? What rights or liabilities were intended to be transferred, created, waived, or suspended by the promisor? Was it to be absolute or conditional?[118] It is not obvious that by promising to pay more or accept less, a promisor *necessarily* intends to extinguish his original rights absolutely and irrespective of changes of circumstances or failure by the promisee to perform under the new arrangement.

Contract orthodoxy sets a threshold of enforceability based on bargain consideration, is restrictive of the scope of excuses for non-performance, and normally enforces to the full extent the promisee's expectations. Expanding the basis for enforcement will necessitate the

[113] M Cohen, 'The Basis of Contract' (1933) 46 *Harv L Rev* 553, 572.

[114] A Kronman, 'Paternalism and the Law of Contract' (1983) *Yale LJ* 763.

[115] E Weinrib, *The Idea of Private Law* (Harvard: University Press Harvard, 1995) 136–40.

[116] P Atiyah, *Essays on Contract* (Oxford: Clarendon Press, 1986) 241.

[117] S Hedley, 'Keeping Contract in its Place: *Balfour v Balfour* and the Enforceability of Informal Agreements' (1985) 5 *Oxford J of Legal Studies* 391.

[118] This is the point made by Longmore LJ in *Collier v Wright* [2007] EWCA Civ 1329, [2008] 1 WLR 643, at [48].

appropriate recalibration of the excuses and remedies and so undermine the internal coherence of contract law. If enforcement is to be
divorced from exchange, it is not obvious what the appropriate remedial response should be. The demands of justice will vary with the
particular *context* (whether commercial, consumer, charitable, family,
and so on) and the particular *reason* for enforcement (whether bargain,
reliance suffered, benefit received, fulfilment of family responsibilities,
and so on).

Thus, German and French law define 'contract' to include gratuitous
promises but recognize special excuses (derived from Roman law) for
the non-performance of gratuitous transactions. These include: the
donee's 'gross ingratitude',[119] the donor's deterioration of circumstances such that 'he is not in a position to fulfil the promise without
endangering his own reasonable maintenance or the fulfilment of obligations imposed upon him by law to furnish maintenance to others',[120]
and the subsequent acquisition of a child by a previously childless
donor.[121] Even completed gifts are revocable in comparable circumstances. Most notably the enforceability of gratuitous promises in German and French law is subject to a stringent formality requirement
unless they are 'synallagmatic' contracts (containing bilateral reciprocal undertakings).[122] This is simply a different way of stating the common law position that an enforceable promise must be supported by
consideration *unless* it is accompanied by the requisite formality.

Phang JA's view that consideration is evidence of serious intention
and that duress, undue influence, and unconscionability can *replace*
consideration assumes what HLA Hart warns against. In *The Ascription of Responsibility and Rights*[123] Hart describes the line of reasoning
that since consent gets you into contract, only lack of consent will get
you out[124] as 'a disastrous over-simplification and distortion' of the
law on the vitiation of transactions. It fails to recognize: (i) that consent
is a *necessary but not sufficient*, condition of transactional liability; and

---

[119] § 530 (1) of the German Civil Code (*BGB*); Arts 953, 955 of the French Civil Code (*Code civil*). This includes, eg, serious misconduct towards the donor or a close relative, infidelity of the donee spouse, filing an unmeritorious petition to declare the donor disabled, and the donee's failure to perform an express condition.

[120] § 519 of the German Civil Code (*BGB*).

[121] See further J Dawson, *ibid*, 53.

[122] §§ 320-26 of the German Civil Code (*BGB*); Art 1102 of the French Civil Code (*Code civil*).

[123] HLA Hart, 'The Ascription of Responsibility and Rights' in *Proceedings of the Aristotelian Society* (1948) 49; also in A Flew (ed.), *Logic and Language—First Series* (Oxford: Basil Black-well, 1952) 145, 173.

[124] *Ibid*, 183.

(ii) that the validity of a transaction is a *two-stage* inquiry, so that even when the language of consent is used in determining both the formation and vitiation stages, they deal with *qualitatively different* concerns. It is a mistake to think 'that there are certain psychological elements required by the law as necessary conditions of contract and that the defences are merely admitted as negative *evidence* of these'. Rather, talk of 'defective consent' in relation to vitiating factors is conclusory, not explanatory; it is merely short-hand for the variety of factors rendering a transaction 'defeasible'.[125] Understanding this allows us to detach the basis for *vitiating* transactions from the basis for *enforcing* them. Space is then opened up to consider values at work *other* than consent and exchange. The question is whether, in the circumstances, a claimant should be relieved of responsibility for the transaction, *despite her consent* to it.[126]

Consistently, Lord Scarman said that '[t]he classic case of duress is… not the lack of will to submit but the victim's intentional submission arising from the realization that there is no practical choice open to him'.[127] Where this results from the defendant's illegitimate pressure, the law does not ascribe the normal responsibility it would to the victim's consent. This view avoids the fiction that the claimant gave no consent despite acting knowingly and intentionally.[128] Rather, it takes the realistic and respectful view that the claimant engaged with reason in consenting,[129] but should nevertheless be excused from responsibility in the circumstances.

In 1994 I criticized *Williams v Roffey* for 'passing the buck' to the doctrine of economic duress because the latter was still too unstable and undeveloped to distinguish appropriate one-sided modifications from the inappropriate.[130] For example, it is unclear how the line can

---

[125] *Ibid*, 145, 174-8 (emphasis in the original). At 180, Hart explains that 'the logical character of words like "voluntary" are anomalous and ill-understood. They are treated in such definitions as words having positive force, yet, as can be seen from Aristotle's discussion in *Book III of the Nicomachean Ethics*, the word "voluntary" in fact serves to exclude a heterogeneous range of cases such as physical compulsion, coercion by threats, accidents, the stakes, etc, and not to designate a mental element or state; nor does "involuntary" signify the absence of this mental element or state.'

[126] *Ibid*, 174.

[127] *Universe Tankships Inc of Monrovia v International Transport Workers Federation (The Universe Sentinel)* [1983] 1 AC 366, at 400.

[128] P Atiyah, 'Economic Duress and the Overborne Will' (1982) 98 *LQR* 197; *Lynch v DPP for Northern Ireland* [1975] 1 All ER 913, 926–38.

[129] Hence the requirement that she has no practicable alternative.

[130] 'Consideration, Practical Benefit and the Emperor's New Clothes' in Beatson and Friedmann (eds), *Good Faith and Fault in Contract Law* (Oxford: Oxford University Press, 1995) 123.

be drawn between the content of 'practical benefit' to the promisor (avoiding the consequences of breach) which points towards enforcement and the promisor having 'no practicable alternative' but to agree (to avoid the consequences of breach) which points against enforcement. However, there is nothing for it but to engage with the task of marking out the appropriate shape of economic duress. Suffice it to say that since scarcity is pervasive, *all* choices are constrained. It is impossible to generate a coherent theory of duress by reference to the internal psychology of the parties. To distinguish acceptable constraints from the unacceptable, we will need to appeal to factors *external* to the will of the parties.

The consideration doctrine cannot be replaced by the vitiating factors of duress, undue influence, and unconscionability. Consideration is not merely a proxy for serious intention to be bound, and despite the justificatory language of the courts, the vitiating factors do not primarily concern the negation of this serious intention.

6. CONCLUSION

Evolution, not revolution, has always been the common law way. Lord Steyn's extra-judicial comment is exemplary:[131]

> I have no radical proposals for the wholesale review of the doctrine of consideration. I am not persuaded that it is necessary. And great legal change should only be embarked on when they are truly necessary.... [T]he courts have shown a readiness to hold that the rigidity of the doctrine of consideration must yield to practical justice and the needs of modern commerce.

The story of the pre-existing duties problem is partly one of the richness, ingenuity, and evolutionary capacity of the common law to overcome obstacles to reaching just and sensible results. Faced with the perceived obstacle of consideration, *Williams v Roffey* widened its scope; *Collier v Wright* circumvented it; and *Antons Trawling* and *Gay v Loh* abolished it. The three approaches are interconnected; there is an order of priority in their application. Expansion of consideration reduces the need to resort to circumvention via promissory estoppel. But abolition of consideration makes the expansion of consideration or of promissory estoppel redundant. Consideration bites before promissory estoppel, but abolition swallows all.

---

[131] 'Contract Law: Fulfilling the Reasonable Expectations of Honest Men' (1997) 113 *LQR* 433, 437.

At the end of the day, the desirable approach to pursue depends on our assessment of the core functions of the doctrine of consideration. The crux of this essay is that enforcement of one-sided modifications *can* be accommodated within the traditional framework by further refinement of the enlargement of consideration recognized in *Williams v Roffey*. To one who promises more for performance already owed, receipt of that performance is superior to the right to sue for it and she should be able to bargain for it. The promise to pay more can be understood as a unilateral offer which becomes binding only if the stipulated performance is rendered. The logic should be extended to relieving promises. The concern to prevent exploitation must be worked out at stage two, under the rubric of economic duress. A coherent resolution of the problem of one-sided modifications eliminates one of the major sources of discontent with the consideration doctrine. This should inform the debate over whether the consideration doctrine should be sustained and rehabilitated or be dismantled wholesale by legislation, or piece by piece in the courts.

A bird in the hand is better than one in the bush. The Emperor who is merely given a repromise of new clothes gets nothing more than he had before; he may still end up naked. But the Emperor who actually gets his new clothes receives something more than he had before. The 'eye of the law' may not see it, but the Emperor, facing a state occasion, will have no doubt.

6

Promissory Estoppel and Debts

BEN MCFARLANE*

1. INTRODUCTION

The purpose of this chapter is to examine just one of the many non-contractual doctrines by which a promise, or a manifestation of consent, may have some legal effect: promissory estoppel. In light of the Court of Appeal's decision in *Collier v P & MJ Wright (Holdings) Ltd*,[1] its particular focus is on the application of promissory estoppel to cases where a creditor, A, is owed a debt by B and accepts, or promises to accept, payment of a lesser sum in satisfaction of that debt. It might be expected that the discussion would focus solely on the problems caused by this particular context. However, the most difficult problems lie with the doctrine of promissory estoppel itself. The courts' current formulation of the doctrine is incoherent. Things have not improved since 1972, when Lord Hailsham, the Lord Chancellor, observed that: 'the whole sequence of cases based on promissory estoppel since the war…raise problems of coherent exposition which have never been systematically explored'.[2] This is not to say that the results of those cases are incorrect, or the reasoning employed is flawed. Rather, it will be argued that the incoherence consists of understanding those cases as resting on one general principle. It will be suggested that the doctrine of promissory estoppel can better be seen as consisting of at least three distinct principles, none of which is the exclusive preserve of promissory estoppel.

---

* Reader in Property Law, University of Oxford; Fellow in Law, Trinity College, Oxford.
[1] [2007] EWCA Civ 1329, [2008] 1 WLR 643.
[2] *Woodhouse AC Israel Cocoa Ltd SA v Nigerian Produce Marketing Co Ltd* [1972] AC 741, at 757.

2. PROMISSORY ESTOPPEL: THREE PRINCIPLES

A popular[3] and concise expression of the requirements and effect of the doctrine of promissory estoppel was given by Robert Goff J in *BP Exploration Co (Libya) Ltd v Hunt (No 2)*:[4]

> The principle, therefore, presupposes three things: (1) a legal relationship between the parties; (2) a representation, express or implied, by one party that he will not enforce his strict rights against the other; and (3) reliance by the representee (whether by action or by omission to act) on the representation, which renders it inequitable, in all the circumstances, for the representor to enforce his strict rights, or at least to do so until the representee is restored to his former position.

In what follows, the party making the representation will be referred to as A and the representee as B. It will be argued that decisions said to be based on promissory estoppel do not in fact depend on the unitary doctrine set out above, but are best explained as applications of one of the three specific principles set out below.

(a) Acceptance by A of substitute performance tendered by B

(i) The principle

The principle is that: (i) if B owes a duty to A; and (ii) B tenders, and A accepts, particular action (or inaction) by B as performance of that duty; then (iii) B's duty is discharged even if, in the absence of such acceptance from A, B's action (or inaction) would not have discharged that duty.

This principle is not promissory in nature: it gives effect to A's *actual* consent in accepting the substitute performance, rather than a promise by A to accept such performance.[5] It should be emphasized that this principle does not depend on the need to avoid B suffering a specific

---

[3] It is, for example, echoed in the formulation adopted by *Chitty on Contracts* (30th edn, London: Sweet & Maxwell, 2008) vol 1, 3-086.

[4] [1979] 1 WLR 783, at 810. Hereafter *BP v Hunt (No 2)*.

[5] This point is important in considering the application of the principle where B's duty arises under a contract required to be made or evidenced in writing. For example, if a contract for the sale of goods were covered by the Statute of Frauds 1677, an oral variation of the contract would not be enforceable. However, A's acceptance of a modified performance would discharge B's duty under that written contract. This distinction between, on the one hand, a variation or new contract and, on the other, an arrangement as to the mode of performance of an existing contract, is noted, for example, by Brett LJ in *Plevins v Downing* (1876) 1 CP 220, at 225.

detriment as a result of his reliance on A. Rather, the principle depends on a broader need for finality. The promotion of finality may, in particular cases, have the effect of preventing B suffering a specific detriment; but it can apply even in a case where such detriment is absent. The virtue of the principle comes from the fact that it *enables* B to rely, if he wishes, on the reasonable belief that his duty to A has been discharged. In pursuance of that aim of finality, the principle extinguishes B's duty.

The principle is clearly similar to that applying where A elects to affirm a contract despite B's breach of a condition. For example, in *BP v Hunt (No 2)*, Robert Goff J described the effect of such an election as based on the 'need for finality in commercial transactions'[6] and also distinguished decisions depending on such an election from those depending on the principle applied in *Hughes v Metropolitan Railway Co.*[7] The possibility of election underlines the need to distinguish carefully between two different types of consent that A may manifest. Where B's failure to perform a particular contractual duty counts as a breach of condition, A has a choice as to whether to affirm or terminate the contract. A can choose to affirm the contract without also choosing to accept B's conduct as substitute performance of B's duty. An affirmation, by itself, simply deprives A of the power to terminate the contract; it does not prevent A from seeking to enforce B's duty, or from claiming damages for its breach. An acceptance of B's conduct as performance of B's duty, in contrast, necessarily entails A's consent to the discharge of B's duty. In theory, the distinction between an election to affirm and the principle discussed in this section is very clear:[8] everything depends on the precise nature of A's consent.[9]

(ii) The principle and promissory estoppel

The principle has some similarities to, but is clearly distinct from, the unitary doctrine of promissory estoppel as defined in the dictum, set out above, from *BP v Hunt (No 2)*. It depends on there being a duty owed by B to A and, to that extent only, it requires a pre-existing legal relationship between the parties. It depends on A, by his words or

---

[6] [1979] 1 WLR 783 at 811. See in particular the discussion there of *Panchaud Freres SA v Etablissements General Grain Co* [1970] 1 Lloyds Rep 53.

[7] (1877) 2 App Cas 439. Hereafter *Hughes*.

[8] The distinction is reflected in s 11(2) of the Sale of Goods Act 1979.

[9] See *Bottiglieri di Navigazione SpA v Cosco Qingdao Ocean Shipping Co ('The Bunga Saga Lima')* [2005] EWHC 244 (Comm), [2005] 2 Lloyds Rep 1 for a commercial case in which A's conduct amounted not only to an election to affirm a contract, but also to acceptance of B's substitute performance as discharging B's duty.

conduct, manifesting his consent to B's substitute performance discharging B's duty to A: to that extent only, it requires a representation, express or implied, by one party that he will not enforce his strict rights against the other. It depends on B's rendering the substitute performance, but does not require any other reliance by B; and its effect is to extinguish, not simply to suspend, any duties of B to A in respect of which A has accepted the substitute performance. Moreover, as noted above, the principle is not promissory in nature, as it depends on A's *actual* consent in accepting the substitute performance.

It is worth asking why this principle has been seen as part of the unitary doctrine of promissory estoppel. The best explanation depends on *Central London Property Trust Ltd v High Trees House Ltd*:[10] the case seen as the modern foundation of that doctrine. The specific principle set out here supports Denning J's obiter view that, had A claimed arrears for 1940 to 1944 (the period in which B had offered, and A had accepted, a reduced rent) such a claim would have failed. Indeed, it provides more effective support than the unitary promissory estoppel doctrine. First, the principle set out here explains why, in *High Trees*, B did not need to show that he had so conducted himself that A's potential claim for arrears for 1940 to 1944 would have caused B a specific detriment. Second, it is also consistent with the fact that B's duty to pay a rent during that period was discharged, and not merely suspended, by A's acceptance of the lower rent.

(iii) Applying the principle to payment of a lesser sum in satisfaction of a debt

There is no inherent reason why the principle cannot apply in a case where A accepts B's payment of a lesser sum in discharge of a debt.[11] Indeed, as noted above, the application of the principle provides the best explanation of Denning J's obiter view in *High Trees* that A was unable to claim arrears for 1940 to 1944. As a matter of authority, however, the reasoning of the House of Lords in *Foakes v Beer*[12] provides a significant obstacle.

---

[10] [1947] KB 130. Hereafter *High Trees*.

[11] It is important to emphasize that the sum must actually be paid by B and accepted by A. The principle is thus consistent with the decision of the Court of Appeal in *Re Selectmove Ltd* [1995] 1 WLR 474.

[12] (1884) LR 9 App Cas 605. Hereafter *Foakes*.

First, the actual decision in *Foakes* does not absolutely preclude the application of the principle to the discharge of a debt.[13] It is important to emphasize that the principle applies only where A has genuinely consented to the discharge of B's duty by means of B's substitute performance. As has been noted by, for example, Treitel,[14] the best explanation for the decision in *Foakes* is that Beer had not in fact consented to the discharge of Foakes's duty to pay interest on the judgment debt owed to Beer.[15]

Second, when applying any non-contractual principle based on A's consent, a court must be particularly alert to ensure that A's consent is genuine and freely given. For example, in *Woodhouse AC Israel Cocoa Ltd SA v Nigerian Produce Marketing Co*,[16] the House of Lords emphasized that the non-contractual nature of the principle does not mean that ambiguous language of A, which could not constitute an offer of a contractual variation, could instead be used as a manifestation of consent such as to trigger the operation of the principle. It may be that the reasoning of the House of Lords in *Foakes* was based on a reluctance to accept that a creditor would genuinely consent to the payment of a lesser sum in discharge of a debtor's obligation. One way to express that reluctance, and to protect creditors, is to prohibit the principle's application to *any* case where, as a substitute for B's performance of a duty to pay a debt owed to A, A accepts a smaller sum of money from B. The lack of benefit to A as a result of such a payment is important not because it entails the absence of consideration: after all, the principle discussed here does not depend on A's making a contractually binding promise. Rather, the lack of benefit is important as it casts doubt on the genuineness of A's consent to the discharge of B's duty.

In cases where B claims that A has consented to accept a lesser sum in discharge of a debt, it is right that a court should carefully scrutinize

---

[13] Similarly, the actual decision in *Pinnel's Case* (1601) 5 Co Rep 117a depended on a point of pleading and so the 'rule' laid down there and applied in *Foakes* was not necessary for the decision in the case itself.

[14] See eg G Treitel, *Landmarks of Twentieth Century Contract Law* (Oxford: OUP, 2003) 25; F Reynolds & G Treitel, 'Consideration for the Modification of Contracts' (1965) 7 *Malaya L Rev* 1, 6–9.

[15] The recital to the agreement suggested that its purpose was simply to give B time for payment, without releasing B from any duty to pay interest (see *per* Earl of Selborne LC (1884) LR 9 App Cas 605, at 610). However, B was able to rely on the rule that the meaning of the document could not be controlled by the recital. That rule may well have been known to B's solicitor, who drew up the document, but not to A. In any case, each of Lord Fitzgerald and Lord Watson preferred to interpret the agreement as *not* involving a promise by A to forgo interest payments, although Lord Watson was nonetheless willing to adopt the contrary interpretation of the Earl of Selborne LC and Lord Blackburn.

[16] [1972] AC 741.

that claim.[17] As a matter of principle, however, it is impossible to justify the blanket prohibition favoured in *Foakes*. The prohibition is self-defeating as it will inevitably catch cases where A *has* genuinely consented to the discharge of B's duty. For the reasons discussed by Lord Blackburn in *Foakes* itself,[18] there *may* be cases in which A is genuinely willing to accept a lesser sum in discharge of B's duty. It is more principled to assess each individual set of facts for the presence or absence of such consent, rather than excluding a whole category of cases, even if the objective probability of A's having consented is lower in such cases.

It can therefore be argued that, in *High Trees*, Denning J was justified, as a matter of logic if not authority, in attacking the prohibition imposed by the reasoning of the House of Lords in *Foakes*. The problem is that, for reasons of authority not logic, his Lordship felt obliged to dress up the straightforward principle discussed here as an application of a wider equitable concept, manifested in earlier decisions such as *Hughes*[19] and *Birmingham & District Land Co v London & NW Railway Co*.[20] Such an approach is deeply problematic—for example, as will be seen in part (b)(i) below, those earlier decisions rest on a clearly distinct principle, one that has no application to a case such as *High Trees*. Further, Denning J's manoeuvre obscures the straightforward nature of the 'acceptance of a substitute performance' principle, by allowing the principle instead to be seen as part of a unitary promissory estoppel doctrine.[21]

The problems caused by Denning J's approach can be seen in an examination of the Court of Appeal's decision in *Collier v P & MJ Wright (Holdings) Ltd*.[22] Collier (B) was one of three former partners jointly liable to a company (A) on a judgment debt. In an application

---

[17] For example, in *Collier v P & MJ Wright (Holdings) Ltd* [2007] EWCA Civ 1329, [2008] 1 WLR 643 (discussed below), Wright suggested it would have been 'bonkers' for him to have accepted a lesser sum in discharge of Collier's liability (*ibid*, at [24]). Longmore LJ also observed at [48] that, where the principle applied in *High Trees* is considered, 'it is perhaps all the more important that agreements which are said to forgo a creditor's rights on a permanent basis should not be too benevolently construed'.

[18] (1884) LR 9 App Cas 605, at 622.

[19] (1877) 2 App Cas 439.

[20] (1888) 40 Ch D 268.

[21] It is not suggested that Denning J's reasoning in *High Trees* itself immediately led to this development: for example, in that case, Denning J expressly distinguished the principle applied from estoppel: [1947] KB 130, at 136. It is rather suggested that Denning J's treatment in that case of *Hughes* and *Birmingham* paved the way for the later assimilation of the principle applied in *High Trees* to a wider doctrine: see eg *per* Lord Denning MR in *W & J Alan & Co v el Nasr Export* [1972] 2 QB 189, at 213.

[22] [2007] EWCA Civ 1329, [2008] 1 WLR 643. Hereafter *Collier*.

to set aside a statutory demand made against him by A, B asserted that A could no longer claim the full debt from him, as B had paid one-third of that debt pursuant to an agreement with A that A would not pursue B for the remainder. Due to the nature of the application, A's allegations of fact could not be fully tested: they had to be accepted as correct if supported by some evidence and not inherently implausible.[23] The question considered by the Court of Appeal was therefore as to the legal effect of A's assumed acceptance of B's payment of the lesser sum on the terms of the alleged agreement.

It was first held that B had provided no consideration for A's alleged promise: B's promise to pay one-third of the sum due was simply a promise to perform a duty already owed to A and so could not, by itself, provide consideration for A's promise to accept the lesser sum in discharge of B's debt. The Court of Appeal then proceeded to examine the 'promissory estoppel point'. Both counsel relied on the unitary model of promissory estoppel as set out in the dictum from *BP v Hunt (No 2)* above. Counsel for B suggested that B had 'conducted his affairs on the premise that his obligation was a several obligation and undertook new commitments based on the belief that he had so conducted his finances as to enable those payments and no more'.[24] It was also claimed that, due to his reliance on A's promise, B had lost a valuable opportunity to make arrangements with his partners, each of whom was now bankrupt.

On the analysis set out here, such arguments, based on the need to show detrimental reliance by B on A's promise, were misconceived. Indeed, B's argument did *not* have to depend on giving any binding force to any promise made by A. It could instead be founded on the discharge of B's duty to A as a result of A's acceptance of B's payment of one-third of his joint liability as full performance by B of his duty to A. Arden LJ explained B's success in *Collier* as resting on the 'brilliant obiter dictum of Denning J, as he was, in the *High Trees* case.'[25] Arden LJ is clearly correct in noting that the same principle that extinguished the tenant's liability to pay rent in respect of the years 1940 to 1944 must, as a matter of logic, also operate to extinguish Collier's duty to the company. The two difficulties come, first, from the House of

---

[23] *Ibid per* Arden LJ, at [21].

[24] *Ibid*.

[25] *Ibid*, at [42]. An alternative explanation for the result in *Collier* is to view B's actual payment of the lesser sum as providing consideration for A's promise not to pursue B for the full sum due: see Chen-Wishart, Ch 5 in this volume. That explanation also views B's actual payment of the lesser sum as crucial. In contrast to the explanation advanced here, however, it depends on broadening the current definition of consideration.

Lords' reasoning in *Foakes*,[26] discussed above and, second, from the application of the principle to joint debtors. The duty owed by Collier to the company was the same as the duty owed to the company by Collier's two partners. Technically, then, it may seem that any conduct of the company that extinguished Collier's duty must also have extinguished the duty owed by those partners. This is why, where joint debtors are concerned, a release is distinguished from a covenant not to sue: a release of one joint debtor releases all, whereas a promise not to sue a particular joint debtor does not affect the liability of the others.[27] The Court of Appeal in *Collier* seems to have accepted, at least impliedly, that the principle discussed here can operate to extinguish Collier's duty whilst preserving the joint liability of the other debtors. That result must be right, as the need for finality which underpins the principle justifies the extinction of only the liability of the particular joint debtor whose performance has been accepted by the creditor.

(b) The *Hughes* principle: limits on A's acquisition of a right as a result of B's action or inaction

(i) *The principle*

This principle may apply where A claims to have acquired a right as a result of particular action or inaction by B. It may be that B's action or inaction was influenced by a promise by A that, if B acted or failed to act in that way, A would *not* acquire, or would not enforce, the right in question. If so, there are good grounds for a rule preventing A's taking or exercising the benefit of that right. The rule has the purpose of ensuring that A does not acquire a benefit contrary to his promise to B.[28] In cases where the right on which A seeks to rely is a right against B, it can also have the effect of allowing B to avoid a detriment that B would otherwise suffer. However, the logic of the principle seems also to apply in a case where, as a result of B's conduct, A acquires a right against C: in such a case, intervention may be necessary even though there is no prospect of B's suffering a detriment.[29]

---

[26] (1884) LR 9 App Cas 605.

[27] This point is discussed by F Reynolds & G Treitel, 'Consideration for the Modification of Contracts' (1965) 7 *Malaya L Rev* 1, 12–13.

[28] This point is emphasized by D Gordon, 'Creditors' Promises to Forgo Rights' [1963] *Cambridge L J* 222.

[29] An analogy can be drawn with cases of fully secret trusts: as a result of a promise made to the testator (B) to hold a right on trust for a third party (C), A acquires a right under the will. To prevent A benefitting as a result of his promise, that promise can then be enforced by C: see eg the discussion of the House of Lords in *McCormick v Grogan* (1869) LR 4 HL 82.

For example, in *Hughes*,[30] A claimed to have a right to forfeit B's lease, arising as a result of B's failure to complete repairs before the end of the required six-month period. During that period, A and B had entered into negotiations as to B's surrender of the lease and A had agreed to B's deferring the repairs whilst the negotiations took place.[31] A had thus led B reasonably to believe that B's inaction in failing to complete repairs before the end of the initial six months would *not* give A a right to forfeit the lease. B's decision not to undertake the repairs in that period was influenced by that belief. A was therefore not allowed to profit from B's inaction by forfeiting the lease on account of B's failure to complete the repairs within the initial six months. The period for completion had to be extended, so that the clock did not run during the parties' negotiations. As B had completed the repairs within the extended period, A had no right to forfeit the lease.

In *Birmingham & District Land Co v London & NW Railway Co*,[32] the question was whether A had a right to remove B from its land as a result of B's failure to build on that land within the time limit agreed by A and B. Under that agreement, B was to acquire long leases of parts of A's land—but only if B built on that land before the end of an agreed period. If B failed to complete the buildings in time, B's permission to remain on the land and its power to acquire long leases would end. As a railway company was interested in acquiring parts of the land and was promoting a private Act of Parliament to do so, A instructed B to cease building, and B complied with that request. A had thus led B reasonably to believe that B's inaction in failing to complete the buildings before the end of the initially agreed period would *not* end B's permission to occupy the land and its power to acquire long leases. B's decision not to continue with building work was influenced by that belief. A was therefore not allowed to profit from B's inaction by removing B from the land and denying B's opportunity to gain the long leases. This meant that the railway company, having acquired A's land subject to B's rights, was under a duty to pay compensation to B: it could not show that, at the time of its acquisition of the land, B's interest in the land had ceased to exist.

There are clear differences between this principle and the principle discussed in part (a) above. First, it is not based on A's acceptance of

---

The principle applying in those cases is also upheld in other parts of the law: see McFarlane, 'Constructive Trusts Arising on a Receipt of Property *Sub Conditione*' (2004) 120 *LQR* 667.

[30] (1877) 2 App Cas 439.

[31] B had written to A proposing to defer the repairs, and A was viewed as having 'acceded to' that proposal: *ibid*, at 445, *per* Lord Cairns LC.

[32] (1888) 40 Ch D 268. Hereafter *Birmingham*.

substitute performance by B. Rather, it gives some legal effect to an express or implied promise made by A. Second, B's action or inaction does not consist of providing substitute performance of a duty owed to A; it instead consists of action or inaction that would otherwise give A a right. For example, in *Birmingham*, B had no duty to build on A's land within a fixed period; it rather had a power to do so. In *Hughes*, both before and after A's promise, B did have a duty to complete the repairs, but A certainly did not accept B's failure to complete the repairs within the initial six months as satisfaction of that duty.

(ii) The principle and promissory estoppel

The principle discussed here resembles, but is distinct from, the doctrine of promissory estoppel as defined in the dictum, set out above, from *BP v Hunt (No 2)*. It depends on the possibility of B's action or inaction leading to A's acquisition of a right and, to that extent only, it depends on there being a legal relationship between A and B. Where B's action or inaction is capable of giving A a right, this will often be a result of a pre-existing contract between A and B. However, a contract is clearly not necessary: it may be, for example, that a statute stipulates that B's action or inaction is capable of giving A a right.[33] The principle depends on A, by his words or conduct, making a promise to B, either that A's right will not be enforced or that such right will not arise. The principle also requires reliance by B, by action or inaction; but, contrary to the formulation in *BP v Hunt (No 2)*, that reliance should not be defined as broadly as any reliance that 'renders it inequitable, in all the circumstances, for [A] to enforce his strict rights, or at least to do so until [B] is restored to his former position'. Rather, B's reliance consists specifically in action or inaction that is capable of giving A a right. The effect of the principle, it seems, is to prevent A from acquiring that right. So, there is no need to see if it is inequitable, in all the circumstances, for A to enforce his strict rights: if the requirements of the principle are met, A's right simply does not arise. As a result, B is necessarily, in a general sense, restored to his former position: for example, in *Hughes*, B was returned, at the end of the negotiations, to the position he was in before those negotiations started: he had a period of six months to complete the repairs, less any time lapsed from A's initial notice to perform the repairs to the start of the negotiations.

---

[33] See eg *Durham Fancy Goods Ltd v Michael Jackson (Fancy Goods) Ltd and another* [1968] 2 QB 839, where, but for the application of the principle discussed here, s 108 of the Companies Act 1948 would have given A a right against B, due to B's signature of a bill of exchange incorrectly stating the name of the company on which the bill was intended to be drawn.

As suggested above, however, the real focus of the principle may not be to protect B but rather to ensure that A does not benefit from B's action or inaction.

The principle, like the 'acceptance of substitute performance' principle, thus differs from the orthodox general formulation of promissory estoppel. Moreover, the principle operates in situations not generally considered to fall within the ambit of promissory estoppel. In particular, it can be seen in parts of the doctrine of common law waiver or forbearance. For example, A may have a power to terminate a contract if B fails to perform by an agreed date. A may then agree to B's performing after that date. If B, in reliance on that promise, fails to perform by the initially agreed date, A has no power to terminate the contract.[34] Further, a closely related principle can be seen in cases relating to licences of land. B's unauthorized presence on A's land ordinarily gives A particular rights against B, such as a privilege to use reasonable force to remove B from the land and a power to claim damages from B. If A invites B onto A's land, A's consent clearly prevents those rights from arising. If B's licence is purely gratuitous, A may choose to revoke his consent at any time. If A does so after B has entered onto A's land, however, A cannot assert a right consequent on B's unauthorized presence on B's land unless A has first given B a reasonable period to leave the land.[35] It is only after that period that B can be said to have chosen to act in the way necessary to give A such a right.

The principle can explain a number of important cases generally said to depend on the application of promissory estoppel, such as *Hughes* and *Birmingham*. It also assists in explaining the notion that promissory estoppel does not give rise to a cause of action. It is first worth noting, as Handley has pointed out,[36] that it may not be technically correct to say that the principle applied in *Hughes* cannot be used to found a cause of action: after all, in *Hughes* itself, it was B (the Metropolitan Railway Company) that brought a claim for an injunction, following A's successful action for ejectment. Nor is the principle purely defensive: for example, consider a case where B plans to make a claim against A. B has a particular period in which to make the claim, before it becomes limitation-barred. Before the expiry of that period, A gives B an extension, promising that he will not rely on

---

[34] See eg *Hickman v Haynes* (1875) LR 10 CP 598. The principle applies even if, for example due to the operation of a formality rule, A's agreement to late performance is not a contractually binding variation: see eg *Levey & Co v Goldberg* [1922] 1 KB 688.

[35] See eg *Minster of Health v Bellotti* [1944] 1 KB 298, at 305-6; J Hill, 'The Termination of Bare Licences' [2001] *Cambridge L J* 89.

[36] K Handley, *Estoppel by Conduct and Election* (London: Sweet & Maxwell, 2006) 13-007.

the limitation bar. As a result, B forgoes the opportunity to bring his claim within the initial period. On the expiry of that initial period, A would otherwise acquire a right: an immunity from B's making a claim. However, the *Hughes* principle operates to prevent A acquiring such a right at the expiry of the initial period. The principle can thus be used in support of B's claim against A. Nonetheless, as applied to the *Hughes* principle, the notion that promissory estoppel cannot operate as a cause of action is essentially correct: the principle aims to prevent A's acquisition of a particular right.

The principle can also make some sense of the difficult idea that promissory estoppel, in some cases at least, has only suspensive effect. That idea is technically inaccurate. For example, in *Hughes*, A's power to terminate the lease for B's failure to repair within the initial six-month period *was* extinguished; similarly in *Birmingham*, A's power to regain possession on the land for B's failure to build within the initially agreed periods *was* extinguished. Nonetheless, it does capture two aspects of the *Hughes* principle. First, there is an important difference between the *Hughes* principle and the acceptance of substituted performance principle discussed in part (a) above. For example, if the latter had applied in *Hughes*, B's duty to perform the requested repairs would have been discharged, and A would have permanently lost the chance to terminate for a breach of that particular duty. But that was not the case, as A had not consented to B's inaction counting as performance of B's duty to repair. So, A could have exercised the power to terminate if the repairs had not been completed within the extended period, taking into account the hiatus for negotiations. That point may be captured by the rather imprecise idea that promissory estoppel may operate suspensively.

Second, the notion of suspensive effect is one way of explaining the possible effect of A's retraction of his promise *before* the point when A's right would otherwise arise. As can be seen in the discussion above of A's revocation of a gratuitous licence acted on by B, the rights A ordinarily acquires as a result of B's unauthorized presence on A's land will arise if B remains on the land after the expiry of a reasonable period from the time of A's revocation. This idea is also present in the factually complex case of *Tool Metal Manufacturing Co Ltd v Tungsten Electric Co Ltd*.[37] A had licensed B to make use of A's patent, on condition that B pay A not only royalties but also additional compensation, due if B sold or used in its production processes more than a certain quantity of particular material not purchased from A or A's licensees.

---

[37] [1955] 1 WLR 761. Hereafter *Tool Metal*.

In 1942, pending negotiations for a new licence agreement, A promised B that it would forgo those additional payments. In 1944, B rejected the new agreement proposed by A. In litigation between the parties, A made a counterclaim insisting on the additional payments. A did not seek full arrears: as in *High Trees* it can be assumed that A was bound by its acceptance of B's substitute performance (payment of royalties alone without the additional compensation) during 1942–1944. A initially claimed that arrears were due from June 1945—a point nine months after B's rejection of the proposed new agreement. A's claim was therefore premised on the view that, even when the end of negotiations between A and B removed the basis on which A had forgone the additional payments, A had to allow B a 'grace period' before reasserting its right to those payments. When it was held by the Court of Appeal that B's rejection of the new agreement did not put B on notice of A's intention to reassert its right,[38] A instead successfully claimed arrears from January 1947—nine months after A's service of its counterclaim.[39]

The necessity of a 'grace period' can be explained by reference to the *Hughes* principle as set out here. The logic of that principle is that A cannot claim a right as a result of particular action or inaction by B, if A has induced that action or inaction by leading B to believe that A's right would not arise, or would not be enforced by A. That principle must also apply if A attempts to revoke such a promise without giving B sufficient time to alter the course of conduct which would otherwise give rise to A's right. In *Tool Metal*, the relevant conduct of B, leading to A's acquisition of a right under the additional compensation clause, consisted of B's sourcing of the material used in its production processes. If B had made particular arrangements as to that sourcing on the basis of A's promise that it would not claim the extra compensation, then the logic of the *Hughes* principle suspends A's right until B

---

[38] Devlin J had found that the grace period began with B's rejection of the proposed new agreement, but the Court of Appeal reversed that finding: (1952) 69 RPC 108.

[39] Pearson J found in A's favour on that new claim, but the Court of Appeal ([1954] 1 WLR 862) reversed that finding, surprisingly concluding that even delivery of the counterclaim did not put B on notice of A's intent to reassert its right to the additional compensation payments. The House of Lords ([1955] 1 WLR 761), however, restored Pearson J's order and so allowed A's claim for payments as from January 1947. By pointing out that A can give effective notice to B of his intention to reassert his right without giving a fixed date from which the right will be reasserted, the House of Lords corrected the Court of Appeal's misunderstanding of the effect of the Privy Council's advice in *Canadian Pacific Railway Co v The King* [1931] AC 414.

has had reasonable time to adjust its conduct in light of A's revocation of its promise.[40]

(ii) Applying the principle to a promise to accept a lesser sum in satisfaction of a debt

The question to be asked here is whether the *Hughes* principle can provide any assistance to B in a case where A promises to accept a lower sum in satisfaction of debt, but then refuses to do so. As argued in *Collier*,[41] it may be that B has made particular arrangements on the basis that the lower sum would be accepted; B may therefore claim it would be inequitable for A to insist on the full extent of the debt, or at least to do so without first allowing B a 'grace period'.

It is clear, however, that the *Hughes* principle is of no assistance to B in such a case. The simple point is that, where A seeks to enforce a pre-existing debt, A is not attempting to enforce a right arising as a result of action or inaction of B induced by A on the basis that A would not acquire, or would not enforce, such a right. A's right to the sum due clearly exists in advance of, and independently of, any action by B in reliance on A's promise. This explains why, in *Foakes*, the House of Lords made no mention of its decision in *Hughes* (even though both the Earl of Selborne LC and Lord Blackburn had served on the Committee of the House of Lords in *Hughes*).[42] Similarly, the *Hughes* principle is perfectly consistent with the decision of the House of Lords in *Jorden v Money*:[43] in that case, the principle did not apply as A's right arose independently of any action by B in reliance on the belief that A would not enforce the debt.

This analysis makes clear that, whenever B's reliance on A's promise does not consist of providing a substitute performance accepted by A, nor of a course of conduct which would otherwise give A a right, neither of the principles discussed in part (a) or part (b) can assist B. Instead, B must attempt to rely on a third principle.

---

[40] See eg *per* Lord Tucker, at 785.

[41] [2007] EWCA Civ 1329, [2008] 1 WLR 643.

[42] In *High Trees*, Denning J ([1947] KB 130, at 135) implied that the *Hughes* principle was overlooked in *Foakes* due to its equitable basis. That suggestion is, however, unconvincing: see eg D Gordon, 'Creditors' Promises to Forgo Rights' [1963] *Cambridge L J* 222.

[43] (1854) 5 HL Cas 185.

**(c) The prospect of B's suffering a detriment as a result of
B's reasonable reliance on A's promise**

(i) The principle

This principle applies where: (i) A has made a promise to B that B has,
or will acquire, a right; (ii) B has reasonably relied on that promise; and
(iii) B would now suffer a detriment if A were wholly free to renege on
that promise. In such a case, B may argue that A is under a duty to B
to ensure that B does not suffer a detriment as a result of his reasonable reliance on A's promise. A's duty, as it is focused on the need to
avoid B's detriment, need not be a duty to put B in the position he
would have occupied had A's promise been performed. In contrast to
the principle discussed in part (a), there is no need for B's reliance to
consist in B's rendering a substitute performance of a duty owed to A.
In contrast to the principle discussed in part (b), there is no need for
B's reliance to take the form of action or inaction that would otherwise
give A a right. And, in contrast to each of the principles discussed in
part (a) and part (b), this third principle operates to impose a new duty
on A to B, rather than merely to extinguish a duty owed by B to A, or
to prevent A from acquiring a right.

(ii) The principle and promissory estoppel

The principle shares some features with the doctrine of promissory
estoppel as defined in the dictum, set out above, from *BP v Hunt (No
2)*. For example, it may be triggered by *any* form of reasonable reliance by B: it does not require B's reliance to take a specific form, such
as the rendering of a substitute performance, or conduct that would
otherwise give A a right. In addition, the notion of limiting A's enforcement of his rights 'at least…until [B] is restored to his former position'
does capture the idea of ensuring that B does not suffer a detriment
as a result of his reliance of A. There are, nonetheless, clear differences between the operation of promissory estoppel and the effect
of the principle. In particular, on the formulation given in *BP v Hunt
(No 2)*, promissory estoppel can apply only where A has promised 'not
to enforce his strict rights' against B. As a result, if B wishes to argue
that the principle imposes a new duty on A to B, B must attempt to turn
to *proprietary* estoppel. For example, in *Crabb v Arun District Council*,[44]
B acted in reliance on a belief, induced by A's conduct, that A would

---

[44] [1976] Ch 179.

grant him a right of way over A's land. As a result, B claimed that A was estopped from denying the existence of that right of way. Lord Denning MR admitted that:

> [w]hen [counsel for B] said that he put his case on an estoppel, it shook me a little: because it is commonly supposed that estoppel itself is not a cause of action. But that is because there are estoppels and estoppels. Some do give rise to a cause of action. Some do not. In the species of estoppel called proprietary estoppel, it does give rise to a cause of action.[45]

The distinction made by Lord Denning MR emphasizes that English law[46] has been reluctant to accept that the principle discussed can operate as a means to impose a new duty on A to B.[47] That acceptance has principally been manifested in the doctrine of *proprietary* estoppel[48] and has thus been generally[49] confined to cases where A's promise is that B has, or will get, a right relating to land.[50] Nonetheless, examples can be found where the principle has been applied and the result instead attributed to the application of promissory estoppel.[51]

---

[45] *Ibid*, at 187.

[46] The principle has, of course, been more fully accepted in jurisdictions in the United States and Australia: see eg Restatement (Second) of Contracts, s 90 and *Waltons Stores (Interstates) Ltd v Maher* (1988) 164 CLR 387.

[47] That reluctance was confirmed by the Court of Appeal in *Baird Textiles Holdings Ltd v Marks & Spencer plc* [2002] 1 All ER (Comm) 737, [2001] CLC 999. In that case, however, even if the principle had been extended, B's claim appeared hopeless, as there was no evidence that A had made a promise that the parties' relationship would continue.

[48] This supports Halson's suggestion that any attempt to extend the application of the principle in English law should not be made by altering the current scope of promissory estoppel: see R Halson, 'The Offensive Limits of Promissory Estoppel' [1999] *LMCLQ* 256.

[49] For an example of proprietary estoppel's application beyond such a case, see *Strover v Strover* [2005] EWHC 860, [2005] NPC 64.

[50] If A's promise is a promise to give B a right in relation to land *and* other property, the principle can also impose a duty on A in relation to that other property: see eg *Re Basham* [1986] 1 WLR 1498.

[51] In *Yeoman's Row Management Ltd v Cobbe* [2008] UKHL 55, [2008] 1 WLR 1752, at [14], Lord Scott made the surprising suggestion that a proprietary estoppel is simply a 'sub-species of a "promissory" estoppel'. That suggestion was based on the view that each doctrine has a purely preclusionary effect. Such an analysis is, however, very hard to square with the ability of proprietary estoppel to impose a new duty on A to B: see further B McFarlane & A Robertson, 'The Death of Proprietary Estoppel' [2008] *LMCLQ* 449. It was also doubted by Lord Walker in *Thorner v Major* [2009] UKHL 18, [2009] 1 WLR 776, at [67] and is, indeed, inconsistent with the use of proprietary estoppel permitted in that case by all members of the Committee of the House of Lords other than Lord Scott: see further B McFarlane & A Robertson (2009) 125 *LQR* 535.

First, there are cases where promissory estoppel has been called in aid due to a misunderstanding as to the limits of proprietary estoppel.[52] For example, in *Maharaj v Chand*,[53] A, a sub-lessee of land held by the Native Land Trust Board of Fiji, promised B, his unmarried partner, that the land would be her permanent home. As a result, B gave up her own flat to move in with A, looked after their children, and contributed to household expenses and bills. The Privy Council seems to have assumed that a successful proprietary estoppel claim would necessarily have led to B's acquisition of a property right in A's land. Such a result would have been problematic as the Native Land Trust Act made it unlawful for A to 'alienate or deal with' the land without the consent of the Board. The Privy Council advised, however, that '[n]either the terms nor the spirit of the section are violated by an estoppel or equity operating *inter partes*' and that B could therefore use *promissory* estoppel to claim a purely personal right against A: a licence to live permanently on the land. The label of promissory estoppel was invoked to justify B's acquisition of a personal rather than a proprietary right. However, that move was unnecessary: there is no reason why the right acquired by a proprietary estoppel claimant cannot be only a personal right against A.[54]

Second, the principle may also explain the results of some promissory estoppel cases, unrelated to land, that lie outside the reach of the principles discussed in part (a) and part (b). For example, in *The Ion*,[55] B, a time charterer, wished to make a claim against A, a ship owner, outside the one-year period permitted by the Hague Rules. B argued that A had indicated, in correspondence with B, that A had no objection to B's claim being made outside that period. The principle discussed in part (b) could not apply, as that communication was made *after* the expiry of the one-year period. Mocatta J nonetheless invoked promissory estoppel to hold that A could not rely on the time bar. His Lordship found that: (i) as a result of A's implied promise not to rely

---

[52] For a recent example, see *Luo v Hui Shui See* [2008] HKEC 996 (Court of Final Appeal of Hong Kong, June 2008): noted Lee & Ho (2009) 125 *LQR* 25. Promissory estoppel was used in that case as A had made a promise to give B a right relating to land owned not by A, but by a company of which A was a director. There is no reason, however, why A's inability to give B the promised right, if unknown to B, should prevent the application of proprietary estoppel: see S Bright & B McFarlane, 'Personal Liability in Proprietary Estoppel' [2005] *Conv* 14.

[53] [1986] AC 898.

[54] See, eg *Jennings v Rice* [2002] EWCA Civ 159, [2003] 1 P & CR 100 (B acquired a right to receive a money payment from A); *Parker v Parker* [2003] EWHC (Ch) 846, (B acquired a licence to use A's land). See further B McFarlane, 'Proprietary Estoppel and Third Parties After the Land Registration Act 2002' [2003] *Cambridge L J* 661.

[55] *Nippon Yusen Kaisha v Pacifica Navegacion SA* [1980] 2 Lloyds Rep 245.

on the time bar, B had not brought his claim more promptly; and (ii) if A were now allowed to renege on the promise, B would suffer a detriment—although it would be able to apply for an extension of time,[56] B's application would be prejudiced by the delay caused by its reliance on A's promise.

(iii) *Applying the principle to a promise to accept a lesser sum in satisfaction of a debt*

Even to the limited extent that it is currently accepted in English law, the principle is prima facie capable of applying to a case in which A promises to accept a lesser sum in payment of a debt. B's reasonable reliance on A's promise, for example by altering his financial arrangements, may lead to B's suffering a detriment if A is free to renege on the promise. And B's claim is not that a new duty has been imposed on A, but rather that, in order to ensure that B does not suffer a detriment, A should be prevented from simply enforcing his pre-existing right against B. It may be that A can discharge his duty to ensure that B suffers no detriment without keeping his promise: in particular, postponing A's right to full payment may suffice to prevent B suffering a detriment as a result of his reliance on A's promise. Of course, in no case will A have to do more than accept the promised lower sum in discharge of the debt: it is clear in principle, and has also been established in cases of proprietary estoppel,[57] that B can have no complaint if A performs his promise.

The approach adopted by the House of Lords in *Foakes*,[58] however, seems to obstruct the application of the principle to a promise to accept a lesser sum. As noted in part (a), if the principle on which B seeks to rely focuses chiefly on A's consent, there may be an argument, albeit an ultimately unconvincing one, in favour of excluding cases in which B claims A has consented to the acceptance of a lesser sum in discharge of a debt. The principle discussed here, however, depends not only on A's promise but also on the need to prevent B suffering a detriment; and that need may also arise where A's promise is to accept a lesser sum. It is true that the mere fact of B's making arrangements to pay the lesser sum should not be grounds on which B can claim a relevant detriment; after all, B had a pre-existing duty to make such a payment and so could not be said to have altered his position in a

---

[56] Such an application could have been made under s 27 of the Arbitration Act 1950.

[57] See, eg *Dodsworth v Dodsworth* (1973) 228 EG 1115, *per* Russell LJ; *Baker v Baker* [1993] 2 FLR 247, at 251, *per* Dillon LJ.

[58] (1884) LR 9 App Cas 605.

legally relevant way. There is no doctrinal reason, however, why other forms of action by B could not constitute the reliance necessary for the principle's application.

For example, in *Collier*,[59] each counsel's interpretation of the 'promissory estoppel point' seemed to focus on this principle, and hence on the need to prevent B suffering a detriment. As noted in part (a)(iii), counsel for B argued that B had relied on A's promise, not only in failing to pursue an arrangement with his now bankrupt former partners, but also in conducting his finances so as to enable payment of one-third of the full liability, but no more.[60] In response, it seems counsel for A spent some time arguing that B's action would not, in fact, cause him any detriment were the full debt to be enforced: indeed, Arden LJ noted that:

> there is no evidence that [B's] position now is in any material respect different from that immediately before the agreement was made. For instance, there is no evidence that he entered into any business venture or made any substantial investment on the strength of the agreement.[61]

As argued in part (a), the question of whether B would suffer a detriment as a result of A's enforcement of the full debt was in fact irrelevant in *Collier*: B's duty to A was discharged by A's acceptance of the lesser sum. Nonetheless, the discussion in *Collier* may provide a foretaste of the position arising, if the principle discussed in this section is to be accepted, in cases where A makes and then revokes (before payment by B) a promise to accept payment of a lesser sum. The tasks of having to determine if B reasonably relied on such a promise and how, if at all, B would now suffer a detriment if A reneged on the promise may not be ones for which a court would have much enthusiasm. Yet the prospect of having to deal with some nebulous allegations of reliance and detriment, such as those made in *Collier*, should not be enough to prevent the application of the principle to promises to accept a lesser sum in payment of debt. After all, courts regularly deal with such allegations when determining proprietary estoppel claims.[62]

---

[59] [2007] EWCA Civ 1329, [2008] 1 WLR 643.

[60] *Ibid*, at [34].

[61] *Ibid*, at [36].

[62] It is true that, in proprietary estoppel cases, reliance and (prospective) detriment may be relatively easy to prove. That is certainly the case if, for example, B builds on A's land in reliance on A's promise that B has or will acquire a right in that land: see, eg *Dillwyn v Llewellyn* (1862) 4 De GF & J 517; *Inwards v Baker* [1965] 2 QB 29. However, it cannot be said that, in proprietary estoppel, it is always a simple matter for a court to establish such reliance and detriment: see, eg *Lalani v Crump* [2007] EWHC (Ch) 47, (2007) EG 136 for a particularly speculative proprietary estoppel claim.

3. CONCLUSION

(a) Specific conclusions: promissory estoppel and debts

This paper has focused on the possible application of promissory estoppel to cases in which a creditor accepts, or promises to accept, payment of a lesser sum in discharge of a debt. It has been argued that there is no unitary doctrine of promissory estoppel, and that cases said to depend on the doctrine are better seen as instead applying one of three principles.

The first principle applies where B is under a duty to A and A accepts substitute performance by B of that duty. It operates to discharge B's duty and its purpose is the promotion of finality. As the principle is based on A's consent, and as there is no need for B to show that the requirements of a contract are present, particular care must be taken to ensure that A has genuinely consented to the discharge of B's duty by means of B's substitute performance. This is particularly true in cases where B's duty to A is a duty to pay a fixed sum to A and the substitute performance consists in B's payment of a lesser sum. The reasoning of the House of Lords in *Foakes* responds to these concerns by setting an absolute prohibition on the application of the principle to such cases. That reasoning was, however, unnecessary for the actual decision in *Foakes* and has been challenged by the analysis of Denning J in *High Trees* and the decision of the Court of Appeal in *Collier*. Certainly, it seems that the absolute prohibition is too blunt an instrument and that the general principle, if applied with due sensitivity to the particular facts of each case, should be permitted to operate so as to discharge B's duty if A accepts a lesser sum in satisfaction of a debt owed by B.

The second principle applies where A claims to have acquired a right as a result of particular action or inaction by B, but B, in choosing to act or not to act in that way, relied on a promise by A that A would not acquire, or would not enforce, the right A now claims. It operates to prevent A acquiring the right in question and its purpose is to prevent A acquiring a benefit as a result of B's reliance on A's promise. In a case involving continuing action or inaction by B, the principle will also operate to ensure that, even if A has retracted his promise, A will only acquire the right if B has been given sufficient time to adjust his conduct in light of A's retraction. In contrast to the first principle, this principle can *never* apply to a case where A has accepted, or promised to accept, a lesser sum in satisfaction of a debt due from B. This is for the simple reason that, in such a case, A's right pre-dates A's promise to B, and so does not arise as a result of any action or inaction by B undertaken in reliance on A's promise. It is for this reason that, in *Foakes*, the House of Lords made no reference to *Hughes*, one of its own (then) recent decisions exemplifying this second principle.

The third principle applies where A promises B that B has, or will acquire, a right and B reasonably relies on that promise with the result that B would suffer a detriment if A were wholly free to renege on the promise. It operates to place A under a duty to B to ensure that B does not suffer such a detriment and its purpose is to ensure B is not made worse off by his reasonable reliance on A's promise. Whilst this principle has gained only limited acceptance in English law, it is, in general, capable of applying where A makes a promise to B not to enforce a particular right against B. Despite this, the logic of the reasoning of the House of Lords in *Foakes* seems to prevent the application of the principle to cases where A promises to accept a lower sum in satisfaction of a debt owed by B. It may be that, as is the case in relation to the first principle, practical concerns provide some support for this restriction: it may be difficult to test B's claims that he has reasonably relied on such a promise and would suffer a detriment if A were wholly free to renege on it. Nonetheless, as is the case in relation to the first principle, this third principle should be capable of applying to such a case—not always to limit B's liability to the promised lower sum, but rather to ensure that B does not suffer a detriment as a result of his reasonable reliance on A's promise.

(b) General conclusions: the scope of promissory estoppel

On the analysis put forward here, the doctrine of promissory estoppel is in fact an unfortunate amalgam of at least three different principles. There is nothing to be gained from seeing those principles through the dark glass of a unitary doctrine of promissory estoppel. First, the language of estoppel is deeply misleading as it suggests a false analogy with estoppel by representation, leading to a false assumption that promissory estoppel can have only a preclusionary effect.[63] Second, the term 'promissory' may also be misleading: the first principle, discussed in part (a), depends on A's actual acceptance of alternative performance, not on A's promise to accept such performance; and, as far as the second and third principles are concerned, the necessary promise by A may be inferred from A's conduct without the need for an express

---

[63] For example, Treitel has noted that, whilst estoppel by representation affects a party's attempt to establish, as a matter of evidence, a particular fact (or matter of fact and law), each of promissory and proprietary estoppel instead concerns the *legal effect* of a promise: see, eg G Treitel, *Landmarks of Twentieth Century Contract Law* (Oxford: OUP, 2003) 37–40.

commitment by A. Third, and most importantly, the use of an umbrella term may lead to confusion between three distinct principles, as well as obscuring links between each of those principles and cases not seen to depend on promissory estoppel. It is not suggested that the disaggregation of promissory estoppel into distinct principles is sufficient to resolve all issues concerning the application of those principles.[64] It is, however, a necessary step towards a better understanding of just some of the various non-contractual doctrines by which A's promise, or manifestation of consent, may have a legal effect.

---

[64] One such question concerns the effect of a change of circumstances after A's consent or the making of A's promise: a point noted in passing by Lord Goff in *Motor Oil Hellas (Corinth) Refineries SA v Shipping Corporation of India (The Kanchenjunga)* [1990] 1 Lloyds Rep 391, at 400 ('If the known danger had become sufficiently different; or if a new and different danger had developed...other questions might have arisen') and raised by Lord Scott in *Thorner v Major* [2009] UKHL 19, [2009] 1 WLR 776, at [19].

7

Liability in Tort for Pre-Contractual Non-Disclosure

JOHN CARTWRIGHT*

The purpose of this paper is to examine the circumstances in which one party to a contract is liable to pay damages in tort for failure to disclose information to the other party during the negotiations. A particular focus of discussion is the suggestion in some recent cases, and in particular the decision in *Conlon v Simms*,[1] that there are circumstances in which a party can claim damages in the tort of deceit for loss suffered by entering into the contract following the other party's failure to disclose relevant information. However, an examination of this topic cannot be made without considering also the relationship between non-disclosure, misrepresentation, and mistake; the remedy of rescission of the contract for misrepresentation and non-disclosure; and the basis of liability in tort for pre-contractual misrepresentation.

1. NON-DISCLOSURE, MISREPRESENTATION, AND MISTAKE

Non-disclosure, misrepresentation, and mistake are linked, and it is important to understand the approach of English law to misrepresentation and mistake in contract in order to understand the approach to non-disclosure. The detail need not concern us here,[2] but in short it can be said that in a claim based on misrepresentation the claimant will assert that in entering into the contract he made a mistake which was caused by the defendant's communication to him of false information; in a claim based on non-disclosure the claimant will assert that he made a mistake or acted on the basis of certain false assumptions which would have been corrected if the defendant had given him (true) information.[3] If the claimant can assert only his own

---

* Professor of the Law of Contract, University of Oxford and Tutor in Law, Christ Church, Oxford; Professor of Anglo-American Private Law, University of Leiden.
[1] [2006] EWHC 401 (Ch), [2006] 2 All ER 1024 (Lawrence Collins J), affirmed on this point (but reversed on other grounds) [2006] EWCA Civ 1749, [2008] 1 WLR 484.
[2] J Cartwright, *Misrepresentation, Mistake and Non-Disclosure* (2nd edn, London: Sweet & Maxwell, 2007) parts I (misrepresentation), II (mistake), III (non-disclosure).
[3] *Ibid*, paras 1.03–1.04, 16.03.

mistake about the facts or circumstances surrounding the contract,[4] he can obtain a remedy only in limited circumstances. English law is notoriously reluctant to allow a party to escape a contract as a result simply of his own mistake of fact;[5] and there is no question of damages being awarded because a claim for mistake does not assert that the defendant has done anything wrong that justifies imposing liability on him. The claim for misrepresentation, though, is quite a different matter. Misrepresentation is active, and causes a mistake on the part of the claimant. The defendant is responsible at least for having caused the mistake, and the remedy of rescission is in principle available for any misrepresentation which induces a contract.[6] The defendant may also be liable to pay damages in tort if the misrepresentation was made fraudulently or negligently.

Non-disclosure, on the other hand, is problematic.[7] It is passive, rather than active. To hold a defendant responsible for non-disclosure is to attribute responsibility to an omission. If the claimant made a mistake which was caused by the defendant (misrepresentation), it is a small step to hold the defendant responsible in law. But if the claimant made a mistake which was not caused by the defendant, but could have been corrected by him, it is not so obvious why the defendant should be held responsible: a source must first be found for the duty to act—the duty to disclose the information in question. And here is the real difficulty for English law: there is no general reason for imposing a duty to disclose; only particular reasons, based either on some pre-existing relationship between the parties[8] or on the nature of the

---

[4] A mistake may also be about the terms of the contract (the basis of the other party's offer) or the identity of the other contracting party: such mistakes raise different issues: Cartwright, above, n 2, para 12.07 and chs 13, 14. The context discussed in this paper is of mistake, misrepresentation, and non-disclosure of material facts.

[5] A unilateral mistake of fact, however serious, does not of itself render the contract void or voidable: *Statoil ASA v Louis Dreyfus Energy Services LP (The 'Harriette N')* [2008] EWHC 2257 (Comm), [2008] 2 Lloyd's Rep 685, following *Smith v Hughes* (1871) LR 6 QB 597. And a common (shared) mistake of fact renders the contract void only if it is so serious that it renders performance of the contract physically or at least commercially impossible: *Great Peace Shipping Ltd v Tsavliris Salvage (International) Ltd (The 'Great Peace')* [2002] EWCA Civ 1407, [2003] QB 679.

[6] *Redgrave v Hurd* (1881) 20 Ch D 1, CA.

[7] Pure non-disclosure, in the sense of simply an omission to communicate relevant information. For the purpose of all remedies for 'misrepresentation' a party may 'make a misrepresentation' not only by false words but also by conduct; or by omitting relevant information from a (true) statement thereby creating a misleading impression: Cartwright, above n 2, paras 3.04, 3.08. But in this paper it is assumed that the non-disclosure is the simple omission to communicate information.

[8] Eg a fiduciary or confidential relationship: *Tate v Williamson* (1866) LR 2 Ch App 55.

contract which they were negotiating which in law carries specific duties of disclosure.[9] The negotiations towards a contract are not a relationship carrying mutual duties of disclosure. Some other legal systems, such as continental civil law systems, can locate the duty of disclosure within the broader, general duty which is recognized to exist between parties negotiating a contract—and which is typically characterized as a duty of good faith.[10] But English law does not accept such a general duty. Indeed, the general starting point is the opposite: it has been said that that the relationship between parties negotiating a contract is inherently adversarial, at arm's length, and that the negotiating party's right to look to his own interests up to the moment of formation of the contract is displaced only if he makes a contractually binding promise or a misrepresentation.[11]

Where there is a duty of disclosure, the mere breach of it—like the mere misrepresentation which induces the contract—gives rise to the remedy of rescission. The additional requirement of the duty to disclose narrows the scope of actionable non-disclosure, and therefore removes the objection that the claimant should take responsibility for his own mistake. However, just as a mere misrepresentation does not give rise to the remedy of damages, but only where the misrepresentation gives rise to an established cause of action in tort, so there is no remedy in damages for mere breach of a duty of disclosure. The question, however, is whether and when the law of tort should apply to a pre-contractual non-disclosure. Assistance in answering this question may be found by considering first the law relating to liability for misrepresentation.

2. LIABILITY IN TORT FOR PRE-CONTRACTUAL MISREPRESENTATION

Broadly speaking, there are three bases of liability in tort for pre-contractual misrepresentation: the tort of deceit, the tort of negligence,

---

[9] Eg a contract of insurance: Marine Insurance Act 1906, s 18; *Pan Atlantic Insurance Co Ltd v Pine Top Insurance Co Ltd* [1995] 1 AC 501, HL.

[10] R Sefton-Green, *Mistake, Fraud and Duties to Inform in European Contract Law* (Cambridge: Cambridge University Press, 2005); J Cartwright and M Hesselink, *Precontractual Liability in European Private Law* (Cambridge: Cambridge University Press, 2008).

[11] *Walford v Miles* [1992] 2 AC 128, HL, at 138 (Lord Ackner). There have been calls to re-think *Walford* in so far as it rejected even *express* duties to negotiate in good faith (see eg *Petromec Inc v Petroleo Brasiliero SA* [2005] EWCA Civ 891, [2006] 1 Lloyd's Rep 121, at [121]) but it would be a complete *volte-face* if the Supreme Court were to go so far as to recognize a general, implied duty to negotiate in good faith along the lines recognized in continental systems; cf Ch 3.

and the claim under s 2(1) of the Misrepresentation Act 1967. Their scope of operation, however, is rather different. Deceit and negligence are torts which operate in, but are not limited to, the pre-contractual context. The claim under the Act is available only for pre-contractual misrepresentations, and is a statutory claim rather than a common law tort, although a successful claim gives rise to damages calculated on the tort measure. The tort of negligence operates over a much wider field than simply 'misrepresentation': making a statement is only one context for the duty of care, which may exist in relation to a wide range of acts and omissions. And, even where the defendant owes a duty of care in making a statement, the fact that his statement is false is not necessarily sufficient for liability since a person may make a misrepresentation but not be negligent if he took reasonable care in making it.[12] By contrast, the misrepresentation is at the core of the tort of deceit.

(a) The tort of deceit

The essence of the tort of deceit is the defendant's fraud by which the claimant was deceived. The defendant was dishonest, in the sense that he knew his statement was false, or did not believe it to be true, or was reckless whether it was true.[13] The policy of making the fraudulent party pay for his dishonesty can be seen throughout the tort, such as in the scope of loss for which the defendant is liable (all consequences, even if they were not foreseeable[14]), as well as in other consequences of fraud in the pre-contractual stage.[15]

---

[12] To that extent, the claim in negligence is not as such a claim for 'misrepresentation': 'misrepresentation is not the cause of action but evidence of the negligence which is the cause of action': *Hedley Byrne & Co Ltd v Heller & Partners* Ltd [1964] AC 465, HL, at 511 (Lord Hodson, quoting Lord Wrenbury in *Banbury v Bank of Montreal* [1918] AC 626, HL, at 713).

[13] *Derry v Peek* (1889) 14 App Cas 337, HL, at 374 (Lord Herschell), reversing CA (1887) 37 Ch D 541 which had held (following earlier cases) that 'fraud' was wider and included making a misrepresentation honestly but without reasonable grounds for believing it to be true (ie, in substance, negligence).

[14] 'It does not lie in the mouth of the fraudulent person to say that [the losses] could not reasonably have been foreseen': Lord Denning MR, *Doyle v Olby (Ironmongers) Ltd* [1969] 2 QB 158, CA, at 167; *Smith New Court Securities Ltd v Citibank* [1997] AC 254, HL, at 266-7 (Lord Browne-Wilkinson), at 282 (Lord Steyn). In negligence, the defendant is liable for only such of the claimant's losses as are of a kind that he could reasonably have foreseen: *Overseas Tankship (UK) Ltd v Morts Dock & Engineering Co (The 'Wagon Mound')* [1961] AC 388, PC.

[15] Rescission is available for fraudulent and non-fraudulent misrepresentations; but there are certain rules relating to that remedy which apply differently in the case of fraud, eg the court is more reluctant to find that rescission is barred by impossibility of restitution, and it has no discretion under s 2(2) Misrepresentation Act 1967 to refuse rescission and make the claimant take damages in lieu: Cartwright, above, n 2, para 4.30.

On the other hand, the defendant's fraud does not attract a remedy unless it achieved its object. Deceit requires a misrepresentation upon which (as the defendant intended) the claimant relied and thereby suffered loss.[16] The misrepresentation may be by words or conduct, but it is the active communication of a falsehood, believed by the claimant, that constitutes the deception.[17]

(b) The tort of negligence

By contrast with the tort of deceit, the courts have only relatively recently accepted that a negligent misrepresentation can give rise to a claim in damages for economic loss. That step was taken by the House of Lords in 1963 in *Hedley Byrne & Co Ltd v Heller & Partners Ltd*,[18] which was applied by the Court of Appeal in 1976 to a pre-contractual misrepresentation.[19] Where the statement was made not fraudulently but only negligently the courts are more reluctant to impose liability[20] and they require a good reason for imposing a duty to take care in making a statement. In effect, the tort of deceit is based on the idea that there is a general duty of honesty in making statements: the proof of dishonesty (fraud) is sufficient to give rise to liability if the claimant relied on the false statement and suffered loss. But there is no such general duty of reasonable care in making a statement: only where there is a 'special relationship' between the parties;[21] where the defendant can foresee the use that might be made of the statement by the claimant and the defendant can reasonably expect the claimant to rely on the statement without independent verification;[22] or where the defendant 'assumed

---

[16] *Bradford Third Equitable Building Society v Borders* [1941] 2 All ER 205, HL, at 211 (Viscount Maugham).

[17] *Peek v Gurney* (1873) LR 6 HL 337, at 391 (Lord Chelmsford), at 403 (Lord Cairns); *Arkwright v Newbold* (1881) 17 Ch D 301, CA, at 324-5 (Cotton LJ); *Smith v Chadwick* (1884) 9 App Cas 187, at 196 (Lord Blackburn: inducement of claimant by the misrepresentation must be proved, but can be inferred on the facts).

[18] [1964] AC 465.

[19] *Esso Petroleum Co Ltd v Mardon* [1976] QB 801, CA.

[20] Cf the discussions in *Hedley Byrne*, above, n 18, about the caution which the courts should exercise in extending the tort of negligence to misstatements causing economic loss: eg Lord Pearce, at 534 ('words are more volatile than deeds. They travel fast and far afield. They are used without being expended and take effect in combination with innumerable facts and other words. Yet they are dangerous and can cause vast financial damage'). See also Lord Reid at 482-3.

[21] *Hedley Byrne*, above, n 18, at 486, 505, 525, 539.

[22] *Caparo Industries plc v Dickman* [1991] 2 AC 605, HL, at 638 (Lord Oliver).

responsibility' to the claimant for the accuracy of the statement, or for the care which he was taking in making the statement.[23]

(c) Section 2(1) of the Misrepresentation Act 1967

The relationship between parties negotiating a contract may be such as to give rise to a duty of care regarding the accuracy of statements where one party has particular access to relevant information and provides it to the other party as an inducement to enter into the contract, the context in which pre-contractual misrepresentations typically arise.[24] In practice, however, little use is made of the tort of negligence here because s 2(1) of the Misrepresentation Act 1967 provides a more attractive remedy. If the claimant can show that he has suffered loss after entering into a contract following a misrepresentation made by the defendant (the other party to the contract) and if the defendant would have been liable if he had been fraudulent, the claimant recovers damages unless the defendant can show that he honestly and on reasonable grounds believed that his statement was true. That is, there is a presumption of liability for pre-contractual misrepresentation which places on the defendant the burden of proving that he was both honest (not fraudulent) and reasonable in his belief (not negligent)—which makes the claim significantly easier than in the tort of negligence.[25] And the measure of damages has been held to be the same as in the tort of deceit, which can extend to a wider range of consequential losses than in the tort of negligence.[26] This last point has been criticized in so far as it appears to 'treat a person who was morally innocent as if he was guilty of fraud',[27] and may be reconsidered in an appropriate case by the Supreme Court. For present purposes, it is sufficient to note that there is no doubt that the presence of *fraud*—dishonesty—is of itself

---

[23] *Hedley Byrne*, above, n 18, at 483, 486, 494, 529, which was extended to cover an assumption of responsibility for the careful performance of a task (eg undertaking a service, as well as giving information or advice) by *Henderson v Merrett Syndicates Ltd* [1995] 2 AC 145, HL.

[24] *Esso Petroleum Co Ltd v Mardon*, above, n 19.

[25] *Howard Marine & Dredging Co Ltd v A Ogden & Sons (Excavations) Ltd* [1978] QB 574, CA.

[26] *Royscot Trust Ltd v Rogerson* [1991] 2 QB 297, CA; cf *The 'Wagon Mound'*, above, n 14.

[27] *Smith New Court Securities Ltd v Citibank* [1997] AC 254, HL, at 283 (Lord Steyn). The interpretation in *Royscot*'s case, above, n 26, appears to be what was intended by the draftsman of the Act, or at least the Law Reform Committee which proposed it, which thought that 'it is not in general the function of the civil law to grade the damages which an injured person may recover in accordance with the moral guilt of the defendant': 10th Report, *Innocent Misrepresentation* (1962), para 22. But it is clear that now the courts do seek to draw distinctions between fraud and non-fraud in attributing responsibility.

enough to justify the intervention of the law, to allow the deceived party not only to rescind the contract but also to claim damages to cover all his losses which flow from the fraud. But if the defendant was not fraudulent, then even though rescission is available, it appears to be less obvious that the party who caused the loss by his misrepresentation, even if he was careless, should have the same scope of liability in damages.

3. NON-DISCLOSURE IN THE PRE-CONTRACTUAL STAGE: THE TRADITIONAL VIEW

There is therefore a well trodden path for a party to a contract to make a claim for damages in tort for loss suffered by entering into a contract following a misrepresentation by the other party: a dishonest misrepresentation has long given rise to a claim in the tort of deceit. And even a negligent misrepresentation may now do so, either in the tort of negligence or under the Misrepresentation Act 1967—although the extension to cover non-fraudulent misrepresentations is relatively recent, and has been taken more cautiously. When we consider claims based not on misrepresentation but on pre-contractual non-disclosure, however, the picture changes.

(a) Section 2(1) of the Misrepresentation Act 1967

It should first be noted that s 2(1) of the Misrepresentation Act 1967—in practice the most useful of the claims for tort damages for pre-contractual misrepresentation—appears to offer no assistance here, at least if it is read literally. The Act provides a remedy 'where a person has entered into a contract after a *misrepresentation* has been *made* to him by another party thereto', and it has been held by the Court of Appeal that the italicized words require an active misrepresentation. Even if the defendant owes the claimant a duty of disclosure sufficient to give the claimant the right to rescind the contract (such as the duty on a party taking out a contract of insurance to disclose material facts to the insurer), the breach of the duty does not give rise to a claim under the Act:[28]

> If section 2(1) is to apply at all, a misrepresentation has to have been 'made' to the complainant by the other party. The expression 'misrepresentation

---

[28] *Banque Keyser Ullmann SA v Skandia (UK) Insurance Co Ltd* [1990] 1 QB 665, CA, at 790. The point was not discussed on appeal to HL, [1991] 2 AC 249.

... made' (which is repeated in several later sections of the Act of 1967) would, in our judgment, on the ordinary meaning of words be inapt to refer to a misrepresentation which had not been made in fact but was (at most) merely deemed by the common law to have been made. If it had been the intention of the legislature that a mere failure to discharge the duty of disclosure in the case of a contract uberrimae fidei would fall to be treated as the 'making' of a representation within the meaning of the Act of 1967, we are of the opinion that the legislature would have said so.

(b) The tort of deceit

The courts have traditionally defined the tort of deceit by reference to 'misrepresentation' which apparently excludes the case of non-disclosure, even if it constitutes a breach of a duty of disclosure. For example, in *Peek v Gurney* Lord Cairns said:[29]

> Mere non-disclosure of material facts, however morally censurable, however that non-disclosure might be a ground in a proper proceeding at a proper time for setting aside an allotment or a purchase of shares, would in my opinion form no ground for an action in the nature of an action for misrepresentation. There must, in my opinion, be some active misstatement of fact, or, at all events, such a partial and fragmentary statement of fact, as that the withholding of that which is not stated makes that which is stated absolutely false.

There have been suggestions to the contrary. In *Brownlie v Campbell*[30] Lord Blackburn said:

> And I go on further still to say, what is perhaps not quite so clear, but certainly it is my opinion, where there is a duty or an obligation to speak, and a man in breach of that duty or obligation holds his tongue and does not speak, and does not say the thing he was bound to say, if that was done with the intention of inducing the other party to act upon the belief that the reason why he did not speak was because he had nothing to say, I should be inclined myself to hold that that was fraud also.

However, this appears not to have been taken up, and more recently the Court of Appeal in *Banque Keyser Ullmann SA v Skandia (UK) Insurance Co Ltd*[31] rejected the argument that the tort of deceit applied in the case of an intentional breach of the duty of disclosure in a contract

---

[29] (1873) LR 6 HL 377, at 403; see also Lord Chelmsford, at 390-1. This statement was obiter, but was followed by CA in *Arkwright v Newbold* (1881) 17 Ch D 301, at 318, 320. See also *Bradford Third Equitable Building Society v Borders* [1941] 2 All ER 205, HL, at 211 (Viscount Maugham).

[30] (1880) 5 App Cas 925, at 950.

[31] Above, n 28, at 788.

uberrimae fidei. It was argued that (i) silence constitutes misrepresentation in a case where the duty of disclose is imposed by law (such as in an insurance contract); and (ii) because judges in such cases have sometimes referred to the wilful failure to disclose as 'fraudulent', this could constitute fraud for the purposes of the tort of deceit. However, this was rejected. Such references to 'fraud' were simply intended to refer to dishonest conduct, and 'lend no support to the proposition that non-disclosure involves an implied representation in such cases'.[32]

(c) The tort of negligence

The tort of negligence can, however, in principle apply to a case of non-disclosure. Since 'misrepresentation' is not a requirement of the tort but only one context in which the duty of care can arise,[33] a claim in negligence does not have to address the problem of whether 'non-disclosure' can in some sense amount to a 'misrepresentation'. Rather, the general test for the existence of a duty of care is applied. However, a duty of care will normally be found only where there is evidence on the facts of the assumption of responsibility[34] by one negotiating party to the other; and this is generally much more difficult to establish than in the case of an active misrepresentation, where the making of the statement can itself be evidence, in context, of the assumption of responsibility by the defendant. To find a duty to provide information requires either some prior conduct by the defendant evidencing his assumption of responsibility towards the claimant in relation to the provision of information, or some pre-existing relationship between the parties giving rise to a duty.[35] Moreover, the courts have recognized

---

[32] *Ibid*. Proposition (i) rested on textbook authority; proposition (ii) on statements in *Carter v Boehm* (1766) 3 Burr 1905, at 1911; 97 ER 1162, at 1165 (Lord Mansfield, referring to concealment as 'fraudulent, if *designed*') and *Blackburn, Low & Co v Vigors* (1866) 17 QBD 553, at 561 (Lord Esher MR). See also *HIH Casualty and General Insurance Ltd v Chase Manhattan Bank* [2003] UKHL 6, [2003] 2 Lloyd's Rep 61, at [75] (Lord Hoffmann: 'non-disclosure (whether dishonest or otherwise) does not as such give rise to a claim in damages').

[33] Above, n 12.

[34] Above, n 23.

[35] *Banque Keyser Ullmann SA v Skandia (UK) Insurance Co Ltd*, above, n 28, at 794-5 ('Can a mere failure to speak ever give rise to liability in negligence under *Hedley Byrne* principles? In our view it can, but subject to the all important proviso that there has been on the facts a voluntary assumption of responsibility in the relevant sense and reliance on that assumption. These features may be much more difficult to infer in a case of mere silence than in a case of misrepresentation.' CA went on to give as examples *Al-Kandari v JR Brown & Co* [1988] QB 665, CA, in which the solicitor's express undertaking to hold the passports of the claimant's husband and child gave rise to (inter alia) the duty to inform the claimant that the

that they should not use the tort of negligence in order to create duties
to provide information or advice which undermine the general principle that there is no duty of disclosure between parties negotiating an
ordinary commercial contract:[36]

> The general principle that there is no obligation to speak within the con-
> text of negotiations for an ordinary commercial contract (though qualified
> by the well known special principles relating to contracts uberrimae fidei,
> fraud, undue influence, fiduciary duty, etc) is one of the foundations of
> our law of contract, and must have been the basis of many decisions over
> the years. There are countless cases in which one party to a contract has
> in the course of negotiations failed to disclose a fact known to him which
> the other party would have regarded as highly material, if it had been
> revealed. However, ordinarily in the absence of misrepresentation, our law
> leaves that other party entirely without remedy.

And the court went further: even if there is a duty of disclosure for the
purposes of the remedy of rescission, this does not of itself give rise to
a concurrent duty in the tort of negligence:[37]

> We do not think that the nature of the contract as one of the utmost good
> faith can be used as a platform to establish a common law duty of care.
> ... The special obligation imposed in contracts of utmost good faith ... does
> not, if we are right, create a duty to speak for breach of which the law attaches
> the consequences which flow from an ordinary breach of duty, whether
> statutory or otherwise. It is a rule of law which provides, and provides
> only, that certain stated consequences (namely the insured party's right to
> avoid the contract) will follow if utmost good faith be not observed.

4. NON-DISCLOSURE IN THE PRE-CONTRACTUAL STAGE: RECENT DEVELOPMENTS

The traditional view that there can be no liability in the tort of deceit
for non-disclosure has recently been revised, although the full implications of the recent cases are not yet certain.

passport was in the hands of the Kuwait Embassy or may be released to the husband; and the
hypothetical example of a father who employs an estate agent for a fee to advise his son on
the proposed purchase of a house and the estate agent negligently fails to inform the son that
a motorway is shortly to be constructed within a few hundred yards of the property). See
also *Hamilton v Allied Domecq plc* [2007] UKHL 33, 2007 SC (HL) 142, at [19]-[23] (no assumption of responsibility on facts, so liability could only be for misrepresentation).

[36] *Ibid*, at 798–9, citing as authority *Bell v Lever Brothers Ltd* [1932] AC 161, HL, at 224 (Lord
Atkin) and *Smith v Hughes* (1871) LR 6 QB 597, at 607 (Blackburn J).
[37] *Ibid*, at 801.

In *HIH Casualty and General Insurance Ltd v Chase Manhattan Bank*[38] Rix LJ left open the question whether a combination of the duty to speak and dishonest non-disclosure can create a cause of action in deceit, although there was no detailed argument about the point, nor were any relevant cases discussed.[39] In the House of Lords, however, Lord Bingham,[40] relying on Lord Blackburn's rather tentative proposition in *Brownlie v Campbell*,[41] regarded it as 'uncontentious' that silence, where there is a duty to speak, may amount to misrepresentation and thought that the deliberate withholding of information, if done dishonestly or recklessly, may well amount to a fraudulent misrepresentation.

The next step was taken by Lawrence Collins J in *Conlon v Simms*,[42] holding for the first time by way of ratio that damages are available in the tort of deceit for fraudulent breach of a duty of disclosure. The duty there arose between partners negotiating their contract of partnership, and the judge said:[43]

> it is clear that where there is a duty to disclose, and the failure to disclose is fraudulent, there will be an action in deceit and damages will be an available remedy. In such cases 'the non-disclosure assumes the character of fraudulent concealment, or amounts to fraudulent misrepresentation, or is otherwise founded on, or characterized and accompanied by, fraud': *Spencer Bower* [*Actionable Non-disclosure* (2nd edn, 1990)] p 249 (para 14.02).

Although Lawrence Collins J's decision was reversed on other grounds, in the Court of Appeal Jonathan Parker LJ agreed expressly with the proposition that where the breach of a duty of disclosure is fraudulent, a party to whom the duty is owed who suffers loss by reason of the breach may recover damages in the tort of deceit. 'Non-disclosure where there is a duty to disclose is tantamount to an implied representation that there is nothing relevant to disclose.'[44] The approach

---

[38] [2001] EWCA Civ 1250, [2001] 2 Lloyd's Rep 483, at [48], [164], [168].

[39] *Peek v Gurney* and *Arkwright v Newbold*, above, n 17, were not cited, and *Banque Keyser Ullmann SA v Skandia (UK) Insurance Co Ltd*, above n 28, was discussed only for its rejection of damages as a general remedy for breach of the duty to disclose. There was no reference to its specific rejection of the argument that the tort of deceit applied in the case of an intentional breach of the duty of disclosure in a contract *uberrimae fidei*: above, n 32.

[40] [2003] UKHL 6, [2003] 2 Lloyd's Rep 61, at [21].

[41] Above n 30, quoted also by Lord Hoffmann, at [72], on the meaning of 'dishonesty'.

[42] [2006] EWHC 401 (Ch), [2006] 2 All ER 1024.

[43] *Ibid*, at [201].

[44] [2006] EWCA Civ 1749, [2008] 1 WLR 484, at [130].

of Lawrence Collins J has also been followed (although rather tentatively) at first instance.[45]

There is therefore some conflict in the authorities. The older cases generally took it as clear that non-disclosure could not of itself give rise to a claim for damages in the tort of deceit. This had been applied explicitly by the Court of Appeal to the case of non-disclosure in breach of a duty to disclose.[46] But now, without a full discussion of those earlier authorities, it is said to be 'clear' that the tort of deceit is engaged by the fraudulent non-disclosure of information which the defendant had a duty to disclose. And this is on the basis that the duty of disclosure is assimilated to misrepresentation: a failure to fulfil the duty to disclose 'is tantamount to an implied representation that there is nothing relevant to disclose'. The Law Commission[47] and textbook writers[48] have not accepted that the new approach in *Conlon v Simms* has overtaken the older approach. And one can criticize not only the failure of the recent cases to address the existing authorities, but also the reasoning by which they have reached the new position. The quotation by Lawrence Collins J from *Spencer Bower*, set out above, is not of itself adequate to justify the general proposition, and must be read in context.[49] What *Spencer Bower* says is not that every dishonest non-disclosure in breach of a duty of disclosure gives rise to damages, but that a non-disclosure does not give rise to damages unless it 'assumes the character of fraudulent concealment, or amounts to fraudulent misrepresentation, or is otherwise founded on, or characterized and accompanied by, fraud'. However, the argument appears to have slid from one (uncontentious) proposition: sometimes the silent concealment of information can amount to a misrepresentation because it misleads the other party; to another (contentious) proposition: if there is a duty of disclosure, the failure to disclose is to be treated as if it

---

[45] *JD Wetherspoon plc v Van de Berg & Co Ltd* [2007] EWHC 1044 (Ch), [2007] PNLR 28, at [17] (Lewison J: one exception to the general rule that mere silence will not support an action for deceit 'is (*or at least may be*) where the person against whom the claim is made has a duty of disclosure and fraudulently fails to do so': emphasis added).

[46] *Banque Keyser Ullmann SA v Skandia (UK) Insurance Co Ltd*, above, n 28.

[47] Consultation Paper No 182, *Insurance Contract Law* (2007) para 2.42.

[48] Treitel, *The Law of Contract* (12th edn, London: Sweet & Maxwell, 2007) para 9.150, fn 681; Beale (ed), *Chitty on Contracts* (30th edn, London: Sweet & Maxwell, 2008) para 6.143.

[49] It should also be noted that the limited authority cited in the footnotes to that section of *Spencer Bower* does not include the older cases which are usually cited against the proposition, and that the edition pre-dates the express rejection by the Court of Appeal of the argument that the tort of deceit applies in the case of an intentional breach of the duty of disclosure in a contract *uberrimae fidei*: *Banque Keyser Ullmann SA v Skandia (UK) Insurance Co Ltd*, above, n 28.

were a misrepresentation; and so every intentional breach of a duty of disclosure gives rise to a claim in deceit. This broad proposition is very far-reaching, and would not be limited to the tort of deceit: if non-disclosure is simply assimilated to misrepresentation, then a pre-contractual non-disclosure would presumably also constitute a 'misrepresentation' for the purposes of s 2(1) of the Misrepresentation Act 1967,[50] and could overturn the case law which has decided that the Act does not apply to non-disclosure.[51] This would mean that every breach of a duty of disclosure would become actionable unless the party in breach could establish that he honestly and reasonably believed the truth of the facts whose accuracy would have been corrected if he had fulfilled his duty. It is not clear that the judges who have assumed in the recent cases that the tort of deceit can apply to breach of a duty of disclosure would have thought that such wide-ranging liability might follow.

At present, therefore, there is no firm basis in the case law for the application of the tort of deceit to non-disclosure, even if the non-disclosure was a breach of a duty of disclosure. On the other hand, it is too easy to stop at that point in the argument, and reject the suggestions in the recent cases that the tort of deceit should apply. Rather, we should consider the broader question of when the party who fails to disclose relevant information during negotiations for a contract should be liable to pay damages in tort to the other party for loss suffered by entering into the contract.

5. WHEN SHOULD THERE BE LIABILITY IN TORT FOR PRE-CONTRACTUAL NON-DISCLOSURE?

The approach to the imposition of liability for pre-contractual non-disclosure must fit with the approach to misrepresentation and mistake, and more generally with the broader policy relating to the allocation of risk and responsibility in pre-contractual negotiations. For example, English law could not sensibly award damages for all loss caused by

---

[50] The tort of negligence is not susceptible to such an argument since 'misrepresentation' is not the basis of the claim: above, n 12.

[51] Above, section 3(a); *Chitty*, above n 48, para 6.143. A counter-argument might be that the statute refers to a misrepresentation which has been 'made'—and this use of an active verb limits its scope to active misrepresentations. Similarly, the closing words of s 2(1) provide a defence if the party making the 'misrepresentation' shows that he honestly and reasonably believed 'that the *facts represented* were true'—a phrase which appears to assume an active representation.

every non-disclosure. Although any misrepresentation (fraudulent, negligent, or wholly innocent) is sufficient to warrant rescission of the contract thereby induced, there is no general remedy of damages for pre-contractual misrepresentation: damages are awarded (assuming that there is no breach of contract) only if a tort or a statutory claim can be established. Non-disclosure is less potent than misrepresentation in being passive rather than active, and therefore in not 'inducing' the contract in the same sense as a misrepresentation. At the very least, it would be very strange to attribute a stronger remedy in damages to non-disclosure than to misrepresentation: it would amount to strict liability for non-disclosure which is not at present thought to be appropriate in the case of misrepresentation.[52]

How, though, could we justify a more focused potential liability in damages for non-disclosure? Drawing by analogy on the law of pre-contractual misrepresentation and the law governing the remedy of rescission, two techniques are evident: defining the responsibility either by reference to the defendant's culpability, or by reference to a duty to disclose.

(a) Liability for fraudulent non-disclosure?

Within the law of misrepresentation, the courts use the defendant's culpability as a primary factor to define the scope of liability. A striking thing about the tort of deceit is how proof of the defendant's dishonesty appears to remove any concern about imposing liability on him. Absent fraud, the common law is cautious about imposing liability in tort for economic losses caused by reliance on statements. The fear is of indeterminate liability—the so-called 'floodgates' argument,[53] and special grounds have to be found to impose a duty to be careful in making statements. But if the defendant was dishonest and intended to cause the claimant's mistake, intended to induce him to enter into the contract, then however trivial the misrepresentation may be, the policy to remedy fraud takes over and the claimant recovers for all the losses which flow from having acted upon the fraud—even if it was not *the* reason for his deciding to enter into the contract, but only

---

[52] Cf *Banque Keyser Ullmann SA v Skandia (UK) Insurance Co Ltd*, above, n 28, at 781, rejecting the (significantly narrower) claim that breach of a duty of disclosure gives rise to a right to damages: 'it would not be right for this court by way of judicial legislation to create a new tort, effectively of absolute liability, which could expose either party to an insurance contract to a claim for substantial damages in the absence of any blameworthy conduct.'

[53] Above, n 20.

a reason.[54] Indeed, it has been held that it is sufficient for the defendant to make a misrepresentation which induces the claimant to persevere in a decision which he had already made—that is, it did not (as in the typical case) induce the claimant's mistake but confirmed it.[55] And the fraudulent defendant is not allowed to argue that the claimant was at fault (contributorily negligent) in making the mistake.[56]

Can this apparently overriding policy to remedy fraud be carried over to non-disclosure, to justify giving a remedy for dishonestly— intentionally or recklessly—allowing the claimant to remain under a relevant mistake and deliberately failing to disclose facts which the defendant knows and knows to be relevant, with a view to inducing the claimant thereby to enter into the contract? This depends upon whether the policy of remedying fraud is sufficient of itself to override the reluctance to sanction non-disclosure. And the answer, according to the traditional view in English law of the relationship between nego-tiating parties, is no. It is inconsistent with the established position set out by Blackburn J in *Smith v Hughes*:[57]

> even if the vendor was aware that the purchaser thought that the article possessed [some particular] quality, and would not have entered into the contract unless he had so thought, still the purchaser is bound, unless the vendor was guilty of some fraud or deceit upon him, and that a mere abstinence from disabusing the purchaser of that impression is not fraud or deceit; for, whatever may be the case in a court of morals, there is no legal obligation on the vendor to inform the purchaser that he is under a mistake, not induced by the act of the vendor.

The case of an arm's length contract of sale, as in *Smith v Hughes*, pro-vides a good test. One could rationally take the position that intention-ally allowing the buyer to misunderstand the facts relating to what he is buying should be remedied—should (in effect) be assimilated to the intentional misrepresentation of those facts, rather than to simple mis-take on the part of the buyer for which he takes the risk. This would in effect impose a general duty to disclose to the other party the fact that he is making a mistake. It may be said that, in practice, this will often be the result anyway: if the seller knows about the buyer's mistake, there may be an implied fraudulent misrepresentation because he will say

---

[54] *Attwood v Small* (1838) 6 Cl & Fin 232, at 502; 7 ER 684, at 785.

[55] *Barton v County NatWest Ltd* [1999] Lloyd's Rep Bank 408, CA, at [55], following *Austral-ian Steel & Mining Corpn Pty Ltd v Corben* [1974] 2 NSWLR 202.

[56] *Standard Chartered Bank v Pakistan Shipping Co (Nos 2 and 4)* [2002] UKHL 43, [2003] 1 AC 959.

[57] (1871) LR 6 QB 597, at 607.

or do something which implicitly confirms the mistake.[58] Or he may
be held impliedly to have warranted that the facts are true by allowing
the sale to go ahead without correcting the misunderstanding.[59] That
is, depending on the facts, the courts may be able to find an implied
representation or an implied contractual term out of fraudulent silence.
But it would be more straightforward to accept that, where the mistake
is one which would have given rise to a remedy if it had been induced
by a misrepresentation made by the defendant, and which is in fact
known by the defendant who deliberately chooses not to disclose
information which would have corrected it, the defendant's fraud is
sufficient to displace the normal rule that each party takes the risk of
his own mistakes. Such an approach would, of course, have to apply
also to the remedy of rescission, since it would be odd to give a remedy
in deceit to a case of non-disclosure without also allowing the mistaken
party to rescind. And this would also then be consistent with another
rule which has not yet been fully resolved.[60] If the claimant is labour-
ing under a mistake which was caused not by the defendant but by an
independent third party, it has been accepted that he may rescind the
contract if the defendant knew of the third party's misrepresentation.[61]
There is still a misrepresentation; but not one for which the defendant
was responsible, and as between the claimant and defendant it was
simply a mistake. But the defendant is not allowed to take advantage
of a contract which has been entered into under a mistake, where he
knows that the mistake was caused by a third party misrepresentation.
It is not a large step to rationalize this into a broader rule that a party
cannot take advantage of a mistake which he knows the other party is
making. And then to say that the knowledge of the mistake also constitutes fraud for the purposes of the tort of deceit.[62]

However, such a development in the law may go too far. It would
abandon a significant distinction on which the decision in *Smith v*

---

[58] *HIH Casualty and General Insurance Ltd v Chase Manhattan Bank* [2003] UKHL 6, [2003] 2
Lloyd's Rep 61, at [71] (Lord Hoffmann).

[59] Cf Sale of Goods Act 1979, s 14 (implied terms of satisfactory quality and fitness for purpose in contract of sale of goods: in effect, this provides an incentive on the business seller to
disclose known defects or limitations on fitness for purpose).

[60] Cartwright, above n 2, para 4.78.

[61] *Royal Bank of Scotland plc v Etridge (No 2)* [2001] UKHL 44, [2002] 2 AC 773, at [40] (Lord
Nicholls), at [144] (Lord Scott of Foscote).

[62] *Etridge* may also apply to allow rescission where the defendant had *constructive* notice
of the third party's representation: see, at [145] (Lord Scott of Foscote). But it does not necessarily follow that constructive notice should suffice for a claim in damages, if the basis for
extending liability to non-disclosure is the defendant's fraud.

Hughes[63] is founded: a party cannot take advantage of a mistake which he knows the other party is making about the *terms* of the contract; but mistakes as to the *facts* or circumstances surrounding the contract are quite different.[64] To require a party as a general rule to disclose a mistake of fact which he knows the other party is making would disturb the well established balance of risk in the negotiations for a commercial contract; it would remove the incentive on each party to ask questions, to check that the facts are as they believe them to be, to take responsibility for their own decisions in the contracting process. And a party should be entitled to remain silent even where he knows that the other party is making a mistake: 'why should I have to tell him? It's his own fault ...'.

(b) Liability for breach of a duty of disclosure?

It may therefore be too much to say that merely keeping silent in the knowledge that the other party is making a mistake of fact should be actionable as deceit. Even other legal systems which admit significantly broader liability for non-disclosure do not generally impose liability simply for failure to disclose the other party's known mistake. Remaining silent can (other systems may say) still be consistent with a party's duty to act in good faith in negotiations.[65] At this point a second argument can be introduced, drawing on the approach taken to non-disclosure in relation to the remedy of rescission. Rescission is available, in principle, for every misrepresentation. But not for every non-disclosure because this would undermine the relationship recognized in law between negotiating parties. Rescission is therefore available only if there is a reason for imposing the duty to disclose the information which the defendant failed to disclose. And such a duty

---

[63] Above, n 57.

[64] Above, nn 4, 5. For criticism, however, of this distinction, at least where the mistake is to a *fundamental* fact, see Treitel, above, n 48, para 8-044.

[65] Above, n 10. Cf the academic Draft Common Frame of Reference (DCFR), which proposes remedies for non-disclosure only where the non-disclosure was either a breach of a duty of disclosure, or where good faith and fair dealing required the disclosure: Study Group on a European Civil Code and Research Group on EC Private Law (Acquis Group), *Principles, Definitions and Model Rules of European Private Law: Draft Common Frame of Reference (DCFR), Outline Edition* (Munich: Sellier, 2009) II.-7:201(1)(b)(ii) (avoidance of the contract for mistake), 205(1) (avoidance for fraudulent non-disclosure), 214 (damages). These provisions are developed from those set out in the Principles of European Contract Law, which followed in general terms the approach taken by European civil law jurisdictions: O Lando and H Beale, *Principles of European Contract Law, Parts I and II* (The Hague: Kluwer Law International, 2000) 256.

arises either from the pre-existing relationship between the parties, or the nature of the contract which is being negotiated.[66] But if there is a duty of disclosure for the purposes of the remedy of rescission, the mere non-disclosure in breach of that duty then gives rise to the remedy—just as any misrepresentation gives rise to rescission. So it is no longer seen as undermining the risk allocation of the negotiations to remedy a breach of the duty to disclose. This does not, of course, show that damages should be available simply for breach of the duty to disclose, any more than damages are available for any misrepresentation. Damages follow from the defendant's culpability, judged here in terms of the law of tort:[67] and a fraudulent misrepresentation gives rise naturally to a claim in the tort of deceit. But the policy of remedying fraud can surely also be furthered, without undermining the risk allocation of the negotiations, where the fraudulent non-disclosure is at the same time a breach of a duty of disclosure. The counter-argument may be along the lines that the pre-contractual duty of disclosure is a creature of equity,[68] devised specifically for the remedy of rescission. But the duty of disclosure arises in relation to the negotiations between the particular parties to the particular contract, and if it is a sufficient non-disclosure to justify rescission of the contract, it is difficult to see why it could not also be treated as a sufficient non-disclosure to justify a concurrent remedy in tort.

There will also be a concern about whether this is the thin end of the wedge. If deliberate non-disclosure—even if limited to deliberate breach of a duty of disclosure—were to be remedied, why not then also negligent non-disclosure? The answer could go either way. A case could certainly be made for liability in damages for negligent breach of a duty of disclosure; but it would be obviously less strong in principle than the case in relation to fraud. On the other hand, there is a parallel in the reasoning: negligent misrepresentation is less potent than fraudulent misrepresentation and therefore a narrower test must be devised to justify the imposition of a duty of care; non-disclosure is less potent than misrepresentation, and therefore a narrower test must be devised to justify the imposition of a duty of disclosure. If the duty of disclosure has been established, does that then also remove the concerns over imposing liability where the non-disclosure is only negligent, not fraudulent? On the other hand, that would also extend the current position, where a breach of a duty to disclose does not give rise to a duty of

---

[66] Above, nn 8, 9.

[67] There may also be possible claims for compensation in equity for breach of trust or fiduciary duty (including breaches which consist in non-disclosure).

[68] Cf *Banque Keyser Ullmann SA v Skandia (UK) Insurance Co Ltd*, above, n 28, at 780.

care in the tort of negligence—for such a duty, the general test of the tort of negligence is separate, and must be applied independently.[69] On the other hand, just as s 2(1) of the Misrepresentation Act 1967 was intended to go beyond the tort of negligence (as it then stood) and allow a claim in damages for non-fraudulent but, broadly, negligent misrepresentation which induced a contract, the parallel logic may be to allow a similar claim where there is a breach of a duty of disclosure where the defendant cannot show that he honestly and on reasonable grounds believed the facts which the claimant misunderstood.

The larger concern in any such development might be that to extend the remedy of damages to non-disclosure would open the door to a reassessment of the very nature of pre-contractual negotiations. However, the award of damages as a remedy for breach of the (well established) duties of disclosure which already justify rescission of the contract, is not a significant inroad on the balance of pre-contractual risk where the damages are limited to an established level of culpability that gives rise to damages in the law of tort. Other legal systems recognize a broader liability in tort for pre-contractual non-disclosure;[70] but that is because they recognize broader duties of disclosure, typically linked to a duty to negotiate in good faith. It does not follow that English law, making such a development, must recognize a general duty of good faith between negotiating parties, nor broader duties of disclosure. It could choose to do so—as Lord Mansfield's propositions in *Carter v Boehm* could have given rise to a broader set of pre-contractual duties of disclosure, rather than being limited to a particular duty of disclosure in insurance contracts:[71]

> The governing principle is applicable to all contracts and dealings.
>
> Good faith forbids either party by concealing what he privately knows, to draw the other into a bargain, from his ignorance of that fact, and his believing the contrary. But either party may be innocently silent, as to grounds open to both, to exercise their judgment upon. Aliud est celare; aliud, tacere; neque enim, id est celare quicquid reticeas; sed cum

---

[69] Above, n 28.

[70] Above, n 10. Eg French law, where broader duties of disclosure are imposed between negotiating parties; deliberate non-disclosure then justifies annulment of the contract (for *dol*) and either deliberate or negligent 'fault' suffices to give rise to liability in tort for loss thereby caused: J Bell, S Boyron, and S Whittaker, *Principles of French Law* (2nd edn, Oxford: Oxford University Press, 2008) 309-11. Cf also DCFR, above, n 65, II.-3:101-105; II.-7:201, 205, 214, which defines both specific and general duties of disclosure (the latter based on the duty of good faith and fair dealing), and provides for avoidance of the contract for non-disclosure, as well as damages where the defendant knew or could reasonably be expected to have known of the ground for avoidance.

[71] *Carter v Boehm* (1766) 3 Burr 1905, at 1909-10; 97 ER 1162, at 1164-5.

quod tu scias, id ignorare emolumenti tui causa velis eos, quorum intersit id scire.[72] ...

The reason of the rule which obliges parties to disclose, is to prevent fraud, and to encourage good faith. It is adapted to such facts as vary the nature of the contract; which one privately knows, and the other is ignorant of, and has no reason, to suspect.

But that is a separate issue, and the argument in this paper does not require any such development.

6. PLACING THE LIABILITY WITHIN THE NOMINATE TORTS

There remains the question of where to place the liability to pay damages for non-disclosure, if it is to be imposed. English law knows no such thing as a general liability for damages for wrongs,[73] but must fit the claim within one of the nominate torts. Damages for a negligent breach of a duty of disclosure can fit relatively comfortably within the tort of negligence, since it is already accepted that there can be liability in negligence if the non-disclosure constitutes a breach of the duty of care. What is necessary, then, is to find the duty of care—which does not hinge upon there being a 'representation'.[74]

On the other hand, there appears to be a difficulty in relation to remedies where the cause of action is defined by reference to a 'misrepresentation'—the tort of deceit or the statutory claim under s 2(1) of the Misrepresentation Act 1967. One objection to the recent cases is that they have claimed that the tort of deceit already covers the fraudulent breach of a duty of disclosure, but this is achieved only by treating the breach of a duty of disclosure as if it were a misrepresentation. It is a neat solution to the need for a remedy, but one which is a fiction—a 'deemed misrepresentation'. It would be better to acknowledge that the tort needs to be developed to cover the case, or at least to be more openly explicit about where the 'deception' lies. One way would be to say that it is not only in causing the mistake, but also in allowing the party to continue to make the mistake—allowing the self-deception to continue in the formation of the contract; or, as the draftsmen of the

---

[72] Cicero, *De Officiis*, Book 3, paras 52, 57: 'Concealment is one thing, silence is another. ... Concealment is not just holding something back in silence, but when, for your own benefit, you intend that those who have an interest in knowing what you know should remain in ignorance of it.'

[73] Cf French law, which imposes liability for, inter alia, loss caused by deliberate or negligent 'fault' (above, n 70); and the DCFR also uses a general test for liability for damages for non-disclosure (*ibid*).

[74] Above, n 12.

DCFR have put it: 'caused the contract to be concluded in mistake by leaving the mistaken party in error'.[75] But, as drafted, the Misrepresentation Act simply does not cover the case of non-disclosure, even where it is a breach of a duty of disclosure. And that seems to be right: such a far-ranging extension of liability for pre-contractual non-disclosure, based on a re-interpretation of the word 'misrepresentation' in the context of fraud, is inappropriate. It is necessary to address head-on the question of whether non-fraudulent breach of a duty of disclosure should give rise to a claim in damages.

7. CONCLUSIONS

In the end, we come to the conclusion that the recent cases are right, but not for the right reasons. They held that the fraudulent breach of a duty of disclosure is actionable within the tort of deceit. The problem with their reasoning is that it did not address the older case law to the effect that deceit requires a misrepresentation by the defendant which caused the claimant to be deceived, and that this simply does not cover the case of an existing mistake which is not corrected by the defendant. They used such reasoning as that breach of a duty of disclosure is 'tantamount to a misrepresentation' and therefore is to be remedied as if it were a misrepresentation, which achieves the object of imposing liability in the tort of deceit, but without taking into account whether it is an appropriate analysis for all purposes for which the law attributes legal consequences to a 'misrepresentation'. And they did not review the broader question of when, and why, the law should impose a liability to pay damages on a party who fails to disclose relevant information. On the basis of the discussion in this paper, it is suggested that there should be liability in the case of a deliberate (fraudulent) breach of a duty of disclosure—and therefore the answer given by the recent cases is justifiable. Such a liability stands at the intersection of two policies which can be seen elsewhere in relation to formation of contracts: sanctioning fraud, and limiting the legal consequences of non-disclosure to cases where there is a particular reason (in the context of the negotiations between these particular parties) to impose a duty of disclosure. Whether the liability should extend to a negligent breach of a duty of disclosure is a further issue which needs to be addressed separately. But a much larger (and quite different) question is whether the scope of the existing duties of disclosure should be broadened—both for the remedy of rescission and for the claim for damages in tort.

---

[75] Above, n 71, II.-7:201(1)(b)(ii).

8

Liability in Unjust Enrichment where a Contract Fails to Materialize

JAMES EDELMAN*

1. THE QUESTION

Two commercial parties, A and B, agree to embark upon a joint venture. They begin negotiations. At B's request, A begins preparatory work towards the joint venture. No contract eventuates. Can A bring a claim against B in unjust enrichment for the value of his services performed in anticipation of a contract? Surprisingly, despite a line of cases dealing with this question stretching back nearly a century, the answer seems far from clear. This chapter suggests that the best way through this thicket is to permit restitution of the value of A's services if, and only if, the objective basis upon which the work was performed was that, in the circumstances which occurred, it would be remunerated. In the language of unjust enrichment, the claimant must show that the unjust factor of failure of consideration is present.

The focus of this chapter is upon the unjust factor of failure of consideration. But a claimant's action for unjust enrichment is not satisfied merely by proof of an unjust factor. It also requires proof that the defendant was enriched and that the enrichment was at the claimant's expense. Since many cases involving pre-contractual services involve a request for those services by the defendant, or other conduct by the defendant which shows that the claimant's work was desired,[1] the issues of enrichment at the claimant's expense will rarely present difficulty. This chapter therefore focuses only on the issue of whether the defendant's enrichment was unjust. The conventional analysis of injustice in these cases focuses upon the question of 'risk'. The thesis

* Professor of the Law of Obligations, Oxford and Fellow of Keble College; Conjoint Professor, University of New South Wales. Barrister, One Essex Court. I am very grateful to Nicholas Strauss QC for comment and criticism from which this chapter has greatly benefitted.

[1] In the words of Mance LJ in *Cressman v Coys of Kensington (Sales) Ltd* [2004] EWCA Civ 47, [2004] 1 WLR 2775, at 2792, the defendant 'was exercising a deliberate preference'. I have discussed elsewhere the nature and meaning of enrichment as the objective value of the desired benefit received by the defendant: J Edelman, 'The Meaning of Loss and Enrichment' in R Chambers, C Mitchell, and J Penner (eds), *Philosophical Foundations of Unjust Enrichment* (Oxford: OUP, 2008) ch 8.

presented in this chapter is that such an approach is question-begging and unhelpful. Instead, the underlying concern in all the cases should be made explicit: did the claimant perform on an objective basis that it was part of an exchange? This should be the only relevant question.

2. THE CONVENTIONAL 'RISK' ANALYSIS

In most of the cases which concern pre-contractual liability for work done, judges express their reasoning in terms of 'risk'.[2] The reasoning is usually as follows: if A takes the risk that no contract will eventuate then A cannot recover the reasonable value of those services. An example is *Regalian Properties v London Docklands Development Corpn*.[3] In that case a tender for the development of land was accepted 'subject to contract' and various other conditions. The developer incurred preliminary expenses of almost $3 million in preparation for the development but subsequent events delayed the preparation of a formal contract including a need for detailed costings, difficulties in obtaining vacant possession, and a falling market. During negotiations the claimant had requested an assurance that it would be compensated for preparatory work. That request was refused.[4] Negotiations broke down when the parties failed to agree on the contract price. The trial judge concluded that where the parties use words such as 'subject to contract' any cost incurred prior to the completion of a contract will be at that party's own risk because each party 'must be taken to know... [that] any cost incurred by him in preparation for the intended contract will be incurred at his own risk'.[5]

There are three difficulties with reasoning which focuses upon 'risk'. First, and most fundamentally, a reference to a party bearing the risk is a legal conclusion which begs the question *why* that party should bear the risk. The conclusion in *Regalian* that the claimant 'must be taken to know' that he has borne the risk is not an explanation. *Why* should the claimant be *taken* to know this? In this regard *Regalian*

---

[2] See, eg *Brewer Street Investments Ltd v Barclays Woollen Co Ltd* [1954] 1 QB 428; *Jennings v Woodman, Matthews & Co* [1952] 2 TLR 409; *Regalian Properties v London Docklands Development Corp* [1995] 1 WLR 212; *Easat Antennas Limited v Racal Defence Electronics Limited* (Unreported, Hart J, Chancery, 28 March 2000), at [70]; *MSM Consulting Limited v United Republic of Tanzania* [2009] EWHC 121 (QB). See also G Jones (ed), *Goff and Jones' Law of Restitution* (7th edn, London: Sweet & Maxwell, 2007) 26-010; *Treitel: The Law of Contract* (12th edn, London: Sweet & Maxwell, 2007) 128–9.

[3] [1995] 1 WLR 212.

[4] *Ibid*, at 229.

[5] *Ibid*, at 231.

contrasts with an Australian decision which had been relied upon heavily by counsel in *Regalian*. In *Sabemo Pty Ltd v North Sydney Municipal Council*[6] the claimant, Sabemo, tendered for a building lease on the defendant council's land. Sabemo won the tender and negotiations commenced for a contract. During three years of negotiations Sabemo performed AUS $426,000 worth of work on the land. Then the council decided to sell the land rather than develop it. It called off the negotiations. In the New South Wales Supreme Court, Sheppard J held that although Sabemo bore the risk that no contract would result, it did not bear the risk that the council might unilaterally withdraw. Once again, this is just a statement of a conclusion, albeit the opposite conclusion from *Regalian*. It does not explain *why* the parties bore, or did not bear, such risks.

The second difficulty with the risk approach is that cases which characterize the claimant as a 'risk taker' do not always deny recovery. The recent decision of *Yeoman's Row Management Ltd v Cobbe*,[7] is a good illustration. Mr Cobbe was a property developer who entered into a joint venture with the defendant company for development of town houses. The joint venture began with an 'in principle' oral agreement between Mr Cobbe and the sole director of Yeoman's Row, Mrs Lisle-Mainwaring. The agreement was that Yeoman's Row would obtain vacant possession of the property and Cobbe would obtain planning approval, buy it from Yeoman's Row, and develop it. Profit share was agreed. Believing that the property would be sold to him to develop, Mr Cobbe engaged architects and other professionals and sought planning permission. Mrs Lisle-Mainwaring encouraged him in these actions. Mr Cobbe succeeded in obtaining planning permission. But the very next day Mrs Lisle-Mainwaring demanded new terms. Mr Cobbe had no claim for breach of contract because the oral agreement was void under s 2(1) of the Law of Property (Miscellaneous Provisions) Act 1989. A claim for proprietary estoppel also failed. In the leading speech, Lord Scott explained that the estoppel claim failed for the same reasons as cases where work was done 'subject to contract':[8] the 'expectation [was] … speculative' and it depended upon contingencies entirely under the control of the other party.[9] Lord Scott held that Mr Cobbe took the risk that the planning permission might be

---

[6] [1977] 2 NSWLR 880.

[7] [2008] UKHL 55; [2008] 1 WLR 1752.

[8] *Ibid*, at [25]-[28]. See also *Attorney-General of Hong Kong v Humphreys Estate (Queen's Gardens) Ltd* [1987] AC 114.

[9] [2008] UKHL 55; [2008] 1 WLR 1752, at [25]. See also *London & Regional Investments Ltd v TBI Plc* [2002] EWCA Civ 355; *Pridean v Forest Taverns* (1996) 75 P&CR 447.

refused and that none of his expenditure would be recovered.[10] But Mr Cobbe succeeded in his claim for unjust enrichment. He was entitled to restitution of the value of the services he had performed.[11] Lord Scott did not explain why Mr Cobbe had borne the risk of not obtaining a contract, and hence was denied his estoppel claim, but had *not* borne the risk in relation to obtaining restitution of the value of the work he performed.

The third problem with the language of 'risk' is that it cannot explain why a claimant who does *not* take the risk *can* recover. The thesis presented here is that such an explanation requires attention to the objective basis upon which the work was done. This point was made in the decision of my colleague, Nicholas Strauss QC, sitting as a deputy judge in the High Court in *Countrywide Communications Ltd v ICL Pathway Ltd*.[12] In that case Countrywide sought remuneration for public relations work performed at the request of a consortium of companies to support their bid to computerize a card system for the provision of benefits. ICL Pathway was the consortium's vehicle for the bid. After ICL Pathway was awarded the contract it replaced Countrywide and refused to remunerate it. The judge held that although no contract had been concluded ICL Pathway was required to make reparation. He emphasized that 'the terms in which the request to perform the services was made may be important in establishing the extent of the risk (if any) which the plaintiffs may fairly be said to have taken that such services would in the end be unrecompensed'.[13]

---

[10] [2008] UKHL 55; [2008] 1 WLR 1752, at [6].

[11] Curiously Lord Scott treated the claims for *'quantum meruit'*, 'unjust enrichment', and 'failure of consideration' under separate headings. However, earlier in his speech (at 1756 [4]) he recognized that each of these is really the same claim as the others: 'an unjust enrichment remedy, a *quantum meruit* remedy and a consideration that has wholly failed remedy are essentially restitutionary in character, concentrating not at all on the value of the expected benefit of which B has been deprived but, as the case may be, on the extent of A's enrichment at B's expense'.

[12] [2000] CLC 324.

[13] *Ibid*, at 349. In one significant respect, however, the analysis in that decision departs from the approach adopted in this chapter. The judge considered that the award in such cases is really for 'a loss unfairly sustained by the claimant' rather than for restitution of unjust enrichment. One difficulty with this suggestion is that awards of *quantum meruit* have always focused upon the reasonable value of work performed; they have never been concerned with the loss of the claimant. Another difficulty is the use of the term 'unjust' as a description of a judicial assessment of fairness rather than a direction to have regard to particular established unjust factors. See also K Hayne, 'Anticipated Contracts that Fail to Materialise' in S Degeling and J Edelman, *Unjust Enrichment in Commercial Law* (Australia: Lawbook Co, 2008) 237, 247.

3. AN ALTERNATIVE ANALYSIS: FAILURE OF CONSIDERATION

(a) The unjust factor of failure of consideration

It is well established that to succeed in an action for unjust enrichment, the requirement of 'injustice' is not an exercise in idiosyncratic judicial discretion. A claimant must prove that the facts of the case satisfy the requirements of an unjust factor such as mistake, duress, undue influence, or failure of consideration.[14]

(i) Definition: failure of basis or purpose

The modern meaning of 'consideration' in an action for unjust enrichment based on 'failure of consideration' was set out clearly in a decision of the House of Lords in 1924. That case was an appeal from Scotland called *Cantiare San Rocco SA v Clyde Shipbuilding and Engineering Co.*[15] The question for the House of Lords was whether to apply, in Scottish law, the English approach to failure of consideration exemplified by the decision in *Chandler v Webster*.[16] The claim in *Chandler* was to recover £100 paid in advance for a room to view the coronation of Edward VII. The Court of Appeal refused the claim even though cancellation of the coronation had frustrated the contract and terminated it *in futuro*. The court held that an action for failure of consideration could succeed only if 'the contract were wiped out altogether'.[17]

In *Cantiare San Rocco SA* the House of Lords rejected this English approach as a matter of Scottish law. A Scottish shipbuilding company had agreed to supply marine engines to an Austrian company. Payments were made in advance under the contract and then the outbreak of war frustrated the contract. In rejecting the English approach, the House of Lords separated the meaning of 'consideration' from the question of contractual validity. In the context of an action for failure of consideration, the Lords held that 'consideration' means the 'basis'

---

[14] *Deutsche Morgan Grenfell Group plc v Inland Revenue Commissioners* [2006] UKHL 49; [2007] 1 AC 558.

[15] [1924] AC 226.

[16] [1904] 1 KB 493. This decision was supported by considerable earlier authority including *Stubbs v The Holywell Railway Company* (1867) LR 2 Exch 311; *Appleby v Myers* (1867) LR 2 CP 651; *Civil Service Co-operative Society v General Steam Navigation Co* [1903] 2 KB 756 at 764; *Blakeley v Muller & Co* [1903] 2 KB 760.

[17] [1904] 1 KB 493, at 499.

or 'purpose' for the claimant's payment or performance. Lord Birken-head LC (with whom Lord Atkinson agreed) said:[18]

> The rule may, I think, be fairly stated thus: A person who had given to another any money or other property for a purpose which had failed could recover what he had given.[19]

Lord Shaw also spoke of failure of consideration as an action 'for recovery of what has been given for a purpose which has failed',[20] and all of their Lordships referred to the *condictio* cited by Celsus and Paul in Justinian's Digest,[21] *condictio causa data causa non secuta*, which translates roughly to 'something given on a basis, that basis not following'.

The applicability of this approach as a matter of English law came before the House of Lords in *Fibrosa Spolka Akcyjna v Fairbairn Lawson Combe Barbour Ltd*.[22] Naturally, the decision in *Cantiare* was at the forefront of the appeal. The House of Lords unanimously overruled *Chandler* and English and Scottish law were brought into 'substantial accord'.[23] Although the House of Lords in *Fibrosa* did not expressly reiterate the meaning of 'consideration' as 'basis' or 'purpose', the *Cantiare* decision plainly informed their approach. More recently, the High Court of Australia has made the *Cantiare* definition explicit.[24]

There are three important points that must be added to this explanation of failure of consideration as the failure of a 'basis', 'purpose', or 'contemplated state of affairs'. The first point narrows the operation of failure of consideration by restricting it to purposes or contemplated states of affairs which are *shared*. The second point is that failure of basis is an objective characterization of the purpose of the parties, not a subjective one. The final point is that the consideration, basis, or purpose can include the legal liability of the parties or either of them, and that the basis can fail immediately or subsequently.

---

[18] [1924] AC 226, at 235.

[19] The only qualification added was that the recipient must also either have been enriched or 'at fault'.

[20] [1924] AC 226, at 252.

[21] Digest XII.4.

[22] [1943] AC 32.

[23] [1943] AC 32, at 71-2 (Lord Wright). The qualification 'substantial' was because Lord Wright reserved his opinion on whether, as in Scottish law, a defendant would have a counterclaim or defence to the extent to which the claimant payer was enriched by a defendant's part performance.

[24] *Roxborough v Rothmans of Pall Mall Ltd* (2001) 208 CLR 516, at 525 (Gleeson CJ, Gaudron, J, and Hayne J) quoting P Birks, *An Introduction to the Law of Restitution* (rev edn, Oxford: Clarendon Press, 1989) 227-8. See also Gummow J, at 557 'the failure to sustain itself as the state of affairs contemplated as a basis for the payments the appellants seek to recover'.

(ii) The basis which fails must be shared

An example of the need for a shared basis is *Burgess v Rawnsley*.[25] Mr Burgess and Mrs Rawnsley met and bought a house as joint tenants, each providing half of the purchase price of £850. Mr Burgess bought the house as a matrimonial home in contemplation of marriage to the defendant but never mentioned marriage to her. Mrs Rawnsley made her contribution for the purpose of obtaining the use of the upstairs flat. They did not marry and Mrs Rawnsley did not move into the house. After Mr Burgess's death, Mrs Rawnsley claimed that the house was hers by survivorship. Mr Burgess's executor countered that the basis on which the house had been bought (marriage) had failed. Although Mr Burgess's executor brought a proprietary claim (for a resulting trust as a tenant in common in equity) the reasoning of the Court of Appeal was equally applicable to a personal claim based on failure of consideration. There was no doubt that if both parties had contemplated marriage then Mr Burgess's executor would have been entitled either to a resulting trust or personal restitution of his contributions when the marriage did not eventuate.[26] But a majority of the Court of Appeal (Lord Denning MR dissenting on this point) held that since Mr Burgess had not communicated that purpose to Mrs Rawnsley, there was no common purpose which had failed.[27] Browne LJ said that[28]

> the basis for this sort of resulting trust is that the purpose for which the trust was created has wholly failed…it seems to me impossible to say that there has been a total failure of consideration or that the trust has failed where a trust is created by two people and where there is a failure of a purpose for which one of them created the trust but which he did not communicate to the other party and which the other did not share.

Although these situations of trusts arising from breakdown of personal relationships are now governed by 'common intention constructive trusts' rather than resulting trusts,[29] the approach of Browne LJ still applies in cases involving breakdown of commercial relationships.

---

[25] [1975] Ch 429.

[26] *Essery v Cowlard* (1884) 26 Ch D 191 and *Ulrich v Ulrich and Felton* [1968] 1 WLR 180, at 185.

[27] The executor, however, succeeded on the separate ground that an earlier oral agreement to sell had severed the joint tenancy.

[28] [1975] Ch 429, at 442.

[29] *Stack v Dowden* [2007] UKHL 17; [2007] 2 AC 432. Compare the forceful dissent of Lord Neuberger who would have applied the traditional analysis of resulting trust.

In such cases there must be a shared basis or purpose which fails.[30] The law does not impose liability upon a defendant for a claimant's unilateral assumptions which turn out to be false.[31]

(iii) The basis is determined objectively

The objective nature of the purpose or basis will be illustrated further below, but it can be briefly illustrated here by the decision in *Upton-on-Severn Rural District Council v Powell*.[32] In that case, the appellant called the Upton police when a fire broke out on his farm. As he had intended, the police called the Upton fire brigade who promptly attended and put out the fire. The Upton fire brigade performed services for free for people in Upton. But it required people outside the area to pay for its services. The uncommunicated, subjective belief of the appellant was that he was entitled to the service for free as an Upton resident.[33] Unfortunately he lived on the wrong side of the border with Pershore which meant that he was entitled to the free services of the Pershore fire brigade, not the Upton fire brigade. The Court of Appeal held that the appellant had to pay the value of the services. The reasoning of the court was that *objectively* the circumstances were such that the basis upon which the services were performed was that they would be remunerated.[34] The Court of Appeal spoke of the result as based on 'implied contract', an expression now commonly regarded as a fiction which conceals an action for unjust enrichment.[35] Although the services were provided on the objective basis that they would be remunerated it could not be said, without fiction, that there was a genuine objective agreement to pay a reasonable sum to the Upton fire brigade.

---

[30] Eg *Gilbert & Partners v Knight* [1968] 2 All ER 248. See further F Maher, 'A New Conception of Failure of Basis' [2004] *RLR* 96, 101.

[31] It is an open question whether a false unilateral assumption which is false at the time it is made can permit restitution if the claimant relies on the unjust factor of mistake. See the further discussion of this point below.

[32] [1942] 1 All ER 220. Cited with approval in *William Lacey (Hounslow) Ltd v Davis* [1957] 1 WLR 932, at 938.

[33] Six hours after it arrived, the Upton brigade was informed by a Pershore fire officer that the property was, in fact, located in Pershore. The Upton brigade continued rendering its services until the Pershore brigade arrived and the Court of Appeal considered this later period no different from the initial period.

[34] See also *Fostif Pty Ltd v Campbells Cash & Carry Pty Ltd* (2005) 218 ALR 166, at 210 where the New South Wales Court of Appeal allowed a class action for recovery of unconstitutional payments to proceed based on failure of consideration even though the individual members of the class action might have had different subjective purposes in making their payments.

[35] *Sempra Metals Ltd v Inland Revenue Commissioners* [2007] UKHL 34; [2008] 1 AC 561, at [107], [111] (Lord Nicholls).

(iv) The basis might be an assumed state of legal affairs

A basis which fails might be an assumed state of *legal* affairs as well as an assumed state of factual affairs. A clear example is the decision of the High Court of Australia in *Roxborough v Rothmans of Pall Mall Ltd*.[36] In that case tobacco retailers purchased cigarettes from wholesalers. The price included a payment which the parties assumed was owed by the wholesalers to the government. When the tax was later held to be unconstitutional the retailer brought an action for restitution relying on failure of consideration. It succeeded because the basis or purpose of the payment by the retailers was that the wholesalers were liable to pay the tax. The decision in *Roxborough* also illustrates that the doctrine applies whether the failure occurs immediately or subsequently. No Justice considered it necessary to address the metaphysical question of whether the retrospective operation of the decision which held the tax to be unconstitutional[37] meant that the purpose of the payment had failed at the time it was paid (immediately) or whether it only failed at the time of the decision (subsequently).

Strangely, with the exception of one lucid analysis,[38] most commentators have assumed that failure of consideration does not apply where the basis or purpose which fails is a shared understanding of legal liability.[39] But failure of a legal basis was the reason for restitution given by two judges in the Court of Appeal in *Guinness Mahon v Kensington and Chelsea RLBC*.[40] In that case, the claimant bank was entitled to recover all the payments it had made to a local council under an interest rate swap contract which had been completed. Robert Walker LJ explained that there was a failure of consideration because 'no enforceable obligation is ever created but the context of a supposed or expected contract is still relevant as explaining what the parties are about'.[41] Morritt LJ said, 'the consideration for each swap which failed was the benefit of the contractual obligation'.[42] In other words,

---

[36] (2001) 208 CLR 516.

[37] *Ha v New South Wales* [1997] HCA 34; (1997) 189 CLR 465.

[38] F Maher, 'A New Conception of Failure of Basis' [2004] *RLR* 96 and F Maher, 'Failure of Basis' (D.Phil thesis, University of Oxford, 2008).

[39] Eg P Birks, *Unjust Enrichment* (2nd edn, Oxford: OUP, 2005) 115; G Virgo, *The Principles of the Law of Restitution* (2nd edn, Oxford: OUP, 2006) 383-4; W Swadling, 'Restitution for No Consideration' [1994] *RLR* 73; B McFarlane and R Stevens, 'In Defence of Sumpter v Hedges' (2002) 118 *LQR* 569.

[40] [1999] QB 215.

[41] *Ibid*, at 240.

[42] *Ibid*, at 227-8. See also at 226 where Morritt LJ said that 'the relevant bargain was for..the legal obligation to make [the payments]'.

the objective purpose or basis of the parties' performance was that the other party's obligation was enforceable.[43]

(b) The failure of consideration explanation of the pre-contractual liability cases

In the context of anticipated contracts which fail to materialize, this analysis makes explicit the exercise which courts are implicitly undertaking when asking which party 'bore the risk' in relation to the work. The question is simply whether the objective basis is that the claimant's performance is part of an exchange. If so, a failure of the counterparty to remunerate the work will mean that the basis upon which it was performed will fail.

We have already seen that the trial judge in *Sabemo Pty Ltd v North Sydney Municipal Council*,[44] held that the claimant had not taken the risk of not being remunerated. His Honour emphasized that the parties had proceeded on a 'joint assumption' that a contract would eventuate and it was not expected that the work would be without remuneration if the council unilaterally withdrew after it was completed. The same is true of the other cases in the area. In *Way v Latilla*,[45] although no separate agreement was ever concluded, Mr Way was entitled to restitution of the value of extra-contractual work he did to obtain a mining concession for the defendant which went beyond his ordinary contractual duties.[46] The House of Lords relied on the fact that the work had been done on the basis that Mr Way would be remunerated handsomely for it even though no separate contract was ever concluded and the parties had reached no agreement on price (reasonable or otherwise).[47] In *Brewer Street Investments Ltd v Barclays Woollen Co Ltd*[48] the claimant landlords spent time making alterations to premises as requested by the defendants, who were prospective tenants. Negotiations for the lease failed and the landlords did not complete the work. Although the Court of Appeal relied heavily on the conventional 'risk' analysis, a crucial factor in their conclusion that the defendants were liable to

---

[43] In *Kommune & Anor v DEPFA ACS Bank* [2009] EWHC 2227 (Comm), at [142] Tomlinson J described this as the 'wider view of failure of consideration'.

[44] [1977] 2 NSWLR 880.

[45] [1937] 3 All ER 759.

[46] Although the relevant contract was with Latilla's company, Latilla had conceded that no distinction should be drawn between him and his company: [1937] 3 All ER 759, at 761.

[47] [1937] 3 All ER 759, at 766 (Lord Wright).

[48] [1954] 1 QB 428.

make restitution[49] was the defendants' agreement to be 'responsible' for payment.[50] In *William Lacey (Hounslow) Ltd v Davis*[51] the defendant was ordered to pay for work done by the claimant for a submission which the defendant used to obtain compensation from the War Commission. Again, the work was done on the basis that it would be remunerated: Barry J observed that the work was not done 'gratuitously merely in the hope that the building scheme would be carried out and that the person who did the work would obtain the contract'.[52] In *British Steel Corp v Cleveland Bridge & Engineering Co Ltd*,[53] the defendant was liable to make restitution of the value of steel nodes supplied to the claimant despite the absence of a concluded contract. A letter of intent provided by the defendant made it plain that the common intention (ie the basis) was that payment was to be made for the nodes.[54] In *Easat Antennas Limited v Racal Defence Electronics Limited*[55] the claimant was entitled to recover its reasonable costs incurred, as requested, toward a Satellite Communications System because 'it was the common understanding' that the claimant would recover its expenditures in the event that a contract did not materialize.[56] In *Vedatech Corporation v Crystal Decisions (UK) Ltd*[57] the claimant was a Japanese subsidiary of an English corporation. The claimant subsidiary did considerable work to assist the defendant companies to introduce their computer program into Japan. No contract was ever reached but Jacob J held that the defendant companies had to make restitution of their unjust enrichment. A central factor in his reasoning was that the work was done on the basis that it would be remunerated.[58]

---

[49] As Lord Denning explained, the claim for restitution was pleaded as a count of money paid rather than *quantum meruit*: [1954] 1 QB 428, at 435-6.

[50] A separate argument, which relates to the issue of enrichment, was that the defendants had only agreed to be responsible for *completed* repairs. Resolution of that issue today would turn upon whether the request is properly characterized as one for an end product (not received) or a service (received in part): *Stocznia Gdanska SA v Latvian Shipping Co Ltd* [1998] 1 WLR 574.

[51] [1957] 1 WLR 932.

[52] [1957] 1 WLR 932, at 939.

[53] [1984] 1 All ER 504.

[54] See esp at 511-2.

[55] (Unreported, Hart J, Chancery, 28 March 2000).

[56] *Ibid*, at [73].

[57] [2002] EWHC 818.

[58] *Ibid*, at [86]: to be remunerated in part on a fee basis and in part by profit participation. That aspect of the decision which suggested that the award should be a share of the actual profit cannot be justified. This fulfils the expectations of the claimant without any contractual restrictions that the defendant might have imposed; it does not make restitution of the value of the benefit received. A proper award of restitution for services provided in

This analysis is also implicit in the *Yeoman's Row* case which was explicitly decided by the House of Lords by relying on the unjust factor of failure of consideration. The trial judge found that Mr Cobbe had expected that if, prior to the planning decision, Mrs Lisle-Mainwaring decided not to proceed with the agreement then he would be reimbursed for all his expenditure. Mrs Lisle-Mainwaring had encouraged this expectation. Although she later decided to repudiate their understanding, she continued to represent to Mr Cobbe that she intended to abide by it.[59] In other words, the objective shared basis upon which the work was done was always that Mr Cobbe's expenditure would be reimbursed if Mrs Lisle-Mainwaring decided not to proceed with the agreement, prior to the planning decision. That basis failed when Mrs Lisle-Mainwaring refused to pay.

In contrast with these cases where the defendant was liable to make restitution of the value of the services performed, are cases where the defendant was not liable. The same failure of basis reasoning underlies or explains these decisions. For instance, in *Regalian Properties v London Docklands Development Corpn*,[60] Rattee J found that the parties had expressly agreed (by the use of the words 'subject to contract') that the work would not be remunerated if no contract materialized as a result of failed negotiations.[61] In *Jennings and Chapman Ltd v Woodman, Matthews & Co*[62] the claimant lessees were refused recovery of the value of work that they did, at the request of sub-lessees, to alter the premises for the sub-lease. The crucial distinction from *Brewer Street Investments Ltd* was that the claimant knew that the consent of the landlord was required for the alterations. Hence the basis for the claimant's work could not have been that it would have been remunerated if (which occurred) the landlord withheld consent and no sub-lease eventuated. Finally, in *MSM Consulting Limited v United Republic of Tanzania*,[63] the claimant was refused recovery of the value of its work in searching for new premises for the Tanzanian High Commission when the work done was not the sort of work for which the Republic of Tanzania would reasonably have expected to pay and no assurance of

---

an industry which relies upon commission is that percentage of the *expected* profit. This was implicitly the approach taken in *Way v Latilla* [1937] 3 All ER 759.

[59] [2008] UKHL 55; [2008] 1 WLR 1752, at 1759-60 [12].

[60] [1995] 1 WLR 212.

[61] For the same reason, a payment made 'subject to contract' is made on the basis that it will be repaid if no contract eventuates. If the counterparty refuses to repay then that basis will fail: *Chillingworth v Esche* [1924] 1 Ch 97.

[62] [1952] 2 TLR 409.

[63] [2009] EWHC 121 (QB), at [171].

payment had been given.[64] Again, the basis was that it would not be remunerated.

In summary, although most of the cases suggest that the focus must be on 'all of the circumstances' and whether the claimant bore the risk, the central issue of importance is whether the basis upon which the work was performed was that it was part of an exchange. Such an approach explains what courts should be looking for when they consider 'all the circumstances' and the factors relevant to the *conclusion* that a claimant did, or did not, take the risk of non-payment.

(c) Failure of basis, not mistake, is the unjust factor in these bilateral transactions

In the law of unjust enrichment generally, the most common unjust factor is mistake. Suppose a claimant mistakenly transfers his cherished number plates to the person who purchases his car. The number plates are not part of the sale and the purchaser, who desires the plates and wishes to keep them, is enriched at the claimant's expense.[65] The claim for the purchaser's enrichment could be brought in two ways. It could be brought as a personal claim for restitution of the value of the number plate which the purchaser received. Alternatively, the claimant might seek restitution of his rights to the number plate, by a claim for rescission or a resulting trust.[66]

The example above involves a non-contractual transfer. But when a contract exists a claim for mistake can never be brought. In contract cases, whether the claim is to recover the value of an enrichment or to effect restitution of rights, unilateral mistake is not sufficient. An objective, shared basis is required. Although this paper is concerned with pre-contractual liability, the concern in contract cases, and the reason why a unilateral mistake is not actionable, is the same for all bilateral transactions: the law is concerned with the joint autonomy of parties, not the impairment of the autonomy of just one of them.

---

[64] *Ibid* at [175], [178].

[65] *Cressman v Coys of Kensington (Sales) Ltd* [2004] EWCA Civ 47; [2004] 1 WLR 2775.

[66] See further J Edelman, 'The Meaning of Loss and Enrichment' in R Chambers, C Mitchell, and J Penner, *Philosophical Foundations of the Law of Unjust Enrichment* (Oxford: OUP, 2009) 211, 226. The law is not yet settled on when such rights-based claims will arise. Some argue that a resulting trust should be a response which is almost always available to unjust enrichment: R Chambers, *Resulting Trusts* (Oxford: Clarendon, 1997) whilst others focus on the power to rescind a transfer B Häcker, 'Proprietary Restitution after Impaired Consent Transfers: A Generalised Power Model' (2009) 68 *CLJ* 324. There may be no difference between the two approaches.

(i) Where a contract governs the event which occurred

The case which establishes the insufficiency of mistake in the contractual context is *Bell v Lever Brothers Ltd*.[67] Bell and Snelling were
executives of Lever Brothers. Lever Brothers wanted to terminate their
contracts of employment so that its business could be reorganized.
They contracted to pay £30,000 compensation to Bell and £20,000 to
Snelling in consideration of termination of their employment contracts.
Lever Brothers later discovered that it could have terminated their
employment summarily because of serious breaches. Lever Brothers
sought restitution of the value of the payments it had made on the
basis of its unilateral mistake.[68] The House of Lords refused the claim.
Lever Brothers might have been mistaken but the basis upon which
they made the payment did not fail. As Lord Atkin said, Lever Brothers 'got exactly what [they] bargained for',[69] namely the termination of
the employment of Bell and Snelling.

Although a unilateral mistake (which is not induced by, or known
to, the other party) will never permit recovery the same is not true
of failure of basis. We have seen that when one party obtains value
under a contract pursuant to a basis which fails then the other party is
entitled to restitution of that value. Usually a contract will have been
terminated *in futuro*, but not *ab initio*. And even termination *in futuro*
is not essential. Provided that the basis for the claimant's performance
has failed, a claim for restitution of value which passes under a contract is possible even if the contract remains extant.[70]

The same contrast exists in relation to claims for restitution of rights
obtained by a defendant under a contract. Although unilateral mistake
does not permit recovery, failure of consideration will cause contractual
rights to terminate for exactly the same reason as the law permits restitution of value or benefits which have passed under a contract.[71] The
failure of basis might be an immediate failure or a subsequent failure.

---

[67] [1932] AC 161.

[68] Bizarrely, a professional jury had found at trial that Bell and Snelling had forgotten
about their breaches at the time they entered the redundancy agreement: see C MacMillan,
'How Temptation Led to Mistake: An Explanation of *Bell v Lever Brothers Limited*' (2003) 119
LQR 625.

[69] [1932] AC 161, at 223.

[70] *Napier and Ettrick (Lord) v Hunter* [1993] AC 713 is a good example of this: the Law Lords
assumed that a claim against the Names for restitution (money had and received) by the
indemnity insurers (whose contracts with the Names had not been terminated) would have
succeeded if it had been brought after the Names had been paid the settlement proceeds.

[71] The effect of misrepresentation in rescinding contracts can also be understood in this
way. A representation by one party, which is relied upon by the other in entering the contract,
is a shared objective basis for the contract.

If there is an immediate failure of basis in relation to the creation of contractual rights then the contract is void *ab initio*. If it is a subsequent failure then the contract is void *in futuro*. These two situations are usually described as fundamental common mistake and frustration.[72] The difference is simply one of timing. In relation to common mistake it has now been emphasized, in the same language as *Cantiare*, that there must be a 'common assumption as to the existence of a state of affairs' which concerns the existence or a vital attribute of the consideration and that matter must not be governed by contract terms.[73] If the agreement provides for a common (objective) basis which relates to a matter which is not a vital attribute of the consideration then the contract terms can be rectified to reflect the common basis and prevent unjust enrichment.[74]

The reason for this distinction between failure of basis and mistake is the concern of the law for party autonomy. The protection of the autonomy of a claimant like Lever Brothers would derogate from the autonomy of defendants like Bell or Snelling. A contractual allocation of rights can only be disturbed if a factor is present which concerns the autonomy of both parties. For instance, although a claimant's unilateral mistake is almost never sufficient to undermine rights objectively created by agreement,[75] the law's concern with the autonomy of both parties is struck in favour of the claimant when the defendant induces the claimant counterparty's entry to a transaction by duress or undue influence, or when the defendant knows that the claimant is entering the contract by duress or undue influence.[76]

(ii) Where no contract governs the event which occurred

The same approach applies to a bilateral case where two parties are negotiating but do not reach final agreement. The reason why there is no room for an additional unjust factor of mistake in these cases

---

[72] Compare the decision of the High Court of Australia in *Roxborough v Rothmans of Pall Mall Ltd* (2001) 208 CLR 516, at [60] where Gleeson CJ, Gaudron, J, and Hayne, J apparently treated the rules for termination of future contractual rights (frustration) in the same way as the failure of basis claim for restitution of value transferred.

[73] *Great Peace Shipping Ltd v Tsavliris Salvage (International) Ltd* [2002] EWCA Civ 1407; [2003] QB 679.

[74] *Chartbrook Ltd v Persimmon Homes Ltd* [2009] UKHL 38; [2009] 3 WLR 267.

[75] In a situation where one party is simply incapable of understanding there is no shared autonomy which can be protected. This is the doctrine of *non est factum*.

[76] A recipient of a gift tainted by duress or undue influence is liable to an action for restitution of the value of the gift (*Bridgeman v Green* (1757) Wilm 58; 97 ER 22) but the same recipient under a contract is not liable unless he knows of the duress or undue influence (*Talbot v Von Boris* [1911] KB 854).

is the same: a concern for the autonomy of both parties. If one party performs then the only question is whether the objective basis was that the work was part of an exchange. If the basis was that it would be remunerated then the failure to do so causes the basis to fail. If the basis was that it would not be remunerated then recovery will be denied even if the claimant labours under a mistake. In the context of pre-contractual negotiations a common example will be where a defendant stipulates that any work done is 'subject to contract'. Even if a claimant misunderstands this expression and mistakenly believes that he will be remunerated for his work, the objective meaning of the expression will govern the situation.[77] Similarly, a payment which is made by mistake but with the purpose of 'closing a transaction' is irrecoverable because the basis upon which it is paid (the closure of a transaction) does not fail.[78]

This approach also explains why the same principle applies in cases where a contract *has been* concluded but work is performed beyond the scope of the contract. The value of that work will only be recoverable if the shared, objective basis upon which it was done was that it would be remunerated. This is most apparent in employment cases where an employer will be liable to pay the value of non-contractual work done only if the objective basis on which the work is done is that it would be remunerated. In *Miles v Wakefield Metropolitan District Council*,[79] a registrar of births, deaths, and marriages for the defendant council, as part of industrial action, agreed to work on Saturdays (as required) but refused to perform marriages on that day. The council responded by telling him not to work on Saturdays and deducted the proportional part of his salary. The House of Lords held that it was entitled to do so since no work had been performed for those days. In obiter dicta, several members of the House of Lords also considered the situation of an employee who, nevertheless, performed limited duties which did not fulfil his contract. Lord Bridge suggested that such an employee would not be entitled to a *quantum meruit* because the original contract of employment would need to have been superseded, and it would not have been.[80] But Lords Brightman and Templeman considered that the employer must surely pay the value of the work.[81] If the employer accepts the work knowing that the employee expects to be paid for it,

---

[77] *Confetti Records v Warner Music UK Ltd* [2003] EWHC 1274, [2003] EMLR 35.

[78] *Maskell v Horner* [1915] 3 KB 106, at 118 (Lord Reading CJ); *Woolwich Equitable Building Society v Inland Revenue Commissioners* [1993] AC 70, at 166 (Lord Goff).

[79] [1987] AC 539.

[80] *Ibid*, at 552.

[81] *Ibid*, at 553 (Lord Brightman), 561 (Lord Templeman).

the basis for the employee's performance will fail unless the employee is remunerated. In contrast, if the employer tells the employee that he will not pay for the work then even if the employee is mistaken in performing he cannot recover. In *Wiluszynski v Tower Hamlets LBC*,[82] the claimant worked for a local council employer and his duties included answering councillors' enquiries on estate matters. As part of an industrial dispute he continued to perform his duties but refused to answer the enquiries. The council explained that he could come to work but that he would not be paid unless he answered the queries. The Court of Appeal held that the employee was not entitled to be paid a *quantum meruit*. Fox LJ (with whom Mann LJ agreed) explained that the 'crucial issue' was whether the council had directed the employee how to perform his work during this period so that the council 'could be said to have displaced or negated the council's previous attitude that it regarded any work done as purely voluntary.'[83]

(iii) Bilateral cases which seem to apply a mistake analysis

Although there is no pre-contractual liability case which has relied upon the unjust factor of unilateral mistake, there are examples where mistake has apparently been considered as the unjust factor in the context of a bilateral relationship. Three of the leading cases which have recognized mistake in such relationships are considered below. Properly understood, all these cases involve failure of consideration, not unilateral mistake.

The first case is *Norwich Union Fire Insurance Society Ltd v WH Price Ltd*.[84] In that case insurers paid out under a bilateral policy of marine insurance thinking that the insured lemons had been damaged in transit. In fact, the lemons had merely ripened. The Privy Council held that the money could be recovered because it had been paid by a mistake of fact. Delivering the opinion of the Board, Lord Wright said that it is[85]

> essential that the mistake relied on should be of such a nature that it can be properly described as a mistake in respect of the underlying assumption of the contract or transaction or as being fundamental or basic.

This 'fundamental mistake' test, which requires the mistake to be an 'underlying assumption of the contract or transaction', is identical to the test for failure of consideration (ie shared, objective basis).

---

[82] [1989] ICR 493.
[83] *Ibid*, at 501.
[84] [1934] AC 455.
[85] *Ibid*, at 463.

Although the requirement of 'fundamental mistake' was rejected by Goff J in *Barclays Bank Ltd v W J Simms Son & Cooke (Southern) Ltd*,[86] his Lordship replaced it, in bilateral transaction cases, with a defence of 'valuable consideration' to any action for restitution. Goff J was using the term 'consideration' in that defence to mean 'basis'. He gave the example of money paid by mistake where the basis for the payment was to discharge a debt which the defendant owed and which did discharge the debt. In such a case, Goff J held, restitution would be denied. In other words, in a bilateral exchange, if the basis for the payment does not fail then a claimant cannot recover the value of a mistaken payment or service. Commenting on this defence, a joint judgment of five justices of the High Court of Australia observed that it may mean that 'the true basal principle which enables recovery of money paid under a mistake, whether of fact or law, is "failure of consideration"'.[87] The judgment explained that the meaning of 'good consideration' in this defence was 'the matter considered in forming the decision to do the act, the state of affairs contemplated as the basis or reason for the payment'.[88]

The second case is *Kleinwort Benson Ltd v Lincoln County Council*.[89] Like *Guinness Mahon*, this case also involved a void interest rate swap agreement between a bank and a local council. The House of Lords allowed the bank to recover its payment in this bilateral transaction by relying on the unjust factor of mistake of law. The decision attracted great controversy over the recognition by a majority of the House of Lords that the claimant could be mistaken even though the law about which it was mistaken was not yet discoverable. As we saw above, the closed swap case of *Guinness Mahon* was decided as a case of failure of consideration. *Kleinwort Benson* could also have been decided in the same way.[90] But a majority of the House of Lords relied upon the

---

[86] [1980] 1 QB 677.

[87] *David Securities Pty Ltd v Commonwealth Bank of Australia* (1992) 175 CLR 353. In *National Mutual Association of Australasia Ltd v Walsh* (1987) 8 NSWLR 586 the claimant sought restitution of insurance commissions paid under a mistake that the policies were regular (and not fraudulent). Recovery was refused because the agents were working for the claimant in 'good consideration' even though they were remunerated for their work and were not contractually entitled to the commission. See also *Lloyd's Bank plc v Independent Insurance Co Ltd* [2000] QB 110.

[88] *David Securities Pty Ltd v Commonwealth Bank of Australia* (1992) 175 CLR 353.

[89] [1999] 2 AC 349.

[90] It was assumed by counsel, erroneously, that the extended limitation period in s 32(1)(c) of the *Limitation Act* 1980 applies only where the cause of action is based on mistake: see *Deutsche Morgan Grenfell Group Ltd v Inland Revenue Commissioners* [2006] UKHL 49; [2007] 1 AC 558, at 610 [147] and J Edelman, 'Limitation Periods and the Theory of Unjust Enrichment' (2005) 68 *MLR* 848.

unjust factor of mistake. One of the members of the majority in *Klein-wort Benson Ltd*, Lord Hoffmann, has subsequently explained what such a 'mistake' requires, in terms identical to failure of consideration. In *Deutsche Morgan Grenfell Group Ltd v Inland Revenue Commissioners*[91] Lord Hoffmann said that, like 'common mistake' it involved a focus on the shared, objective circumstances:

> The real point is whether the person who made the payment took the risk that he might be wrong. If he did, then he cannot recover the money. ... It would be more rational if the question of whether a party should be treated as having taken the risk depended upon the objective circumstances sur-rounding the payment as they could reasonably have been known to both parties, including of course the extent to which the law was known to be in doubt...

The final case is *Dextra Bank & Trust Company Limited v Bank of Jamaica*.[92] In that case Dextra was induced by fraudsters to pay nearly US $3 million to the defendant bank ('BOJ'). Dextra thought it was making a loan and BOJ thought it was entering into a foreign exchange trans-action. Both were defrauded and the fraudsters paid Dextra's cheque to BOJ and disappeared with BOJ's foreign exchange. One claim for restitution by Dextra was based upon its mistake in thinking that BOJ had previously agreed to take a loan. The Privy Council accepted that this was a mistake of fact, but held that it was not causative of the pay-ment because Dextra had insisted that the fraudsters only hand over the money upon receipt of a valid promissory note from BOJ.[93] This causation reasoning is difficult to understand. Although Dextra had asked for (but never received) the additional security of a promissory note, its mistaken belief that BOJ had agreed to a loan was nevertheless causative: the mistake was a factor in Dextra's decision, but for which the money would never have been paid to the fraudsters and BOJ.

The causation concern of their Lordships was, in any event, met by Dextra's argument that it was also mistaken at the time of payment of its cheque to BOJ by the fraudsters because at that time it was still ignorant of the true facts, that the fraudsters were acting beyond their authority. This argument also failed. Nor could Dextra recover based on its 'misplaced reliance' on the fraudsters.[94] As the Privy Council explained, all of these claims based on mistake could 'only succeed,

---

[91] [2006] UKHL 49; [2007] 1 AC 558, at [26]–[28]. See also Lord Brown at [175] who preferred to describe the unjust factor as failure of consideration.

[92] [2002] 1 All ER (Comm) 193.

[93] *Dextra Bank & Trust Co Ltd v Bank of Jamaica* [2002] 1 All ER (Comm) 193, at [30].

[94] *Ibid*, at [29].

if at all, on the basis of the circumstances in which the BOJ acquired the cheque'.[95] But in circumstances where Dextra had 'failed to communicate directly with the BOJ to make sure that the BOJ understood that the money was being offered as a loan'[96] it could not recover. In other words, a unilateral mistake in a bilateral transaction is insufficient. There must be a shared, objective basis which fails.

4. CONCLUSION

In a recent extra-judicial consideration of this area of law, Justice Hayne, of the High Court of Australia, suggested that there may be no single principle which can explain cases involving pre-contractual liability where a contract fails to materialize. He proposed instead that the reason for liability might be found by 'a basis that makes some objective assessment of the circumstances and imposes the obligation as a consequence of that analysis'.[97] The short point of this chapter was that this is precisely the single principle which should be applied. The motivating concern, and underlying principle, in the cases is that a defendant who requests or accepts work from a claimant in circumstances where a contract fails to materialize will be liable to pay for the value of that work if, and only if, the objective basis upon which the work was done was that in the circumstances which occurred it was part of an exchange.

One postscript must be added to this chapter to respond to an objection that this argument is mere prestidigitation. The objection is that this analysis—which focuses on an objective, shared understanding that work is part of an exchange—is simply contract by another name. The rabbit, it is said, was always in the hat. To paraphrase H L Mencken, this objection is simple, elegant, and wrong. First, the very reason why claims for a reasonable sum arise in these cases is because a court has decided that a contract was *not* concluded. As we have seen this might be because there is too much uncertainty about the bargain. Or it might be because legislation has rendered a bargain void or unenforceable. Second, there is a difference between a shared understanding that work is part of an exchange (with no agreement about the price in exchange) and an agreement that the work would be remunerated at a reasonable price. In cases where work is done before

---

[95] *Ibid*, at [33].

[96] *Ibid*, at [29].

[97] K Hayne, 'Anticipated Contracts that Fail to Materialise' in S Degeling and J Edelman, *Unjust Enrichment in Commercial Law* (Australia: Lawbook Co, 2008) 237, at 249.

a contract is concluded the parties may have wildly different views concerning the appropriate remuneration or exchange, even though they had a shared basis that it would be remunerated. The remuneration which one party believed to be reasonable might be considered entirely unreasonable by the other. It is a fiction to suggest that the parties agreed upon a reasonable rate as determined by the court.[98] Thirdly, if this principle were truly contractual then decisions of the highest courts in the Commonwealth would have to be condemned for making awards of restitution despite having found a legislative prohibition against contractual enforcement.[99] In contrast, those decisions can be easily understood, and justified, once the restitutionary award is seen as *imposed* upon the parties irrespective of the price that they might have agreed. Finally, and simply as a matter of authority, as explained above, it is a principle which has been recognized for more than half a century that the award of restitution of money paid or the value of performance rendered when a basis fails is an *imposed* award. We now recognize such imposed awards as part of the law of unjust enrichment not the law of contract.

---

[98] For instance, '[t]here is no material in the present case upon which any court would decide what was the share which the parties must be taken to have agreed. But, while there is, therefore, no concluded contract as to the remuneration…the work was not to be gratuitous': *Way v Latilla* [1937] 3 All ER 759, at 763 (Lord Atkin). Of course, in other cases it is possible that the parties might expressly or impliedly reach agreement that the price be 'reasonable' (eg Sale of Goods Act 1979 s8(2)) but where the parties have differing views on the price in a continuing negotiation (and thus differing views on what is 'reasonable') it is a fiction to suppose they have agreed a 'reasonable' price to be determined by the court.

[99] *Pavey & Matthews Pty Ltd v Paul* (1987) 162 CLR 221; *Deglman v Guaranty Trust Co of Canada and Constantineau* [1954] SCR 725; *Dimond v Lovell* [2002] 1 AC 384 (reaching the opposite conclusion but only on the construction of the legislation which extended to an exclusion of unjust enrichment).

PART C

Parties

9

Problems in Assignment Law: Not Yet Out of the Wood?

ANDREW TETTENBORN*

Despite the appearance of two excellent books on the subject in the last three years,[1] the topic of the assignment of rights continues to cause problems for academics and puzzlement for practitioners alike. Hence this chapter. In it we concentrate on what is perhaps the most basic issue within assignment law—namely, assignability, or what rights are capable of assignment and when.

On the surface the matter seems straightforward. If you ask an educated English lawyer what the rules on assignability are, he is likely to sum up the accepted position in something like these four propositions:

(1) Legal rights have a proprietary character. This is true whether they are rights under a contract, rights to sue in tort, or other kinds of rights.[2] It follows that all rights are prima facie assignable just as tangible items of property are transferable.
(2) By way of exception, an assignment must not offend the principles derived from the law of maintenance, champerty, and possibly general public policy. If it does, it will not be given effect.
(3) By way of further exception, some personal obligations are intransmissible by nature. Notable examples are contracts where the identity of one or other party is vital—such as a contract of employment, or a contract to paint a picture—and also the right to sue for at least some torts of a personal nature, such as assault or slander.
(4) Lastly, even where an assignment would otherwise be valid, a suitably-drafted anti-assignment clause will prevent it being given effect.

The above statements, if laconic, at least sound straightforward. Looked at more closely, however, all of them bar (1) raise potential difficulties, which are described below.

---

* Bracton Professor of Law, University of Exeter.

[1] See G Tolhurst, *The Assignment of Contractual Rights* (Hart, 2006), and M Smith, *The Law of Assignment: the Creation and Transfer of Choses in Action* (OUP, 2007). In addition Scots law gets its first specialist treatment: R Anderson, *Assignation* (Edinburgh Legal Education Trust, 2008).

[2] For example, a right to recover money paid in error on the basis of unjust enrichment.

1. MAINTENANCE, CHAMPERTY, AND ASSIGNMENT

(a) History

A logical system of law would say that if a right is not personal, or expressly or impliedly made unassignable, it must therefore be transferable (subject to the usual caveat concerning extraordinary circumstances, blatant illegality, and the like.[3] Scots law, indeed, largely takes just this approach.[4] England, by contrast, is not logical. Here it is universally accepted that an assignment otherwise good may still fail on the somewhat enigmatic ground that it savours of maintenance or champerty.[5] It is (so it is said) for this reason that, for instance, a tort claim cannot simply be sold to the highest bidder,[6] nor an action for enormous damages for breach of contract be disposed of for a song to someone prepared to take the risk of bringing it.[7] Now, this argument looks nebulous and awkward, and indeed it is (as will appear). It is also intellectually very curious, in that we have a coupling together of two doctrines—unassignability and maintenance—without any really plausible connection between them. One, assignability, involves a straightforward issue of substantive rights: how far, as a matter of legal policy, should A's right to sue be capable of becoming B's claim instead? The other institutions, by contrast—maintenance and champerty—are essentially procedural vices.[8] Summed up, maintenance consists in financially backing somebody else's lawsuit without good reason; champerty, supposedly a more sinister sub-species, involves not only maintaining the suit but also arranging to take a cut of its proceeds as and when won.[9] In any case both logically require

---

[3] It is not easy to think of such a case: but one example might be an assignment of a debt which transpired to be a payment for cocaine or terrorist AK-47s supplied by the assignee.

[4] On which see Ross Anderson's laconic reference to the 'unparalleled willingness of Scots lawyers to assign anything and everything': *Assignation*, para 5-48.

[5] Tolhurst, *The Assignment of Contractual Rights*, para 6.59 ff; Chitty, *Contracts* (29th edn), para 19-048. For those who prefer statements in the case law see, eg, *Master v Miller* (1791) 4 TR 320, at 340 (Buller J, citing earlier authority from Coke); *Trendtex Trading Corp v Crédit Suisse* [1982] AC 679, at 703 (Lord Roskill).

[6] *Trendtex Trading Corp v Crédit Suisse* [1982] AC 679, at 702 (Lord Roskill).

[7] A nice example being *Advanced Technology Structures Ltd v Cray Valley Products Ltd* [1993] BCLC 723 (£10 million potential worth of claim transferred by company to ex-controller in supposed requital of £10,000 debt owed to him: assignment not recognized).

[8] Vices in that, despite their suppression more than 40 years ago as crimes or torts, statute makes it clear that they may still taint a transaction: Criminal Law Act 1967, s 14(2).

[9] As good an account as any comes in Winfield, *Textbook of the Law of Tort*, 654-660 (published in 1937, when both were still torts).

a muscling-in on litigation in support of *another*'s right, whereas an assignee *ex hypothesi* does not buttress someone else's claim, but rather vindicates his own.

Why, then, use maintenance and champerty to restrict assignment? The answer, not surprisingly, is long on history and short on logic.

One explanation lies in the mediaeval fear of litigational malpractices, and in particular that those with money and clout would sweet-talk or strong-arm local judges into deciding in their friends' favour.[10] As long as this fear was justified, it did indeed make no sense to distinguish between those who merely pulled the purse strings (maintainers) and those who supposedly guarded their position by formally taking over the rights concerned (assignees). This being so, the common law's decision to harden its stance against assignment[11] on principle is less surprising.[12]

A more significant explanation, however, lies (it is suggested) in the intellectual contortions arising from the practical necessity to allow some form of assignment of an intangible, whether the common law liked it or not. The job, as we know, was done in Chancery, where from the seventeenth century the law of trusts neatly sidestepped the Temple's intransigence.[13] Briefly, whenever an obligee, A, expressed an intent to transfer his right to B, equity imposed a trust[14] on it and thus ensured that B, even if disenfranchised at common law, could compel A to exercise his right to sue for his benefit. But here came the bind. If B asked equity's help, equity understandably extracted from him, as the real party in issue, a promise to pay the costs;[15] and it is suggested

---

[10] See the classic, if hyperbolic, reference in *Lampet*'s case (1613) 10 Co Rep 46b, 48a to 'the great wisdom and policy of the sages and founders of our law, who have provided, that no possibility, right, title, nor thing in action, shall be granted or assigned to strangers, for that would be the occasion of multiplying of contentions and suits, of great oppression of the people, and chiefly of terre-tenants, and the subversion of the due and equal execution of justice'.

[11] Which originally had been more doctrinal than anything, common lawyers being simply unable to understand an obligation as anything other than personal to the parties: see Holdsworth, *History of English Law*, vii, 520 and authorities there cited.

[12] See *Co Litt* 266a: Marshall, *The Assignment of Choses in Action*, 52-3; Holdsworth, *History of English Law*, vii, 524; *Re Kenneth Wright Distributors Pty Ltd (in liq); WJ Vine Pty Ltd v Paul* [1973] VR 161, 166; *Glegg v Bromley* [1912] 3 KB 474, 489-90 (Parker LJ).

[13] Equity lawyers 'from the earliest times thought the doctrine [of unassignability at common law] too absurd for them to adopt': —Buller J in *Master v Miller* (1791) 4 Durn. & El. 320, at 340.

[14] See, eg, *Fulham v M'Carthy* (1848) 1 HLC 703, at 722 ('The assignor of a legal interest still has an interest, being trustee for the assignee'—Lord Campbell). The better view is that this is a constructive trust: Smith, *The Law of Assignment*, para 6.12.

[15] For a rare statement of what must have been universally regarded as obvious, see Blackburn J in *Jeffs v Day* (1866) LR 1 QB 372, at 374.

that this, to a common lawyer, must have inexorably suggested both maintenance and champerty. After all, the whole point of the arrangement was that B was not enforcing a right of his own, but rather bankrolling A to enforce A's claim in exchange for a cut (here 100 per cent) of the proceeds. The only counter to this was yet more legal legerdemain. Assignees duly seized on an ancient rule that acts done with good reason or justification did not infringe the laws against maintenance,[16] and reasoned that at least some assignees had a legitimate interest in enforcing the obligation concerned. Thus where this was so the plea of champerty or maintenance could be met by a plea that the assignee had acted with due justification.[17]

What has just been said explains (even if it does not really justify) the maintenance-based limitations on assignability. Unfortunately, even when thus explained, the maintenance limitation itself remained problematical. In particular, by 1979 the authorities were in utter chaos on the issue of when an assignee did or did not have the requisite legitimate interest. Thankfully, in that year the House of Lords in *Trendtex Trading Corp v Crédit Suisse*[18] cut the Gordian knot. An effectively insolvent commodity trader owed its bank large sums, and its only asset was a massive damages claim against a Nigerian defendant. The bank took an assignment of that claim as representing what looked like its best chance of salvaging something from the wreck. Rather than troubling to enforce it, it then resold it for a small cash sum to a Swiss financier, who shortly afterwards settled it at an enormous profit. When the original trader sought to impeach the assignments (unsuccessfully, for reasons irrelevant here),[19] the House took the opportunity to lay down a simple, general rule: for an assignment to escape the maintenance limitation, the assignee had to have a 'genuine commercial interest in enforcing the claim of another' (Lord Roskill's words[20]) or a 'genuine and substantial interest' (Lord Wilberforce's phrase[21]). In *Trendtex* itself, the House agreed that the bank's desire to assure payment to itself was just such an interest; but that the sub-assignee financier, being a mere speculator, had no adequate excuse for taking it; and

---

[16] On which see Winfield, *Textbook of the Law of Tort*, 656 ff.

[17] Neatly summed up by Lloyd LJ in *Brownton Ltd v Edward Moore Inbucon Ltd* [1985] 3 All ER 499, at 509: ('[t]here is no difference between the interest required to justify maintenance of an action and the interest required to justify the taking of a share in the proceeds, or the interest required to support an out-and-out assignment.').

[18] [1982] AC 679.

[19] More precisely, that Swiss law, which was held to govern the validity of the assignments, found them unobjectionable.

[20] [1982] AC 679, at 703.

[21] *Ibid*, 694.

further that that the bank, having obtained the claim not to enforce it but to sell it to him, had also acted illegitimately.

Trendtex, it will be noticed, studiedly retains the formal tie between assignment and champerty. But the inference is irresistible that the link is pretty nominal, and that incantations of 'champerty' as a ground of attack now cloak a much more general 'public policy' criterion. Indeed, Baroness Hale in the Privy Council effectively let this cat out of the bag in *Massai Aviation Services v Attorney General of the Bahamas*.[22] Following a corporate reorganization, an action for breach of contract was brought not by the original contractor but by the associated company to whom some of its assets had been transferred. The defendant plausibly but unmeritoriously challenged the plaintiff's title to sue. Her Ladyship said that in such a case it was 'essential to look at the transaction as a whole, and to ask whether there is anything in it which is contrary to public policy',[23] decided there was not, and thus summarily saw off the plea.

One further point needs to be made concerning the recasting of the law in *Trendtex*. Before that case, it had often been said that the assignment of some claims was unaffected by the 'commercial interest' requirement altogether. One was liquidated claims, such as debts,[24] and possibly unjust enrichment claims too.[25] Another was claims to the proceeds of a cause of action as and when obtained[26] (which, since a successful damages claim would in its nature spawn a liquidated judgment debt, came to much the same thing). The reasoning behind these exclusions[27] was never entirely satisfactory, since elsewhere the common law condemned maintaining any sort of claim, without discriminating between debt, damages, or anything else. Nevertheless, despite occasional cases taking the logical view and rejecting blanket exclusions of this sort,[28] these exceptions have continued to be accepted

---

[22] [2007] UKPC 12, [2007] 5 LRC 179.

[23] *Ibid*, at [19].

[24] A neat example being *Fitzroy v Cave* [1905] 2 KB 364 (upholding the purchase of debts by an assignee who not only had no conceivable interest in buying them, but admitted with engaging candour that his only aim was to bankrupt the debtor). See too the earlier *Comfort v Betts* [1891] 1 QB 737.

[25] See Mason P in *Fostif Pty Ltd v Campbells Cash & Carry Pty Ltd* (2005) 63 NSWLR 203, at 232.

[26] *Glegg v Bromley* [1912] 3 KB 474.

[27] Which tended to be of the bootstrap variety. Typical was Cozens-Hardy LJ's unconvincing argument in *Fitzroy v Cave* [1905] 2 KB 364, at 372 that a debt was an item of property in its own right; that the assignee as owner could do as he liked with his own; and that it somehow followed that maintenance and champerty must be irrelevant.

[28] Notably Megaw J's decision in *Laurent v Sale & Co* [1963] 1 WLR 829, actually disallowing the assignment of a debt on the basis that it smacked of champerty. In the light of what

in Australia[29] and England.[30] In other words, debts and similar claims can invariably be traded, however cynically or speculatively.

(b) The maintenance limitation today

So much for the history. Turning to the present status of the maintenance limitation, its recent developments seem, if taken *au pied de la lettre*, to ease life mightily for practitioners. Thus assignment of debts has been confirmed as unproblematical; and even as regards non-debt claims, it now seems apparent that, unless something positively obnoxious appears, virtually all the old restrictions on assignment[31] have gone. Hence it seems that an assignment with almost any plausible commercial explanation can be safely recommended to a client. And, indeed, a number of cases suggest just this. Thus the need to ensure payment from an otherwise judgment-proof debtor will suffice (as in *Trendtex* itself[32]), even where there has been no previous involvement between assignor and assignee,[33] as where a buyer of substandard goods in the commodity markets takes an assignment of its bankrupt seller's claim against its own supplier.[34] Again, even before

appears below, it is suggested that this case must now be regarded as wrong. Note also that when *Trendtex Trading Corp v Crédit Suisse* [1980] QB 629 was in the Court of Appeal, Lord Denning MR at 656 made disparaging comments about the supposed immunity from attack of assignments of proceeds claims.

[29] *Re Daley, ex p National Australia Bank Ltd* (1992) 37 FCR 390.

[30] See *Camdex International Ltd v Bank of Zambia* [1998] QB 22 (debts) and *Sears Tooth (A Firm) v Payne Hicks Beach (A Firm)* [1997] 2 FLR 116 (proceeds claims). In *Camdex* there are suggestions that there might be an exception where the assignment was not 'bona fide' or 'colourable' (see [1998] QB 22, at 39, 40). What these exceptions mean—if anything—is obscure.

[31] For example, there used to be a heresy that an action in tort could not be assigned (eg Farwell LJ in *Defries v Milne* [1913] 1 Ch 98, at 109; *Poulton v Commonwealth* (1953) 89 CLR 540, at 602). This is now well explored: see *24 Seven Utility Services Ltd v Rosekey Ltd* [2003] EWHC 3415 (QB) and eg *PSC Industrial Services Canada Inc v The Queen in right of Ontario* (2005) 258 DLR (4th) 320.

[32] See *Re Timothy's Pty Ltd* [1981] 2 NSWLR 706, at 712 (Needham J: 'the principle of the *Trendtex* case can be applied to an assignment of a right of action by a debtor to a creditor where the evidence shows that, without that assignment, the creditor is not likely to be paid his debt.').

[33] So held in Australia (see *Re Timothy's Pty Ltd* [1981] 2 NSWLR 706, above, and *Beatty v Brash's Pty Ltd* [1998] 2 VR 201); and in Canada (*Edmonton (City) v Lovat Tunnel Equipment Inc* (2000) 260 AR 140). In England compare *Total Liban SA v Vitol SA* [1999] 2 Lloyd's Rep 700 (substandard goods sold by A to B to C: when B insolvent, no objection taken to C taking assignment of B's right against A so as to substitute a solvent debtor for a bankrupt one).

[34] *Total Liban SA v Vitol SA* [1999] 2 Lloyd's Rep 700. See too the Canadian *Edmonton (City) v Lovat Tunnel Equipment Inc* (2000) 260 AR 140 (similar result where two defendants sued

the point was put beyond doubt by *Massai Aviation Services v Attorney General of the Bahamas*,[35] corporate reorganization or restructuring was fairly consistently accepted as an adequate excuse for assignment: thus assignment of a cause of action by a closely-held corporation to its shareholder was good,[36] even if the assignee was not otherwise a creditor.[37] Again, in an important if underestimated case in 1985 the Court of Appeal approved the tactic of one co-defendant settling with a claimant and in exchange taking over the latter's rights against the other co-defendants.[38] In a similar vein, there is probably no objection under *Trendtex* to the common US practice[39] whereby a claimant releases an under-insured defendant in exchange for an assignment of the latter's claim against some third party—such as an insurer, broker, or even his own lawyer. Although this does not seem to have been tested in England, the Canadian courts have upheld such assignments under *Trendtex*.[40] And finally, it is pretty clear that the pre-1979 safe havens, such as they were, remain: for example, the right of the buyer of an asset,[41] or a person taking over a project, to accept with it a transfer of associated claims against third parties, and the right of a person entitled to subrogation to bolster that right with an express transfer.

and D1 assigned to claimant rights against D2 for indemnity). And cf *Advanced Technology Structures Ltd v Cray Valley Products* [1993] BCLC 723 (employee with right to payments from bankrupt employer taking over employer's contract suit against third party: although assignment ineffective for other reasons, legitimate interest in principle).

[35] [2007] UKPC 12, [2007] 5 LRC 179.

[36] See *Norglen Ltd v Reeds Rains Prudential Ltd*, 3 February 1994 (unreported) (Morritt J), accepted as correct in the Court of Appeal ([1996] 1 WLR 864, at 873); also *Circuit Systems Ltd v Zuken-Redac (UK) Ltd* (1994) 11 Const LJ 201. Both cases went to the House of Lords together on other grounds, where this conclusion was unquestioned (see *Norglen Ltd (In Liquidation) v Reeds Rains Prudential Ltd* [1999] 2 AC 1).

[37] *Massai Aviation Services Ltd v Attorney-General for the Bahamas* [2007] UKPC 12, [2007] 5 LRC 179. See too *528650 Ontario Ltd v Hepburn* (2003) 124 ACWS (3d) 16 (Canada); *Re Daley, ex p National Australia Bank Ltd* (1992) 37 FCR 390 (Australia), to much the same effect.

[38] *Brownton Ltd v Edward Moore Inbucon Ltd* [1985] 3 All ER 499. This was a commercial claim: but a Canadian court has treated a personal injury suit in the same way (see *Margetts v Timmer Estate* (1999) 178 DLR (4th) 577).

[39] Common, but not uncontroversial. In the context of the assignment of legal malpractice claims, see Walters, 'The unwitting attorney, the desperate client, and the perpetuation of the New York power play: a proposal to ban voluntary assignments of legal malpractice claims' 3 *Cardozo Pub L Pol'y & Ethics J* 543 (2005), and cf the sour comment on one such assignment in *Zuniga v Groce, Locke & Hebdon*, 878 SW2d 313, at 317 (1994) ('a transparent device to replace a judgment-proof, uninsured defendant with a solvent defendant').

[40] See *Fredrickson v Ins Corp of BC* (1988) 28 DLR (4th) 414 (insurers) and *453416 Ontario Inc v White* (1984) 42 CPC 209 (brokers).

[41] *Ellis v Torrington* [1920] 1 KB 399; *Re Kenneth Wright Distributors Pty Ltd (in liq)*; *WJ Vine Pty Ltd v Paul* [1973] VR 161.

However, despite this good news there do remain pitfalls. In at least some cases one still cannot be sure an assignment will be upheld, even if it is otherwise done with good reason.

To begin with, whatever might have been said in *Trendtex*, the actual result in that case still casts a shadow. At least outside plain debts, speculation in claims (traditionally dismissed as 'trafficking in litigation') apparently remains a no-go area. Any purchase in these circumstances is in danger of being regarded as ineffective and thus open to attack either by the defendant (if the assignee tries to sue), or for that matter by the assignor himself. Admittedly, it has now been made wholesomely clear that an assignment will not fail the 'speculation' test merely because the assignee stands to make a profit from it.[42] Nevertheless, difficulties may still arise where the profit is unusually handsome: the assignee in such a case remains in danger of assimilation to someone with no adequate interest at all, and of having the transfer disallowed on the basis of public policy.[43] Moreover, it seems this may be true even if he would otherwise have a good reason for taking an assignment of some sort: thus an insolvent company's assignment of a £10 million third party claim to a creditor was struck down when it appeared that the creditor's claim was worth only some £10,000.[44]

Secondly, some impeccably non-speculative arrangements may also still present dangers. Sometimes this arises from narrow readings by courts of what is, after all, the fairly open-ended criterion of a 'genuine commercial interest'. Thus even if a liable defendant can settle with a claimant by transferring to the latter his own claim to contribution against others, there remains doubt whether this scheme remains effective where the defendant concerned settles not on the basis of probable liability but for more general commercial reasons, such as a desire to keep the claimant sweet as regards future relationships.[45]

---

[42] See *Brownton v Edward Moore Inbucon Ltd* [1985] 3 All ER 499, 504, at 509 (Megaw and Lloyd LJJ); *Massai Aviation Services v Attorney General (Bahamas)* [2007] UKPC 12, [2007] 5 LRC 179, at [17] (Baroness Hale).

[43] '[F]or a minority shareholder to buy a substantial claim for a nominal sum in the hope of making a substantial profit may well be contrary to public policy'—Baroness Hale in *Massai Aviation Services Ltd v Attorney-General for the Bahamas* [2007] UKPC 12, [2007] 5 LRC 179, at [21].

[44] *Advanced Technology Structures Ltd v Cray Valley Products Ltd* [1993] BCLC 723. See too the Canadian *Re Rizzo & Rizzo Shoes Ltd* (1998) 38 OR (3d) 280, esp at [33] (ground for disallowing assignment to creditor that taken 'for the purpose of obtaining more than what the assignee is legally entitled to').

[45] See the New South Wales decision in *Rickard Constructions Pty Ltd v Rickard Hails Moretti Pty Ltd* (2004) 188 FLR 278. Whether this strict approach would be followed in England is not clear. But this is the problem. One can hardly advise a client to enter into a transaction where any doubt of this sort remains.

Furthermore, it has to be remembered that arguably it is the interest of the assignee only that counts for these purposes, and hence the fact that an assignment serves a legitimate purpose of the *assignor* may not be enough. Thus while the creditor of a doubtful debtor can protect himself by taking an assignment from the debtor, he cannot, it seems, achieve the same result by selling his own claim to someone who owes his debtor money and would thus have an insolvency set-off.[46] Yet again, a series of Commonwealth cases seems to discountenance the technique of claims consolidation—ie the practice, where a number of connected claimants have potential interlocking claims against a defendant, of assigning these claims to one claimant to prosecute.[47]

It is not easy, if one may say so, to see what good these remaining limitations on assignment do. For example, to say that the only relevant interest is the assignee's may well be historically true: it was, after all, his potential liability in maintenance that caused the problem in the first place. Nevertheless, whether we ought still to say this is questionable: if we are moving to a simpler question of whether the assignment offends public policy, it should not matter whose legitimate interests we are talking about. Again, it seems curious that the maintenance limitation should apply to assignments of rights to damages, but not to debt claims. Why should it be less objectionable to speculate in (say) a contested debt claim than in a simple claim for damages for breach of contract? And if the ready assignability of the former does not seem to have caused problems in practice, why should it be any different with the latter?

Indeed, one can wonder (no doubt unthinkably) if even the central prohibitions in *Trendtex*—speculation or trafficking in litigation—remain appropriate as separate grounds of objection at all. Since *Trendtex*, the courts have gamely upheld them, the recent tendency being to say that such speculation has to be regarded as offending public policy.[48] Just what the public policy is, however—apart perhaps from a puritanical distaste for profiteers, which seems a pretty slender

---

[46] See the Australian decision in *Monk v Australia & New Zealand Banking Group Ltd* (1994) 34 NSWLR 148 (assignee in such a case has no sufficient interest to justify reliance on the assignment).

[47] See the Commonwealth decisions in *Waste Not Wanted Inc v The Queen in right of Canada* [1988] 1 FC 239 (residents plagued by nuisance caused by dumping cannot assign individual causes of action to public interest group incorporated for the purpose). See too *Tacan v Canada* (2003) 124 ACWS (3d) 684 (Indians cannot assign claims against government to band for more efficient prosecution). But the decisions are not all one way: a similar arrangement was upheld in Australia in *Campbells Cash & Carry Pty Ltd v Fostif Pty Ltd* (2006) 229 CLR 386.

[48] Eg Baroness Hale in *Massai Aviation Services Ltd v Attorney-General for the Bahamas* [2007] UKPC 12, [2007] 5 LRC 179, at [21], above, n 42.

ground—remains unclear. It is all very well to say (for example) that 'nobody wants a futures market in personal injury claims'[49] but why? There would certainly be much clarity and coherence gained if courts ceased objecting to speculative transfers as such and instead demanded evidence of specific objectionability[50] before disallowing them. Indeed, it is worth noting that in one area—insolvency law—precisely this has been done. A trustee in bankruptcy or liquidator has long had statutory power to dispose of the debtor's rights,[51] and this has consistently been construed as ousting any champerty-based (or speculation-based) objection.[52] No particular ill effects seem to have arisen from this right in an insolvency practitioner to hawk the debtor's claims to the highest bidder almost without restriction: and, if so, it seems unlikely that much more harm would result from its extension to any potential assignor.

2. INTRANSMISSIBLE OBLIGATIONS: A SEPARATE CATEGORY?

Maintenance and champerty (or something like them) clearly represent one restriction on assignment. Implicitly personal contracts, and those containing explicit anti-assignment clauses, represent another (of which more later). But at this point another question arises. Are these the only restrictions, or can we go further and say that there are obligations which are by their nature outside the whole assignment regime altogether, so that they remain intransmissible whatever the circumstances? The answer is often regarded as 'Yes', but (to anticipate) it is suggested that this needs to be regarded with a good deal of scepticism.

Assertions that there is indeed a hard core of naturally intransmissible obligations are not difficult to find. Most often this category is exemplified by 'personal tort' claims such as libel, assault, or pain

---

[49] Or, perhaps more accurately, very few. For an absolutely serious defence of just such a solution see Shukaitis, 'A Market in Personal Injury Tort Claims', 16 *J Legal Studies* 329 (1987).

[50] Such as an explicit contractual promise to give particular evidence in court: see, eg *Deloitte Touche Tohmatsu v Cridlands Pty Ltd* (2003) 204 ALR 281.

[51] See para 6 of Pt III of Sch 4 of the Insolvency Act 1986 (company liquidator's power 'to sell any of the company's property by public auction or private contract with power to transfer the whole of it to any person'). For the bankruptcy power, see Sch 5, Pt II, para 9.

[52] An interpretation introduced by *Seear v Lawson* (1880) 15 Ch D 426, consolidated by *Guy v Churchill* (1889) 40 Ch D 481, and regarded as canonical ever since.

and suffering arising from personal injury.[53] At first sight this seems in accordance with principle. It looks outlandish and unsavoury to allow A to recover for some injury to B, or for some calumny affecting B's reputation, however willing B may have been to assign to A his right to complain. It looks even more unattractive for personal injury suits for pain and suffering to be able to be trafficked in the fashion of sub-prime debt or pork bellies. Moreover, a general category of unassignable obligations of this sort also chimes in neatly with a very long-accepted rule in insolvency: namely, the principle denying creditors access to the proceeds of claims for what are essentially personal wrongs to the debtor.[54]

This is all very well. However, it is noteworthy that, however commonplace, assertions of a class of completely intransmissible rights almost all appear in obiter dicta (one exception being an entertaining Manitoba case airily seeing off a hopeful driver who sued a negligent third party as assignee of his passenger's traffic injury claim).[55] More to the point, there is in fact some Commonwealth authority to the contrary, where even claims of this sort have been regarded not as unassignable but as merely subject to the *Trendtex* 'legitimate interest' test. Thus even as regards that most personal of claims, defamation, at least one Canadian court saw no problem when, in a corporate reconstruction, one company assigned the benefit of a defamation claim to its designated successor together with the rest of its assets.[56] Again, take the case of negotiated settlements of complex litigation. If a co-defendant can settle a *commercial* claim in exchange for a takeover of the claimant's would-be rights against another defendant,[57] there is no obvious reason why the same should not apply merely because the underlying claim concerned pain and suffering or assault. And indeed, a couple of Canadian decisions have allowed just this to happen. *In Margetts v Timmer Estate*[58] in 1999, passengers injured in a car accident sued their driver and, in addition, sued the Crown as highway

---

[53] Typical is Fletcher Moulton LJ's statement in *Glegg v Bromley* [1912] 3 KB 474, at 488: 'We are all agreed that you cannot assign a cause of action for a personal wrong.' See too *Trendtex Trading Corp v Crédit Suisse* [1980] QB 629, at 656 (Lord Denning MR); also in the HL at [1982] AC 679, at 702; *24 Seven Utility Services Ltd v Rosekey Ltd* [2003] EWHC 3415 (QB), at [25]; and in addition the Australian decision in *Beatty v Brash's Pty Ltd* [1998] 2 VR 201.

[54] Ie the rule encapsulated in *Beckham v Drake* (1849) 2 HLC 579: see too *Rose v Buckett* [1901] 2 KB 449 and *Ord v Upton* [2000] Ch 352.

[55] See *Compton v Allward* [1912] 1 WWR 452.

[56] *PSC v Ontario* (2005) 258 DLR (4th) 320.

[57] Which he can: see *Brownton Ltd v Edward Moore Inbucon Ltd* [1985] 3 All ER 499, no above, n 38.

[58] (1999) 178 DLR (4th) 577.

authority; the latter, as part of a settlement with the passengers, took over their rights against the driver. The Alberta Court of Appeal robustly dismissed a challenge to the competence of this assignment, pointing out that the Crown had a more than adequate interest in taking it, and that there was nothing else obnoxious about the arrangement. In similar vein, the British Columbia Supreme Court did much the same thing in *CW v Norton*.[59] Where a trainee prison guard was brutalized by a college instructor, Morrison J approved without hesitation an arrangement under which the college paid a large sum to settle the trainee's claim and in exchange accepted an assignment of his right to sue the instructor for battery.

Whether these decisions would be followed in England remains an open question. But it is suggested that there is much to be said in their favour, and that at least as regards causes of actions arising out of past wrongs there is no objection in principle to the idea of assignment. Of course, in the nature of things it will not be often that anyone will have adequate reason to take over a 'personal tort' claim (the settling defendant is one of the few plausible examples): but if there is, there seems no reason to strike down the assignment as a matter of principle.

3. PERSONAL CONTRACTUAL RIGHTS AND CONTRACTS WITH EXPRESS ANTI-ASSIGNMENT CLAUSES

(a) Anti-assignment clauses generally

In *Linden Gardens Trust Ltd v Lenesta Sludge Disposals Ltd*,[60] the House of Lords finally cemented the rule[61] allowing contractors to prohibit assignment, made clear that this was a matter for the contractors alone,[62] and confirmed that an assignment in disregard of such a provision was entirely ineffective.[63] They thus held that where a building contract forbade assignment by the client, a purchaser of the building who had purported to accept an assignment of the client's rights could

---

[59] [2001] BCTC 478.

[60] [1994] 1 AC 85.

[61] Previously expressed in *Helstan Securities Ltd v Hertfordshire County Council* [1978] 3 All ER 262.

[62] To the assignees' argument that the courts should supervise such clauses for reasonableness or some similar feature, Lord Browne-Wilkinson's response was pithy: 'there is no public need for a market in choses in action.' ([1994] 1 AC 85, at 107).

[63] Rather than merely wrongful but effective (an interpretation suggested as possible in Goode (1979) 42 *MLR* 553): see in particular [1994] 1 AC 85, at 104 (Lord Browne-Wilkinson).

have no conceivable cause of action against the builders. It also confirmed that, in contrast to the Uniform Commercial Code (which drastically limits the effect of such clauses, especially where pure receivables are concerned)[64] the right to prevent assignment is an absolute one.

In addition to *Linden Gardens*, there is also clear authority that a contract which by nature depends on the personal characteristics of one party cannot be assigned, even if it contains no explicit prohibition. Straightforward examples are contracts of employment (hence the decision in *Nokes v Doncaster Amalgamated Collieries Ltd*[65] that a long-serving employee apparently ceased to be an employee at all following a technical corporate reorganization which would have changed the identity of his employer)[66] and contracts where the personality, skill, or creditworthiness of one or other party is crucial.[67] These two categories of non-assignability are dealt with together here because it is suggested that they are essentially expressions of the same principle, the only distinctive feature of the latter case being that the prohibition is implicit rather than express.[68]

(b) Problems with unassignable contracts: pre-existing agreements to assign receivables

Despite the apparently absolute pronouncements in *Linden Gardens* and elsewhere, two problems nevertheless continue to arise for lawyers wishing to be assured that an express or implicit 'no-assignment' clause will actually be effective.

The first arises from a curious decision in the Court of Appeal, which seems to suggest that even an express anti-assignment clause will not prevent assignment where the would-be assignee claims (as nearly all financiers do) under a pre-existing agreement by the assignor to assign future receivables. In *Foamcrete (UK) Ltd v Thrust Engineering Ltd*[69] the court was concerned with payments due under a joint venture agreement, the issue being whether these were caught by a previously-agreed floating charge when it crystallized despite the

---

[64] Art 9-406(d). This view is gaining converts on this side of the Atlantic: it appears in the proposed *Principles of European Contract Law*, in the shape of Art 11:301(c).

[65] [1940] AC 1014. More recently, see *UNISON v Allen* [2007] IRLR 975.

[66] See too the earlier *Brace v Calder* [1895] 2 QB 253 (same result following change in composition of employing partnership).

[67] Eg *Griffith v Tower Publishing Co Ltd* [1897] 1 Ch 21 (publishing agreement).

[68] Thus just as specific agreement may prevent an assignment otherwise permissible, conversely it can make even an entirely personal agreement transferable: see *Devefi v Mateffy Pearl Nagy* (1993) 113 ALR 225, at 235 (also at [1993] RPC 493, at 503).

[69] [2002] BCC 221.

presence of an anti-assignment clause.[70] It was held that they were. The grounds of decision were somewhat enigmatic. But essentially the argument was that an assignment in the face of an anti-assignment clause was invalidated because it involved a breach of contract by the assignor; that the assignee obtained an interest in the chargor's receivables at the time of the floating charge agreement; and that because this agreement had been concluded before the joint venture agreement, the former could not amount to a breach of the latter.

Foamcrete, if taken seriously, in practice emasculates anti-assignment clauses in the context of finance (unless the financier is unlucky enough to be claiming under a floating charge that post-dates the contract concerned). Nevertheless, although it seems for the moment to be the last word,[71] it is submitted that its reasoning is highly doubtful, and that further challenge can by no means be ruled out.

To begin with, while an agreement to assign a chose in action can come into being before the chose itself, the actual assignment of it (which allegedly would constitute the breach) cannot. The suggestion in *Foamcrete* that the future chose in action stood assigned in equity as soon as the floating charge was signed is thus simply false.[72] On a proper interpretation the assignment should have been regarded as taking place at the later date when the floating charge crystallized—which of course was after the joint venture agreement came into effect.

Secondly, it is suggested that in any case *Foamcrete* misinterprets the reason why an anti-assignment clause is effective. The reason why such a clause precludes a successful assignment is (it is submitted) not that the creditor technically breaks his contract by trying to assign, but more simply that a contractor is entitled to decide whom he is willing to contract with. Despite the Court of Appeal's attempt to pray *Linden Gardens* in aid in *Foamcrete*,[73] Lord Browne-Wilkinson's opinion if anything stresses the point being made here: the reason why English law was willing to give effect to prohibitions on assignment

---

[70] In fact it was held that the clause was inapplicable to these payments, for reasons not relevant here. But the decision was equally explicit on what the position would have been had the clause applied.

[71] A search in February 2009 revealed not so much as a single subsequent citation in England, Canada, or Australia.

[72] See cases such as *Biggerstaff v Rowatt's Wharf Ltd* [1896] 2 Ch 93 (assignment under floating charge takes place for purposes of set-off at time of crystallization). The authority cited in *Foamcrete*, the Australian *Re Margart Pty Ltd* [1985] BCLC 314, is not in point, holding merely that proceeds of property subject to a floating charge can be paid to the chargeholder unaffected by the equivalent of s127 of the Insolvency Act 1986.

[73] The case is quoted from at some length at 224-5.

lies in the very genuine commercial interest of a contractor in deciding whether he is prepared to contract at all and, if so, whom he wishes to contract with.[74]

(c) Problems with unassignable contracts: trusts

The second difficulty facing drafters of anti-assignment clauses (if *Foamcrete* was not enough) revolves around a series of cases that apparently allows assignees an end-run around many anti-assignment clauses by way of the creation of a trust. In other words, they suggest that even if an obligation is otherwise unassignable there can still be an enforceable trust of the benefit of it, with much the same legal result as if there had been an assignment in the first place.

The first of these cases was *Don King Productions Ltd v Warren*.[75] Two boxing promoters went into partnership, agreeing that the benefit of all their contracts with individual boxers should be brought in. When the partnership fell to be dissolved, it had to be decided what the status of these rights was. The partner who had provided the more lucrative contracts argued that they could not be treated as partnership assets, since if they were they would have been effectively assigned; but that this could not be, since (a) they were essentially personal contracts; and (b) for good measure, most of them contained express anti-assignment clauses. Lightman J disagreed. Partly this was for the entirely unexceptionable reason that, however unassignable an agreement might be, there was nothing to stop parties agreeing to treat the profits from it *as if* they were partnership assets. But he also said, worryingly, that even if the contracts were too personal to be transferred, or forbade assignment outright, this did not bar the promisee from agreeing to hold the benefit of them on trust for someone else. True, a trust of an obligation might bind the obligee to enforce it as the beneficiary's catspaw in just the same way as an equitable assignment might once have done.[76] But this did not matter: a trust was not an assignment. On appeal, the Court of Appeal upheld Lightman J on this point (though Morritt LJ also said, even more enigmatically, that although an otherwise inalienable obligation might be held in trust, this would not necessarily give the beneficiary any right to insist on its enforcement).[77]

Don King was strictly obiter on the question of whether trust beneficiaries could indeed avoid anti-assignment clauses by invoking

---

[74] See [1994] 1 AC 85, at 107.
[75] [2000] Ch 291.
[76] Before the Judicature Acts simplified matters.
[77] See [2000] Ch 291, at 335-6.

the difference between trusts and assignments.[78] But the court made its view quite clear. The same goes for a later Court of Appeal decision, *Barbados Trust Co v Bank of Zambia*.[79] Simplified slightly, Bank of America (BoA) held Zambian bonds that prohibited assignment to anyone but a bank. BoA purported to assign them to a non-bank; and after further transfers they ended up in the hands of yet another non-bank Barbados Trust (BT), which sought to sue on them. To overcome the restriction on assignment (which, if effective, meant that BoA was still entitled rather than BT), BoA obligingly declared itself trustee for BT, whereupon BT sued, joining BoA as a nominal defendant.[80] Bank of Zambia (BoZ) understandably objected to this as a stratagem to give BT by the back door a status it could not get directly. In the event BT did lose, on the separate ground that (for reasons that do not matter here) BoA's own title had been defective all along. Langley J nevertheless upheld BoZ's other objection, as did Hooper LJ in the Court of Appeal, the latter making the obvious point that however much trust might theoretically differ from assignment, the result of letting BT sue as trust beneficiary was identical to recognizing their title as equitable assignees. But the majority of the Court of Appeal,[81] like the Court of Appeal in *Don King*, was having none of it. This was a trust, not an assignment: the bonds said nothing about trusts; hence the bar on assignment was beside the point.

With respect, the view in *Don King* and *Barbados Trust* seems perverse. To begin with, it was suggested above that the object of permitting no-assignment clauses at all is fundamentally one of freedom of contract: to allow people to decide in advance who they wish (and do not wish) to contract with. This is important. Not only does one have a very legitimate interest in avoiding contractual relations with those one dislikes or mistrusts. More to the point, contracts in practice pre-eminently involve negotiation over performance, and a contracting party has an even more vital claim to decide whom he is, and whom he is not, prepared to negotiate with. The result of *Don King* and *Bank*

---

[78] Two subsequent decisions following it equally did not trench on this point. See *Swift v Dairywise Farms Ltd* [2000] 1 WLR 1177 (trust could be used to allow hypothecation to lender of proceeds of otherwise untransferable milk quota); *John Taylors (A Firm) v Masons (A Firm)* [2001] EWCA Civ 2106 (application of the rule in *Keech v Sandford* (1726) Sel Cas t King 61 to renewals of unassignable licenses).

[79] [2007] EWCA Civ 148, [2007] 1 Lloyd's Rep 495.

[80] This practice was long-standing and implicitly approved in *Les Affréteurs Réunis SA v Leopold Walford Ltd* [1919] AC 801 (see too *Performing Right Society Ltd v London Theatre of Varieties Ltd* [1924] AC 1 and *Vandepitte v Preferred Accident Insurance Corporation of New York* [1933] AC 70, at 74).

[81] Waller and Rix LJJ.

of Zambia is to set this at nought, or very nearly so. It is true that there are dicta in both cases suggesting (though not stating) that if a contract says 'no assignments *or trusts* are permitted' this may be given effect,[82] and hence that the result is not as disastrous as it looks. But this will not really do. Contracts are, as the House of Lords has emphasized[83] and indeed Lightman J in *Don King* accepts,[84] to be interpreted in a businesslike and realistic way: to tell a contractor that a no-assignment clause will not prevent effective assignment unless he adds a no-trust clause as well is technicality run mad.

Moreover, even on technical grounds it is suggested that *Don King* and *Zambia* are suspect in insisting that assignments and trusts are essentially different things. Traditionally it has been accepted that the opposite is true, and that an equitable assignment is a form of trust (admittedly constructive rather than express, but nothing can turn on that).[85] What, then, are the differences we are meant to find? Equitable assignments can be summed up in something like four propositions. First, A[86] prevails against the creditors of C if insolvent.[87] Secondly, A can insist that the right be now exercised for his benefit, and hence take control of its enforcement. Thirdly, A takes 'subject to equities'—ie he can only enforce the right 'warts and all', subject to any defences available to D against C,[88] and takes subject to certain rights of set-off—broadly, all connected counterclaims[89] and some unconnected ones arising before notice.[90] And fourthly, he is immune to post-notice

---

[82] See in particular Lightman J in *Don King Productions Inc v Warren* [2000] Ch 291, at 321; and Rix LJ in *Barbados Trust Co v Bank of Zambia* [2007] 1 Lloyd's Rep 495, [2007] EWCA Civ 148, at [88].

[83] *Investors' Compensation Scheme Ltd v West Bromwich Building Society* [1998] 1 WLR 896, at 912-913 (Lord Hoffmann).

[84] See *Don King Productions Inc v Warren* [2000] Ch 291, at 310-11.

[85] See above, n 14.

[86] In this section A means the assignee, C the creditor/assignor, and D the debtor.

[87] He is, of course, subject to specific limitations, with doctrines such as the insolvency rules providing for the annihilation of transfers in fraud of creditors. But so is the transferee of any other asset, so this means nothing.

[88] See, eg *Athenaeum Life Ass'nce Co v Pooley* (1853) 3 D & J 294; *Graham v Johnson* (1869) LR 8 Eq 36.

[89] *Newfoundland Government v Newfoundland Railway Co* (1888) LR 13 App Cas 199. More precisely, the opposable claims are those that between D and C would amount to equitable or 'transactional' set-off.

[90] *Watson v Mid-Wales Ry Co* (1867) LR 2 CP 593 (more exactly, this covers claims otherwise covered by the Statutes of Set-off). The reason for limiting this susceptibility to pre-notice cross-claims is that a debtor who gives credit to his creditor not knowing of an assignment should not lose any rights of set-off he would otherwise get, but a debtor who knows of the assignment deserves no such indulgence.

set-off arising between C and D[91] and post-notice agreements between them to change the contractual rights involved.[92] If one looks closely, it is suggested that every one of these also applies to a trust. We can take them in turn.

First, the beneficiary's interest trumps those of the trustee and his creditors. This point is so obvious that we do not need to waste further time on it.

Secondly, the beneficiary of a bare trust of a right must logically have the right to control its enforcement, using the rule laid down in *Vandepitte v Preferred Accident Insurance Corporation of New York*.[93] For the trustee of a right to refuse point-blank to enforce it when asked,[94] thus effectively destroying the trust property, would seem as blatant a breach of trust as anyone could imagine. It is true that a curious throwaway line of Lightman J in *Don King v Warren*[95] aimed at dealing with this point suggests the contrary, and that one can have a trust without the right of enforcement,[96] but this cannot be right. The authority cited does not support it.[97] Furthermore, if Lightman J is right, and the beneficiary of a trust of a chose in action cannot insist that the trustee actually exercise it, this seems almost entirely to defeat the point of the trust in the first place. Put shortly, if the beneficiary does not have this right, what rights worth having does he possess?[98]

Thirdly, although there is little authority, it seems very likely that the 'subject to equities' rule applies to trusts. This must obviously be true of the 'warts and all' principle,[99] for the simple reason that you

---

[91] *Ibid*.

[92] *Brice v Bannister* (1878) 3 QBD 569.

[93] [1933] AC 70. *Barbados Trust* accepts as much: see Rix LJ at [2007] 1 Lloyd's Rep 495, [2007] EWCA Civ 148, at [99].

[94] Assuming adequate arrangements made for costs, etc.

[95] [2000] Ch 291.

[96] *Ibid*, at 321.

[97] The authority was *Re Brockbank* [1948] Ch 206, which was said to show that beneficiaries, even if unanimous, could not tell a trustee what to do with the trust property. On a proper reading, however, it merely holds that beneficiaries cannot order a trustee to depart from the terms of the trust. In that case they were doing just that, by purporting to tell a surviving trustee whom to appoint as a new trustee, something which was specifically left up to the trustee's own discretion.

[98] '... there is an irreducible core of obligations owed by the trustees to the beneficiaries and enforceable by them which is fundamental to the concept of a trust. If the beneficiaries have no rights enforceable against the trustees there are no trusts'. —Millett LJ in *Armitage v Nurse* [1998] Ch 241, at 253.

[99] Which, it should be noted, has been held to apply in the case of subrogation: see *The Front Comor* [2005] 1 CLC 347, [2005] EWHC (Comm) 454, and *The Jay Bola* [1997] CLC 993 (subrogee bound by arbitration provision).

only declare yourself trustee of a right you actually have.[100] In so far as there would have been a defence had the original creditor sued, the trustee cannot fare any better. Moreover, exactly the same argument applies to connected counterclaims (ie those arising out of equitable set-offs which would have been available as between debtor and trustee), since they would have amounted to an equitable defence *pro tanto* against the creditor himself—a solution which reflects common sense, since the rationale of allowing such a set-off is that the connection between the right being sued on and the debtor's cross-claim is so close that it would be inequitable to the debtor to determine the former without the latter. If this is right, it should make no odds that the person seeking to enforce the right is acting as trustee for someone else who actually stands to benefit. And indeed, this has been held to be the case both in Australia[101] and later by Laddie J in England.[102]

What about unconnected counterclaims against the trustee? In the assignment context, these are (as mentioned above) available against an assignee if created before the debtor knew of the assignment, on the basis that they would have afforded a defence under the Statutes of Set-off had the assignor sued, and that an assignment of which the debtor was unaware at the relevant time should not alter the position. There seems no authority deciding whether the same thing applies to a trust of the obligation: but it is submitted that the assignment reasoning must apply equally here.[103] A debtor who thinks he is obtaining a set-off ought to be no more affected by an unknown trust than by an unknown assignment.

Lastly, it is suggested that logically a trust beneficiary, just like an assignee, must be insulated from post-notice cross-claims or changes. In the assignment context, what is now the established rule arose in the days before fusion, from the Court of Chancery's practice of supporting the assignee's right with certain ancillary orders, notably

[100] This also seems to be implicit in *Murphy v Zamonex Pty Ltd* (1993) 31 NSWLR 439, referred to below. If a beneficiary takes subject to certain counterclaims, it must follow *a fortiori* that he takes subject to defences.

[101] *Murphy v Zamonex Pty Ltd* (1993) 31 NSWLR 439 (claim on loan by trustee suing as such: trade practices claim by borrower against trustee's predecessor personally pleadable as equitable set-off). See too *Doherty v Murphy* [1996] 2 VR 553.

[102] *Penwith District Council v V P Developments Ltd* [2005] 2 BCLC 607 (unsatisfied arbitration costs order against construction company: claim by company in related arbitration to recover alleged underpayments: latter available for set-off so as to prevent winding-up on basis of costs order, irrespective of fact that company insolvent and suing entirely as trustee for benefit of its creditors).

[103] And indeed, is assumed to do so in Derham, *Set-off* (3rd edn, OUP), § 17.96, where it is stated (though without authority) that the rules of statutory set-off are the same for obligations held on trust as for assigned ones.

injunctions restraining the debtor from invoking either the Statutes of Set-off or, as the case might be, on any agreement to release or reduce the rights of the original creditor.[104] Since fusion, life is more straightforward: these rights of the assignee are directly cognized, and set-offs otherwise available to the debtor are simply shut out. But if there is no difference—apart from that between express and constructive trusts—between the interest of an assignee and a trust beneficiary, there is no reason to distinguish between them—as at least one authority indirectly suggests.[105]

It is true that there is one possible counter-argument. With an active trust, as one of a landed estate, or one supporting a bond issue, no-one would seriously argue that a debtor to such a trust, even if he knew he was dealing with a trustee, should be unable to deal with, and if necessary compromise, the trust's claims against him without the express permission of every beneficiary. If this were so, it would negative the whole point of such arrangements, which is to leave the day-to-day management of the estate, or whatever, to the trustees' informed discretion.[106] On the other hand, it is suggested that this argument cannot apply to a bare trust: here there is no object to defeat, and hence no reason to disapply the obvious rule.

In short, it is suggested that the supposed distinction between bare trusts and assignments is one without a difference, and that therefore the only other plank in the reasoning in *Don King* and *Barbados Trust* disappears.

---

[104] See Note 16 above.

[105] 'A mere agreement between A. and B. that B. shall pay C. (an agreement to which C. is not a party either directly or indirectly) will not prevent A. and B. from coming to a new agreement the next day releasing the old one. *If C. were a cestui que trust it would have that effect.*' – Jessel MR in *Re Empress Engineering Co* (1880) 16 Ch D. 125, 129 (Jessel MR) (emphasis supplied). See too M Smith, *The Law of Assignment*, § 13.11; and compare *Scott on Trusts*, 3d ed, vol IV, p 2517 to the same effect. There is one apparently contrary authority, *Gibson v Winter* (1833) 5 B & Ad 96; but this was doubted by Lord Campbell in *De Pothonier v De Mattos* (1858) E B & E 461, 483 and by the Supreme Court of Canada in *Culina v Giuliani* [1972] SCR 343.

[106] Even on occasion to the extent of disregarding the express wishes of the beneficiary: see *Re Brockbank* [1948] Ch 206, above, n 44. Moreover, it can also be pointed out that in at least one arguably analogous situation, the beneficiary is not protected. Whereas an assignment plus notice to the debtor locks the assignee's rights in against subsequent alterations, an insurer's subrogation to claims of the assured does not. On the contrary: it is well established that even where an insurer does have subrogated rights, those rights can be validly released or altered by the assured, and if they are, the insurer's only remedy is against the assured. See *West of England Fire Insurance Co v Isaacs* [1897] 1 QB 226.

4. PRACTICAL CONSIDERATIONS

There is not much to be done about the continued uncertainty referred to at the beginning of this chapter over what is assignable and what is not. On the other hand, even accepting as authoritative—for now—the curious decisions in *Foamcrete, Don King*, and *Barbados Trust*, there may be useful draftsman's solutions to give anti-assignment clauses the effect everyone previously thought they had.

Let us start with the *Foamcrete* problem—that is, the suggestion that despite *Linden Gardens*, a prohibition on assignment is ineffective as against a prior agreement to assign. It is worth noting that in *Foamcrete* the anti-assignment clause was brief and unadorned ('neither of the parties to this agreement shall be entitled to assign this agreement …'). This suggests that it may be possible to reinforce such a provision to increase its effectiveness. Two additions seem particularly appropriate. First, it would be as well to make it clear, not only that assignment is prohibited, but that any forbidden assignment is to be wholly ineffective in law and in equity, and that no duty of any kind shall exist towards anyone other than the original obligee. Logically this should circumvent any argument based on the date of the assignment. If the contract says that an assignment is not only wrongful but ineffective, the question whether the assignment amounted (or not) to a breach of the assignor's obligations must be irrelevant. Indeed, one might profitably go even further: there seems no reason why the clause should not also preclude further argument by saying explicitly that any assignment of it shall be of no effect whether the agreement or instrument purporting to create it was executed before or after the contract itself.

The trust point in *Don King* and *Barbados* is less straightforward, but arguably not insuperable. To begin with, it was suggested in both cases that, had there been a prohibition covering not only assignments but also trusts, this might have made a difference.[107] Although these statements were obiter, it is suggested that they must be correct on principle. True it is that because a person cannot be prevented from dealing with his property once he has it, equity will enforce, *as between assignor and assignee*, an agreement to hand over any proceeds of the enforcement of a chose in action,[108] whatever the position as regards assignments or trusts of the obligation itself. But this does not mean that it will go further and ensure that the right is enforced *against*

---

[107] Above, n 81.
[108] *Glegg v Bromley* [1912] 3 KB 474.

the obligor,[109] or allow the assignee to sue if he joins the assignor as a technical party. The reason, it is suggested, it is that here the obligor can convincingly raise a further argument: namely, that there is no equity in granting a remedy that will render nugatory a legitimate third party right,[110] such as a debtor's right to decide whom he is willing to contract with.

On the other hand, preventing the assignee suing on the debt is not necessarily enough, given that as often as not the debtor is more concerned with being able safely to negotiate with, and win concessions from, the creditor without reference to any third party. With this in mind, a further clause is probably appropriate, to the effect that the debtor will not be obliged to recognize any trust or assignment, or the title or interest of any trust beneficiary or assignee,[111] and that performance rendered to, or release by, the creditor will discharge any obligation of the debtor. Such a clause might seem unnecessary: but the object of it is to ensure that if, for some reason, the assignee or trustee does get an interest despite the assertion in the contract that he cannot, he can obtain no rights that the creditor did not himself have.

5. CONCLUSION

The conclusion of this paper is essentially that one of the problems of assignment—the delineation of what is, and is not, assignable—is difficult to do much about until the courts themselves make matters clearer. On the other hand, there may be a drafting solution to the difficulties of anti-assignment clauses. True, that involves a very complex formula to deal with what ought on principle to be a simple problem: but then arguably that is the courts' fault.

---

[109] *Linden Gardens Trust Ltd v Lenesta Sludge Disposals Ltd* [1994] 1 AC 85.

[110] For analogous situations, see, eg equity's clear power to refuse specific performance where the effect of giving it would be to defeat a contractual stipulation entered into by the defendant in favour of a third party (*Warmington v Miller* [1973] QB 877), and to refuse to lend its aid to an equitable chargee where, to the knowledge of the chargee, this would defeat a negative pledge clause previously agreed with a third party (*English & Scottish Mercantile Investment Co Ltd v Brunton* [1892] 2 QB 700).

[111] A term not without precedent. It is, for example, commonplace in any contract for the issue of securities.

10

Agency Law for Muggles: Why There is no Magic in Agency

THOMAS KREBS[*]

1. TWO CONVENTIONAL MODELS OF AGENCY

The law of agency is usually regarded as distinct from the general law. A person is liable on a contract even though it was not made by him, but by his agent. Similarly, he might be held liable for his agent's torts, or be asked to make restitution even though it is not he, but his agent, who has been enriched. In fact, there is much to be said for a view which refuses to accept this special role of agency law, a view which maintains that the rights and liabilities of the parties must generally be derived from and explained by an application of the general rules of contract, tort, and unjust enrichment. However, such a much more ambitious claim must wait for another day—this essay focuses merely on the relationship between agency and contract law.

In agency, contractual formation is mediated by the agent, whose contractual communications with the third party (commonly the exchange of offer and acceptance) are then attributed to his principal. Attempts to account for this phenomenon can be divided into broadly two schools: first, there are those who regard 'consensual agency' as the 'paradigm case'.[1] In the words of *Bowstead & Reynolds on Agency*, 'the basic situation of agency is treated as being that in which the principal agrees that the agent should act for him and the agent expressly or impliedly agrees to do so.'[2] The clearest judicial statement of this approach is probably the following dictum by Lord Pearson in *Garnac Grain Co Inc v HMF Faure and Fairclough Ltd*:[3]

> The relationship of principal and agent can only be established by the consent of the principal and the agent. They will be held to have consented

---

[*] University Lecturer in Commercial Law and Fellow of Brasenose College, Oxford. The term 'Muggle' has recently officially become part of the English language—the Oxford English Dictionary defines it as follows: 'In the fiction of J. K. Rowling: a person who possesses no magical powers. Hence in allusive and extended uses: a person who lacks a particular skill or skills, or who is regarded as inferior in some way.' Readers with children or no aspirations for the High Court Bench can safely ignore this footnote, of course.

[1] *Bowstead & Reynolds on Agency* (18th edn, Sweet & Maxwell, 2009) 6.

[2] *Ibid*.

[3] [1968] AC 1130.

if they have agreed to what amounts in law to such a relationship, even if they do not recognise it themselves and even if they have professed to disclaim it [...]. But the consent must have been given by each of them, either expressly or by implication from their words and conduct.

This 'consensual' approach to agency has come under sustained attack by a number of commentators belonging to the second school. They regard agency not so much as based on the consent of principal and agent, but arising by operation of law. Their main argument is that consent cannot account for instances of 'apparent' authority which, they argue, can arise irrespective of or even against the will of the principal. It arises where the principal so conducts himself that the third party, with whom the agent is dealing, is led to believe that the agent is acting on the principal's behalf and with the principal's authority, so that by contracting with the agent contractual relations between principal and third party can be brought about. In such circumstances the principal will normally be bound even if, vis-à-vis the agent, no such authority was ever given or indeed expressly withheld or limited.[4] It follows, the argument goes, that consent, though relevant, is not required to give rise to the agency relationship and, therefore, is not required to give rise to contractual relations between principal and third party. This conclusion is further supported by cases such as *Boardman v Phipps*,[5] in which the House of Lords held that, even parties never authorized at all by their supposed principals could be treated as 'self-appointed agents'.[6]

The 'agency by operation of law' school of thought runs into considerable difficulty, however, when it comes to explaining why and in what circumstances the law gives rise to an agency relationship. Most accounts are at best descriptive, at worst obscure. Thus, Montrose writes:

The power of an agent is not strictly conferred by the principal but by the law: the principal and agent do the acts which bring the rule into operation, as a result of which the agent acquires a power.[7]

Dowrick, writing some 15 years later, is no more explicit:

The agent is invested with a legal power to alter his principal's legal relations with third persons, while the principal is under a correlative liability to have his relations altered.[8]

---

[4] Fridman, *Law of Agency* (7th edn, London: Butterworths, 1996) 15.
[5] [1967] 2 AC 46.
[6] Fridman, *Law of Agency* (7th edn, London: Butterworths, 1996) 15.
[7] (1938) 16 *Can Bar Rev* 756, 761.
[8] (1954) 17 *MLR* 24, 36.

Although the adherents of the 'power-liability' model of agency are self-declared opponents of the consensual model, McMeel has recently pointed out that there is in fact little contradictory about the two schools of thought: in fact, they are simply doing different things. While the power-liability model seeks to describe the legal phenomenon of agency, the consensual model seeks to explain and rationalize it.[9]

The argument put forward in this paper is that the whole debate is indeed beside the point. What both models of agency seek to do is identify a definition of agency which can determine in any given case whether a certain party is or is not an agent. This attributes much more importance to the characterization of a relationship as agency than is its due. While a definition might be helpful for purposes of exposition and pedagogy, the characterization of a relationship as one of agency rarely has any mandatory consequences. Thus, it is not always the case that the agent drops out of the contractual relationship between principal and third party, or that the agent does not guarantee performance by the third party to his principal. Although agents will regularly owe fiduciary duties to their principals, it is not their agency which has this consequence, but the fiduciary nature of their relationship with the principal.

What we need to explain, therefore, is not how a person becomes another's agent, but in what circumstances and on what grounds an intermediary can bring about rights and obligations between two others, namely the principal and the third party. The model offered here is a straightforward offer and acceptance model. This requires some explanation.

Both the conventional models of agency focus on the power of the agent and how this arises out of the relationship between principal and agent. They focus on the status of the intermediary as an agent, and not on the actual contractual parties, the principal and the third party. Fictions are sometimes taken to the extreme of saying that somehow the legal personalities of principal and agent become fused, that effectively principal and agent become one person, or that the agent somehow becomes the principal's alter ego.[10]

It is suggested, however, that it is not the power of the agent which needs to be explained, but the creation of contractual rights and liabilities between principal and third party. It is that relationship, therefore, which needs to be focused on. Agency is frequently listed as one of the

---

[9] McMeel, 'Philosophical Foundations of Agency' (2000) 116 *LQR* 387.

[10] Hence the Latin maxim: 'qui facit per alium facit per se'.

exceptions to the privity rule recognized by English law.[11] It is suggested that this is misleading. Let us assume that T wishes to assert a contractual claim against P, having entered into a contract with A openly acting on P's behalf. In order to find a contract, English law looks for two matching manifestations of consent, namely an offer and an acceptance.[12] Regarding agency as an exception to privity suggests that somehow the contract is not made by P and T, but by A and T. If the benefit and burden of that contract are P's, then this is explained by the 'magic' of agency: by the fiction that principal and agent have become a single legal person. This appears to assume that, in English law, offer and acceptance must be exchanged directly between the parties in order to give rise to a binding contract, and that an exception to privity (such as agency) is needed if this is not the case. This is, however, manifestly incorrect. Contracts can be entered into either by parties reaching agreement face to face, or *inter absentes*, the contract by correspondence being regarded as the paradigm case of this.[13] In both cases, the parties' communications will be interpreted objectively—in other words, in both cases there is the real possibility that the parties' minds are never subjectively *ad idem*, but that nevertheless one will be held to the objective interpretation of his communication as understood by the other party to the contract. Contracts concluded through agents are normally not analysed in these terms. This leads to particular problems when there is a mismatch between the parties' expressed intentions in two of the three relationships involved, namely between P's intentions as communicated to A on the one hand and to T on the other. We have already seen that the law of agency refers to such situations as 'apparent' or 'ostensible' authority. It is suggested here that the law has as much trouble to explain P's liability to T in these situations as it does because the basis of agency generally in a straightforward offer and acceptance model has not been fully appreciated.

One consequence of adopting the offer and acceptance model advocated here is a stricter division between internal and external aspects of agency, putting English law in line with the majority of civilian

---

[11] See eg *Chitty on Contracts* (30th edn, 2008) 18-077; *Dunlop Pneumatic Tyre Co v Selfridge* [1915] AC 847; *Scruttons v Midland Silicones Ltd* [1962] AC 446.

[12] Consideration is normally unproblematic, but not always. Thus, in *Dunlop Pneumatic Tyre Co v Selfridge* [1915] AC 847 the third party's claim failed against the principal on the basis that no consideration had been furnished *by the third party to the principal*. Again, this emphasizes that the relationship we must focus on is that between the third party and the principal.

[13] Stoljar, *The Law of Agency* (Sweet & Maxwell, 1961) 32 ff.

systems, in particular Germany,[14] Switzerland,[15] Japan,[16] Italy,[17] Greece,[18] and France.[19] These systems distinguish sharply between the relationship of principal/agent on the one hand and the relationships of principal/third party and of agent/third party on the other.[20] This approach, which goes back to an article written by Paul Laband in the latter half of the nineteenth century (and which must be regarded as one of the most influential pieces of academic legal writing ever),[21] prevents us from falling into the error of conflating the different relationships. It explains why, even though an agent is forbidden by the principal from entering into a contract with a third party, the principal can nevertheless find himself bound if the agent does not follow his instructions, with the consequence that the principal must seek redress from the agent, for breach of the contract forming the core of the *internal* relationship, while being contractually bound to the third party (who would otherwise be the one suing the agent, for breach of warranty of authority). However, this 'principle of abstraction', while it describes the different relationships in much better focus than English law currently does, still does not explain *why* third party and principal end up in a contractual relationship. For instance, German law distinguishes sharply between an agent (who possesses 'authority' to bind his principal following the exercise of his own discretion) and a messenger, who has no discretion whatsoever.[22] It is argued here that this distinction can be overestimated and is, at least insofar as English law is concerned, merely a matter of degree.

[14] §§ 167–168 BGB.
[15] Art 32 Swiss OR.
[16] § 99 Japanese Civil Code.
[17] Art 1387 Italian Civil Code.
[18] §§ 211 Greek Civil Code.
[19] While the French Civil Code does not yet draw the distinction, which was developed well after its inception by the German jurists Jhering and Laband, current French literature does: cf eg Ghestin/Billiau,*Traité de droit civil. Les obligations, les effets du contrat: interprétation—qualification—durée—inexécution—effet relatif—opposabilité* (3rd edn, 2001), 789.
[20] Kötz (transl Weir), *European Contract Law* (1997) 334.
[21] Laband, 'Die Stellvertretung bei dem Abschluss von Rechtsgeschäften nach dem Allgemeinen Deutschen Handelsgesetzbuch' (1866) 10 *Zeitschrift für das Handelsrecht* 183.
[22] Even though the BGB does not define the term 'messenger' (there is a brief mention of him in § 120, in the context of mistaken communications by a messenger), the distinction is widely acknowledged to be fundamental: cf Medicus, *Allgemeiner Teil des BGB*, (7th edn) 339.

2. AN OFFER AND ACCEPTANCE MODEL OF AGENCY

As long ago as 1891, Oliver Wendell Holmes, in the first of his two seminal articles on agency,[23] maintained that, as far as an agent's actual authority was concerned, the contract brought about through his inter-mediation between principal and third party 'would need no explana-tion and introduce no new principle'.[24] Holmes's proof that this is so is ingenious. Nobody can dispute, he argues, that a contract concluded through a messenger is a valid contract between offeror and offeree. The offer is the offeror's, the acceptance the offeree's. Likewise, where the parties agree that the price for goods is to be determined by an independent expert or referee, a contract is brought about to which the referee is but a stranger. Combine the two and you have a typi-cal agency scenario, namely 'the case of an agent with discretionary powers, no matter how large they may be'. Holmes continues:

> So far as he expresses his principal's assent to be bound to terms to be fixed by the agent, he is a mere messenger; in fixing the terms he is a stranger to the contract, which stands on the same footing as if it had been made before his personal function began.[25]

The language of agency thus tends to obscure the essentially simple and straightforward nature of the subject—as simply an application of ordinary contractual rules on offer and acceptance. Once it is appreci-ated, however, that a contractual offer does not need to be communi-cated personally, and that there is no need for a contractual acceptance to be communicated at all, provided the terms of the offer do not require communication of the acceptance, it quickly becomes obvi-ous that the third party's contractual liability towards the principal can be explained on straightforward contractual grounds. To demon-strate that this must be so, we might replace the agent with a notional machine or computer. As we know from *Thornton v Shoe Lane Parking*, it is quite possible to contract through a ticket machine. Lord Den-ning MR, in that case, analysed the transaction in the following terms: 'the offer is made when the proprietor of the machine holds it out as being ready to receive the money. The acceptance takes place when the customer puts his money into the slot.'[26] The first point to note is that no actual communication of the acceptance to the proprietor of

---

[23] Holmes, 'Agency', (1890-91) 4 *Harv L Rev* 345. The second article, which is really the second part of the same article, can be found at (1891-92) 5 *Harv L Rev* 1.

[24] *Ibid*, 346.

[25] *Ibid*, 348.

[26] *Thornton v Shoe Lane Parking* [1971] 2 QB 163, at 169.

the machine ever takes place: a contract comes about even though it does not have any notice at all of having entered into one. The machine in question, back in 1964, was, of course, a fairly unsophisticated, mechanical one. Would it make any difference to Lord Denning's analysis, one may ask, if the machine was a modern ticket computer as we find them in train stations today? Does it really make a difference that the machine can now make offers on different terms, depending on the time of day, the number of passengers, or on whether a ticket has been pre-booked or not? If it does, then we would have to expand the law of agency to include 'electronic agents', with their very own 'magical' powers to bind their principals. In reality, of course, the fact that the machine is running through a number of algorithms, however complicated these may be, can make no difference to the essentially contractual analysis. I would suggest that an agent with discretionary powers to fix the terms of an offer or an acceptance on behalf of his principal is in no different a position. As long as he operates according to the objectively manifested will of his principal, the latter is bound by the consequences for that reason alone.

This begs the question whether the above analysis can explain the whole of what we know as 'the law of agency', and indeed whether there is any need for a separate subject by that name. This was the point of Holmes's article. He concluded that agency was indeed a subject in its own right, mainly because of four doctrines which could not be explained by ordinary contract: that a principal might be liable for the torts of his agent, that an agent might bring about a contract while ostensibly contracting in his own name, that a principal might ratify unauthorized acts of his agent, and that a principal might be regarded as possessing goods which were really in the possession of his agent. In England, the first of these, vicarious liability, is best categorized as belonging to the law of torts, and it is now well established that it derives from the employer/employee rather than the principal/agent relationship. The third, contrary to Holmes's assertion, can, it is argued here, be explained using the above offer and acceptance model,[27] while the fourth, that goods can be possessed indirectly or 'constructively', is a general rule of personal property law which is not peculiar to agency.[28] This leaves the doctrine of the undisclosed principal. It must be conceded that this doctrine cannot be explained using the offer and acceptance model. However, it is argued here that this is not in fact necessary. In the following, this paper will

---

[27] See below, p 13.
[28] Thus constructive possession can be exercised through a warehouseman or ship's master, neither of whom is generally thought of as the agent of the constructive possessor.

first explain why this is so. It will then look at three additional problematic areas. The first, mentioned by Holmes, is the doctrine of ratification. Two additional problems not referred to in Holmes's articles
will then be examined: apparent authority and the interpretation of an
agent's actual authority.

3. UNDISCLOSED AGENCY

The doctrine of the undisclosed principal allows an agent to enter into
contracts with third parties ostensibly on his own behalf, but in reality
on behalf of his undisclosed principal. It is well established that the
principal will be able to sue the third party directly on such contracts
and vice versa. This result has been called 'surprising',[29] in that it does
not sit at all well with the general rules of contract law: the third party
never makes any promise to the supposed principal, nor does the principal ever express his intention to be bound to the third party. Many have
tried and failed to explain the doctrine as part of the law of agency.[30]
Worse, attempts to account for agency as a phenomenon have been
hampered and misdirected by the perceived necessity to account for
undisclosed agency as part of the same theoretical framework.[31] It
may be necessary to admit that 'general' agency has in fact little in
common with undisclosed agency, and that the failure of a theoretical
model to account for undisclosed agency does not render that model
less useful as far as agency proper is concerned. It is suggested here
that undisclosed agency is mainly used in order to protect principal
and third party against the insolvency of an intermediary who would
otherwise be directly liable on the relevant contract. The language and
conceptual framework of agency are convenient tools to bring about
a reallocation of insolvency risks and very little more. That this is so
follows from an examination of the practical goals of undisclosed
agency, of its historical development and its current rules.

   There are essentially two situations in which there will be a commercial need to hide the fact that the intermediary is acting on behalf

---

[29] *Bowstead & Reynolds on Agency*, (18th edn, Sweet & Maxwell, 2009) 8-071.

[30] See eg Barnett, 'Squaring Undisclosed Agency Law with Contract Theory' (1987) 75 *Cal
L Rev* 1969 (he does not really square it at all); Müller-Freienfels, 'Comparative Aspects of
Undisclosed Agency' (1955) 18 *MLR* 33.

[31] One commentator not open to this charge is McMeel, above, n 9, who simply excludes
undisclosed agency from the scope of his inquiry (n 7 to his article)—I propose to do
the same!

of somebody else:[32] the principal may wish to enter the market without this being known (for a variety of reasons—frequently because he places a premium on goods which would be reflected in the price were his identity known); similarly, the intermediary may wish to avoid that the third parties he is dealing with will in future deal with the principal directly, cutting him out of the transaction. These goals could be achieved by a chain of contracts (P-A-T), with each party being liable and entitled to the person next to him in the chain only, and this is the solution adopted in civilian jurisdictions under the heading 'indirect representation'. These legal systems then provide rules which, to a greater or lesser extent, make the third party directly liable to the principal if the intermediary becomes insolvent, so that the difference between those systems and the common law is not as great as may at first sight appear.[33] Historically, the undisclosed agency doctrine appears to have been developed to deal with precisely the insolvency of an intermediary who had been acting in his own name but on somebody else's account.[34] The modern doctrine bends over backwards to protect the third party from nasty surprises, so that its rules are a long way removed from the rules applicable to disclosed agency scenarios. Thus, the undisclosed principal is barred from ratifying contracts entered into by the agent in excess of his authority—had the agency been disclosed, he would be able to do so. In addition, the agent does not 'drop out'—he remains liable and entitled alongside the principal. The third party can avail himself of any defences—including set-off—which he would have against the agent. Finally, the contract may, by its express or implied terms, exclude the possibility of an undisclosed principal. It is thus arguable that undisclosed agency has rather more in common with assignment than it does with agency proper. It is for this reason that I feel it is justified to leave undisclosed agency out of account when it comes to identifying the doctrinal underpinnings of general, disclosed agency law: just because undisclosed agency cannot manage without magic, the same is not necessarily true for agency law proper.

To sum up: in this paper I propose an explanation of agency law which is based on a straightforward offer and acceptance model. This model can account for most rules of modern agency law, with the notable exception of undisclosed agency. It is possible to go a step further and argue that there is in fact no agency law properly so-called, but

---

[32] See *Bowstead & Reynolds on Agency* (18th edn, Sweet & Maxwell, 2009) 8-073.

[33] Kötz, *Europäisches Vertragsrecht I*, p 367; *Bowstead & Reynolds on Agency* (18th edn, Sweet & Maxwell, 2009) 377.

[34] Stoljar, *The Law of Agency* (Sweet & Maxwell, 1961) 203-11.

simply a set of concepts which are used to express what are essentially straightforward contractual rules in three-party scenarios. For example, while, under the view put forward here, the concept of 'authority' does not have any independent significance, the language of authority sums up rather well the underlying contractual framework: the principal makes an offer to the third party to enter into a contract with him through the intermediation of the agent, provided the terms of that contract remain within certain parameters.

4. RATIFICATION

Where an agent enters into a contract on his principal's behalf, but exceeds his authority, the principal will not be bound unless he ratifies the contract. If he does, his ratification is said to take effect retrospectively—in other words, the law pretends that the agent had authority all along. The practical effect of this is that even where the third party, on discovering the agent's lack of authority, makes it clear that he no longer wishes to be bound, the principal is nevertheless free to ratify and bind the third party to the contract. If this is correct, it is difficult to square ratification with the offer and acceptance model defended in this essay: at no point are the parties *ad idem*; at first, the principal has not expressed his intention to be bound—later on, the third party has expressly disavowed any such intention.

The leading case which is usually cited as authority for the above proposition is *Bolton Partners v Lambert*.[35] It concerned a contract to take a lease. Lambert wrote to Scratchley, a director of Bolton, offering to take a lease from it. Scratchley replied to Lambert, accepting this offer. The very next day, Lambert sought to withdraw from the contract. It appears from the report that he did not at that point know that, in accepting the offer, Scratchley had exceeded his authority. When Bolton later sued for specific performance, this circumstance became clear and Lambert argued that he had, on that ground alone, been entitled to withdraw from the contract. The Court of Appeal disagreed. To Cotton LJ, the correct analysis of the situation was as follows:

> I think the proper view is that the acceptance by *Scratchley* did constitute a contract, subject to its being shewn that *Scratchley* had authority to bind the company. If that were not shewn there would be no contract on the part of the company, but when and as soon as authority was given to *Scratchley* to bind the company the authority was thrown back to the time when the

---

[35] (1889) LR 41Ch D 295.

act was done by *Scratchley*, and prevented the Defendant withdrawing his offer, because it was then no longer an offer, but a binding contract.[36]

One explanation of the result in *Bolton v Lambert* is that Lambert originally sought to withdraw from the contract because he believed that the negotiations had not yet reached the stage in which a binding contract had been formed, or, arguably, because he thought he could get out of a bad bargain by simply refusing to proceed. However, this explanation runs into the difficulty that, in English law, a party can withdraw from a contract citing an invalid reason for doing so, provided he can later demonstrate that at the time of the withdrawal a valid reason was in existence.[37] It therefore seems that the rule in *Bolton v Lambert* is binding on English courts up to the Court of Appeal.

Cotton LJ appreciated the practical difficulties which the fiction that ratification had retrospective effect might cause, and 'how favourable the rule was to the principal, because till ratification he was not bound, and he had an option to adopt or not to adopt what had been done'.[38] He then went on to assert, however, that he was bound to apply the fiction and find in favour of the principal. The result has been widely criticized. Thus, in the Australian case of *Davison v Vickery's Motors Ltd*, Isaacs J, obiter, strongly expressed the view that the decision was wrong. He said:

> The basic assumption on which the novel and special doctrine of *Bolton Partners* ... rests is that a person may by the act of another become party to a bilateral contract without his authority or knowledge and possibly contrary to his express decision. The assumption connotes that there is no instant binding effect on the supposed principal and yet that the other party is instantly bound .... You cannot have a contract which at the same time is no contract ... Even in the case of a direct communication between A and B, an arrangement however specific between them personally which merely leaves one of them open to buy or sell does not constitute a contract. Only when the election is made and the gap closed can there be said to be a contract. And then, only if thereby the conjoint wills concur ... The basic assumption of the case cannot, therefore, in my opinion, be supported.[39]

---

[36] At 307 *et seq.*

[37] *Boston Deep Sea Fishing and Ice Co v Ansell* (1888) 39 Ch D 339. See also *Bowstead & Reynolds on Agency* (18th edn, Sweet & Maxwell, 2009) 86.

[38] At 307, citing *Hagedorn v Oliverson* (1814) 2 M & S 485, an insurance case in which Lord Ellenborough CJ pointed out that the retrospective effect of ratification meant that a principal could avoid paying an insurance premium where no loss was suffered, while taking the benefit of the insurance in the event of a loss by ratifying his agent's unauthorized entering into the policy on his behalf. However, that situation did not in fact arise in that case, and as such the dicta relied on by Cotton LJ are obiter.

[39] *Davison v Vickery's Motors Ltd* (1926) 37 CLR 1, 18–19.

There are two observations which can be made about this passage. The first is that Isaacs J, interestingly, seeks to draw an analogy with contractual negotiations directly conducted between the intended parties to the contract. He does not regard a contract entered into through an agent as in any way different conceptually: what matters is that 'the conjoint wills concur', in the same way as in general contract law. The second observation is that Isaacs J is concerned about contracts which bind one party but not the other. While he is probably wrong in saying that such contracts are conceptually impossible, the difficulty in the context of ratification is that the third party never consents to be unilaterally bound—this merely comes about because of the agent's lack of authority. This can lead to unfortunate results. Thus, if the supposed rule in *Bolton v Lambert* were applied without exception, the principal would be able to speculate at the third party's expense: assume A, purporting to act for P, but in excess of authority, offers T some shares. T accepts the offer. P can now lean back and watch the market: if the share price goes up (ie the bargain turns out to be a bad one for him), he does nothing and then refuses to be bound by the contract, citing A's lack of authority. If the share price goes down (ie the bargain turns out to be a good one for him), he ratifies A's act and insists on payment of the price originally agreed by T. The problem is exacerbated by the finding in *Bolton* that even if T finds out that A was acting without authority, and that T is therefore in a precarious position vis-à-vis P, this does still not give him a ground to withdraw from the contract.

In *Bolton v Lambert* itself, Cotton LJ acknowledged that the fiction was subject to exceptions: 'An estate once vested cannot be divested, nor can an act lawful at the time of its performance be rendered unlawful, by the application of the doctrine of ratification.'[40] Another possible exception, the precise scope of which is unclear, is that it is not possible to ratify an unauthorized act which had to be done within a certain time after the time limit has elapsed. In *Dibbins v Dibbins*[41] the terms of a partnership provided that a surviving partner could purchase the deceased partner's share of the partnership within a period of two weeks. When one of the partners died, the other was of unsound mind, so that when his solicitors purported to exercise the option on his behalf, they lacked the authority to do so as a result. A ratification of their act after the two-week period had elapsed was held to be invalid, distinguishing *Bolton v Lambert* on the ground that

---

[40]   At 307.
[41]   [1896] 2 Ch 348.

in that case there had been no time limit. A time limit revokes an offer automatically at a certain time. Is it justifiable to have one rule for automatic revocations and another (the rule in *Bolton v Lambert*) for revocations that are actually communicated to the offeree? The basis of the (correct) decision in *Dibbins* is that, in laying down a time limit, the offeror seeks to have certainty about whether or not the offeree is bound. However, the third party in *Bolton v Lambert* had exactly the same interest, which was no less worthy of protection.

Finding it difficult to reconcile *Dibbins v Dibbins* and a number of other cases with *Bolton v Lambert*, Bowstead & Reynolds put forward a general standard according to which ratification becomes impossible where to allow it would 'unfairly prejudice a third party'.[42] In the best case scenario, this very wide exception deprives the rule in *Bolton v Lambert* of all practical relevance, in the worst case scenario, however, it gives the court a wide-ranging discretion the exercise of which is difficult to predict. There seems to be unanimity that the rule is anomalous and undesirable. The Privy Council, in *Fleming v Bank of New Zealand*,[43] reserved the right to reconsider the case, while it has never been accepted in the United States.[44]

The problems with the fiction in *Bolton v Lambert* flow from the fact, recognized by Isaacs J in *Davison v Vickery's Motors Ltd*, that the case is simply irreconcilable with the ordinary rules of contract law. Assume R, a rogue, writes to S, offering to buy goods at a certain price, and forging the signature of C, a long-standing customer of the company. S writes to C, accepting the offer. It is now beyond any doubt, following *Shogun Finance v Hudson*,[45] that there is no contract of any kind in this situation. However, C may well decide to treat S's acceptance as an offer to sell it the goods on the terms set out therein. It is equally clear, however, that S can withdraw that offer at any time until C has actually accepted it. Can it make any difference to this scenario if R, rather than pretending to be C, pretended to be acting *on behalf and with the authority of* C? The law, it is suggested, cannot possibly reach contradictory results in the two cases.

It must be admitted, however, that as it stands the rule in *Bolton v Lambert* is inconsistent with the offer and acceptance model defended in this essay. This can mean two things: either the model is wrong and needs to be revised in order to accommodate the case, or the case is wrong and must be overruled and explained as anomalous until it is.

---

[42] *Bowstead & Reynolds on Agency* (18th edn, Sweet & Maxwell, 2009) Art 19.
[43] [1900] AC 577, at 587.
[44] American Law Institute, *Restatement of Agency (Third)* § 4-05(1).
[45] [2004] 1 AC 919.

I suggest that it is in fact *Bolton v Lambert* which is wrong, and not the offer and acceptance model of agency.

5. 'APPARENT' AUTHORITY

The possibility of ratification only arises where the agent has exceeded his authority. By ratifying, the principal can take advantage of any such contract entered into by his agent. But what of the third party? Can he ever sue on the contract, even though the agent, in making it, exceeded his authority? In general, the answer is 'no'. This is because the principal has never expressed his willingness to be bound on those terms. To draw an analogy with the 'non-agency' law of contract, it is as if the third party had accepted an offer contained in a forged letter: the principal is not bound. A third party dealing with an agent is thus taking a risk, and the more important and valuable the transaction, the more careful the third party is going to be in managing that risk. This can be done in two ways: the third party can either put his trust in the agent, whose solvency may be beyond question, or with whom he has dealt many times in the past. Alternatively, he can make sure that the agent's assertions as to his own authority are true—by seeing documentary proof (such as a power of attorney or letter of authority), or by contacting the principal directly. If the principal then confirms that the third party can deal with the agent, all the elements of a contract are present if the third party does so: the agent's offer (or acceptance of the third party's offer) is 'covered' by the principal's assurance that the agent's manifestations of consent will bind him. If we think back to Oliver Wendell Holmes's analogy with a messenger on the one hand and a referee (deciding terms) on the other, in this situation the agent is acting less as a messenger and more as a referee, the principal essentially making an offer to the third party to contract with the agent on terms to be agreed between third party and agent, and this offer is accepted by the third party doing so. It is thus in fact easier to analyse the situation in terms of offer and acceptance than an agency scenario in which the third party takes the agent's word for it that the agent is authorized to bind the principal. And yet English law seems to find it very difficult to accept the contractual analysis in this scenario, preferring to base the outcome (that the third party can sue the principal) on estoppel. There are, it is suggested, two reasons for this. The first is that the law of agency developed at a time when the will theory of contracting was still struggling with the more modern objective theory for universal acceptance, the second that the language of 'authority' has become to be taken at face value, so that authority is essentially something which the agent either possesses or not. Thus, where the principal tells the agent one thing and the third party another, the agent's 'true' or 'actual' authority is derived from the principal's communication to the agent. Fridman in particular is adamant that this must be so:

> There are circumstances in which the relationship [of agency] arises (at least for certain purposes) against the real wishes of one, if not both, of the parties. In situations of this kind the agency relationship, as far as certain of its effects are concerned, has no contractual, or even consensual, basis. Indeed the conduct which gives rise to the particular effects in question may have occurred without the cognizance, let alone the approval of the person who is treated as the principal, and possibly without the agent's intending to act for the benefit of such a principal. The contrast here is between agency arising by consent, and agency arising from estoppel.[46]

This passage demonstrates both of the errors mentioned above. Fridman first ignores that the modern law of contract has moved on. The 'real' wishes of contractual parties matter but rarely, if ever: the law of contracts looks to the intentions of the parties as *objectively manifested* to the other party to the contract. Once this is appreciated, the distinction between 'actual' and 'apparent' authority falls away. Similarly, it is simply beside the point to focus on the agent's consent to act as an agent. This may, of course, be relevant to the relationship between principal and agent—if the agent never consented to act, he cannot very well be held liable for his failure to act. However, it is entirely irrelevant to the relationship between principal and third party (although it must be admitted that scenarios in which an agent binds the principal 'accidentally', with no appreciation of the effects of his acts, will be rare).

Most cases of 'apparent' authority do not involve any direct communication between the third party and the principal. Instead, the principal will generally be found to be bound because of implied manifestations of consent, be it by placing the agent in a certain position (such as the manager of a bank branch, or as a general purchasing agent), by a regular course of dealing, or in any other of the myriad ways in which implied statements can be made. Dicta in the case law base the principal's liability to third parties in such cases squarely on the doctrine of estoppel. Thus, Pollock CB in *Reynell v Lewis*, said:

> Agency may be created by the immediate act of the party, that is, by really giving the authority to the agent, or representing to him that he is to have it, or by constituting that relation to which the law attaches agency; or it

---

[46] Fridman, *Law of Agency* (7th edn, London: Butterworths, 1996) 15.

may be created by the representation of the defendant to the plaintiff, that the party making the contract is the agent of the defendant, or that such relation exists as to constitute him such; and if the plaintiff really makes the contract on the faith of the defendant's representations, the defendant is bound; he is estopped from disputing the truth of it with respect to that contract; and the representation of an authority is, *quoad hoc*, precisely the same as a real authority given by the defendant to the supposed agent. This representation may be made directly to the plaintiff, or made publicly so that it may be inferred to have reached him, and may be made by words or by conduct.[47]

In *Rama Corpn v Proved Tin and General Investments Ltd*[48] Slade J said:

Ostensible or apparent authority […] is merely a form of estoppel, and you cannot call in aid an estoppel unless you have three ingredients: (i) a representation, (ii) a reliance on the representation and (iii) an alteration of your position resulting from such a reliance.

All three of these requirements, as they are applied in the cases, are very weak indeed: the most general representations are sufficient, and it is not clear whether any reliance (other than the attempt to enter into a contract via the agent) is required, far less whether such reliance must indeed be a change of position in the sense that the third party incur some detriment.[49] The requirement of reliance appears to be satisfied merely by the third party entering into the contract.[50] This is puzzling, because, if the agent indeed has no 'real' authority, it is difficult to see why entering into the contract is detrimental to the third party. Of course, there is the possibility that, had the third party known the truth, it would have entered into a different contract with somebody else, but the courts do not require this to be shown or even asserted by the third party. It could—possibly—be argued that there is a potential detriment in entering into the contract after all, namely that, under the rule in *Bolton v Lambert*, the principal might decide to ratify the contract. The detriment could thus be seen in the one-sided option given to the principal. However, this argument is both tenuous (and has never been relied on in any case that I have been able to find in supporting a claim of apparent authority) and trying to justify one bad rule by another. As pointed out above, the rule in *Bolton v Lambert* arose precisely because of the kind of fiction which the notion of apparent authority is based on.

---

[47] *Reynell v Lewis*, (1846) 15 M & W 517, at 527 *et seq.*
[48] [1952] 2 QB 147, at 149 *et seq.*
[49] *Bowstead & Reynolds on Agency* (18th edn, Sweet & Maxwell, 2009) 8-029.
[50] See eg *Cleveland Mfg Co Ltd v Muslim Commercial Bank Ltd* [1981] 2 Lloyd's Rep 646, at 650; *Arctic Shipping v Mobilia* [1990] 2 Lloyd's Rep 51, at 59.

However, the rule in *Bolton v Lambert* is indeed a necessary corollary of apparent authority being regarded as based on estoppel. This is because a principal cannot rely on his own representation to found an estoppel against the third party. If the agent's authority in such a case is indeed based on estoppel, the principal would be subject to a one-sided liability. This is not normally a problem, given that the principal can always simply ratify the agent's contract. However, in the absence of the rule in *Bolton v Lambert*, this would allow the third party to speculate at the expense of the principal (as opposed to vice versa in situations where the agent possessed no authority at all). Let me explain. It will often be the case that a principal will only realize that his agent has exceeded his authority when the third party first contacts him. Where the agent had apparent authority, the third party will not, without more, be bound, and is thus in the desirable position of being able to decide well after the contract was meant to be concluded whether the deal struck represents a good or a bad bargain for him, thus speculating at the expense of the principal. Of course, if the principal knew about the contract, he could ratify straight away—but given that he will normally only find out about it when it is too late, this is not an option available to him. As long as English law bases apparent authority (that is, authority declared to the third party rather than the agent) on estoppel, it thus faces a stark choice between alternative unilateral liabilities: if *Bolton v Lambert* is good law, this allows the principal to speculate at the expense of the third party where the agent has no authority whatsoever. If *Bolton v Lambert* is held to be an aberration, the third party is able to speculate at the principal's expense whenever the agent is clothed with apparent authority.

Bowstead & Reynolds regard the contractual approach to apparent authority as having 'much to commend it',[51] but ultimately reject it for the very reason that it would allow the principal to sue the third party directly, without having to ratify and being subject to the safeguards of ratification.[52] It is difficult to see why this is regarded as preferable.

6. CONSTRUCTION OF AUTHORITY

Most contractual issues in agency law come down to interpretation. If a dispute arises, the court needs to decide whether a contract between principal and third party has come about and, if so, on what terms.

---

[51] *Bowstead & Reynolds on Agency* (18th edn, Sweet & Maxwell, 2009) 345.
[52] *Ibid*, 346.

While the concept of authority does some useful work in this context, it must never obscure the need for matching manifestations of consent by both principal and third party. The question the law has to answer is in every case: could the third party reasonably believe that the principal had consented to the contract, based on manifestations of consent made to either the agent or the third party? The fact that an agent is involved does have some impact on this exercise,[53] but should not normally change the result. The concept of authority should be our servant, not our master.

In the recent case of *Fiona Trust & Holding Corporation v Privalov*[54] the House of Lords lost sight of this. A charterparty had been entered into through the ship owners' agent, and it was alleged by the owners that the agent had been bribed. The contract contained an arbitration clause. The validity of that arbitration clause was in issue before the House of Lords. The owners, in court proceedings to restrain arbitral proceedings commenced by the charterers, argued that the arbitration clause, along with the charter as a whole, was liable to be rescinded by them. The House of Lords held that, under s 7 of the Arbitration Act 1996 the arbitration clause had to be regarded as an agreement separate from the charterparty. While the agent might not have had authority to enter into the charterparty, this did not mean that he had not had authority to enter into the arbitration agreement.

Section 7 of the Arbitration Act 1996 reads:

> Unless otherwise agreed by the parties, an arbitration agreement which forms or was intended to form part of another agreement (whether or not in writing) shall not be regarded as invalid, non-existent or ineffective because that other agreement is invalid, or did not come into existence or has become ineffective, and it shall for that purpose be treated as a distinct agreement.

In applying this section to the dispute before him, Lord Hoffmann admitted that:

> there may be cases in which the ground upon which the main agreement is invalid is identical with the ground upon which the arbitration agreement is invalid. For example, if the main agreement and the arbitration agreement are contained in the same document and one of the parties claims that

---

[53] In the sense that the principal's communications to the agent must be interpreted from the point of view, and with the reasonable background knowledge, of the agent rather than of the third party: this could be a modern interpretation of *Ireland v Livingston* (1871–72) LR 5 HL 395 in the light of *Investors' Compensation Scheme Ltd v West Bromwich Building Society* [1998] 1 WLR 896.

[54] [2007] Bus LR 1719. I am grateful to Dr Andrew Scott of All Souls College for first drawing this case to my attention.

he never agreed to anything in the document and that his signature was forged, that will be an attack on the validity of the arbitration agreement. But the ground of attack is not that the main agreement was invalid. It is that the signature to the arbitration agreement, as a 'distinct agreement', was forged. Similarly, if a party alleges that someone who purported to sign as agent on his behalf had no authority whatever to conclude any agreement on his behalf, that is an attack on both the main agreement and the arbitration agreement.

Lord Hoffmann concluded that, because in the present case the agent had merely exceeded his authority, rather than acting wholly without authority, the principle of severability in s 7 applied and the arbitration agreement stood. The problem with this approach is that it draws a distinction between 'no authority' and 'excess of authority'. It assumes that an intermediary who can call himself an 'agent' has some special quality (his authority!) which allows him to enter into contracts even though he knows full well that he is not allowed to enter into such contracts. This is presumed to be the case even in circumstances in which the third party knows that the agent is acting outside his authority. In the words of Lord Hoffmann, in order for the arbitration agreement to be affected, it 'would have to be shown that whatever the terms of the main agreement or the reasons for which the agent concluded it, he would have had no authority to enter into an arbitration agreement'.[55] In an excellent case note,[56] Adam Rushworth observes that, in contrast:

> the question must be whether the agent has actual authority to enter into an arbitration agreement collateral to a contract that he knows is harmful to his principal. If he does not have such actual authority, and the third party knows this, the arbitration agreement itself does not come into existence and is thus ineffective. It is not immediately obvious that a reasonable principal would afford such authority to his agent.[57]

Let us analyse the facts of *Fiona Trust* in terms of the offer and acceptance model advocated here. The owner's agent is approached by a potential charterer and negotiations commence. The agent is induced to enter into a contract with the charterer by bribery. Can it be said that, objectively speaking, the principal is making an offer to the third party charterer to (i) enter into the charter; and (ii) submit all disputes arising from or to do with the charter to arbitration? Surely, both the agent and the third party know or ought to know that no such offer

---

[55] At [18].
[56] Rushworth, 'The scope and validity of arbitration agreements' (2008) *LQR* 195.
[57] At [198].

by the principal is on the table in such circumstances. In other words, the situation is analogous to Lord Hoffmann's example of a contract concluded by forging another person's signature—nothing in that contract can bind that person, it is a complete nullity. While the policy behind the decision is clearly an expansion of arbitrability of disputes (and a reduction in the workload of the Commercial Court), the reasoning of the decision, to the extent that it is based on agency, is very questionable indeed. It is suggested that this is because their Lordships failed to appreciate that agency is governed by ordinary contractual principles.

7. CONCLUSION

The claim put forward in this paper is modest, but should be seen against the background of a much more ambitious one: obligations in English law are created by consent, wrongs, unjust enrichment, and miscellaneous other events. Agency is not a miscellaneous other event in this Birksian list; on the contrary, some agency cases will be contractual, some wrongs-based, others again based on unjust enrichment. In this paper this wider model was applied to the contractual relationship between a principal and a third party, where the contract is mediated by an agent. The argument put forward here was that all cases of agency proper obey the same rules of contract law which apply to all other contracts in English law. It is important to realize this, because only if we know what we are doing and where on the legal map we are located can we treat like cases alike and thus produce just and coherent outcomes.

11

A Review of the Contracts (Rights of Third Parties) Act 1999

HUGH BEALE*

When the Law Commission Report proposed what became the Contracts (Rights of Third Parties) Act 1999, the majority of commentators seemed to support reform along the lines proposed, but there were a number of critics. The criticisms were broadly of two kinds. Some took the line that the proposals were unprincipled, or at least inconsistent with the principles that are accepted as underlying the rest of the law of contract.[1] Others were of a more practical nature: the Act was unnecessary because developments in case law meant that the promisee could always ensure that the third party obtained the intended benefit; that the Act would create new difficulties; or simply that the Act would not be used.

Ten years after the passing of the Act, it seems appropriate to look at its operation. There is not the space in this volume to attempt anything like a complete review, nor to deal with the question of the promisee's remedies.

1. DIFFICULTIES WITH THE ACT

Commentators have rightly identified a number of uncertainties and potential difficulties with the Act. So far few of them have been reflected in any decided case, and it seems appropriate to deal principally with those that seem particularly likely to cause trouble. The main ones concern the necessary intention to confer an enforceable benefit on a third party: in particular, the question of when will a term 'purport to confer a benefit on him' within s 1(1)(b) and the linked

---

* Professor of Law, University of Warwick; Visiting Professor at the University of Oxford and the University of Amsterdam.

[1] Many of the critical essays are contained, and some that had already been published are most helpfully reprinted, in P Kincaid, *Privity: Private Justice or Regulation* (Ashgate, 2001). See also Kincaid's earlier articles 'Third Parties: Rationalising a Right to Sue' [1989] *CLJ* 243, 'The Trident Insurance Case: Death of Contract?' (1989) 2 *JCL* 160, 'Privity and the Essence of Contract' (1989) 12 *UNSWLJ* 59, and 'The U.K. Law Commission's Privity Proposals and Contract Theory' (1994) 8 *JCL* 51. The other major critique is by R Stevens, 'The Contracts (Rights of Third Parties) Act 1999' (2004) 120 *LQR* 292.

question of when, despite purporting to confer a benefit, the parties
will be held not to have intended the term to be enforceable by the
third party within s 1(2).[2]

There is an important difference between the draft Bill in the Law
Commission Report and the Act. Clause 1 of the Law Commission Bill
referred to the third party having the right 'to enforce the contract',
whereas the Act refers to the third party having the right to enforce 'a
term of the contract'. I do not know who should be credited with this
change—the Commissioners or Parliamentary Counsel—but I think
it is a great improvement. For example, in the construction sector
there were serious concerns that third parties might be able to claim
all sorts of rights under the contract—for example, that the original
parties could not vary the work, or terms of the contract that would
have little direct relevance to the third party, without the third party's
consent. The new formula makes it much clearer that the third party
may acquire the right to enforce only certain terms of the contract, and
the contract must be taken 'term by term'.

Indeed, I wonder whether this approach should have been taken
further. 'Term' is ambiguous. It may refer to a particular obligation
(for example, to use materials of satisfactory quality) or it may refer to
a particular clause in the document which may impose more than one
obligation. In such a situation some obligations under the term may be
enforceable by the third party but not others. It might have been better
to adopt the drafting style of the *Principles of European Contract Law*,[3]
and to refer to the third party being entitled to require performance of
an obligation under the contract.[4]

Nonetheless, there will be difficult cases. In the cases of a construction project involving sub-contractors, does a sub-contract which
requires work to be carried out on the employer's land to construct
something which the employer will own and use 'purport to be for the
benefit of the employer', so that the employer will acquire rights unless
the presumption is rebutted under s 1(2)? Does it make a difference
whether the employer is named in the sub-contract particulars? Is the

[2] See Stevens (2004) 120 *LQR* 292, 306–9.

[3] O Lando and H Beale (eds), *Principles of European Contract Law, Parts I and II* (The Hague:
Kluwer, 2000). Study Group on a European Civil Code and Research Group on EC Private
Law (Acquis Group), *Principles, Definitions and Model Rules of European Private Law: Draft
Common Frame of Reference (DCFR), Outline Edition* (Munich: Sellier, 2009), arts II.-9:301-9:303
take a different approach which refers to the contract conferring 'a right or benefit on a
third party'. This seems to raise all the difficulties of 'incidental' beneficiaries that the Law
Commission's report was so carefully seeking to avoid.

[4] Art 6:110.

mere fact that the employer is identified sufficient to raise a presumption, or do the words or the circumstances have to indicate something more before they will 'purport to confer a benefit' on the third party? Sooner or later the courts will have to deal with a sub-contract that is ambiguous or silent on the point. Fortunately, as we will see, it is easy to avoid these problems arising, and my view is that the risk of doubts arising in construction contracts is easily justifiable by the convenience of an easy mechanism to give third parties rights when that is what the parties want. In most cases the contract will state expressly which terms or obligations the third party shall have the right to enforce—and if it does, then s 1(2) does not arise.

The question of whether the contract purports to confer a benefit on a third party seems more likely to be problematic with less formal agreements such as consumer contracts. *Treitel's Law of Contract* suggests that whether a holiday contract for a party is within s 1(1)(b) may depend on whether the members of the party are named.[5] What about a consumer who buys goods and contracts for them to be delivered to a named third person? I think that might well fall within s1(1)(b);[6] and there will be little to go on to decide whether the presumption is rebutted under s 1(2).

I do have some concern over the meaning of 'expressly' in s 1(1)(a). In *Prudential Assurance Co Ltd v Ayres*[7] the trial judge referred to the Oxford English Dictionary definition:

> That which is conveyed or expressed, esp. by a formal document; bearing, tenor, import, effect; meaning, substance, sense.

'Import' seems to include implications, but I do not think an implication should suffice to bring the case within s 1(1)(a), and thus exclude consideration under s 1(2) of whether this is a correct construction of the contract, unless the implication is completely clear. But no doubt the courts would insist on that anyway.

As to s 1(2) itself, I am glad to see the courts taking the line that the mere fact that the third party might have an alternative remedy will not suffice to rebut the presumption;[8] nor the fact that there is a chain of contracts.[9] Though it is possible to read the Law Commission report

---

[5] E Peel, *Treitel's Law of Contract* (12th edn, Sweet and Maxwell, 2007) para 14-099.

[6] This seems to have been the Law Commission's view: see Law Com No 242 para 7.41.

[7] [2007] EWHC 775 (Ch), [2007] L & TR 35; reversed [2008] EWCA Civ 52, [2008] L & TR 30.

[8] *Nisshin Shipping Co Ltd v Cleaves & Company Ltd* [2003] EWHC 2602, [2004] 1 Lloyd's Rep 38.

[9] *Laemthong International Lines Company Ltd v Artis (The Laemthong Glory) (No 2)* [2005] EWCA Civ 519, [2005] 1 Lloyd's Rep 688, at [53]–[54].

as suggesting that the presumption will be rebutted if there is a chain of contracts[10]—in other words, it will be assumed that the parties intend the only actions to go 'up and down the chain'—I do not see that if the contract does purport to benefit the third party (for example, it clearly requires a sub-contractor to do the work on the property of a named employer) the mere existence of the chain should rebut the presumption. However, in contracts of any sophistication there will be other factors which may well show that the employer was not intended to have direct rights against the employer: for example, if the employer's architect has the right to require the contractor to arrange the re-doing of defective work whether it was the contractor or the sub-contractor who was at fault.

Section 1(3) provides that the third party must be identified in the contract by name, as a member of a class or as answering a particular description but need not be in existence when the contract is entered into. The Law Commission Report states that:

> … a third party who is to receive money or services under a contract would need to be capable of being ascertained with certainty at the time at which the promisor's duty to perform arose.

As has been pointed out, this would be awkward when the parties wish to give third parties, such as future owners of the building, the right to enforce (ie to sue for breach of) a term such as that work be carried out with reasonable care and skill, as the duty to carry out the work will arise long before the building is compete, let alone sold to a new owner.[11] No doubt the problem could be overcome by giving the third party the right to enforce a term that the work has been carried out with reasonable care and skill. In any event, it has been correctly pointed out[12] that the Act does not seem to impose the limitation mentioned in the Law Commission report.

Given the difficulties that led the Law Commission in its Report to exclude arbitration clauses from the scope of the Act, it might have been expected that the subsequent decision to include s 8 would give rise to difficulties. However, the only reported case dealing with s 8 does not suggest major problems.[13]

At the Colloquium, Professor Robert Stevens asked a question that has not, so far as I know, arisen in practice but which raises an issue of

---

[10] Law Com No 242, para 7.18 (iii).

[11] Merkin, *Privity of Contract* (2000) para 8-71.

[12] *Ibid*.

[13] *Nisshin Shipping Co Ltd v Cleaves & Company Ltd* [2003] EWHC 2602, [2004] 1 Lloyd's Rep 38.

principle worth discussing.[14] In a contract between A and B, A undertakes to build a house for C for the sum of £ 1 million to be paid by B, and the contract confers on C the right to enforce A's promise (rather than, as we will see later is sometimes done, giving C the right to claim against A for any defects in the house). C communicates his assent. Later A repudiates the contract and B accepts the repudiation. Does C have a claim against A and, if so, how is it to be measured? There seemed to be general agreement that C should not be entitled to claim the full value of the house (or the full cost of having it built by someone else); that would mean that A would have to pay damages equivalent to the cost of performing without being paid, since B no longer has an obligation to pay and C has never undertaken to pay himself. Just as if the contract had been to build the house for B and B had been the claimant, it seems right that C should not recover more than the loss of value over the price to be paid (or the additional cost of having the work done by another builder), plus losses caused by any delay in having the building completed. It is not immediately obvious how this result is to be reached under the Act, but like Professor Burrows' principal suggestion in his oral response, I believe the answer lies in ss 1(4) and (5). Section 1(4) provides that:

> This section does not confer a right on a third party to enforce a contract otherwise than subject to and in accordance with any other relevant terms of the contract.

A's obligation to build is conditional in the sense that, unless the contract states otherwise, A does not have to perform unless B is ready and willing to pay when the time comes, and B's acceptance of A's repudiation means that B is not ready and willing to pay. Section 1(5), which states that C will have 'any remedy that would have been available to him ... if he had been a party to the contract' reinforces this. Had C been a party (in other words, had it been a tri-partite agreement under which A undertook to B and C jointly that he would build for C, and B undertook responsibility to pay the price[15]) I am sure that the court would hold that A's obligation to build would be conditional

---

[14] See also Stevens (2004) 120 *LQR* 292, 301–2.

[15] In this case it seems not to matter that C was not providing consideration: *Coulls v Bagot's Executor and Trustee Co Ltd* (1967) 119 CLR 460; though see Coote, 'Consideration and the Joint Promisee' [1978] *CLJ* 301, 307. It has been said that as B cannot sue A without joining C, C must have a right of action: see E Peel, *Treitel's Law of Contract* (12th edn, 2007) para 13-032, though this is disputed by Stevens (2004) 120 *LQR* 292, 314. Where A's undertaking is to B and C jointly and severably it is less clear that C can sue without having provided consideration: *Treitel's Law of Contract*, para 13-034, but a dictum of Lord Atkin suggests that he can: *McEvoy v Belfast Banking Co Ltd* [1935] AC 24, at 43.

on B still being willing to pay, and C's remedies would be limited accordingly.

Another way of reaching the same result is to say that, when B accepts A's repudiation, A's primary obligation to build is replaced by a secondary obligation to pay damages for non-performance,[16] and these will be measured in the normal way. In the case of the contract for the benefit of a third party, the effect will be to treat C (unless the contract states otherwise) as if C, not B, had been the promisee.[17]

2. USE OF THE ACT

It is evident from the case law that the doctrine of privity caused difficulties when parties to a contract wanted to extend the protection given to the parties themselves by exclusion and limitation of liability clauses and the like to third persons who were also involved in the performance of the contract. Many of the cases involved carriage by sea, where very elaborate clauses were developed in order to provide stevedores with the protection of the clauses in the bill of lading.[18] In fact the original 'Himalaya clause' case involved the liability of the ship owner's employees to an injured passenger,[19] and there have been other cases involving employees;[20] while similar issues have arisen with sub-contractors in construction projects.[21] These may be called the 'negative benefit' cases. The Law Commission's Report suggested that the Act would also bring practical advantages in at least two areas in which the parties may want to confer positive benefits on third persons: construction contracts and insurance. It referred also to schemes that seek to provide indemnities to cover a number of different legal actors all involved in a project.[22]

To what extent have parties started to employ the Act as a way of overcoming the difficulties caused by the doctrine of privity of contract? At the time the Act was passed, some commentators argued that it would simply not be used. Ways had been found of dealing with the problems thrown up by the doctrine of privity in particular contexts,

---

[16] Cf Lord Diplock's well known statement in *Photo Production Ltd v Securicor Transport Ltd* [1980] AC 827, at 848–50.

[17] In effect, as Stevens suggests, this element of C's loss is 'capped' by the loss suffered by B: (2004) 120 *LQR* 292, 302.

[18] *New Zealand Shipping Co Ltd v AM Satterthwaite & Co Ltd (The Eurymedon)* [1975] AC 154.

[19] *Adler v Dickson* [1955] 1 QB 158.

[20] Eg *Gore v Van der Lann* [1967] 2 QB 31.

[21] Eg *Southern Water Authority v Carey* [1985] 2 All ER 1077.

[22] Law Com No 242, paras 3.9–3.27.

and practitioners would prefer to continue to use these rather than to risk the uncertainty of the new legislation.

Initial reports seemed to confirm this suggestion. We were told that many firms were simply adding a clause to all their precedents to the effect that the Act would not apply to the contract. The question is whether this has changed.

It has not proved easy to get information about this. Published sources tell us only so much, and refer to possible uses rather than actual use. However, practitioner colleagues have provided some valuable information about actual use, at least in general terms.[23]

(a) Negative benefits

(i) Exclusion and limitation clauses

Before the Act, ways had been found of extending the protection of exclusion or limitation of liability clauses to employees and sub-contractors. Some 'Himalaya clauses' relied on agency or trust devices to do their work, and on occasions these were successful. However, they were prone to difficulty and occasionally failure. For example, there might be doubts about whether the promisee had authority to agree to the clause on behalf of stevedores.[24] In one case the stevedores were not protected because they had damaged the goods while they were unloading goods stored on top of damaged goods, and thus before they had accepted the consignor's offer that they would have limited liability if they carried out the performance requested of them.[25] In another it was held that a sub-contractor could not ratify what had been done in its name by the main contractor if at the time the clause was agreed the contractor could not have identified the sub-contractor.[26]

---

[23] I am particularly grateful to Richard Calnan of Norton Rose LLP, Sarah Cameron of Pinsent Masons LLP, Sam Krafft of Allen and Overy LLP, and Jeremy Winter of Baker & MacKenzie LLP (and the many colleagues in those firms who in turn helped them) for information on a variety of contexts; to Julian Burling, Counsel to Lloyd's and Peter Hinchliffe, Lead Insurance Ombudsman, for information on insurance; and to colleagues at the Colloquium.

[24] See *Port Jackson Stevedoring Pty Ltd v Salmond & Spraggon Pty (Australia) Ltd (The New York Star)* [1981] 1 WLR 138.

[25] *Raymond Burke Motors Ltd v Mersey Docks and Harbour Board Co* [1986] 1 Lloyd's Rep 155.

[26] *Southern Water Authority v Carey* [1985] 2 All ER 1077.

Now s 1(6) of the Act means that employees,[27] stevedores, sub-contractors, and the like can be given the protection of the clauses of the contract easily and reliably: it will suffice that that the clause is stated to be for the benefit of the third party. I suspect that for carriage of goods by sea the pre-Act standard documents continue to be used[28] but that is probably unnecessary: the clauses clearly indicate an intention to benefit the stevedores, etc and so they will work. The real question is whether to eliminate unnecessary provisions. What I am told is that in other contexts s 1(6) of the Act is frequently relied on to provide protection to officers and employees of companies.[29]

It is worth noting that a third party may avail himself of an exclusion or limitation of liability in a contract for the carriage of goods by sea even though in other respects s 1 of the Act does not apply to contracts for the carriage of goods by sea.[30] The reason for excluding such contracts from the operation of the Act in other respects was to avoid any conflict with the provisions of the Carriage of Goods By Sea Act 1992, which permits subsequent holders of bills of lading, and the holders of ships' delivery orders and sea waybills, to enforce the terms of the contract of carriage, but with different consequences to those that would obtain were the 1999 Act to apply: for example, the holder becomes liable for unpaid freight or demurrage, while the original promisee ceases to have a right of action.[31] The 1992 Act was not intended to give rights of enforcement to other parties, which might be the result were the 1999 Act to apply. But the 1992 Act was not addressed to exclusion or limitation of liability clauses and that explains why the new Act does apply to such clauses.[32]

Contracts sometimes contain choice of forum or exclusive jurisdiction clauses. This is particularly common in contracts for the carriage of goods by sea. A carrier may require, for example, that any claim

---

[27] Art IV bis of the Hague-Visby Rules now extends the protection given to the carrier to servants or agents of the carrier who are not independent contractors: see *Carver on Bills of Lading* (2nd edn by Treitel and Reynolds, 2005) paras 9-286–9-298.

[28] I am grateful to Professor Andrew Tettenborn for information on this point.

[29] A partial search of the *Encyclopaedia of Forms and Precedents* on LexisNexis suggests that the only common use of the Act made in forms and precedents is to exclude the liability of third parties, eg 'Boilerplate and Commercial clauses: Sub-contracting 42.7: "It is hereby declared that any sub-contractor of {the Carrier} and the servants and agents of {the Carrier} … are third parties to this contract within the meaning of the [Act] and shall be entitled to enforce this contract accordingly."' However, the same clause seems to contemplate conferring positive rights on a third person who derives rights from the consignor, see below.

[30] s 6(5).

[31] See Law Com No 242, para 12.8.

[32] Law Com No 242, para 12.10.

against it be brought in a particular forum and wish the same benefit to be extended to claims against its sub-carriers or stevedores.[33]

Although choice of forum or exclusive jurisdiction clauses may in part purport to confer negative benefits on the third parties, they are closely analogous to arbitration clauses. It will be recalled that the Report recommended that third parties should not have rights of enforcement in respect of agreements to submit disputes to arbitration. Though this was not stated explicitly in the Bill, it seems it would have been possible to make the third party's right to enforce some other term of the contract subject to arbitration.[34] However, an agreement that any claim against the third party should be by way of arbitration would not have given the third party the right to insist that this be done. The reason was essentially because this would have to involve also imposing obligations on the third party in relation to the arbitration proceedings. It would not be right to allow the third party to insist on arbitration unless he were also bound to arbitrate. Jurisdiction agreements were treated in the same way.[35] At a later stage it was decided that where a third party has the right to enforce a term subject to arbitration, the third party should be treated as a party to the arbitration agreement so that the third party will be obliged to take the necessary steps;[36] and also to provide rather similarly for the case where the parties have agreed that any claim by the promisor against the third party (eg a tort claim for negligent damage) shall be subject to arbitration, provided that the third party exercises the right to insist on arbitration.[37] One might have expected choice of forum or exclusive jurisdiction agreements in general to have been treated in the same way, but it seems to have been thought that this might be incompatible with art 17 of the (then) Brussels Convention.[38]

Even if that had been done, however, such clauses in contracts for the carriage of goods by sea would not have been affected for a separate reason. The Act's provisions on arbitration do not apply generally to contracts for the carriage of goods by sea, since s 8 applies only

---

[33] *The Pioneer Container* [1994] 2 AC 324 of course involved a choice of forum clause, but in that case the clause was contained in the sub-carrier's conditions and the question was whether the sub-carriers could rely on it as against the owners of the goods.

[34] See Burrows, 'Reforming Privity of Contract: Law Commission report No 242' [1996] *LMCLQ* 467, 481–2.

[35] Law Com No 242, para 14.18.

[36] s 8(1).

[37] See s 8(2).

[38] See Explanatory Note to the Act para 32; Burrows, 'The Contracts (Rights of Third Parties Act 1999 and its implications for commercial contracts' [2000] *LMCLQ* 540, 552 fn 28.

when there is an enforceable right under s 1 and, as we have seen, s 1 has only a very limited application to such contracts.

(ii) Settlements

A closely related use of the Act may occur in settlement agreements. It may not always be clear which company in a group or involved in a project is the correct defendant, or whether several defendants may be jointly and severably liable for a particular loss. Rather than join all the possible parties in any settlement of the claim, the settlement may be expressed to be for the benefit of all the possible defendants.

(b) Positive benefits

(i) Indemnity clauses

The first situation is closely related to the use of the Act to provide negative benefits, ie to limit the liability of officers and employees. The exclusion or limitation of liability will frequently be coupled with an indemnity to the officer or employee; and rather than (or in addition to) this being a right as against the company/employer under the contract of appointment or employment, the right to indemnity may be provided by the other party to the contract with the company/employer, as a third party right under that contract.

The Law Commission's Report referred to difficulties that had been experienced in the off-shore oil and gas industry, where

> major oil companies and their advisers have attempted to minimize litiga-tion arising from drilling contracts in the North Sea. This has largely been achieved by the use of cross indemnities between oil companies and con-tractors, which to be effective, must not only benefit the parties to the con-tracts in question but also all other companies in their respective groups, their employees, agents, sub-contractors and co-licensees. This is because, for example, it will often be unclear at the outset of project which member of a client company's group will operate a platform and will thus be caused loss by any failings on the part of the contractor. An indemnity should therefore ideally benefit all companies likely to be affected.[39]

I have no information about use of the Act in the oil and gas industry in particular, but I was told that the Act is regularly used to reduce the need for complex schemes of indemnity. In the field of carriage of goods by sea, it is not uncommon for owners to agree to release goods

---

[39] Law Com No 242, para 3.23.

without production of the bill of lading, against letters of indemnity. In *The Laemthong Glory*[40] letters of indemnity had been issued by both the charterers and the receivers of the cargo. Whereas the letter issued by the charterers was addressed to the owners, the letter issued by the receivers had been addressed to the charterers. It was held by the Court of Appeal that on its wording the receivers' letter purported to confer a benefit on the owners, who were therefore able to enforce the indemnity.[41]

(ii) Insurance

Many insurance contracts are partly or wholly intended for the benefit of persons who are not parties to the contract. Some of these are covered by specific statutory exceptions, such as s 83 of the Fire Prevention (Metropolis) Act 1774, s 11 of the Married Women's Property Act 1882, and s 148(7) of the Road Traffic Act 1948, which in effect give the beneficiaries the right to enforce the policy.[42] Where the insured under a liability policy has become insolvent before or after incurring liability to a third party, the Third Parties (Rights Against Insurers) Act 2010 (replacing the 1930 Act of the same name)[43] gives a third party the right to bring a direct action against an insurer. But the Privity Report pointed out that there are many situations in which there is no relevant exception and the beneficiary of a policy has no right to proceed against the insurer. The Report mentioned life insurance policies for the benefit of dependants other than spouses and children (for example, a cohabitee or a step-child); insurance taken out by a company to cover its subsidiaries or its contractors and sub-contractors; and an employer who takes out private health insurance for its employees.[44]

Needless to say, an insurance company is unlikely to refuse point-blank to pay a claim simply because the beneficiary is not a party to the contract. The company's commercial reputation would be severely damaged.[45] But when a claim is disputed, the beneficiary may find

---

[40] *Laemthong International Lines Company Ltd v Artis (The Laemthong Glory) (No 2)* [2005] EWCA Civ 519, [2005] 1 Lloyd's Rep 688.

[41] At [48].

[42] See Law Com No 242, paras 2.53–2.57.

[43] Implementing the Joint Report of Law Commission and the Scottish Law Commission, *Third Parties—Rights against Insurers* (Law Com No 272, Scot Law Com No 184, 2001).

[44] LC No 242, para 3.25.

[45] I wonder whether attitudes will differ with insurance schemes that are in 'run-off', ie where no fresh business is being accepted. These are often transferred to other companies with different names.

they cannot challenge the insurer's refusal to pay, whether in part or in full, because they have no right of action against the insurance company. *Mulchrone v Swiss Life (UK) Plc*[46] concerned a group income protection scheme taken out by Norton Rose in favour of its employees. The claimant had been suffering from repetitive strain injury and had received payments under the scheme, but the insurers ceased payments on the ground that she no longer met the definition of disablement under the policy. She sought to take the issue to arbitration; but Swiss Life declined to arbitrate with her. It accepted that she would have a right to arbitrate if the Act applied, but it argued that the insurance in question pre-dated the coming into force of the Act, which applies only to contracts made after 11 May 2000. Thus, it was said, the only parties to the insurance (and presumably the arbitration agreement also) were the insurer and Norton Rose and therefore the claimant had no cause of action or rights against the insurer. It was held that the relevant contract had been entered before 11 May 2000 and so the claimant had no right of action.

It should be explained, however, that this was not a case of simple refusal by the insurer to pay. The claimant had already taken her case to the Financial Ombudsman Service, which had determined that she was fit to resume work. For that reason, Norton Rose understandably refused to allow the claimant to bring an action in its name.[47]

The existence of the Financial Ombudsman Service (FOS) has in practice rendered discussion of privity of contract irrelevant in the context of consumer insurance, including group insurance for employees. The rules of the scheme (which are set out in the Financial Services Authority Handbook)[48] require it to ensure that customers are treated fairly and enable it to deal with complaints from the beneficiaries of policies whether or not they have a right of action under the policy. The lead Ombudsman tells me that:

> I believe that following an assertive stance on our part 3-4 years ago, the major providers of protection and medical cover under group employee schemes are likely to be dealing directly with employees who are entitled to the benefit of the policy even though they are third parties.

In other words, it is for most consumer claims irrelevant whether the policy confers a legal right of enforcement on the intended beneficiary or excludes it—though it would be interesting to know whether insurers exclude the Act in order to prevent claims by beneficiaries

---

[46] [2005] EWHC 1808 (Comm).
[47] See at [7]–[10].
[48] See <http://fsahandbook.info/FSA/html/handbook/DISP>.

such as Ms Mulchrone who wish to challenge the decision of the Ombudsman Service or who decline to use it.

Although the FOS will deal with complaints from some small businesses as well as from consumers, the bulk of commercial insurance contracts are not affected by it. It seems equally plausible that in such policies insurers should routinely be excluding the Act or they should now use it to create direct rights in the intended beneficiaries of, say, global policies to cover contractors and sub-contractors. One can imagine that the third party beneficiaries would seek to obtain direct rights so that, in the event of a dispute, they do not have to depend on the cooperation of the policy-holder, and some insurers might find it worthwhile to offer such rights. On the other hand, when a single incident may give rise to potential claims by several beneficiaries, or simply in case they cannot reach agreement with a beneficiary, the insurer may well prefer to have to deal only with the policy-holder. Certainly this seems to happen in the retail sector. The Lead Ombudsman also told me that:

> there is presently a concern about the handling of claims that insurers receive from those who have been in an accident with or incurred liability as a result of their insured's fault. In both motor and public liability insurance, insurers will contact such third parties directly and attempt to settle the claim against the insured party very quickly. When a dispute breaks out, lack of contractual arrangement between the parties can be queried by insurers as a reason for denying any liability or culpability to the third party, notwithstanding their direct dealings.

I have been able to find little published discussion of the use being made of the Act in insurance. The only information that I have gleaned privately is that a senior insurance lawyer has 'more often seen the Act excluded than employed'. I am not sure, however, whether this allows for the fact that a policy will not need to mention the Act in order to rely on its provisions to create enforceable rights. Normally it will be sufficient that the beneficiary is named in, or is identifiable from, the policy. If insurers are issuing policies in favour of third party beneficiaries without excluding the operation of the Act—and my contact has kindly sent me an example, of a travel policy which does just that—it is presumably because they are willing for the beneficiaries to have direct rights of action.

It was also suggested that the Act might have the effect of making 'cut-through' agreements in reinsurance contracts enforceable by the insured against the reinsurer.[49] These are clauses which allow the

---

[49] Eg *MacGillivray on Insurance* (11th edn, 2008) para 20-068.

insured and the reinsurer to deal with each other directly in the event
of the insurer's insolvency. I am told by practitioner colleagues that
they do sometimes see the Act used in this context, but the take-up is
not wide. This may be because the major texts on insurance[50] seem to
have accepted the argument made by Henley[51] that, though the Act
on the face of it applies, the cut-through arrangement will fail because
it infringes the principle in *British Eagle International Airlines Ltd v
Compagnie Nationale Air France*,[52] by giving one creditor (the insured)
an advantage over the others. This seems debatable. It cannot be the
case that a debtor who arranges for payment of one of his creditors
by making a contract with another person (the 'promisor') that the
promisor will pay the creditor (who thus becomes the third party beneficiary) will fall foul of the *British Eagle* case, or it would be impossible
to confer rights on third party 'creditor beneficiaries'. It is not easy to
see why it matters that the creditor beneficiary is only to have rights in
a certain situation, for example if the reinsurer decides to operate the
cut-through clause. It is true that this would divest the insurer of
the right to the relevant reinsurance monies, but it can be argued that
the effect of the clause is simply that the insurer's claim against the
reinsurer is a form of flawed asset, always liable to be defeated by
the exercise of the cut-through clause.[53] In addition, the rights that
would be given were a cut-through agreement to be enforceable by the
insured against the reinsurer do not seem very different to the right
given by the Third Parties (Rights Against Insurers) Act 1930 to the
injured party to proceed directly against the insurer when the insured
has become bankrupt. This might suggest that public policy would
not be infringed by the cut-through arrangement allowing the insured
to proceed directly against the reinsurer. It is true that, quite apart
from the fact that the 1930 Act does not apply to reinsurance,[54] there
is a difference between this case and the typical case that may have
been envisaged by the 1930 Act: whereas the insured will have chosen
whether or not to deal with the insurer and can have estimated the
chances that the insurer will remain solvent, many claimants under

---

[50] *MacGillivray on Insurance* (11th edn, 2008) para 20-068; Clarke, *Law of Insurance Contracts*
(looseleaf) para 5-1A.

[51] In Merkin, *Privity of Contract* (2000) paras 9-65–9-67.

[52] [1975] 1 WLR 758.

[53] Cf the discussion of direct payment clauses in construction contracts by M Bridge,
'Collectivity, Management of Estates and the Rule in Winding-up' in J Armour and H Bennett, *Vulnerable Transactions in Corporate Insolvency* (Oxford: Hart Publishing, 2003) 1, esp
26-30. However, as Bridge points out, some courts have held that direct payment clauses do
infringe the *British Eagle* principle, eg *A-G v McMillan v Lockwood Ltd* [1991] 1 NZLR 53.

[54] s 1(5).

the 1930 Act will be the victim of a tort committed by the insured and have had no choice as to whether or not to deal with the insured. However, the 1930 Act will also apply when the insured's liability to the third party is in contract. But in the light of the doubts about the efficacy of cut-through clauses, it would not be surprising to find that they are seldom used.

(iii) Construction contracts

In the arena of construction contracts there are a number of situations which it was thought that parties might want to use the Act. The simplest one is where A is employed by B to carry out work on C's property, for example where C is an elderly relative of B. Another is the issue that lay behind *Linden Gardens Trust Ltd v Lenesta Sludge Disposals Ltd*:[55] where a subsequent owner or tenant of the building may want to bring an action against the builder, should defects emerge in the building. The same issue can arise with design defects; and the claimant may be a funder rather than the owner or tenant. A third situation is that of the employer who wishes to bring an action directly against a sub-contractor who has not carried out work properly or a supplier who has supplied materials that are defective. That may happen because the contractor itself is not responsible for the default;[56] or because the contractor has become insolvent; or because the contractor can rely on a conclusive certificate that the work has been carried out in accordance with the contract, issued before the problem emerged.[57]

On the other hand, the industry was very concerned to avoid unintended liabilities. For example, the employer should be free to vary the work without having to get the consent of any third party; and it seems also to be generally accepted that sub-contractors (even nominated sub-contractors) should not be given the right to sue the employer directly for payment.[58]

---

[55] [1994] 1 AC 85.

[56] As in *Gloucester CC v Richardson* [1969] 1 AC 480 (normal implied term as to quality excluded where contractor had no right to object to nomination of supplier and latter would supply only on limited liability terms).

[57] This may have been the problem in *Junior Books Ltd v Veitchi Co Ltd* [1983] 1 AC 520.

[58] Many contracts do give the right to the employer to make payments directly to sub-contractors if the main contractor has failed to pass on money paid in respect of sub-contract work, presumably to stop the sub-contractor walking off the job; but these provisions often do not purport to give the sub-contractor any rights and usually they cease to apply if the main contractor becomes insolvent, for fear of the *British Eagle v Air France* principle: see Bridge, note 53 above.

At least in sophisticated construction contracts, the industry had come up with a solution before 1999 which achieved the desired results without giving rise to unintended rights or liabilities. The contractor, and often also significant sub-contractors, would be required to issue a 'collateral warranty'. These are described briefly in the Law Commission's Report.[59] It is worth looking in a bit more detail at what is presumably a typical collateral warranty, the standard warranty provided by the Joint Contracts Tribunal as part of the Standard Building Contract 'family' of contracts. I will summarize in the next two paragraphs the warranty designed for contractors to give to subsequent purchasers and tenants of the building.[60] (For simplicity's sake I will refer simply to the purchaser rather than 'purchaser or tenant'.)

In consideration of the payment of £1, the contractor warrants that, with effect from practical completion, he has carried out the work in accordance with the contract[61] and has used proper materials.[62] If the warranty is broken the contractor will be liable for the costs of repair, renewal, or reinstatement incurred by the purchaser, but not for any other losses unless it has been agreed in the particulars that the contractor will be liable up to a stated maximum figure. Further, by agreement the contractor's liability may be limited to what it would be 'just and equitable' to require the contractor to pay on the assumption that consultants and sub-contractors have given similar warranties and have paid their just and equitable shares to the purchaser. Further, as against the purchaser, the contractor is not only entitled to rely on any term of the contract but also to raise any defence he would have had against the employer.[63] On the other hand:

> The obligations of the Contractor under or pursuant to this paragraph ... shall not be diminished by the appointment of any person by the Purchaser ... to carry out any independent enquiry into any relevant matter.[64]

I understand the purpose of this to be to prevent the contractor arguing that the purchaser employed a surveyor to inspect the building before he bought it and that the purchaser's recovery should be reduced because of defects the surveyor either found or should have found.

The purchaser has no right to issue any direction or instruction to the contractor. The contractor agrees to maintain insurance, provided

---

[59] Law Com No 242 para 3.15.
[60] CWa/P&T (2005).
[61] Cl 1.1.
[62] Cl 2.
[63] Cl 1.4.
[64] Cl 1.5.

that it remains available at commercially reasonable rates. If it ceases to be available, the parties should discuss the means of best protecting their respective positions.[65] The agreement may be assigned by the purchaser without the consent of the contractor, and by the first assignee to a second; but no further assignment is permitted. No proceedings may be brought on the warranty more than six years after the date of practical completion, or 12 years if the warranty is under deed.[66] For the avoidance of doubt, the contractor is not liable to the purchaser for delay.[67] And for completeness, nothing in the agreement confers any right on any person who is not a party to it.

Initially it was thought that the industry would continue to use warranties of this type and would simply spurn the Act, inserting clauses to ensure that it did not affect their contracts. And indeed this is the line still taken by some leading textbooks on construction contracts. But others pursued a more thoughtful approach. For example, while *Winward Fearon on Collateral Warranties*[68] might, from its title, be expected to have taken the party line, in fact it contains a very thoughtful discussion of how the Act may be used to avoid the need for collateral warranties. The authors point out that while it is unwise simply to let the Act apply by not excluding it, it is not necessary to exclude it totally. Rather, they conclude that it is possible

> to create express third party rights under the contract to a limited, and expressly stated, class of third parties and, at the same time, exclude the potentially uncertain rights that would otherwise be created by s 1(1)(b).

They go on to explore what such a provision might contain. And recently at least two families of contracts have changed their approach. Both the JCT contracts and the New Engineering Contract 3 now take just the approach advocated.[69] I will describe the Standard Building Contract already mentioned.[70]

We should perhaps begin with assignment, since the current JCT contract is in fact much more flexible than those of us who are not experts on construction law may expect. Clause 7 starts with the usual prohibition on either party assigning the contract or any rights under

---

[65] Cl 5.

[66] Cl 8.

[67] Cl 9.

[68] 2nd edn by Cornes and Winward, 2002, paras 3.56–3.60.

[69] Ho, 'Third Way', (2006) *SJ* 150, 151 states that the British Property Federation has 'made the Act its default mechanism to create third party rights under its recently introduced Consultancy Agreement.'

[70] There are similar provisions in other versions, eg the Major Project Construction Contract Revision1, 2007.

it without the consent of the other, but there is an exception. If it has been agreed that clause 7.2 shall apply, the employer, if it transfers its freehold interest or creates a leasehold interest in the works or a section of them, may grant or assign to the transferee or lessee the right to bring proceedings in the name of the employer to enforce any terms of the contract made for the benefit of the employer. It is carefully provided that the assignee is stopped from disputing any enforceable agreement made by the contractor and employer before the date of the assignment.

This provision of itself would have prevented most of the problems in the *Linden Gardens* case. However, it is clear that only a form of equitable assignment is contemplated; the new purchaser will have to join the employer in any action. Moreover, it will be of limited value if different parts of the building are to be sold or let to different purchasers or tenants and the division does not reflect the sections of the work set out in the contract particulars. (I believe that in practice works are divided into sections primarily when they are to be completed at different dates, so for example small retail units in a shopping centre might not each be treated as a separate section.)

So what of third party rights? The contract states at an early stage that nothing in it confers or is intended to confer any right to enforce any of its terms on any person who is not a party to it, other than any rights that may be conferred on any purchaser or tenant under clause 7A or a funder under clause 7B.[71] These clauses apply only when this is stated in the contract particulars; and they are alternatives to collateral warranties, which are dealt with by clauses 7C (P/Ts) and 7D (funders). If it has been agreed that clauses 7C or 7D shall apply, the employer may give a notice requiring the contractor to enter into a collateral warranty of the kind already described with the purchaser, tenant, or funder.

If clause 7A is stated to apply, rights will vest in the purchaser when the employer gives notice to that effect to the contractor.[72] Before that point the employer and contractor may rescind or vary the terms of the contract, and the employer may terminate the contractor's employment.[73] Once that notice has been given, the purchaser acquires the rights set out in a schedule, and neither these rights nor clause 7A itself may be varied without the purchaser's consent.[74] The rights that the purchaser acquires are virtually the same as the purchaser would have

---

[71] Cl 1.6.
[72] Cl 7A.1.
[73] Cl 7A.2.
[74] Cl 7A.3.

under the collateral warranty described earlier, and are subject to the same limitations.

So the JCT contract now gives parties the possibility of granting rights to purchasers and tenants. What is remarkable is the way in which the rights are carefully delineated. It is perhaps a pity that those of us engaged in the Law Commission privity project did not draw up a document like this to show to the construction industry during the consultation period. I think it would have reassured many of the doubters.

There seem to be good reasons for using the new clauses in place of the collateral warranties that have become traditional. A separate warranty has to be issued for each tenant or purchaser, and it is said that this is time-consuming, particularly for the contractor or consultant, and is easily overlooked.[75] The third party rights approach using the 1999 Act merely requires completion of the contract particulars plus any amendments that the parties wish to make to the schedule setting out the third parties' rights: one document for all. Thereafter all that is needed is for the employer to serve the relevant notices—which can easily be made a standard part of granting tenancies or selling units. On the other hand, the third party 1999 Act approach does assume that the employer and contractor can settle once and for all what rights all third parties will get. I have heard that sometimes different warranties are issued to different purchasers or tenants, according to their bargaining power and the state of the market.[76] But unless the different warranties are agreed at the outset, the contractor will not be under any obligation to issue a 'better' warranty to a particularly demanding purchaser, so I am not sure that this is a real advantage of warranties.

Whatever the merits, there is bound to be some reluctance to change ways of doing business. In practice, are parties making use of clauses 7A and 7B or their equivalents in other forms? The answers I have received vary from firm to firm, some reporting that they have seen some examples of third party rights being conferred both on purchasers and tenants and on funders, but that collateral warranties remain the norm; others report that third party rights are now 'largely used' in place of warranties.[77]

Given the JCT's approach to third party rights for purchasers, tenants, and funders, I was surprised to find that the JCT did not take

---

[75] Ho, 'Third Way', (2006) *SJ* 150. The sheer number of warranties required on a large project may be a problem: Murdoch and Hughes, *Construction Contracts* (4th edn, 2008) 325.

[76] See R Merkin (ed), *Privity of Contract* (2000) para 8-72.

[77] Likewise, A Minogue, [2006] *Building* 47 reports that most big City projects are successfully using third party rights.

the same approach in order to give the employer direct rights against sub-contractors, the third situation in which it was thought that the Act might be used. The standard form of sub-contract provides that third parties are not to acquire any rights under it. Instead there is provision for collateral warranties: if the contract particulars call for these to be given, the sub-contractor must execute and deliver warranties when notified.[78] Why third party rights were not thought appropriate in this case I do not know.

(iv) Intellectual property rights and services for the benefit of a group

It is apparently quite common for a company to take out a licence to use intellectual property rights for itself and other companies in the same group. This right, and its associated warranties and any obligation to indemnify the authorized users against liability to third parties for infringement, may be extended to other companies in the same group by using the provisions of the 1999 Act. The same is true when a company contracts for services (such as accounting or IT maintenance) that are intended to benefit not just itself but also other companies in the group.

Part of the reason for making this type of arrangement is that it may be hard to predict exactly which company will suffer loss if there is a breach of contract—or even after the event to show exactly on whom the loss fell. A defendant may not think it worthwhile to pursue arguments that the loss caused by its breach did not fall on the claimant company but on some other member of the group if the other member of the group also has the right to sue.

(v) Contracts of carriage: parties deriving title from the consignor

I have found a precedent for a contract of carriage which contemplates giving rights to those who derive title from the customer (presumably meaning the consignor).[79] This would be useful in contracts for carriage by road (not covered by the Carriage of Goods by Road Act 1965 which are excluded from the 1999 Act),[80] for which there are no

---

[78] Standard Building Sub-contract (SBC Sub/C) cl 2.26.

[79] *Encyclopaedia of Forms and Precedents*, LexisNexis, 'Boilerplate and Commercial clauses: Sub-contracting 42.7: "It is hereby declared that any sub-contractor of {the Carrier} and the servants and agents of {the Carrier} and also any person deriving title to the goods from {the Customer} are third parties to this contract within the meaning of the [1999 Act] and shall be entitled to enforce this contract accordingly."'

[80] By s 6(5)(b).

equivalents to the rights given to the holder of a bill of lading, etc by the Carriage of Goods by Sea Act 1992.[81]

(vi) *Replacement for multi-partite agreements*

I am told that the Act is also used for transactions which in the past might have been set up as multi-partite arrangements, but where the interests of some of the parties involved are really only in being sure that the agreement is carried out properly.

(vii) *Outsourcing of financial services*

When financial or other services are 'outsourced', in other words sub-contracted, the firm that employs the sub-contractor will itself be responsible for any deficiencies and there will be no need to use the Act. However, regulators may not have direct control over the sub-contractor. A fascinating use of the Act is to give the Financial Services Authority the right to demand access and information direct from the firm to which financial services work is outsourced. The FSA 'MIFID Connect' Guidelines on the application of the outsourcing requirements under its rules implementing the Markets in Financial Information Directive[82] require the outsourcing firm to:

> ensure access for the firm, its auditors and the relevant competent authorities to data related to the outsourced activities, as well as to the business premises of the service provider, and the competent authorities must be able to exercise those rights of access[83]

and state that, in order to meet the requirement that competent authorities must be able to exercise their rights of access, they may need to be given third party rights of action in any outsourcing agreement.

(viii) *Efficient structures*

Lastly, it is said that the Act is quite often used when for legal or tax reasons a body does not want to contract directly. This sort of issue is

---

[81] For international carriage the Carriage of Goods by Road Act 1965 makes the consignee a party to the contract: s 14(2): see *Chitty on Contracts* (30th edn, 2008), Vol II, para 36-133.

[82] Directive 2004/39/EC, OJ L 145, 30 April 2004.

[83] Para 4(e), referring to SYSC 8.1.8R(9).

familiar from previous cases such as *Darlington BC v Wiltshier Northern Ltd*[84] and *Alfred McAlpine Construction Ltd v Panatown Ltd*.[85]

3. CRITICISMS OF PRINCIPLE

When the Law Commission's report was issued, there were a number of criticisms of principle, both of the proposal and of the way in which the Law Commission justified it. I have to be highly selective. I will deal only with points on which the information about the use of the Act seems to help resolve the arguments.

The first is that the Law Commission report claimed that its proposals would stop the doctrine of privity from thwarting the intentions of the parties.[86] Critics argued that the (now) Act cannot be justified in terms of giving effect to the intention of the parties in the plural. The promisor does not need to have his intention made binding; he can fulfil his intention by simply performing.[87] I think the use that the JCT forms make of the Act show that this is misguided. Contractors—the promisors in the relevant scenario—want work. The more marketable the building will be, the more likely the employer is to commission the work. And the building will be more marketable if purchasers can be given enforceable rights against the contractor in the event of a defect. So it is in the contractors' interest, and therefore it is their intention, to enter binding commitments. This is just another version of the point made long ago by Posner in relation to gratuitous promises—a promise which is binding on the promisor is more valuable than one that is not, not only to the promisee but also to the promisor.[88] If purchasers were content to rely on the contractor's intention to perform, there would be no collateral warranties.

The second point is raised most forcefully by the critic who did so much to try to generate a principled debate on reform, Peter Kincaid;[89] and an additional reason for dealing with it is that, no matter how selective space requires this review to be, his arguments at least should be considered. He points out quite correctly that contract law does not simply give effect to the intentions of the parties. It is normally only those intentions which are incorporated into a bargain that will be

---

[84] [1995] 1 WLR 68.
[85] [2001] 1 AC 518.
[86] LC No 242, para 3.1.
[87] Eg Stevens, 'The Contracts (Rights of Third Parties) Act 1999' (2004) 120 *LQR* 292, 293.
[88] Posner, 'Gratuitous promises in economics and law' (1977) 6 *JLS* 411.
[89] See above, n 1.

enforced; and he argues that the way in which the Act creates rights in third parties is inconsistent with the bargain principle. In brief, the bargain principle requires that obligations are created only to those to whom promises were made and who have provided consideration for them. If the Act can be justified at all, it must on one of two other grounds. One is imposing liability in order to protect justifiable reliance by the third party: though he rejects the notion that this would be liability in tort,[90] he says that this reliance liability would be 'outside contract.' But in that case the third party's rights should depend on it having relied, and its recovery should be limited to the reliance interest. The Act allows the creation of unvariable rights in the third party even without the third party's reliance; and gives the third party the same (expectation-interest) remedies as if it were a party to the contract. The other ground of justification must be in terms of a public interest in the performance of contracts.

I will make only two points, both aimed at showing that the provisions of the Act can be justified as a matter of private law, without resorting to notions of public interest save in the most general sense that parties on whom it is intended that rights be conferred should have efficient remedies.

First, if the third party's right were inconsistent with the bargain principle, I think it could be justified as a useful exception. We already recognize the deed (and contracts in which the consideration is purely nominal[91]) as exceptions to the bargain principle. Kincaid rightly points out that in these cases the promise is at least made to the third party—though in the case of a promise by deed, the beneficiary need not accept or even know of it. The promise under deed is often seen by continental lawyers with whom I have discussed it as an example of a 'unilateral juridical act' which is wholly justified by the will theory. I do not see why we should not welcome another will-based exception to the bargain principle. If one thinks of it as a case in which a deed is not required because the safeguards imposed by the doctrine of consideration (evidentiary, channelling, and cautionary) are already satisfied by the requirement that there be consideration between promisor and promisee, it seems to me to be unexceptionable.

However, I do not see that the Act is inconsistent with the bargain principle. The argument that only a person who has provided

---

[90] See (1997) 12 JCL 47, 63; *Privity*, 79.

[91] Kincaid ((1997) 12 *JCL* 47, 58-9 replied to my earlier argument to this effect by saying that nominal consideration follows from '... the very idea of individual liberty ... the promisor can state his own price'. But that would not prevent the law from refusing enforcement in cases in which the price is obviously sham.

consideration should be able to enforce a promise[92] seems to depend on a particular view of the meaning of the bargain principle, for example whether consideration is seen as something justifying the claim (in which case it is logical to say that it must have been provided by the claimant) or as something justifying the imposition of liability on the defendant. On the latter view it seems to be enough that there was consideration for the defendant's promise, albeit coming from the promisee rather than the third party claimant.[93]

As to the point that only a promisee should be able to enforce the contract, reluctance to admit the possibility of creating rights in a third party may be linked to our pre-occupation with liability and damages rather than with the obligations created by the contract.[94] The promisor should not be able to deny the third party's claim because creating an obligation in favour of the third party is precisely what he agreed to in the contract. To put it another way, what the promisor expressly or impliedly[95] undertook was to create a right in the third party to enforce the relevant term of the contract to the extent permitted under the Act. If that is not the outcome, he has not done what he undertook.

I suspect Kincaid would reply that this should give the promisee a remedy, but not give the third person a right to sue. But that seems to me to require an unnecessary detour around the houses. Take the example of the employer who wants subsequent purchasers or tenants to have the right to claim directly against the contractor for defects in the building. Quite apart from the 1999 Act, had the contractor promised to grant a collateral warranty to the third party purchaser when notified to do so by the employer, as provided for by clauses 7C and 7D of the JCT form considered earlier, then (provided the terms of the warranty were sufficiently defined) the employer could get an order of specific performance.[96] Since by that stage the third party would probably already have purchased the property, the warranty would

---

[92] An approach shared by other commentators: eg C Mitchell, 'Searching for the Principles behind Privity Reform' (Kincaid, *Privity* 104) and S Smith, 'In Defence of the Third Party Rule' (1997) 17 *OJLS* 643.

[93] See likewise R Flannigan, 'Privity—The End of an Era (Error)' (1987) 103 *LQR* 564, 569-72 and Sir Anthony Mason, 'Privity—A Rule in Search of a Decent Burial' in Kincaid, *Privity*, 88, 91; and also J Beatson, 'Reforming the Law of Contracts for the Benefit of Third Parties: A Second Bite at the Cherry' [1992] *CLP* 1, 5.

[94] Cf Beatson [1992] *CLP* 1, 4.

[95] I understand s 1(1)(b) and its accompanying restriction in s 1(2) as a way of saying that the third party is to have a right if that was a clear implication of the agreement.

[96] *Winward Fearon on Collateral Warranties*, para 10.4. I imagine that the court would even execute the warranty in the contractor's name in the same way it will execute a conveyance of land.

probably be by deed to avoid any problems of consideration—and there is no doubt that the warranty would be enforceable although it formed no part of a bargain with the third party. Alternatively, if this were permitted under the contract, the employer would have to assign its rights to the third party.[97] Again the third party would not provide any consideration to the promisor. Why should either extra step be necessary? The answer might be made that rights conferred by deed or by subsequent assignment are different to rights conferred (or not) by a bargain. I think that would be to sacrifice obvious commercial convenience on the altar of doctrinal purity. It should equally be possible to create third party rights by initial agreement, either immediately or, as the JCT contracts provide, on the employer notifying the particulars of the third party to the contractor. In either case, it will be noted, the original parties may vary their intentions before the notice is given; but once it has been given, the rights—either the third party rights or those conferred by the collateral warranty—are (and should be) irrevocable.

The analogy of the collateral warranty made by deed suggests another way of putting it. Some liken rights under a deed (since they do not depend on the beneficiary's agreement) as a form of property right. Would it not help to think of the right created in the third party as a form of property which the promisor, by making the contract and (typically) notifying the third party, is conferring on the third party? That is the performance promised under the contract and (save where revocation is permitted), why should the promisor be able to withdraw that right any more than it can take back goods delivered to a third party? Waters has likewise suggested that the third party right can usefully be seen as a form of intangible property.[98]

I think we need to be very careful here. First, I am certainly not suggesting that the third party be treated as obtaining a proprietary right enforceable against other persons, for instance the promisor's other creditors. (That would follow if the promisor were to declare a trust in favour of the third party, but I think that should require an express declaration.) Secondly, the 'property' is defeasible, in the sense that the promisor and promisee may agree to revoke it before acceptance or reliance by the third party. So my argument is only one by analogy to property, not that the third party obtains a property right in the technical sense. Nonetheless I find it useful to think of the third party's right in these terms, just as we may think of the action in tort for inducing

---

[97] See LC No 242, para 3.19.
[98] A Waters, 'Privity, Property and Pragmatism' in Kincaid, *Privity* 309, 333–6.

a breach of contract as a form of protection of a contracting party's property in their contract rights.[99]

The other point goes to Kincaid's argument that any remedy should be based on reliance. I find it telling that the schemes which have been drafted by the JCT—a neutral body, since both sides of the industry are represented on it—are not 'reliance-based'. They come into effect by agreement, not when there has been reliance, and they contemplate an expectation measure of recovery, not one limited to reliance losses. Although in practice it will only be a purchaser who has actually bought the property who will ever seek to enforce their third party rights (or their rights under a collateral warranty), there is no requirement that the third party should have relied before the rights come into existence. There seems nothing to prevent the employer from notifying the name of a prospective purchaser, even if the third party would in practice be unable to prove a loss unless they have purchased. More tellingly, the purchaser's rights are not affected by what they may have been told by a surveyor before they purchased—so the fact that they may have obtained a reduced price for the building is irrelevant to the contractor's liability for repairs or for further losses if it was agreed that these should also be covered up to the contract maximum. Again, I think the point is that it is in the interests of all the parties that the third party should have irrevocable rights irrespective of reliance and that the third party's recovery should not be limited to its reliance loss.

4. CONCLUSION

While it is perhaps too soon to claim that the Contracts (Rights of Third Parties) Act 1999 has been an outstanding success, in that as yet its use seems to be limited, I think we can say that it has certainly not been a failure. Rather I regard it as useful but still underused.

---

[99] Cf S Waddams, 'Joanna Wagner and the Rival Opera Houses' (2001) 117 *LQR* 431, 449.

Index

The notation 191n46 and n47, for example, refers to footnotes 46 and 47 on page 191.

acceptance *see* email: offer and acceptance; websites: offer and acceptance
agency 11–12, 66, 224
  authority
    'apparent' 206, 208, 218–21
    construction of 221–4
  by operation of law/power-liability model 206–7
  civil law 209, 213
  consensual model 205–6, 207
  electronic 62–3, 211
  'Himalaya clauses' 231
  offer and acceptance model 207–12, 213–14, 217–18, 223–4
  ratification 211, 213, 214–18
  two conventional models of 205–9
  undisclosed 211–13
agreements in principle *see* letters of intent
Amazon.co.uk 85, 86
anti-assignment clauses 11, 192, 194–5
  practical considerations 203–4
  pre-existing agreements to assign receivables 195–7, 203
  trusts 197–202, 203–4
anticipated contract fails to materialize *see* unjust enrichment
arbitration 48, 228, 233–4
agreements 222–4
assault and battery
  assignment of rights 192–3, 194
assignment of rights 11, 183, 204
  anti-assignment clauses 11, 192, 194–5
    freedom of contract 196–7, 198
    practical considerations 203–4
    pre-existing agreements to assign receivables 195–7, 203
    trusts 197–202, 203–4
  construction contracts 241–2
  intransmissible obligations 192–4
  maintenance and champerty 183
    history 184–8
    maintenance limitation today 188–92

personal contractual rights 183, 192, 195
  practical considerations 203–4
  pre-existing agreements to assign receivables 195–7, 203
  trusts 197–202, 203–4
  undisclosed agency 213
Australia
  agency 215–16
  assignment of rights 188, 190n45, 191n46 and n47
  trusts 201
  comfort letters 34
  estoppel 130n46
  preparatory work: unjust enrichment 161, 164, 167, 168, 173n72, 176, 178
  revocation of unilateral offer 100, 101

bankruptcy 109, 188n34, 192
bare agreements to negotiate 42
  objective restriction agreed 47–50
  otherwise enforceable contracts 43–7
bare trusts 200, 202
battery
  assignment of rights 194
'best endeavours' fallacy 40–2
bills of lading 230, 232, 235
breach of trust 154n67, 200
British Airways (ba.com) 85n93
burden of proof
  good faith and negotiations 58
  Misrepresentation Act 1967: s 2(1) 142

Canada
  assignment of rights 188n33 and n34, 190n44, 193–4
    consolidation of claims 191n47
    under-insured defendants 189
  Ontario Law Reform Commission 97
carriage of goods
  by road 244–5
  by sea 230, 232–5

champerty and maintenance 183
  history 184–8
  maintenance limitation today 188–92
children
  step-children 235
choice of forum clauses 232–3
choses in action
  assignment of rights 196, 200, 203–4
co-defendants
  assignment of rights 189, 193–4
  settlement agreements 234
confidentiality agreements 36
cohabitees 235
comfort letters 4–5, 33–6
companies
  agency 12
  assignment of rights 189, 190, 193, 195
  parent company
    letters of comfort 4–5, 33–6
  quasi-partnership 25–6
  reorganizations/reconstructions 189,
    193, 195
  third party rights
    efficient structures 245–6
    indemnity clauses 234
    insurance 235–7
    intellectual property rights and
      services for benefit of group 244
    outsourcing of financial services 245
    settlement agreements 234
condition, breach of
  affirm or terminate contract 117
conditions precedent 27
confidential relationship 138n8
**consideration and contract
  modifications** 7, 8–9, 89–91, 112–13
  abolishing consideration 8–9
  in adding modifications 105–7
  outright 107–12
  bird in the hand: actual
    performance 92–6, 113, 121n25
  promissory estoppel 102–5, 112
  revocation of unilateral offer 99–102
  unilateral contract device 7, 9, 96–8, 105,
    107, 113
  Williams v Roffey, award in 98–9
**consideration: failure of and unjust
  enrichment** 10, 159–60, 178–9
  conventional 'risk' analysis 160–2, 168
  failure of basis as unjust factor 171
    bilateral cases and mistake

    analysis 175–8
    contract 172–3
    no contract 173–5
  pre-contractual liability cases 168–71
  unjust factor of failure of
    consideration 163–8
consideration, nominal 247
consolidation of claims 191
construction contracts
  third party rights 226–7, 228, 230, 231–2,
    239–44, 246, 248–9, 250
    collateral warranties 240–1, 242, 243,
      244, 246, 248–9, 250
constructive notice 152n62
constructive possession 211
constructive trusts 165, 199, 202
consumer contracts 227
contra proferentem 44n37
contributory negligence 151

damages
  assignment of rights to 187–8, 191
  breach of an agreement to negotiate 56–9
  condition, breach of 117
  deceit 140–1, 147–8, 150–1, 154, 156
  expectation 13, 58–9, 94n22
  gain-based 93–4
  licences of land 125
  misrepresentation 138, 150
    Misrepresentation Act 1967 140,
      142–3, 155
  mistake 138
  non-disclosure and 137, 138, 139, 142–3,
    147–8, 149–50, 154–7
  non-performance 230
  primary remedy for breach of
    contract 109
  punitive 31–2, 94n22
  reliance 58–9, 250
  third party rights 13, 230, 250
  unilateral offer, revocation of 101–2
debts
  assignment of 187–8, 191
  promissory estoppel and *see separate entry*
deceit, tort of 39, 137, 140–1, 156, 157
  pre-contractual non-disclosure 144–5,
    146–9, 150–3, 156
  remedy 140–1, 147–8, 150–1, 154, 156
deeds 247, 249
defamation
  assignment of rights 192–3

defendants
  assignment of rights 189, 193–4
  settlement agreements 234
disclosure, duty of 9–10, 51, 137, 157
  approach to imposition of tort liability for
    non-disclosure 149–50, 157
    breach of duty of disclosure 153–6
    fraudulent 150–3
    placing liability within nominate
      torts 156–7
  civil law systems 139
  misrepresentation, mistake and
    non-disclosure 137–9
  misrepresentation, tort liability for
    pre-contractual 139–40
    deceit 140–1
    Misrepresentation Act
      1967: s 2(1) 142–3
    negligence 141–2
  non-disclosure in pre-contractual
    stage 143
    deceit 144–5, 146–9
    Misrepresentation Act
      1967: s 2(1) 143–4
    negligence 145–6
    recent developments 146–9, 157
  reasons for imposing 138–9
  remedies
    damages 137, 138, 139, 142–3, 147–8,
      149–50, 154–7
    rescission 137, 138, 139, 140n15, 143,
      146, 150, 152, 153–4, 157
discretion
  contractual party: exercise of 51–2, 54
duress 90, 91, 96, 98, 107, 110–12, 113, 163, 173

economic loss and tort
  reliance on statements 141, 150
electronic data interchange (EDI) 62–3
email: offer and acceptance 6–7, 26, 86–7
  European Union 72
  firewall 77–8
  garbled contents 78
  inbox full 78
  incorrect email address 77
  junk-mail, deleted as 77–8
  multiple email addresses 78–9
  offeror: time of receipt of email
    acceptance 70
    able to access 72–3
    arrives on server 70, 71–3, 76

    downloaded 70n40
    ought reasonably to have come to
      offeror's attention 70, 73–6
    read 70–1
  'ordinary business hours' 74, 75
  other countries 70
    Germany 75n63
    United States 64n14, 69n37, 71–2
  place contracts made 69–70
  postal rule 64–70, 71, 76n66
  server, problem with 78
  things go wrong 76–9
    email address incorrect 77
  United Nations 63n7, 71, 72, 73n54,
    75n61
  'vacation reply' 75n64
  viruses 78
employees
  bankrupt employer
    assignment of rights 188n34
    remuneration 174–5
  third party rights
    exclusion or limitation of liability 230,
      231–2
    indemnity 234
    insurance 235–7
  vicarious liability 211
employment contracts 183, 195
estate agents 100
estoppel by representation 135
  agency: 'apparent' authority 218–21
estoppel, promissory 7–8, 9, 102–5,
  115–16
  acceptance by A of substitute
    performance by B 134, 135
    payment of lesser sum 118–22
    principle 116–17
    promissory estoppel and
      principle 117–18
  conclusions
    debts 134–5
    expansion of consideration 112
    scope of promissory estoppel 135–6
  Hughes principle: limits on A's acquisition
    of a right 134–6
    payment of lesser sum 128
    principle 122–4
    promissory estoppel and
      principle 124–8
  prospect of B's suffering a
    detriment 135–6

estoppel, promissory (*cont.*)
    payment of lesser sum 132–3
    principle 129
    promissory estoppel and
        principle 129–32
estoppel, proprietary 130–1, 132, 133,
    161–2
European Union
    Draft Common Frame of Reference
      (DCFR) 19n6, 39, 153n65, 155n70, 157
    electronic commerce 72, 83, 84n91, 85
    Principles of European Contract Law 39,
      153n65, 195n64, 226

factoring of receivables 11
faxes 67n29, 68, 77n68
fiduciary duty/relationship 138n8, 146,
    154n67, 207
Financial Ombudsman Service
    (FOS) 236–7
Financial Services Authority
    outsourcing of financial services 245
floating charges 195–6, 203
forgery 217
France
    agency 209
    comfort letters 4–5, 35
    gratuitous promises 110
    pre-contractual disclosure duties 155n70
    remedies 95n35
freedom
    of choice 108–9
    of contract 196–7, 198
frustration 163, 173

Germany
    agency 209
    email: offer and acceptance 75n63
    gratuitous promises 110
    remedies 95n35
good faith, agreement to negotiate in 5–6,
    19, 37–40, 59–60, 139, 155
    analysis 50–1
      obligation 51–6
      remedy 56–9
    other countries 39, 55, 139, 153, 155
      United States 40
    scope 40
      bare agreements to negotiate 42–50
      'best endeavours' fallacy 40–2
gratuitous promises 246

Greece 209
group of companies
    efficient structures 245–6
    letters of comfort 4–5, 33–6
    reorganizations/reconstructions 189,
      193, 195
    services for benefit of group 244
guarantees
    parent company 4–5, 34, 35

heads of agreement *see* letters
    of intent
'Himalaya clauses' 230, 231
holiday contracts 227
Hong Kong
    estoppel 131n52

illegality 82, 90, 184
indemnities 230, 234–5
injunctions 202
insolvency 109, 191, 192, 193, 199
    construction contracts 239
    insurance 235, 238
    undisclosed agency 212–13
instant messaging 62
insurance contracts 139n9, 143, 145, 146
    construction projects 240–1
    third party rights 230, 235–9
intellectual property rights and services
    for benefit of group 244
intent, letters of 3–5, 17–21, 36
    contract 26–32
    no contract 21–6
    other countries 18–19, 21–2
      Australia 34
      France 4–5, 35
      New Zealand 35
      United States 19, 28–31
    some legal effect
      agreements regarding negotiations 36
      followed by performance 33
      letters of comfort 4–5, 33–6
      'un-gentlemen's agreement' 21
intention to create legal relations 34–5,
    90, 109
interim contracts 33
internet *see* email: offer and acceptance;
    websites: offer and acceptance
invitation to treat
    websites 81–2, 85
Italy 209

Japan 209
joint and several liability 234
juries 31–2
jurisdiction clauses, exclusive 232–3

land
  licences 125, 126
  proprietary estoppel 130–1, 132, 133, 161–2
Law Commission
  consideration 89–90
  email: offer and acceptance 68, 72
  gazumping 18
  postal rule 68
  pre-contractual non-disclosure 148
  third party rights 225, 226, 227–8, 230, 235
    construction contracts 230, 240, 243
    criticisms of principle 246
    offshore oil and gas industry 234
Law Reform Commission, Ontario
  consideration and contract
    modifications 97
Law Revision Committee (1937)
  consideration and contract
    modifications 89, 97, 103
letters of comfort 4–5, 33–6
letters of intent 3–5, 17–21, 36
  contract 26–32
  no contract 21–6
  other countries 18–19, 21–2
    Australia 34
    France 4–5, 35
    New Zealand 35
    United States 19, 28–31
  some legal effect
    agreements regarding negotiations 36
    followed by performance 33
    letters of comfort 4–5, 33–6
    'un-gentlemen's agreement' 21
libel
  assignment of rights 192–3
licences of land 125, 126
life insurance policies 235
liquidated claims, assignment
  of 187–8
liquidators 192
lock out agreements *see* **good faith,**
  agreement to negotiate in

maintenance and champerty 183
  history 184–8
  maintenance limitation today 188–92

memorandums of understanding
  see **letters of intent**
messaging, instant 62
misrepresentation
  Misrepresentation Act 1967: s 2(1) 140,
    142–3, 155
    pre-contractual non-disclosure 143–4,
      149, 156–7
  negotiating in good faith and 37, 38–9,
    51, 52, 55, 56, 59, 60
  non-disclosure, mistake and 137–9,
    151–2
  remedies
    damages 138, 140, 142–3, 150, 155
    rescission 137, 138, 140n15, 143, 150
    tort liability for pre-contractual 139–40
      deceit 140–1
      Misrepresentation Act 1967: s 2(1) 140,
        142–3
      negligence 140, 141–2
mistake
  misrepresentation, non-disclosure
    and 137–9
  unjust enrichment 163, 166n31, 171–8
mitigation of loss 94n22
modifications *see* **consideration and**
  contract modifications
multi-partite agreements,
  replacement of 245
    negative pledge clauses 204n110

negligence 141–2
  pre-contractual non-disclosure 145–6,
    156
New Zealand
  abolishing consideration in adding
    modifications 105–7
  comfort letters 34
nominal consideration 247
non est factum 173n75
non-disclosure *see* **disclosure, duty of**

offer and acceptance model of agency
  see **agency**
offer and acceptance *see* **email: offer and**
  acceptance; websites: offer and
  acceptance
oil and gas industry 234
ombudsman 236–7
'ordinary business hours' 74, 75
outsourcing of financial services 245

parent companies
  letters of comfort 4–5, 33–6
  see also groups of companies
patent licence 126–7
performance of contracts
  best endeavours 41, 42n28
personal contractual rights 183, 192, 195
  practical considerations 203–4
  pre-existing agreements to assign
    receivables 195–7, 203
  trusts 197–202, 203–4
personal injury claims
  assignment of rights 189n38, 192, 193–4
personal property law 211
postal rule
  email 64–70, 71, 76n66
  websites 84
pre-contractual non-disclosure
  see disclosure, duty of
preparatory work: contract fails to
    materialize *see* unjust enrichment
principals *see* agency
privity of contract 230–1, 246
  agency and 208
  consumer insurance 236
promissory estoppel 7–8, 9, 102–5, 115–16
  acceptance by A of substitute
    performance by B 134, 135
    payment of lesser sum 118–22
    principle 116–17
    promissory estoppel and
      principle 117–18
  conclusions
    debts 134–5
    expansion of consideration 112
    scope of promissory estoppel 135–6
  Hughes principle: limits on A's acquisition
    of a right 134–6
    payment of lesser sum 128
    principle 122–4
    promissory estoppel and
      principle 124–8
  prospect of B's suffering a
    detriment 135–6
    payment of lesser sum 132–3
    principle 129
    promissory estoppel and
      principle 129–32
proprietary estoppel 130–1, 132, 133, 161–2
public interest 247
public policy

assignment of rights 183, 187, 190, 191–2
'cut-through' agreements in reinsurance
    contracts 238
punitive damages 31–2, 94n22

quantum meruit 162n11 and n13, 174–5
quasi-partnership 25–6

reinsurance contracts 237–9
remedies
  damages *see separate entry*
  injunctions 202
  quantum meruit 162n11 and n13, 174–5
  rescission *see separate entry*
  specific performance 94n22, 95, 96, 109,
    204n110, 248
remoteness of damage 94n22
reorganizations/reconstructions,
    corporate 189, 193, 195
repudiation 54
rescission
  fraud 140n15, 143
  misrepresentation 137, 138, 140n15, 143,
    150, 152, 154
  mistake 171
  non-disclosure 139, 146, 153–4, 157
restraint of trade 109
resulting trusts 165, 171
risk: preparatory work and contract fails to
    materialize *see* unjust enrichment
road, carriage of goods by 244–5
Roman law 110, 164

Scotland 184
sea, carriage of goods by 230, 232–5
secret trusts, fully 122n29
settlement agreements 234
shareholders
  assignment of rights to 189, 190n43
  shareholders' agreements 25–6
Singapore
  consideration 107
slavery contracts 109
specific performance 94n22, 95, 96, 109,
    204n110, 248
step-children 235
stevedores 230, 231–3
'subject to contract' 18, 42, 160, 170, 174
subrogation 189, 200n99
subsidiaries
  letters of comfort 33–6

Switzerland 209
'synallagmatic' contracts 110

taxation
  efficient structures 245–6
  failure of consideration:
    unconstitutional 167
telegraph 65
telephone calls 65, 67n29, 84
telexes 65–7, 68, 71, 72, 73, 74, 77n67
third party rights: 1999 Act 12–13, 223, 250
  arbitration clauses 228, 233–4
  carriage of goods
    by road 244–5
    by sea 230, 232–5
  chain of contracts 227–8
  construction contracts 226–7, 228, 230,
    231–2, 239–44, 246, 248–9, 250
  consumer contracts 227
  criticisms of principle 246–50
  difficulties with the Act 225–30
  efficient structures 245–6
  employees 230, 231–2, 234, 235–7
  exclusion and limitation clauses 231–4
  exclusive jurisdiction clauses 232–3
  holiday contracts 227
  indemnities 230, 234–5
  insurance 230, 235–9
  intangible property 249
  intellectual property rights and services
    for benefit of group 244
  multi-partite agreements,
    replacement of 245
  outsourcing of financial services 245
  settlements 234
  stevedores 230, 231–3
  'term of the contract' 12–13, 226
  use of the Act 230–1
    negative benefits 231–4
    positive benefits 234–46
time limits
  agency
    authority exceeded: ratification 216–17
tort 247, 249–50
  liability for pre-contractual non-
    disclosure *see* disclosure, duty of
trusts
  breach of trust 154n67, 200
  constructive 165, 199, 202
  declaration of trust 11, 249
  'Himalaya clauses' 231

resulting 165, 171
unassignable contracts 197–202, 203–4

uberrimae fidei contracts 144, 144–5, 146,
  147n39, 148n49
unconscionability 107, 110–11, 112
undisclosed agency 211–13
undue influence 107, 110–11, 112, 146,
  163, 173
unfair terms
  websites: offer and acceptance 86n96
unilateral contract device 7, 9, 96–8, 105,
  107, 113
  revocation of unilateral offer 99–102
unilateral mistake 171–3, 175
  of fact 138n5
United Nations
  offer and acceptance
    automated message systems 63n7
    email 63n7, 71, 72, 73n54, 75n61
    websites 81
United States
  agency 217
  assignment of rights
    anti-assignment clauses 195
    under-insured defendants 189
  email: offer and acceptance 64n14, 69n37,
    71–2
  estoppel 130n46
  good faith, agreement to negotiate in 40
  letters of intent 19, 28–31
unjust enrichment 10, 159–60, 178–9,
  205, 224
  assignment of rights 187
  conventional 'risk' analysis 160–2, 168
  failure of consideration 178–9
    failure of basis as unjust factor 171–8
    pre-contractual liability cases 168–71
    unjust factor of 163–8

vending machines 79–80, 210–11
vicarious liability 211
void and voidable contracts 138n5

waivers 8, 125
websites: offer and acceptance 6, 61–3, 79,
  86–7
  customer: time of receipt of email
    acceptance
    arrives on server 84
  downloading digital products 79–80

websites: offer and acceptance (*cont.*)
  European Union 83, 84n91, 85
  invitation to treat 81–2, 85
  order placed but performance later 80
    acceptance 82–4
    control by retailer 84–6

  offer 80–2
  postal rule 84
  unfair terms 86n96
  United Nations 81
***Wednesbury* unreasonableness** 52
will theory 247